THE CONSTITUTION AND THE FUTURE OF CRIMINAL JUSTICE IN AMERICA

The Constitution and the Future of Criminal Justice in America draws together leading scholars from law, psychology, and criminology to address timely and important topics in U.S. criminal justice. The book tackles cutting-edge issues related to terrorism, immigration, and transnational crime, and to the increasingly important connections between criminal law and the fields of social science and neuroscience. It also provides critical new perspectives on intractable problems such as the right to counsel, race and policing, and the proper balance between security and privacy. By putting legal theory and doctrine into a concrete and accessible context, the book will advance public policy and scholarly debates alike. This collection of chapters is appropriate for anyone interested in understanding the current state of criminal justice and its future challenges.

John T. Parry is Professor of Law at Lewis & Clark Law School. He is the author of *Understanding Torture: Law, Violence, and Political Identity* (2010), as well as numerous articles on issues relating to criminal law, foreign relations law, and transnational and international criminal law. He is also coauthor of *Criminal Law: Cases, Statutes, and Lawyering Strategies* (2005, 2d ed. 2010) and a member of the American Law Institute. Parry's scholarly work focuses broadly on legal structures that restrain or permit the exercise of state power on individuals, with a particular emphasis on criminal law, civil rights law, and foreign relations law.

L. Song Richardson is Professor of Law at the University of Iowa College of Law. Her legal career includes work as a state and federal public defender, as an assistant counsel at the NAACP Legal Defense Fund representing capital defendants in habeas cases, and as a partner in a boutique criminal law firm. She is a member of the American Law Institute. Her research explores the legal implications of mind sciences research on criminal procedure, criminal law, and policing. Her work has been published by law journals at Yale, Berkeley, Duke, Northwestern, and Cornell, among others.

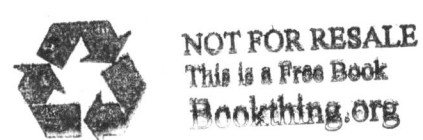

The Constitution and the Future of Criminal Justice in America

Edited by

JOHN T. PARRY
Lewis & Clark Law School

L. SONG RICHARDSON
The University of Iowa College of Law

CAMBRIDGE
UNIVERSITY PRESS

32 Avenue of the Americas, New York, NY 10013-2473, USA

Cambridge University Press is part of the University of Cambridge.

It furthers the University's mission by disseminating knowledge in the pursuit of education, learning, and research at the highest international levels of excellence.

www.cambridge.org
Information on this title: www.cambridge.org/9781107605220

© Cambridge University Press 2013

This publication is in copyright. Subject to statutory exception and to the provisions of relevant collective licensing agreements, no reproduction of any part may take place without the written permission of Cambridge University Press.

First published 2013

Printed in the United States of America

A catalog record for this publication is available from the British Library.

Library of Congress Cataloging in Publication data
The constitution and the future of criminal justice in America / edited by John T. Parry, Lewis & Clark University Law School, L. Song Richardson, The University of Iowa College of Law.
    pages cm
Includes bibliographical references and index.
ISBN 978-1-107-02093-1 (hardback) – ISBN 978-1-107-60522-0 (pbk.)
1. Criminal justice, Administration of – United States. 2. Constitutional law – United States. I. Parry, John T., 1964– editor of compilation. II. Richardson, L. Song, 1966– editor of compilation.
KF9223.C66   2013
364.973–dc23   2013007965

ISBN 978-1-107-02093-1 Hardback
ISBN 978-1-107-60522-0 Paperback

Cambridge University Press has no responsibility for the persistence or accuracy of URLs for external or third-party Internet Web sites referred to in this publication and does not guarantee that any content on such Web sites is, or will remain, accurate or appropriate.

Contents

Notes on Contributors		*page* vii
Acknowledgments		xi
Introduction		
	John T. Parry and L. Song Richardson	1

PART I FOUNDATIONS – THE SCOPE OF CRIMINAL LAW AND ACCESS TO COUNSEL

1. The Past and Future of the Right to an Attorney for Poor People Accused of Crimes 13
   Stephen B. Bright

2. Criminal Justice in America: Constitutionalization without Foundation 27
   Markus D. Dubber

PART II RACE AND CRIMINAL PROCEDURE

3. The Challenges of "Quality of Life" Policing for the Fourth Amendment 45
   Susan A. Bandes

4. Implicit Racial Bias and the Fourth Amendment 59
   L. Song Richardson

PART III POLICING AND PRIVACY

5. The Exclusionary Rule: Its Effect on Innocence and Guilt 79
   Tonja Jacobi

6. Consent, Dignity, and the Failure of Scattershot Policing 93
   Janice Nadler

7. Neurotechnologies at the Intersection of Criminal Procedure and Constitutional Law 109
   Amanda C. Pustilnik

   PART IV TECHNOLOGY AND THE SURVEILLANCE SOCIETY

8. Information and Social Control 137
   Wayne A. Logan
9. Is the Fourth Amendment Relevant in a Technological Age? 152
   Christopher Slobogin

   PART V CONFESSIONS AND *MIRANDA*

10. False Confessions and the Constitution: Problems, Possibilities, and Solutions 169
    Richard A. Leo
11. The Foggy Future of *Miranda* 187
    Emily Hughes

    PART VI CONVICTION, SENTENCING, AND INCARCERATION

12. Collateral Consequences of Criminal Conviction 205
    Gabriel J. Chin
13. Psychopathy, Criminal Responsibility, Punishment, and the Eighth Amendment 222
    Adam R. Fox and Reid Griffith Fontaine

    PART VII EMERGENCIES AND BORDERS – IMMIGRATION, TERRORISM, NATIONAL SECURITY, AND TRANSNATIONAL CRIME

14. Preemption and Proportionality in State and Local Crimmigration Law 241
    Juliet P. Stumpf
15. Embattled Paradigms: The "War on Terror" and the Criminal Justice System 260
    Susan N. Herman
16. The Civilianization of Military Jurisdiction 287
    Stephen I. Vladeck
17. Crime across Borders: Globalization, Executive Power, and the Transformation of Criminal Justice 310
    John T. Parry

Index 333

Contributors

Susan A. Bandes is the Centennial Distinguished Professor of Law at DePaul University College of Law. She is a prolific scholar in the areas of criminal procedure, government accountability, and the role of emotion in law. Her articles appear in the Yale, University of Chicago, Michigan, and Stanford law reviews, among others. Her book *The Passions of Law* was published by New York University Press in 2000. Prior to joining the DePaul faculty, she was staff counsel for the ACLU of Illinois and a staff attorney for the Illinois Office of the State Appellate Defender.

Stephen B. Bright is President and Senior Counsel of the Southern Center for Human Rights in Atlanta and Visiting Lecturer at The Yale Law School. He has represented people facing the death penalty at trials and on appeals and prisoners in challenges to inhumane conditions and practices; written essays and articles on the right to counsel, racial discrimination in the criminal justice system, judicial independence, and other topics that have appeared in scholarly publications, books, magazines, and newspapers; and testified before committees of both the U.S. Senate and House of Representatives. He received the American Bar Association's Thurgood Marshall Award in 1998, the American Civil Liberties Union's Roger Baldwin Medal of Liberty in 1991, and the National Legal Aid & Defender Association's Kutak-Dodds Prize in 1992, among others.

Gabriel J. Chin is Professor of Law at the University of California Davis School of Law, where he writes and teaches in the areas of criminal law, race and law, and immigration. He is a former public defender and prosecutor, and his articles have appeared in the Cornell, UCLA, University of Pennsylvania, and Harvard Civil Rights–Civil Liberties law reviews, among others. His work has been cited by numerous courts, including the U.S. Supreme Court. He served as Reporter on the ABA Standards for Criminal Justice on Collateral Sanctions and Discretionary Disqualification of Convicted Persons, as well as on the Uniform Collateral Consequences of Conviction Act promulgated by the Uniform Law Commission.

Markus D. Dubber is Professor of Law at the University of Toronto. His scholarship focuses on theoretical, comparative, and historical aspects of criminal law. He is the author or editor of several books, including *The Police Power: Patriarchy and the Foundations of American Government* (Columbia University Press 2005), *The New Police Science: The Police Power in Domestic and International Governance* (edited with Mariana Valverde; Stanford University Press 2006), and a casebook on American criminal law.

Reid Griffith Fontaine is a Visiting Research Fellow in the Social Science Research Institute, Center for Child and Family Policy, at Duke University. He has authored more than thirty-five articles in law and psychology. His book *The Mind of the Criminal: The Role of Developmental Social Cognition in Criminal Defense Law* was published by Cambridge University Press in 2012.

Adam R. Fox is a lawyer and interdisciplinary philosophy and law scholar. He received his law degree at the University of Arizona and is currently a graduate student in the Department of Philosophy at Georgia State University.

Susan N. Herman is Centennial Professor of Law at Brooklyn Law School and President of the American Civil Liberties Union. She writes extensively on constitutional and criminal procedure topics for scholarly and other publications, ranging from law reviews and books to periodicals and online publications. Her most recent book, *Taking Liberties: The War on Terror and the Erosion of American Democracy*, was published by Oxford University Press in October 2011.

Emily Hughes is Professor and Bouma Fellow in Law at the University of Iowa College of Law. Her coauthored book, *Federal Habeas Corpus: Cases and Materials* (Carolina Academic Press), is in its second edition. She thanks University of Iowa College of Law students Susan Elgin, Will Gyauch, Jessica Hlubek, Bradon Smith, and Tiffany Spoor for their assistance with various phases of this chapter. She also thanks her dean, Gail Agrawal, for her support, and the Iowa law faculty for commenting on an early draft.

Tonja Jacobi is Professor of Law at Northwestern University School of Law. She specializes in judicial behavior and strategy, examining how judges respond to institutional constraints and attempt to shape the incentives of parties before the court. She has a Ph.D. in political science from Stanford University and a law degree from the Australian National University. She has published in more than twenty peer-reviewed and law review journals and is currently working on a book about the causes and mechanisms of constitutional stability.

Richard A. Leo is a Professor of Law and Dean's Circle Research Scholar at the University of San Francisco. He is the author of dozens of academic articles on police interrogation, false confessions, and/or wrongful convictions, as well as several books on these subjects, including *Police Interrogation and American Justice* (Harvard University Press 2008); *The Wrong Guys: Murder, False Confessions and the Norfolk Four* (New Press 2008, with Tom Wells); and, most recently, *Confessions of Guilt: From Torture to Miranda and Beyond* (Oxford University Press 2012, with George C. Thomas III). He has received numerous individual and career achievement awards for his research and publications, as well as Soros and Guggenheim Fellowships. In 2011 he was elected to the American Law Institute.

Wayne A. Logan is Gary & Sallyn Pajcic Professor of Law at Florida State University. He is author of *Knowledge as Power: Criminal Registration and Community Notification Laws in America* (Stanford University Press 2009).

Janice Nadler is Research Professor at the American Bar Foundation and Professor of Law at Northwestern University School of Law. She received a J.D. from the University of California at Berkeley and a Ph.D. in social psychology from the University of Illinois, Urbana-Champaign. Her scholarly interests lie at the intersection of law and psychology, and her research focuses on moral intuitions, compliance with the law, perceptions of injustice, negotiation, and dispute resolution.

John T. Parry is Professor of Law at Lewis & Clark Law School. He is the author of *Understanding Torture: Law, Violence, and Political Identity* (Michigan 2010), as well as numerous articles on issues relating to criminal law, foreign relations law, and transnational and international criminal law. He is also coauthor of *Criminal Law: Cases, Statutes, and Lawyering Strategies* (Lexis 2005, 2d ed. 2010) and a member of the American Law Institute. He thanks Tung Yin for helpful comments and Jenny Logan for research assistance.

Amanda C. Pustilnik is an Associate Professor at the University of Maryland's Francis King Carey School of Law, where she developed a course on law and neuroscience and teaches criminal law and evidence. She previously taught as a lecturer at Harvard Law School. She is the editor of the SSRN ejournal *Law & Neuroscience* and publishes and blogs on the intersections of neuroscience and criminal law.

L. Song Richardson is Professor of Law at the University of Iowa College of Law. Her legal career includes work as a state and federal public defender, as an assistant counsel at the NAACP Legal Defense Fund representing capital defendants in habeas cases, and as a partner in a boutique criminal law firm.

She is a member of the American Law Institute. Her research explores the legal implications of mind sciences research on criminal procedure, criminal law, and policing. Her work has been published in law journals at Yale, Berkeley, Duke, Northwestern, and Cornell, among others.

Christopher Slobogin occupies the Milton Underwood Chair at Vanderbilt University Law School. He has written extensively about the Fourth Amendment and surveillance, including articles in the Chicago, Minnesota, and UCLA law reviews. In 2007 the University of Chicago Press published his book *Privacy at Risk: The New Government Surveillance and the Fourth Amendment*.

Juliet P. Stumpf is Professor of Law at Lewis & Clark Law School. Her scholarship explores the intersection of immigration law with criminal law and other substantive areas including constitutional law, civil rights, and employment law. Her research is interdisciplinary, examining the insights that sociology, psychology, and political science contribute to the study of immigration law. Representative publications include *Doing Time: Crimmigration Law and the Perils of Haste*, 58 UCLA L. Rev. 1705 (2011); *Fitting Punishment*, 66 Wash. & Lee L. Rev. 1683 (2009); *States of Confusion: the Rise of State and Local Power over Immigration*, 86 N.C. L. Rev. 1557 (2008); and *The Crimmigration Crisis: Immigrants, Crime, and Sovereign Power*, 56 Am. U. L. Rev. 367 (2006). For helpful comments and conversations, she thanks Jennifer Chacón, Jack Chin, Ingrid Eagly, Lucas Guttentag, Mary Holland, Anil Kalhan, Hiroshi Motomura, Jenny Roberts, Mike Wishnie, and participants at workshops at Cornell University and the Law and Society Association's 2012 Annual Meeting.

Stephen I. Vladeck is Professor of Law and Associate Dean for Scholarship at American University Washington College of Law. He was part of the legal team that successfully challenged the Bush administration's use of military tribunals at Guantánamo Bay, Cuba, in *Hamdan v. Rumsfeld*, 548 U.S. 557 (2006), and he has coauthored party and amicus briefs in a host of other major lawsuits, many of which have challenged the U.S. government's surveillance and detention of terrorism suspects. Vladeck is a coeditor of Aspen Publishers' leading national security and counterterrorism law casebooks, a member of the American Law Institute, a senior editor of the peer-reviewed *Journal of National Security Law and Policy*, a senior contributor to the Lawfare blog, the Chair of the Section on Federal Courts of the Association of American Law Schools, the Supreme Court Fellow at the Constitution Project, and a Fellow at the Center on National Security at Fordham University School of Law. He thanks Gal Bruck and Pasha Sternberg for research assistance.

Acknowledgments

Many people helped produce this book. First and foremost are the participants in the conference "The Constitution in 2020: The Future of Criminal Justice," held at Florida State University College of Law in October 2010, a group that includes many of the people who have contributed to this book. In particular, Susan A. Bandes, Jack Balkin, Reid Griffith Fontaine, Wayne A. Logan, Dan Markel, and the American Constitution Society made that conference possible. Thanks are due as well to our respective institutions: Lewis & Clark Law School and the University of Iowa College of Law. At Lewis & Clark, particular thanks are due to Dean Robert Klonoff and Associate Dean Brian Blum, as well as to Ed Brunet, Lisa Frenz, Andy Marion, and Sue Page. At the University of Iowa, thanks are due to Dean Gail Agrawal and to law students Solomon Chouicha and Taylor Whitten for their valuable assistance with advancing this book to completion. Finally, the support of John Berger at Cambridge University Press has been invaluable.

Introduction

John T. Parry and L. Song Richardson

What is the future of criminal justice in the United States? There is ample room for pessimism, especially with the constitutional aspects of criminal law. No one doubts that the Warren Court era of the early 1950s through the 1960s was a high point for the constitutional rights of criminal defendants. Nor is there serious dispute that, on balance, the Supreme Court since then has adopted a more restrained attitude toward the constitutional rights of criminal defendants.

Changes in constitutional criminal law reflect more than judicial appointments and judicial attitudes, however. They also derive from political decisions and popular attitudes. Since the mid-1960s, national and local politicians have tended to support the idea of a "war on crime" that puts a premium on toughness toward lawbreaking and offenders (or suspected offenders) at the expense of individual rights.[1] By and large, the voting public has supported these efforts.

The political decisions associated with the war on crime have had several concrete and negative results. More and more conduct has been criminalized, often through multiple statutes that define overlapping crimes (sometimes overlapping state and federal crimes) for the same basic conduct. Incarceration rates have expanded, especially among young black men;[2] maximum and supermax security prisons have proliferated;[3] mandatory minimums ensure lengthy prison sentences for nearly all felonies in many jurisdictions;[4] and the consequences of criminal convictions are dire. Police and prosecutors continue to enjoy wide discretion to control the outcomes of criminal cases,[5] and the development of new surveillance technologies expands their ability to gather evidence in ways that erode traditional notions of personal privacy. Politicians and commentators urge people to live in fear of violent crime and to be suspicious of people who act in unusual ways or who just seem to be out of place.[6] Undocumented immigrants automatically become criminals through the act of crossing a national border. These developments are important in their own right; they are also causes and effects of judicial decisions to rethink the scope of constitutional rights and other constitutional and structural limitations on criminal law and punishment.

The reaction to the September 11, 2001, terrorist attacks has elevated the level of fear and added new fuel to the political responses to criminal justice. The resulting "war on terror" joined the war on crime and put increased pressure on courts to adapt constitutional rights and substantive law to meet the perceived new challenge.[7] Because antiterror activities are international in scope and involve military as well as police action, they also shine a spotlight on international and transnational criminal law, on the choice between military and law enforcement responses to disorder, and on the interactions between the civilian and military criminal justice systems.[8]

The overall picture, however, is more complicated than we have suggested so far. Alongside these developments eroding the constitutional rights of criminal defendants are Supreme Court decisions placing some limits on the power of the political branches to eliminate or restrict the scope of these rights. For instance, to the surprise of many, the Court struck down Congress's attempt to overrule *Miranda v. Arizona*,[9] the landmark decision requiring police to inform suspects of their rights to counsel and to remain silent before a custodial interrogation.[10] In another unexpected decision, the Court overruled a prior decision that gave the police virtually unchecked discretion to conduct a warrantless search of a vehicle's passenger compartment after an arrest of the vehicle's occupant.[11] Most recently, a unanimous Supreme Court ruled that officers must obtain a warrant before attaching a GPS device to an automobile.[12]

In light of this varied landscape, what is the future of constitutional criminal law in the United States? The chapters in this collection, each written by an expert in the field, address this question. They are grouped around a series of themes: the scope of the criminal law and access to counsel; policing and privacy; race and criminal procedure; technology and the surveillance society; confessions and *Miranda*; conviction, sentencing, and incarceration; and finally, immigration, terrorism, national security, and transnational crime. Each chapter addresses an important topic in constitutional criminal law, first summarizing the current state of the law and then offering an insightful glimpse into its future direction.

The first two chapters, which address foundational issues in criminal justice, compose Part I. Stephen B. Bright begins the book by detailing the contemporary crisis in the right to counsel. Too few lawyers are available, and they have opportunity to provide effective representation to their clients. The criminal justice system ends up processing cases through plea deals, and the potentially meritorious issues that might emerge if lawyers had the time to think even briefly about cases instead are lost. The solution, Bright maintains, is not only obvious but also required by any meaningful commitment to equal justice and the right to counsel: "adequately funded, independent public defender offices." From the perspective of criminal procedure, a meaningful right to counsel is central to the future of criminal justice.

In his chapter, Markus D. Dubber addresses a different, but equally important issue: the lack of any constitutional foundation for the American criminal justice system and, particularly, for the substantive criminal law. Dubber explains that, in contrast to European countries, there has never been a meaningful debate in the United States about "the legitimacy of punishment in a self-governing polity." What this means, moreover, is that the effort to provide such a foundation must focus on the present and the future. Dubber calls for an inquiry into the ways in which the Constitution could structure the criminal justice system and limit its scope. He finds a glimmer of hope for such an effort in the Supreme Court's 2003 *Lawrence v. Texas* decision, which suggested that "autonomy of self" is central to constitutional liberty[13] and which could support limiting doctrines similar to those developed by the Canadian Supreme Court and the German Constitutional Court.

The second part of the book considers race and criminal procedure. Susan A. Bandes assesses the impact of another landmark Warren Court decision: *Terry v. Ohio*,[14] which clarified the circumstances under which police can stop and frisk a person who they suspect might be engaged in criminal activity. The Court attempted to balance individual and law enforcement interests, but the impact of *Terry* has been to license the intensive – and all too frequently unjustified – policing of certain classes of people, typically black and Latino males, and certain kinds of neighborhoods, typically those with higher concentrations of minority and/or poor residents. Bandes considers a range of possible solutions, from changes in legal doctrine (which she doubts will be forthcoming), to legislative and administrative action (including investigations of local police departments by the federal Department of Justice), to changes in police culture. She is less than sanguine about the prospects for beneficial change, but she holds out the hope that informed, good faith dialogue could foster the political will necessary to move forward.

L. Song Richardson's chapter uses lessons from the field of psychology to analyze police practices and the Supreme Court's decision in *Terry v. Ohio*. More than four decades of research demonstrate that most individuals, regardless of their race, have implicit, that is, unconscious, racial biases that can influence behaviors toward and judgments of nonwhites. She argues that these unconscious racial biases can explain why police disproportionately subject nonwhites to stops and frisks even though "stops and searches of whites are more often successful in yielding evidence of criminal activity." She also sheds light on how the *Terry* decision reinforces and magnifies the effects of that bias. Richardson considers several changes in legal doctrine but ultimately concludes that structural changes in the operation of police departments and in officer training are more likely to address the effects of unconscious racial biases on police behavior and offers some suggested reforms.

Part III turns to the intersecting issues of policing and privacy. Tonja Jacobi's chapter takes aim at the exclusionary rule, which as a constitutional remedy imposed on state courts for police violations of the Fourth Amendment is one of the most significant accomplishments of the Warren Court's criminal procedure revolution. Jacobi's criticisms, however, do not follow the familiar path of arguing that the exclusionary rule results in acquitting the guilty. Rather, marshaling social science evidence, she contends that the exclusionary rule's effects are far more perverse. Because juries and judges tend to assume that gaps in the prosecution's evidence result from exclusion of evidence, the rule does help the guilty, but it does so "at the expense of the actually innocent – the exclusionary rule actually *decreases* the chance of finding a reasonable doubt for those defendants most likely to be innocent." She insists that a rational system of criminal procedure would adopt "rules that aid screening between innocent and guilty defendants, and forgo rules [such as the exclusionary rule] that blur those categories."

In her chapter, Janice Nadler addresses a different Fourth Amendment issue – the widespread use of "consent searches." While the Constitution certainly permits law enforcement officials to conduct searches when a person freely consents, Supreme Court case law allows police to obtain consent under coercive circumstances. The Court's doctrine ignores the power imbalance between a police officer and, for example, a person on a bus that has been stopped by police. Even more, Nadler suggests, the Court's refusal to recognize the power imbalance expresses and shapes a set of undesirable attitudes on the part of both police and populace. Rather than pursue a policy of coerced consent that treats the subject of such a search as presumptively guilty, Nadler argues that police should act in ways that not only cultivate their legitimacy in the eyes of the public but also increase the chances of genuine cooperation.

Amanda C. Pustilnik explores the increasing role that neurotechnology will play in criminal investigations. As researchers and investigators become more and more confident of their ability to analyze brain waves or blood flow in the brain, they will seek to use these technologies to supplement – and perhaps even in some cases to replace – more familiar forms of interrogation and search. Pustilnik first explains developments in neuroscience that support the use of these technologies to assist the investigation of crime. She then considers the ways in which Fourth and Fifth Amendment doctrine could intersect with these efforts, particularly with respect to notions of privacy. She concludes that the inevitable expansion of these technologies "will require reexamining the relationship among physical, information, and spatial intrusions," and she details the difficult choices that will confront courts in the years ahead.

Part IV focuses on technology and the surveillance society. Wayne A. Logan discusses the use of information, particularly the information generated by registration and community notification laws, to monitor offenders who are no longer incarcerated and to inform the public about their movements. Although this example focuses on a specific form of postconviction monitoring, Logan's argument sweeps more broadly. He highlights the curiously passive role the judiciary has played as information gathering and sharing have increased, despite the fact that this information explicitly is used as a method of social control. But he also avoids treating social control through information as a negative development – as he points out, "compared to the manifold negative consequences of physical imprisonment, increased resort to any information-based, noncarceral strategy is a potential cause for optimism." That is to say, whether the gathering and sharing of information will become parts of a comprehensive, effective, but also humane response to criminal activity is, as Logan emphasizes, the critical issue.

For his part, Christopher Slobogin considers the increased use of monitoring technologies to monitor, track, and gather information about suspects. Most important to his analysis is the fact that contemporary Fourth Amendment doctrine has very little to say about these activities. As he explains, Fourth Amendment doctrine focuses largely on "physical searches" even as police increasingly are relying on "virtual searches ... that do not require physical access to premises, people, papers, or effects and can often be carried out covertly from far away." Slobogin urges courts to bring the Fourth Amendment into the twenty-first century by including virtual searches within its confines so that courts can consider the reasonableness of the proposed activity. Equally important, he insists that constitutional criminal procedure has something to say about police practices in general, whether or not those practices conform to traditional models.

The chapters in Part V address the constitutional law of police interrogation. Richard A. Leo examines the problem of false confessions. His survey of this critical problem identifies three primary errors made by police: misclassification of an innocent person as guilty, the use of psychologically coercive methods, and the disclosure of nonpublic facts to suspects, such that the false confession appears to contain "persuasive indicia of reliability." Turning to the law of false confessions, Leo points out that contemporary doctrine concerns itself with the process that produces the confession, such as whether or not the suspect received the *Miranda* warnings and had access to counsel, and not enough with the actual truthfulness of the confession that results from the process. If courts paid greater attention to reliability, Leo argues, the resulting doctrine would force changes in police practices while also reducing the number of false confessions and wrongful convictions.

Emily Hughes takes up the topic of the *Miranda* doctrine in its current form, as it applies to truthful statements obtained under circumstances that implicate the privilege against self-incrimination. Her chapter focuses on the 2003 decision in *Missouri v. Seibert*[15] that addressed a police tactic of interrogating without the *Miranda* warnings, obtaining a confession, then giving the *Miranda* warnings and having the suspect repeat the confession. The Supreme Court held that the confession was inadmissible, but its ruling made clear that cases will turn on their specific context. Justice Souter's plurality opinion proposed a multifactor inquiry to determine when "Miranda warnings delivered midstream could be effective enough to accomplish their objective."[16] Hughes highlights the ambiguity of *Miranda* law after the *Seibert* decision by presenting seven variations on the facts of *Seibert*. The ambiguities flowing from *Seibert*, she observes, support the conclusions that the Supreme Court is deliberately undermining *Miranda* and creating incentives for police and state judges to ignore the underlying principles of the *Miranda* doctrine. The Supreme Court is able to announce and adhere to clear rules. It is not too late, Hughes suggests, for the Supreme Court to turn the *Miranda* doctrine in that direction.

The chapters in Part VI address topics related to conviction, sentencing, and incarceration. Gabriel J. Chin canvasses the collateral consequences of criminal convictions, which range widely from loss of the right to vote, to possible deportation, restrictions on employment, registration requirements, and more. With few exceptions, the Supreme Court has allowed these consequences to proliferate without constitutional regulation, on the theory that they are not punishment. Furthermore, Chin suggests, the high levels of criminal convictions in most states, coupled with the costs of mass incarceration, create strong incentives for governments to use collateral consequences as an alternative sanction since they are less costly. Chin argues that the Supreme Court should revisit its general refusal to intervene in this area and, instead, should "recognize that systematic subjection to collateral consequences is constitutional punishment." At the very least, he urges, judges should warn defendants about the possible consequences of the decision to plead guilty.

Adam R. Fox and Reid Griffith Fontaine address the intersection of mental illness and criminal responsibility, and the implications of this intersection for Eighth Amendment doctrine. They note that the Supreme Court recently has been receptive to specific claims about the reduced responsibility of juveniles and mentally handicapped individuals. Their chapter considers whether these rulings should extend to psychopathic individuals, a possibility that they recognize "is considerably less likely to attract public sympathy." After describing the behavioral features of psychopathy and the kinds of criminal behavior in which psychopaths are more likely to engage, they discuss the evidence that psychopathy has a neurological basis that diminishes the moral agency and responsibility of psychopaths for criminal conduct – albeit to different degrees for different individuals. They suggest that Eighth Amendment doctrine supports the conclusion that courts should take into account the diminished responsibility of psychopaths at various stages in the criminal process.

Part VII introduces several topics that too often are excluded from discussions of criminal justice but that are increasingly central to the operation of federal criminal law. Juliet P. Stumpf's chapter, for example, examines the rise of "crimmigration" – the increasing intersection of criminal law and immigration law. Much of crimmigration law is federal, punishing people who have not complied with federal immigration law (often, the lack of compliance takes the form of illegally entering the country). However, her chapter explores some of the ways in which state law contributes to the crimmigration phenomenon. Stumpf identifies "a submerged norm of proportionality" that should play a role in evaluating the legitimacy of state criminal law responses to illegal immigration. She argues that to the extent that a person's unlawful presence in the United States also includes "the potential for lawful integration," state criminalization of immigration not only has the potential to frustrate the purposes of federal immigration regulation, but also threatens to burden that person with the label of criminal even as he or she still has the "potential for redemption through legalization."

Susan N. Herman's chapter covers the so-called war on terror. She argues that the response to the September 11 attacks "has profoundly changed American criminal law in two very different ways." First, it has fostered a system of military detention and military commission trials for people who, before 9/11, would have gone through the ordinary criminal justice system. Second, the creation of these extraordinary processes creates pressure to dilute the protections that typically accompany prosecution in the ordinary system. She warns that these changes place the ordinary criminal justice system at risk, so that all defendants, in whatever forum, will have to make do with "exceptions and watered down rights." Herman provides significant examples of how these pressures are playing out in American criminal justice. However, she also reminds readers of the web of laws and doctrines that have undergirded criminal law for decades, a structure that is capable of handling the challenges posed by the war on terror, if only officials – and the public – will trust it. Whether the future will see a return to the pre-9/11 structure, or whether the processes set in motion by the response to those events will continue to reshape the criminal justice system, is a critical but still unanswerable question.

Stephen I. Vladeck's chapter considers a related development: the convergence of the civilian and military justice systems. Vladeck notes that the typical account of this process extolls the extent to which the military justice system has become more like the civilian one, gradually developing greater procedural protections and making room for independent appellate review by civilian judges, including the Supreme Court. But his chapter focuses on a different convergence: the gradual increase in the criminal jurisdiction of military courts to include conduct previously reserved for civilian courts. Courts-martial now prosecute service members for any offense, even those unrelated to their military service. In addition, Congress has expanded the ability of military courts to try civilians who serve with or accompany the armed forces overseas. Vladeck's third example is the use of the military commissions established at Guantánamo Bay Naval Base to prosecute noncitizens for war crimes, including crimes that are not subject to military jurisdiction under international law. Vladeck cautions against this expansion and urges a return to the principle that military jurisdiction should be confined to where it is necessary.

The final chapter, by John T. Parry, considers the growth of transnational and international law enforcement efforts. Parry suggests that, in general, globalization leads to an increase of executive power at the expense of legislative power. In the area of crime control, this expansion also draws on the already immense and increasing executive power over criminal prosecutions. The rise of what Parry calls the "national security sovereign" – an executive branch that claims the authority to manage seemingly frequent foreign relations crises and advance the national security interests of the United States – completes the picture. Taken together, these developments pose several risks, such as diluted procedural rights and new or redefined substantive offenses that will generalize beyond the national security context. Even more, Parry argues, these developments will increase the politicization of criminal law and will erode traditional rule of law values. Only a multifaceted opposition, or the unlikely development of self-restraint on the part of the executive branch, can stop or reverse the growth of the national security sovereign.

The Constitution and the Future of Criminal Justice in America puts cutting edge issues of theory and doctrine into concrete and accessible context. Our goal is not only to advance academic debate but also to influence a broader conversation about public policy in these areas. By looking to the future, this collection seeks to shape an ongoing dialogue about criminal justice and the Constitution.

Every book of this kind has gaps. This is a collection of essays about the Constitution and criminal law. It is not a book that focuses on criminology or criminal law more generally (either philosophically or doctrinally),[17] although several chapters touch on these topics. Most of the time, the chapters in this book focus unapologetically on legal doctrine. Courts create, apply, and change doctrine, and they do it in specific cases that have direct impacts on the interests of individuals. Judicial decisions, made within the parameters of legal doctrines, send people to jail or release them. Legal doctrines shape the reasoning of judges and the arguments of lawyers. They also impact police policies, training, budgets, and political decisions. And, not least important, these doctrines also impact the ways in which people think about their civil rights and liberties. This book exists precisely because constitutional law matters to criminal justice. Looking forward, the overarching goal of this book is to make sure that the ongoing interaction between the two is beneficial.

Notes

1. For an early and pessimistic assessment, see James Vorenberg, *The War on Crime*, THE ATLANTIC MONTHLY, May 1972. For a more recent and even more pessimistic assessment, see HENRY RUTH & KEVIN R. REITZ, THE CHALLENGE OF CRIME: RETHINKING OUR RESPONSE (2003).
2. MICHELLE ALEXANDER, THE NEW JIM CROW: MASS INCARCERATION IN THE AGE OF COLORBLINDNESS (2010).
3. E.g., SHARON SHALEY, SUPERMAX: CONTROLLING RISK THROUGH SOLITARY CONFINEMENT (2009).
4. For a useful introduction to the debate over and effect of mandatory minimums in the context of federal sentencing, see U.S. Sentencing Commission, *Report to Congress: Mandatory Minimum Penalties in the Federal Criminal Justice System* (Oct. 2011), available at http://www.ussc.gov/Legislative_and_Public_Affairs/Congressional_Testimony_and_Reports/Mandatory_Minimum_Penalties/20111031_RtC_Mandatory_Minimum.cfm (last visited May 1, 2013). For the specific issue of life without parole as a sentencing option, see LIFE WITHOUT PAROLE: AMERICA'S NEW DEATH PENALTY? (Charles J. Ogletree & Austin Sarat eds., 2012).
5. This is a major theme in WILLIAM J. STUNTZ, THE COLLAPSE OF AMERICAN CRIMINAL JUSTICE (2011).
6. See JONATHAN SIMON, GOVERNING THROUGH CRIME: HOW THE WAR ON CRIME TRANSFORMED AMERICAN DEMOCRACY AND CREATED A CULTURE OF FEAR (2007).

7 E.g., William J. Stuntz, *Local Policing after the Terror*, 111 YALE L.J. 2137 (2002).
8 For many useful early perspectives on these issues, see *Symposium: Law and the War on Terrorism*, 25 HARV. J. L. & PUB. POL'Y 399–834 (2002).
9 *Miranda v. Arizona*, 384 U.S. 436 (1966).
10 *Dickerson v. United States*, 530 U.S. 428 (2000).
11 *Arizona v. Gant*, 556 U.S. 332 (2009), overruling *New York v. Belton*, 453 U.S. 454 (1981).
12 *United States v. Jones*, 132 S. Ct. 945 (2012); see also *Kyllo v. United States*, 533 U.S. 27 (2001) (holding that use of a thermal imaging device to scan a residence "is a 'search' and is presumptively unreasonable without a warrant").
13 *Lawrence v. Texas*, 539 U.S. 558 (2003).
14 *Terry v. Ohio*, 392 U.S. 1 (1968).
15 *Missouri v. Seibert*, 542 U.S. 600 (2003)
16 *Id.* at 615.
17 For useful recent books on these topics, see CRIMINAL LAW CONVERSATIONS (Paul Robinson et al., eds. 2009); THE PHILOSOPHICAL FOUNDATIONS OF CRIMINAL LAW (R. A. Duff & Stuart Green, eds. 2011); CRIME AND PUBLIC POLICY (James Q. Wilson & Joan Petersilia, eds. 2011).

Part I

FOUNDATIONS – THE SCOPE OF CRIMINAL
LAW AND ACCESS TO COUNSEL

1

The Past and Future of the Right to an Attorney for Poor People Accused of Crimes

Stephen B. Bright

The Supreme Court declared more than a half-century ago that "there can be no equal justice where the kind of trial a man gets depends on the amount of money he has."[1] The Court later recognized that representation by lawyers is "fundamental and essential" for fairness in criminal cases.[2] It required that lawyers be provided to people accused of crimes who could not afford them in all cases where there is a possible loss of liberty.[3]

The legal system is so complex and contains so many procedural traps that a layperson accused of a crime can no more navigate it alone than a passenger can fly a plane in the absence of the pilot. Those accused of crimes rely upon lawyers to protect all of their legal rights, investigate thoroughly the facts, test the prosecution's case against them through cross-examination of witnesses and other means, produce evidence that casts doubt upon guilt, and, for those found guilty, present information about the client and argue for a sentence that takes into consideration the individual circumstances of the client. This is fundamental to a fair, legitimate, and credible criminal justice system that produces reliable verdicts.[4]

Nevertheless, most people who cannot afford a lawyer do not receive this kind of representation. The kind of justice people receive depends very much on the amount of money they have. And, although the right to a lawyer for those who cannot afford one was not established until midway through the twentieth century, the situation today does not differ largely from what one newspaper recognized at the end of the nineteenth: "Nobody but a simpleton believes the ancient fiction that one man's life and liberty are as highly

In addition to the authorities cited, this essay is based on and includes the author's observations from being a public defender; litigating capital cases, challenges to indigent defense systems and ineffective assistance of counsel claims; teaching and counseling defense attorneys; and studying and trying to improve the legal representation provided to poor people accused of crimes over the last 35 years.

esteemed by the law as another's; and that one man, without reference to the linings of his pockets, has the same chance before the law as his neighbor who may be able to fee lawyers."[5] While the wealthy could delay cases indefinitely, "the poor wretch, white and black, is promptly forced to trial, ready or not ready, and as promptly convicted and punished. Such inequalities in the enforcement of our criminal laws have destroyed public confidence in the integrity and impartiality of our courts."[6]

The same could be said about the processing of people through the courts today. Many courtrooms look as if a slave ship is docked outside the courthouse. A large number of men – almost all of them people of color – wearing orange jumpsuits are led in, handcuffed together. One or more lawyers talk to each one of them. Of course, the conversations are not confidential – the defendants are handcuffed to each other. The conversations are generally not very long. Usually, they go something like "here is what the plea offer is, and this is what you will get."

A short time later, the judge takes the bench. Each defendant hobbles up to the podium in chains, pleads guilty, answers the judge's questions, waives his rights – probably without understanding either the rights or the consequences of the plea being entered – and is sentenced. Sometimes the guilty pleas are taken in groups. Some plead guilty to get out of jail, even if innocent. That is called "meet 'em and plead 'em," and that is all the representation some people receive. It is not legal representation; it is processing people through the courts in a way that resembles the operations of a fast food restaurant.

Without zealous and effective representation for the accused, there is no adversary system. Instead, there is the pretense of one. It is not fair and it does not produce reliable verdicts. The criminal courts are failing in their most basic responsibility – separating the guilty from the innocent. There have been 281 exonerations since 1989 based on the results of DNA testing – 17 of those exonerated were on death row.[7] But there is biological evidence subject to DNA testing in only 10 percent of cases. The same number of mistakes are being made in the other 90 percent, but no one finds out. Innocent people remain in prison; perpetrators of crimes remain free to commit other crimes.

Todd Willingham was convicted of arson in Texas after his house burned down and his three children died in the fire.[8] An assistant fire chief and a deputy fire marshal testified that in their opinion the fire was arson. Another man, Ernest Ray Willis, also was sentenced to death in an almost identical arson case. But Willis was fortunate – a law firm from New York represented him in post-conviction proceedings. The firm devoted more than a dozen years to the case and spent millions of dollars on fire consultants, private investigators, and forensic experts to analyze the evidence in his case and point out that the expert testimony at his trial was based on theories and assumptions that had been completely discredited.[9]

Those same theories were the basis for the opinions in Willingham's case that the cause of the fire was arson. For example, an expert told the jury that intricate patterns of cracks on glass – "crazed glass" – recovered from the scene were proof that an accelerant had been used to start the fire.[10]

However, studies have found that crazed glass results from cold water hitting hot glass, such as when a fire department sprays streams of water on a fire, trying to put it out.[11] There were similar explanations for other testimony given in both the Willis and Willingham cases.[12]

When the law firm took its evidence to the prosecutor in Willis's case, the prosecutor consulted his own expert and concluded that there had not been arson.[13] Willis was released. An expert who examined the evidence in Willingham's case reached the same conclusion – that there had been no arson. Willingham did not kill his one-year-old twin girls and his two-year-old girl when he had no motive to do so. But Willingham's case had already been through the courts. Texas executed Willingham on February 14, 2004. A switch of the lawyers in the two cases could have changed the outcomes. It is likely that if the New York law firm had taken Willingham's case, he would be alive today, and Willis would be dead.

James T. Fisher Jr. spent 26 ½ years in the custody of Oklahoma – most of it under sentence of death – without ever having a competent lawyer and, as a result, without ever having a fair and reliable determination of whether he was guilty of any crime. Fisher, a black man, was convicted in 1983 of the murder of a white man on the basis of the dubious testimony of the man originally charged with the murder. The lawyer assigned to represent him tried Fisher's case and twenty-four others during September of 1983, including another capital murder case the week before Fisher's trial.[14] The lawyer called no witnesses at either the guilt or penalty phase of trial other than Fisher. He made no opening statement or closing argument at either phase. The lawyer said *only nine words* during the entire sentencing phase of the trial.[15] Four of the words were "the equivalent of judicial pleasantries" and the other five "formed an ill-founded, unsupported and ultimately rejected objection to one portion of the prosecutor's closing argument."[16] The nine words contained no advocacy on behalf of Fisher.

On appeal, the Oklahoma Court of Criminal Appeals pronounced itself "deeply disturbed by defense counsel's lack of participation and advocacy during the sentencing stage," but it was not disturbed enough to reverse the conviction or sentence.[17] It held that the outcome would not have been different even without the incompetent representation.[18]

Nineteen years after Fisher's trial, a federal court of appeals set aside the conviction, finding that Fisher's lawyer was "grossly inept" and disloyal to his client by "exhibiting actual doubt and hostility toward his client's case."[19] It found that the lawyer "destroyed his own client's credibility and bolstered the credibility of the star witness for the prosecution" and "sabotaged his client's defense by repeatedly reiterating the state's version of events and the damaging evidence he had elicited himself."[20] The court observed that the prosecution's case against Mr. Fisher "was not overwhelming" but "in essence a swearing match between Mr. Fisher and [the state's witness], either of whom could have committed the murder."[21]

Oklahoma gave Fisher a second trial in 2005 and a lawyer who was drinking heavily, abusing cocaine, and neglecting his cases.[22] The lawyer physically threatened Fisher at a pretrial hearing and, as a result, Fisher refused to attend his own trial.[23] He was convicted and sentenced to death again. This time both the state trial court and the Oklahoma Court of Criminal Appeals recognized that Fisher had again been denied his right to counsel and that it made a difference.[24] His conviction was reversed again. Prosecutors agreed to Fisher's release in July 2010, provided that he be banished from Oklahoma forever.[25] Fisher may not have been guilty of any crime – he never had a constitutional trial – but he spent 26½ years in custody.

Other capital cases, which involve the highest stakes and the greatest demands on both lawyers and the legal system, also provide shameful examples of deficient legal representation of the accused.[26] There have been three cases in Houston alone where the defense lawyers slept at capital murder trials. In one of those cases, the defendant, Carl Johnson, was executed.[27] In another, Calvin Burdine was given a new trial by the *en banc* Fifth Circuit Court of Appeals,[28] after a panel of that court had upheld his conviction and death sentence.[29] George McFarland's conviction and death sentence have twice been upheld by the Texas Court of Criminal Appeals even though McFarland's lead counsel slept during trial.[30]

The need for competent legal representation is about more than fair determinations of guilt or innocence. It is critically important at every stage of the process from bail hearings to sentencing. Jacqueline Winbrone was arrested in 2007 in one of many New York counties that appoint individual lawyers to represent the poor. Her bail was set at $10,000.[31] No lawyer represented her at the bail hearing, and Winbrone, who was the sole caretaker of her husband, could not reach her court-appointed lawyer to seek a bail reduction in order to care for her husband, who needed transportation to dialysis treatment several times per week.[32] Days later, her husband died.[33] Ms. Winbrone was also unsuccessful in trying to reach the lawyer to obtain a bail reduction or even a temporary release from jail to attend his funeral. Eventually, she contacted a prisoners' rights organization, and an attorney from it secured her release on her own recognizance.[34] Ultimately, the charge against Winbrone – possession of a firearm found in the family car – was dismissed.[35]

As Ms. Winbrone's experience illustrates, the process of arrest and pretrial incarceration may be a severe punishment, regardless of guilt or innocence. Whether one has counsel from the outset may depend upon the amount of money he or she has. A person who can afford a lawyer will usually hire one within hours of arrest. The lawyer will attempt to secure the person's release from jail, often successfully; start an immediate investigation of the charges; and then represent the client through the complex legal system. People who cannot afford lawyers may languish in jail long after arrest without seeing a lawyer.

A person who stays in jail for days or weeks after being arrested may lose his or her job and home as a result even if the charges are ultimately dismissed. People may go from being right on the margins of making it in society to being homeless. Some – struggling to overcome enormous challenges, such as mental illness or limitations; addiction; lack of family, friends, or any other support system; or extreme poverty – may never be able to get their lives back on track.

The availability and quality of lawyers for poor people accused of crimes vary from state to state and even from county to county within a state. While there is good, even exemplary representation in some places, most states and counties are more concerned with limiting costs than providing high-quality representation and ensuring fairness in their courts.

In order to provide competent attorneys to defend the poor, states must at least provide adequate funding for lawyers, investigators, and consultations with experts; structure, such as public defender offices;[36] training so lawyers know what they are doing;[37] and independence from the judiciary and the prosecution.[38] The problem in most states is inadequate funding, which leads to crushing caseloads that leave lawyers without the time needed to give clients individual attention and to investigate their cases thoroughly and consult with experts.[39] Insufficient funding and lack of structure in some places result in representation by grossly incompetent lawyers, who do not know the law, ignore their clients, fail to investigate and present critical evidence, and provide only perfunctory representation.[40]

States trying to fine, imprison, and execute people have not been enthusiastic about paying for good legal representation that might frustrate those objectives. The prosecution's chances of obtaining a conviction improve if the defendant is poorly represented. Besides, as Attorney General Robert F.

Kennedy observed in 1963, the poor person accused of a crime has no lobby.[41] As a result, funding for representation for those who cannot afford lawyers has not kept up as the number of those imprisoned has grown from 200,000 in the 1970s to 2.3 million today.[42] The United States has the highest incarceration rate of any country in the world and more than 7 million people on probation, on parole, or in community programs.[43] All of these people pass through the criminal courts.

It costs between $65 and $75 billion to hold so many people in jails and prisons.[44] About 60 percent of inmates are held by state governments, about one-third are held by local governments, and less than 10% are held by the federal government.[45] State and local governments are willing to pay an average cost of $26,000 per prisoner per year,[46] but they are unwilling to pay for legal representation that would ensure fairness in the process that results in people going to prison or jail. The latest available data on spending for legal representation for the poor indicated approximately $3.5 billion was spent in 2005.[47] Even if that amount had doubled by 2013 – which is doubtful – it is still less than 10 percent of what is spent on prisons and jails.

There are also marked disparities in funding for the prosecution and the defense. A study in Tennessee found that funding for the prosecution of poor people was $130 to $139 million, while funding to provide lawyers in those cases was only $56.4 million, a difference of $73 million.[48] A comparison of prosecution and defense budgets in California found that indigent defense was funded less than the prosecution by at least $300 million dollars in 2006 and 2007.[49]

The system is further out of balance as a result of the millions of dollars the federal government showers on prosecutors and law enforcement for various programs such as drug enforcement, highway safety, and domestic violence and the access that state prosecutors have to many federal, state, and local resources such as law enforcement agencies, crime laboratories, and expert witnesses.[50] Programs such as drug task forces result in many more arrests. Those arrested will need lawyers when they are prosecuted in the criminal courts. But the federal government seldom provides any funding for that purpose. For example, in 2010, prosecutors and law enforcement in Dade County, Florida, received $4.3 million in federal Byrne and Justice Assistance grants; the public defender received $150,000.[51] What is unusual about this is that the public defender received anything.

Public defender offices, with structure, specialization, training, and organization, are the most cost-effective way to provide good-quality representation. Public defenders develop an expertise in defending the accused and are regularly at the courthouse and the jail. Private attorneys must also be part of a program of providing representation to the poor. They represent clients in cases where there is a conflict of interest and other cases that the public defender cannot take because of workload or other reasons. They can use their expertise to do as much as possible with the time and resources they have for each case.

Many states and localities have established and funded public defender offices – the New York Legal Aid Society and the Los Angeles County Public Defender Office have been representing clients since around 1915, but other counties in those states have not followed their example. Florida set up public defender offices in each of its judicial circuits in 1963, in response to the Supreme Court decision from that state declaring a right to counsel,[52] but Georgia did not get around to it until 2005, and Montana established its system in 2006. Other jurisdictions – including Alabama, Michigan, Texas, and much of New York and Pennsylvania – still have not set up public defender programs to this day and rely primarily on the appointment of lawyers by judges or administrators or contracts with lawyers to handle a certain number of cases for a fixed fee.

Regardless of structure and specialization, funding influences what a public defender office can do and how well it does it. The workload of Missouri's statewide public defender program increased by more than twelve thousand cases in a six-year period, but the program received no additional staff during that time.[53] At the end of 2011, it was sixty-six lawyers short of what it needed to handle its current workload.[54] The director of the state public defender commission wrote in the program's annual report, "triage has replaced justice in Missouri's courts." People languish in jail "for weeks or even months with no access to counsel," and attorneys are forced to take "shortcuts that lead to wrongful convictions."[55]

The public defenders in Miami-Dade County, Florida, have twice sought relief for excessive caseloads. In one case, they asked to be allowed to decline representation in third-degree felony cases until their caseloads were under control so their lawyers could give each client the individual representation that the Sixth Amendment requires.[56] In the other, a single public defender sought to withdraw from a single case because his obligations to 164 clients in pending felony cases prevented him from being able to represent yet another client, one who faced a first-degree felony charge that carried a sentence of life imprisonment as a habitual offender.[57] The public defenders prevailed on both cases before trial courts that were familiar with their situations. However, they lost both cases before an intermediate appellate court.[58]

It is hard to imagine the state having any interest in seeking reversal of a judge's decision allowing a public defender to decline a single complex case except to take advantage of the public defender's excessive workload. It is apparent how discouraging the reversal must be to the conscientious public defender with 164 clients, as well as to his colleagues. Members of the legal profession, including public defenders, are prohibited by ethical standards from taking on more work than they can competently handle.[59] But public defenders are forced by judges to do it every day.

Surely, the judges who required that the public defender take the case recognized that some of the best and most diligent public defenders will have no alternative except to resign if they are forced to take on more cases than they can competently and ethically handle. Once good lawyers start leaving a public defender office because effective representation is no longer possible, a downward spiral begins, as the office loses its most dedicated and experienced lawyers, its supervisors and mentors. The large caseloads must then be given to newly hired, inexperienced lawyers. It becomes harder to hire and keep good lawyers as the job becomes more and more impossible. The decision, if allowed to stand, will significantly increase violations of the right to counsel by driving conscientious lawyers out of public defender offices.

One judge on the Florida Court of Appeals, concurring in the denial of allowing the public defenders to decline third degree felonies until they had reasonable caseloads, said that the case was "nothing more than a political question masquerading as a lawsuit."[60] But it is not a political question to be taken to the legislatures. It is a *constitutional* question to be resolved by the courts. The right to counsel is guaranteed by the Sixth Amendment to the Constitution and is not subject to the whim of legislators. Judges have the responsibility to enforce it. Most legislators – like most people – do not understand the importance that those accused of crimes be well represented. It is an issue constantly exploited by demagogues, who say that governments should not waste money defending people who have committed crimes. They play on fear and ignorance.

When cost is the only consideration, counties may contract with lawyers or law firms to defend the accused on the basis of the lowest bid. The budget of a contract lawyer in one California county was only 27 percent of the prosecution's budget in 2005.[61] Nevertheless, he lost the contract the next year when he was undercut by a bid that was almost 50 percent less from a law firm that contracts with several other counties and has been described as the "Walmart of defense representation."[62] Twenty-four of California's fifty-eight counties use contractors.[63]

In order to make a profit, contractors must handle a very high volume of cases and spend as little time as possible on each case. One California contract lawyer said that he pled 70 percent of his clients guilty at the first court appearance after spending about thirty seconds explaining the prosecutor's plea offer to them.[64]

Contracts to handle individual cases give lawyers the same incentive to spend as little as possible on the defense. A contract lawyer was paid an $80,000 flat fee that included $60,000 for defense expenses by Fresno County, California, to represent Keith Doolin at his death penalty trial.[65] The lawyer was allowed to keep any of the money not spent. As one member of the California Supreme Court observed, "The contract thus had a built-in incentive for counsel to spend as little as possible on the defense so he could pocket more money."[66] He did just that. Instead of conducting necessary investigations and consulting experts, the lawyer spent less than 20 percent of the money allocated for defense expenses and kept the remaining funds for himself.[67] Doolin was sentenced to death.

In another California case, a lawyer lied to Kenneth Earl Gay to convince him to abandon the public defender who was representing him and then had the trial court appoint him. The California Supreme Court found the lawyer ineffective at the penalty phase for misleading the defendant into confessing to robberies, failing to investigate and discover mitigating sentencing evidence, and using an incompetent mental health expert.[68] A concurring justice summed up the representation provided:

> The lawyer engineered his appointment ... by extraordinary, dishonest means, and for the apparent purpose of quickly obtaining a fee while expending as little time and effort on the case as possible. The attorney carried out his plan by strictly limiting the amount of background investigation and psychological evaluation he authorized his expert to consider or undertake, and generally by preparing and presenting only a rudimentary case in mitigation.[69]

Prosecutors have not only tolerated this sad state of affairs; they have exploited it. They take advantage of inadequate representation to obtain convictions and severe sentences despite their responsibility to see that justice is done.[70] That requires a working adversary system, as attorneys general of twenty-three states recognized in 1963 in filing an *amicus curiae* brief in the Supreme Court in support of establishing a right to counsel in the state courts. But today, there is no such support from prosecutors for the right to counsel. Instead, depriving the accused of competent representation has become a strategy to win cases for some prosecutors.

Finally, the United States Supreme Court has not enforced the right to counsel and has given no encouragement to lower courts to do so. It has adopted a standard of effective assistance of counsel, which provides that no matter how bad a lawyer's representation may be, a conviction is to be upheld if judges believe the lawyer's incompetence probably did not affect the outcome.[71] This standard fails to take into account many of counsel's more critical responsibilities, such as meeting with the client within hours of being assigned the case; promptly arguing for pretrial release; building an attorney-client relationship of trust; counseling the client about the case and his or her options; negotiating with the prosecutor regarding discovery, resolution of the case, and other matters; if necessary, developing a client-specific sentencing proposal; and performing scores of other tasks that may have nothing to do with a fair trial but everything to do with the client being properly informed and the lawyer providing the advocacy throughout the case that anyone accused of a crime should receive.

Moreover, judges cannot possibly know whether the outcomes of trials might have been different because they do not see the witnesses who testified at trial. Nevertheless, courts shrug off one travesty after another on the basis of a guess that incompetence of the lawyers did not matter. James Fisher was almost executed because the Oklahoma courts concluded the first time they reviewed the case that the outcome would not have been different even if he had been represented by a good lawyer. But the second time, they found it would have been. As Justice Marshall pointed out, the court adopted a "malleable" standard – whether representation is "effective" is in the eye of the beholder.[72]

The solution to these problems is no secret. Programs like the Public Defender Service in Washington, D.C.,[73] federal public defender programs all over the country, and some statewide public defender systems, such as Colorado's, provide models. The American Bar Association has published ten principles for a defense delivery system.[74] Among them are sufficient funding, reasonable workloads, training, supervision, and independence.

Adequately funded, independent public defender offices can ensure that every person arrested has a lawyer at the initial bail hearing to argue for pretrial release, and at every subsequent hearing. They can also employ investigators and social workers and retain experts so that cases are thoroughly investigated and clients receive individual representation at every stage of the process. That includes sentencing for those found guilty. Advocacy backed up by information about the client may result in probation instead of prison or some other sentence that takes into account the individual characteristics of the person.

These are not just good ideas; they are required by the Constitution if its promises of equal justice and the right to a lawyer mean anything. But the outlook is bleak, as shown by the indifference states have shown to living up to their constitutional responsibility and their willingness to pay for prison and jail cells, but not competent legal representation for the poor. So long as courts, public officials, the bar, and the public remain indifferent, representation of the poor will remain a scandal and the criminal courts will lack credibility and legitimacy.

Notes

1 *Griffin v. Illinois*, 351 U.S. 12, 19 (1956).
2 *Gideon v. Wainwright*, 372 U.S. 335, 344 (1963).
3 See *Alabama v. Shelton*, 535 U.S. 654 (2002); *Argersinger v. Hamlin*, 407 U.S. 25, 37–8 (1972).
4 See *United States v. Cronic*, 466 U.S. 648, 654 (1984) (Of all of the rights that an accused person has, the right to be represented by counsel is by far the most pervasive, for it affects his ability to assert any other rights he may have.)
5 Greensboro Herald and Journal, Jan. 19, 1895, quoted in EDWARD L. AYERS, VENGEANCE AND JUSTICE: CRIME AND PUNISHMENT IN THE 19TH-CENTURY AMERICAN SOUTH 227 (1984).
6 *Id.*
7 The Innocence Project, *Facts on Post-Conviction DNA Exonerations*, available at www.innocenceproject.org/Content/Facts_on_PostConviction_DNA_Exonerations.php (last visited on Dec. 30, 2011).
8 David Grann, *Trial by Fire: Did Texas Execute an Innocent Man?* New Yorker, Sept. 7, 2009 at 42, available at http://www.newyorker.com/reporting/2009/09/07/090907fa_fact_gann (last visited Dec. 30, 2011).
9 *Id.* at 56.
10 *Id.*
11 *Id.* at 58–9.
12 *Id.* at 59–62.
13 *Id.* at 62.
14 *Fisher v. Gibson*, 282 F.3d 1283, 1293 (10th Cir. 2002).
15 *Id.* at 1289.
16 *Id.* (quoting the district court).
17 *Fisher v. State*, 739 P.2d 523, 525 (Okla.Crim.App.1987).
18 *Id.*
19 *Fisher v. Gibson*, 282 F.3d at 1298.
20 *Id.* at 1308.
21 *Id.*
22 *Fisher v. State*, 206 P.3d 607, 610–11 (Okla. Crim. App. 2009).
23 *Id.* at 610.
24 *Id.* at 612–13.
25 See Dan Barry, *In the Rearview Mirror, Oklahoma and Death Row*, N.Y. TIMES, August 10, 2010. For additional discussion of James T. Fisher's case, see *Man Spends 26 Years on Oklahoma's Death Row without Ever Receiving Effective Counsel*, available at http://www.secondclassjustice.com/?p=198 (last visited Jan. 15, 2012).
26 See Stephen B. Bright, *Counsel for the Poor: The Death Sentence Not for the Worst Crime but for the Worst Lawyer*, 103 YALE L. J. 1835 (1994); Bruce A. Green, *Lethal Fiction: The Meaning of "Counsel" in the Sixth Amendment*, 78 IOWA L. REV. 433 (1993).

27 See David R. Dow, *The State, The Death Penalty, and Carl Johnson*, 37 B.C. L. Rev. 691, 694–5 (1996) (describing attorney Joe Frank Cannon, who slept while representing Johnson and whose "ineptitude ... jumps off the printed page").
28 *Burdine v. Johnson*, 262 F.3d 336 (5th Cir. 2001) (en banc).
29 *Burdine v. Johnson*, 231 F.3d 950, 959 (5th Cir. 2000), *vacated and rev'd en banc*, 262 F.3d 336 (5th Cir. 2001).
30 *Ex Parte McFarland*, 163 S.W.3d 743, 752–759 (Tex. Crim. App. 2005) (en banc) (upholding conviction in post-conviction proceedings and rejecting challenge based on counsel's sleeping); *McFarland v. State*, 928 S.W.2d 482, 499–507 (Tex. Crim. App. 1996) (en banc) (upholding conviction and sentence despite counsel's sleeping); *id.* at 527 (Baird, J., dissenting) (arguing "[a] sleeping counsel is unprepared to present evidence, to cross-examine witnesses, and to present any coordinated effort to evaluate evidence and present a defense").
31 *Hurrell-Harring v. State*, 883 N.Y.S.2d 349, 360 n.3 (N.Y. App. Div. 2009) (Peters, J., dissenting), *aff'd as modified*, 930 N.E.2d 217 (N.Y. 2010).
32 *Id.*
33 *Id.*
34 *Id.*
35 *Id.*
36 See Charles J. Ogletree, Jr., *Beyond Justifications: Seeking Motivations to Sustain Public Defenders*, 106 Harv. L. Rev. 1239, 1285–9 (1993) (describing the Public Defender Service for the District of Columbia and how it trains and motivates its lawyers).
37 See Jonathan A. Rapping, *National Crisis, National Neglect: Realizing Justice through Transformative Change*, 13 U. Pa. J. Law & Soc. Change 331, 351–4 (2009–10).
38 See American Bar Association, *Ten Principles of a Public Defense Delivery System*, at 1, 2 (2002) (independence is the first of the ten principles).
39 See National Right to Counsel Committee, *Justice Denied: America's Continuing Neglect of Our Constitutional Right to Counsel* (2009), available at http://www.constitutionproject.org/manage/file/139.pdf (last visited Dec. 30, 2011).
40 See, e.g., Kenneth Williams, *Ensuring the Capital Defendant's Right to Competent Counsel: It's Time for some Standards!* 51 Wayne L. Rev. 129 (2005); William S. Geimer, *A Decade of Strickland's Tin Horn: Doctrinal and Practical Undermining of the Right to Counsel*, 4 Wm. & Mary Bill of Rts. J. 91 (1995).
41 Anthony Lewis, Gideon's Trumpet 211 (1964).
42 *Too Many Laws, Too Many Prisoners*, Economist, July 22, 2010, available at www.economist.com/node/16636027 (last visited Jan. 15, 2012) (reporting that one in every 100 adults in America is in prison, which, as a proportion of total population, is five times more than in Britain, nine times more than in Germany, and 12 times more than in Japan); The Pew Ctr. on the States, *One in 100: Behind Bars in America 2008* at 5 (2008) (reporting that, at the start of 2008, American prisons and jails held more than 2.3 million adults, while China had 1.5 million inmates and Russia had 890,000).
43 Bureau of Justice Statistics, *Correctional Population in the United States, 2010* at 1–3 (2011).

44 John Schmitt, Kris Warner & Sarika Gupta, Center for Economic and Policy Research, *The High Budgetary Cost of Incarceration* at 2 (June 2010) (projecting that based on costs for 2006, that federal, state, and local governments spent about $75 billion on corrections 2008) available at www.cepr.net/documents/publications/incarceration-2010–06.pdf (last visited on Dec. 30, 2011); Justice Policy Institute, *Pruning Prisons: How Cutting Corrections Can Save Money and Protect Public Safety* at 1 (May 2009) (federal, state and local governments are spending a combined $68 billion dollars on corrections) available at http://www.justicepolicy.org/images/upload/09_05_REP_PruningPrisons_AC_PS.pdf (last visited Dec. 30, 2011).
45 Schmitt, Warner & Gupta, supra note 44, at 10.
46 *Id.* at 11.
47 National Right to Counsel Committee, supra note 39.
48 *Id.*, supra note 39, at 61.
49 *Id.*
50 *Id.* at 61–2.
51 National Legal & Defender Association, *Congressional Summit Offers Federal Recommendations to Stem Indigent Defense Crisis* (June 16, 2010), available at http://www.nlada.net/jseri/blog/gideon-alert-congressional-summit-offers-federal-recommendations-stem-indigent-defense-cr (last visited Dec. 30, 2011) (quoting Miami-Dade County Public Defender Carlos Martinez).
52 See Lewis, supra note 41, at 202–3. *Gideon v. Wainwright*, 372 U.S. 335 (1963), the case which established the right to counsel, was brought by a Florida prisoner, Clarence Earl Gideon, who had been denied counsel at his trial in Panama City.
53 *State ex rel. Missouri Public Defender Commission v. Pratte*, 298 S.W.3d 870, 877 (2009).
54 Missouri Public Defender Commission, *Fiscal Year 2011 Annual Report* 13 (2011), available at http://www.publicdefender.mo.gov/about/FY2011AnnualReport.pdf (last visited Dec. 30, 2011)
55 *Id.* at second unnumbered page (Memorandum of Cathryn R. Kelly to Governor and other officials at (Oct. 1, 2011).
56 *State v. Public Defender*, 12 So.3d 798 (Fla. Dist. Ct. App. 2009) (per curiam), *review granted*, 34 So.3d 2 (Fla. May 19, 2010).
57 *State v. Bowens*, 39 So.3d 479 (Fla. 3d DCA 2010).
58 *State v. Bowens*, 12 So.3d at 805–6; *State v. Bowens*, 39 So.3d at 480–2.
59 American Bar Association, *Model Rules of Professional Conduct* 1.1 (2007). A comment is quite explicit: "A lawyer's workload must be controlled so that each matter can be handled competently." *Id.* at Rule 1.3, cmt. 2.
60 *State v. Public Defender*, 12 So.3d at 806 (Shepherd, J., concurring).
61 Laurence A. Benner, *The Presumption of Guilt: Systemic Factors That Contribute to Ineffective Assistance of Counsel in California*, 45 CAL. W. L. REV. 263, 306 (2009).
62 *Id.*
63 *Id.* at 300.
64 *Id.* at 305.

65 *People v. Doolin*, 198 P.3d 11, 60 (Ca. 2009) (Kennard, J., concurring and dissenting).
66 *Id.*
67 *Id.*
68 *In re Gay*, 968 P.2d 476, 827–30 (Ca. 1998).
69 *In re Gay*, 968 P.2d at 514 (Werdegar, J., concurring).
70 See *Berger v. United States*, 295 U.S. 78, 88 (1935).
71 *Strickland v. Washington*, 466 U.S. 668, 687, 693–96 (1984).
72 *Id.* at 707 (Marshall, J., dissenting).
73 See Ogletree, supra note 36.
74 American Bar Association, *Ten Principles*, supra note 38.

2

Criminal Justice in America

Constitutionalization without Foundation

Markus D. Dubber

Criminal justice in America lacks foundation in three senses: *historical*, *political*, and *substantive*. The U.S. Constitution will continue to fail to place meaningful limits on American penal power without a radical reconceptualization of the challenge of state punishment in a modern democracy, that is, ultimately as a fundamental question of political legitimacy.[1] This question was not framed in American constitutional history, as neither the American Revolution nor the Civil War generated any interest in the legitimacy of punishment in a self-governing polity, in stark contrast to the continental Enlightenment, which seized on punishment as the most drastic, most visible, and most tangible manifestation of state power. Instead, attention in the United States was limited to procedural aspects of the exercise of the state's penal power, that is, to secondary questions of application, rather than to the fundamental question of legitimacy, to the how, not to the whether.

To put it differently, and more precisely, what is needed is not a fundamental reconceptualization of the challenge of state punishment in a supposedly self-governing polity, but a conceptualization of that challenge in the first place. The search for historical foundations of the legitimation of American criminal justice reveals an absence, rather than an insufficient presence. There is no account of American criminal justice as justice, and more specifically as justice in a political community that regards self-government, or autonomy, as the touchstone of political legitimacy. Without such an account, a constitutional law of American criminal justice would itself be without foundation; a constitutional criminal law would have no principles of criminal justice to stand on.

In the following, I explore the lack of historical, political, and substantive foundations of American criminal justice. I then conclude by exploring the prospects for a constitutionalization of American criminal law, with some comparative glances at developments in other countries, notably Canada and Germany.

1. HISTORICAL

To say that there is no conception of American criminal justice qua justice is not to say that there is no conception of American penality, but it is a conception in terms not of justice, but of *police*, in the old, broad sense of both the end and the means of patriarchal household governance, which is still reflected in the concept of "police power" (and "police science," on the Continent, or "peace, order, and good government," and "peace, welfare, and government" in the constitutional law of other former British colonies).[2] As the most comprehensive, least definable, never mind curtailable state power, the police power is a mode of governance, rather than one form of power among others, a way of regarding the very act of governing itself and, ultimately, the nature of sovereignty.

This conception of sovereignty is nothing new; nor is it specifically American; instead it is grounded historically and conceptually in the discretionary and essentially unlimited power of the householder over his household, familiar at least since the days of the Greek *oikonomikos* and his *oikos*, and the Roman *paterfamilias* and his *familia*. Any limits that may be placed upon this power of a governor who is qualitatively different from, and superior to, the governed derive not from the objects of his (and later "its") power, and certainly not their rights, but from the governor himself. The police governor's power is only subject to the power of another, superior, governor-householder who (or that) will decide to exercise its own discretionary police power vis-à-vis the microhouseholder if the latter proves radically incompetent at the exercise of his power over his microhousehold – a power now conceptualized as delegated from the macrohouseholder to the microhouseholder, rather than as an original, sovereign, power.

The American Founding Fathers, while framing their revolution generally in terms of the principle of autonomy and as a pursuit of justice rather than good government, did not subject the state's penal power to the critical analysis that figured so prominently in the work of continental Enlightenment figures such as Beccaria or Kant. Instead, they took the traditional account of penal power for granted and, rather than pushing to replace police power with justice power, continued to regard penality as an instance of the householder's power to govern his household. In the realm of penality, the American Revolution merely eliminated the macrohouseholder (the king), who might have exercised, at least in theory, some control over the exercise of the delegated power to discipline by his colonial agents.

After the revolution, American penal power thus was less constrained, not more. There would be no more missives from the king to his colonial subjects, reminding them that those under their control as microhouseholders were in the end members of his macrohousehold as well and reserving the right to interfere on behalf of, for instance, slaves who had to suffer the malicious incompetence and excessive discipline of their masters.[3]

The identity of the householder had changed (as the new sovereign, the people, had replaced the old, the king), but the mode of governance had not. The police power of the king remained the police power of the people, and the conception of punishment changed as little in quality as did the conception of crime. Crime remained a violation of the peace, except that the peace violated was now the peace of the new sovereign, the people, rather than that of old, the king. Crime was not, in other words, the violation of the victim's individual rights, but the violation of public peace; in fact, criminal law was defined precisely as that branch of the law that concerned itself not with personal, or private, harm, but with public harm (unlike private law), so that, for instance, a nuisance became criminal if, and only if, it affronted the public, rather than an individual.

Having thrown off the macropolicer, the American revolutionaries-turned-governors simply assumed the sovereign penal power they had taken from the king, perhaps stripping it of its more recent excesses, which they regarded as evidence of an abuse of the police power. There was no need to replace the police power with a different foundation for penality, one more attuned to the radical new conception of state power and its legitimacy measured by the touchstone of personal self-government; instead, improvements in the exercise of the police power sufficed. What was needed in the penal realm was not more justice, but better police. And better police, in the absence of new ideas, meant – to a large extent – older police, that is, returning to a time before the corruption of sovereign power.

In other words, and especially for Thomas Jefferson, who gave more thought to the question of punishment than any other member of his generation, what was needed was a healthy dose of Coke. Jefferson's Bill for Proportioning Crimes and Punishments (1777–9) is by far the most concerted effort by a member of the founding generation to consider what a criminal justice in America might look like.[4] The bill formed part of a wholesale reform of the laws of Virginia in light of the revolutionary principles laid out by Jefferson himself in the Declaration of Independence:

> our whole code must be reviewed, adapted to our republican form of government, and, now that we had no negatives of Councils, Governors & Kings to restrain us from doing right, that it should be corrected, in all it's parts, with a single eye to reason, & the good of those for whose government it was framed.[5]

The bill, in its preamble, starts ambitiously, promising to a bill "deducible from the purposes of society," the "principal" purpose being to "secure enjoyment" of men's "lives, liberties and property." In the end, however, the bill turns out to be a gloss on Coke, whom Jefferson revered as the humble alternative to the suspiciously elegant and systematizing Blackstone, because Coke contented himself with merely commenting upon an account of the common law, rather than elevating himself to the position of its master scientist-scholar.

The bill apes Coke in form and in substance. In form, Jefferson copied Coke's practice of adding extensive marginalia, and even used antiquated spelling (at one point going through the manuscript to change the spelling of *forfeit* to *forfiet*). The bill includes so many quotes from ancient texts that Jefferson's editor had to enlist an expert in Anglo-Saxon to decipher them.[6]

In substance, the bill provided for castration as the punishment for "rape, polygamy, or sodomy" for men; a woman instead was to have "cut thro' the cartilage of her nose a hole of one half inch diameter at the least." Murder by poison was punished by poisoning, and maiming by maiming in kind.

Murder by dueling was punished by hanging, the dead body then to be placed in a gibbet – with further punishment for anyone who removed it, and instructions to replace it. Petit treason – the ultimate police offense of killing one's householder – remained a crime separate from, and more serious than, murder. Petit treason was punishable by hanging, followed by dissection by "Anatomists," a punishment thought to be particularly dishonorable at the time. In fact, there were several petit treason cases in eighteenth-century Virginia, against slaves, which resulted in horrific punishments, including beheading and displaying the severed head on a stake.[7] Ducking, whipping, and the pillory were retained for offenses including witchcraft and larceny.

Later in life, Jefferson expressed regret about the bill's strict adherence to talionic rule.[8] At the time, however, the talion was the only norm that had emerged from the discussion of criminal law among the handful of commissioners (including George Wythe, Edmund Pendleton, George Mason, and Thomas Lightfoot Lee) who met on a day in January 1777 to discuss their grand revision project. Criminal law had been assigned to Mason; Jefferson took it on only after Mason had resigned from the revision committee.[9]

Jefferson had no interest in criminal law, and it showed. He apparently used the bill as an opportunity to practice his penmanship; Dumas Malone remarked that "no other document that Jefferson ever drew better exhibits his artistry as a literary draftsman."[10]

Some members of the revolutionary generation did develop an interest in matters of penality. The Bill of Rights does of course include various procedural provisions. They were not considered novel protections derived from some revolutionary American conception of the state's penal power, however, but rather were contemporary reminders, and even restatements, of ancient rights of Englishmen.[11] (The same applies to the Eighth Amendment, a provision that might have been thought to reflect a new substantive view if not of crime, then at least of its punishment, but was, without discussion, lifted out of the English Bill of Rights of 1689.)[12] Moreover, they are not concerned with the legitimation, nature, or scope of penal power, but only with its application, and in particular its application against the ex-revolutionaries themselves by colonial agents of their royal ex-sovereign. The paradigmatic offense driving concern about norms governing its investigation was not murder – or, more specifically, parricide, as captured in the memorable opening of Foucault's *Discipline and Punish* – but precisely the political offenses that the Founding Fathers, and those with whom they empathized across the Atlantic, were suspected of having committed, such as treason. Tellingly, while the founding generation objected to the conception of "constructive" treason, which extended treason's reach to the protection of the authority of royal officials, they did not challenge the idea of treason itself, as an act of disloyalty toward the sovereign; the sovereign changed, but treason remained the same. (In fact, Jefferson's bill retains the offense of petit treason, created in the Treason Act 1351, which treats as treason killing of the householder by a household member, including of the husband by his wife.)

2. POLITICAL

One might not be surprised to find no constitutional provisions directly addressing the nature and limits of the state's penal power, since, after all, the nature and limits of the state's penal power would derive from the nature and limits of the state's power, period. What is surprising, however, is that – apart from Jefferson's aborted preamble – that derivation, or "deduction" in his words, attracted no interest whatsoever. As the foundations of state power were subjected to intense, and certainly extensive, scrutiny, resulting in elaborate schemes of horizontal and vertical power sharing (or rather separation and division), driven by an outrage about taxation *without representation*, it occurred to no one that the best place to start a substantive critique of state power would be the state's power to punish its constituents, that is, to deprive those of life, liberty, and property whose life, liberty, and property it existed to protect or, put another way, to threaten, impose, and inflict penal pain to the point of death on those whose capacity for self-government it existed to manifest.

There was, in other words, a failure to recognize the problem of state punishment as a fundamental *political* problem, that is, as a problem of state power in a democracy. The state's penal power, or rather its exercise, instead at most raised problems of administration, that is, of procedure.

There were those in the revolutionary generation who turned their attention to the third and final aspects of the penal process (beside the substantive realm of definition and the procedural one of application, or imposition), the infliction of punishment. The late eighteenth century witnessed the construction of the Walnut Street Jail (in 1776) in Philadelphia and general efforts to reform the practice of imprisonment (i.e., the form in which the punishments threatened in the substantive aspect of the penal process and imposed in its, strictly speaking, procedural aspect, were inflicted). These efforts, however, were not driven by political ideas, but by religious conviction. They had nothing to do with the institution of a system of popular self-government; nor did they reflect a political reconceptualization of crime, or its punishment, or the state's penal power. They instead reflected religious, and in particular Christian (and, more particularly still, primarily Quaker, along with Unitarian and Methodist) ideas about human nature, and notably man's relation to his Creator and to his "unfortunate fellow-creature[s]."[3] "There but for the grace of God, go I" was the motivating sentiment that established an empathic connection between reformers and those unlucky souls who found themselves in prison.

The prisoner, in the eyes of religious reformers, was not a fellow citizen, or a fellow moral person endowed with the distinctive capacity for self-government, but a wretched man who had strayed from the righteous path. Prison reforms thus stressed the importance of religious instruction, and the Bible became the prisoner's constant companion and manual, and instrument, of rehabilitation.

As religiously motivated, these reform efforts soon lost steam as the experience of empathic identification grew fainter and fainter, particularly as the icon of unlucky suffering, the debtor, saw his lot improve over time. Debtors were first moved out of the general population, to separate them from the truly wretched, the incorrigible criminal population; the intermingling of the unlucky and therefore corrigible inmates from the essentially malicious and therefore incorrigible ones was among the main objections raised by the celebrated Quaker-dominated Philadelphia Society for Alleviating the Miseries of Public Prisons. Eventually, imprisonment for debt was abolished altogether, depriving the prison reform movements of its iconic object of empathy. Once prison housed no more "worthy characters ... reduced by misfortune," leaving behind only the "wretches who are a disgrace to human nature," the reformist zeal waned.[4]

This religious reform moment not only was short-lived; it also never penetrated the legal, never mind the political, discourse. Political discourse, that is, discourse about the nature and limits of state power, did not reach the infliction of penal pain. The state's power to punish in general was beyond political scrutiny and taken for a granted as an exercise of the unlimited patriarchal power of the householder over his household, now transferred onto the state, breaking down the distinction between private heteronomy (in the *oikos*, the *familia*) and public autonomy (in *agora*, the *forum*). If anything, the spread of imprisonment as a sanction removed the infliction of penal sanctions – the sharp point of the state's penal power where the most acute (if certainly not the only) violation of its constituents' right to liberty occurs – not only from political discourse, but from the political gaze as well.

The prison itself was conceptualized as a disciplinary household, with the inmate at best a rightless object of the discretionary power of the warden-householder and at worst as "slave of the state" under the control of the warden-overseer.[15] As slave of the state is precisely how the prisoner appeared in legal discourse on prison management, which was content to note its nonexistence, the prisoner was not a legal subject and therefore beyond the realm of legal discourse. The lack of legal subjecthood here only served as the manifestation in the realm of law of the more fundamental lack of political personhood, which marked the criminal, and therefore criminal law, as beyond political discourse.

To the extent that constitutional discourse marks the interface of legal and political discourse, of legality and legitimacy, it is worth recalling that the Civil War amendments, which marked either the first, or the second, moment of American constitutional birth, made a point of excluding offenders from its grand expansion of subjecthood (or the long overdue affirmation of subjecthood previously recognized): The Thirteenth Amendment's solemn and geographically sweeping declaration that "neither slavery nor involuntary servitude ... shall exist within the United States, or any place subject to their jurisdiction" did not apply to "punishment for crime whereof the party shall have been duly convicted."

3. SUBSTANTIVE

Unlike prison law, which to this day remains a subject in name and an oxymoron in effect, criminal law of course has been the subject of legal discourse for centuries. But that is precisely the point. The American Revolution did not produce a radical reconsideration of criminal law, as law. Instead American criminal law was happy to continue not only the political project of state punishment (as an exercise of the discretionary and limitless police power), but also the legal project of rearranging the same handful of concepts, or rather

Latin maxims, familiar from English criminal law: "non facit reum nisi mens sit rea" being the most significant one, supplemented by others such as "ignorantia legis non excusat" (as opposed to "ignorantia facti," which does "excusat"). Never mind that these maxims, and in particular the Ur-maxim about the essential requirement of *actus reus* and *mens rea*, were mysterious in scope and origin and honored in their breach;[16] these were all English maxims, however empty, that were developed in the very system of government that the Americans had launched a revolution, and a war, to discard. There was no effort to generate a system of criminal law in a republic democracy, nor even to adapt the traditional English doctrinal tools for a completely new legal and political discourse.

This lack of interest in criminal law as a subject of law reflected the failure to see state punishment as a fundamental – and fundamentally – political challenge, as a presumptively illegitimate exercise of state power in a self-governing polity rather than as a discretionary, and fearsome, tool of public household discipline, wielded if, when, and however appropriate. Criminal law, in a system of penal police, has no legitimatory function because the problem of legitimating state punishment does not arise. Perhaps doctrines of criminal law may help identify, or at least classify, those who show contempt for the sovereign's authority by disobeying its commands, or otherwise interfering with its peace. But they do not, in the end, legitimate the sovereign's penal power, nor constrain it.

In fact, the first and only effort to take a serious look at American criminal law did not occur until the mid-twentieth century, almost two hundred years after the American Revolution, when the American Law Institute – having taken note of the incoherent heap of doctrine amassed after centuries of legal neglect – launched the Model Penal Code project. The Model Penal Code, drafted between 1952 and 1962 under the leadership of Herbert Wechsler, was ambitious, and remarkably successful, not only as a model code – a mere Restatement, as in torts or contracts, was thought insufficient, if not impossible, given the state of American criminal law – but also as a systematic statement of American criminal law. Today it remains the most sophisticated textbook of American criminal law; it has reshaped American criminal law scholarship and teaching along with American criminal lawmaking.

The Model Penal Code, however, was not a foundational document. It was a product of two schools of legal thought, one substantive, the other formal. Formally, the Model Penal Code was a legal process document. Its goal was to produce a blueprint for the penal process that assigned appropriate discretion at various points to the appropriate decision maker in pursuit of the unquestioned, and unquestionable, goal of the penal process: crime reduction. Substantively, the Model Penal Code was driven by a treatmentist ideology that sought crime reduction through the penocorrectional treatment of those its threats of punishment had not managed to deter, either through rehabilitative treatment (for corrigibles) or through incapacitative treatment (for incorrigibles). The criminal law was reconceptualized as a set of crude diagnostic tools applied by nonexpert officials (judge and jury) who were ill equipped to generate reliable diagnoses of criminal dangerousness. Guilty verdicts and provisional sentences, the outcome of the judicial aspect of the process, were only the beginning of a professionalized system for the diagnosis and treatment of the criminally dangerous, driven by penological experts (and laid out in some detail in the almost completely ignored parts III and IV of the "Model Penal *and Correctional* Code," to use its now forgotten full title). The penal process, thus, was in the end an administrative process; criminal law was part of the administration of criminal justice; and the Model Penal Code was a good government proposal.

The Model Penal Code drafters had no interest in posing, never mind addressing, the question of what legitimates state punishment in a liberal democracy; they did not begin their task with an exploration of the constitutional foundations of, or limits on, the state's penal power. Foundational questions, they were convinced, were settled, and their task was, in good Legal Process fashion, to modernize, rationalize, and render consistent, drawing on the orthodoxy of the day, treatmentism (the doctrinal implications of which Wechsler had worked out, for the law of homicide, as early as 1937).[17] The entire Model Penal and Correctional Code thus should be read from back to front, beginning with the professional treatmentist regime laid out in the Correctional Code (parts III and IV), for which the Penal Code (parts I and II) sets the amateurish stage. The Penal Code's general part and special part (I and II, respectively) appear as a layman's *DSM* for criminal dangerousness. (The *DSM*, incidentally, was first published in 1952, the year the Model Penal Code project was launched[18]).

Ironically, while the Model Penal Code did not concern itself with the constitutional law of crime, in either its general part (setting out general conditions for the assessment of criminal liability, i.e., for the diagnosis of criminal dangerousness) or its special part (containing definitions of specific offenses, *i.e.*, of manifestations of criminal dangerousness), it did have an indirect, and presumably unintentional, effect on the only pocket of constitutional law that concerned itself in any detail with the substantive law of crime, if only insofar as it affected the availability of a particular sanction, the death penalty (under the Eighth Amendment's "cruel and unusual punishments" clause). The Supreme Court's revival of capital punishment after *Furman v. Georgia* drew on the Model Penal Code's capital sentencing provision, setting out mitigating and aggravating circumstances, which the drafters had placed in brackets to express their unwillingness to endorse capital punishment as an available sanction (without, however, suggesting that this sanction was unconstitutional). The American Law Institute (ALI) recently withdrew the relevant section in the course of its reconsideration of the Model Penal Code's sentencing provisions "in light of the current intractable institutional and structural obstacles to ensuring a minimally adequate system for administering capital punishment" (without, again, suggesting that capital punishment was either illegitimate or unconstitutional as a matter of substance, rather than of administration).

4. CONSTITUTIONAL?

Given the long history of neglect of substantive criminal law in the United States, a history marked by missed opportunities to face the political challenge of state punishment in a democratic republic and design a body of law that attempts to meet this legitimatory challenge, it is no surprise that American constitutional law has failed to engage with criminal law in any meaningful or sustained way. This point has been made often, but so far to little effect.[19] Apart from the First Amendment law, which asserts its firstness also in this realm by insisting that speech not be chilled, American constitutional law has virtually ignored substantive criminal law, both in its general part and in its special part. As Henry Hart, Wechsler's fellow legal process traveler, put it in 1958, while the Model Penal Code project was still under way, "What sense does it make to insist upon procedural safeguards in criminal prosecutions if anything whatever can be made a crime in the first place?" It is true that American constitutional law (federal and state) has shown remarkably little interest in this question of what "can be made a crime in the first place" and instead has concerned itself with procedural matters, especially during the Warren Court years (1953–69), though that concern has dissipated greatly since then, as subsequent Courts have been engaged in a concerted effort to cut back on what came to be seen as the Warren Court's expansive view of constitutional criminal procedure, to the point where protective constitutional norms are so limited in scope and, even if applicable, are so riddled with exceptions as to raise the question whether the Court still "insist[s] on procedural safeguards in criminal prosecutions."

The question is not, however, whether it "makes sense" to focus on procedural criminal law while ignoring substantive criminal law. The problem is not inconsistency, or even incoherence. The problem instead is lack of interest, or rather a failure to recognize that the legitimacy of state punishment depends on the development of a set of legal norms that reflect the fundamental principle of legitimacy in a democratic republic, the capacity for self-government, or autonomy, of its constituents. Until the constitutional challenge of criminal law is seen as a problem of legitimation, rather than of application, as a problem of foundations, rather than of implementation, it matters little whether the Court focuses on questions of substance, procedure, or infliction.

The problem of legitimation of state punishment is not limited to the special part, that is, to the what, but also extends to the general part of criminal law, that is, to the who. While there may be precious little constitutional law (apart from occasional First Amendment concerns) that limits the scope of the criminal law, there is even less that grounds the prerequisites for criminal liability. *Actus reus* and *mens rea* remain the central concepts in the general part of American criminal law, without a solid constitutional foundation. The constitutional law on defenses is rigidly formalistic, concerned less with the question of whether the constitution requires the recognition of certain defenses than with the classification of an issue as one of offense or of defense (a classification left to legislative discretion), which then determines the analysis of the procedural question of who must prove what and under what standard.[20] In general, the U.S. Supreme Court sees its function in criminal law as one of statutory interpretation (in the case of federal law) and of deference to legislative intent in the spirit of experimentation (in the case of state law), or both. Nothing has changed since the time of Hart's essay, which included an extended analysis of the Supreme Court's decision in *Morissette v. United States*, in which the Court declined the invitation to explore the constitutional basis of culpability and instead engaged in a convoluted act of statutory interpretation, gleefully ridiculed by Hart.[21]

The most promising starting point for a constitutionalization of substantive criminal law is Justice Kennedy's majority opinion in *Lawrence v. Texas*, in particular its opening paragraph:

> Liberty protects the person from unwarranted government intrusions into a dwelling or other private places. In our tradition the State is not omnipresent in the home. And there are other spheres of our lives and existence, outside the home, where the State should not be a dominant presence. Freedom extends beyond spatial bounds. Liberty presumes an autonomy of self that includes freedom of thought, belief, expression, and certain intimate conduct. The instant case involves liberty of the person both in its spatial and more transcendent dimensions.[22]

This passage in *Lawrence*, in which the Court struck down Texas's "deviate sexual intercourse" statute, is framed broadly enough to leave room for the development of a constitutional law of the general and special parts of criminal law, that is, of the conditions of punishability (who) and the scope of the criminal law (what). The passage, of course, does many other things besides, and it is noncommittal about its animating constitutional principle (or principles). If a concern about privacy is taken to be paramount, then *Lawrence* adds nothing to a long line of Supreme Court cases expressing that concern (to varying degrees, and different effects). At any rate, privacy may generate some constraints on the scope of criminal law, as it arguably did in *Lawrence*, but says nothing (or very little) about the interests or rights that the state may – rather than may *not* – constitutionally safeguard, or manifest, through criminal law (except for an interest in privacy, the interference with which has in fact been subjected to criminal punishment). If, however, the case is taken to turn on "autonomy of self," it suggests a line of analysis that could lead to the constitutionalization of both the foundation and the limits of criminal law (by limiting its scope to violations of another's "autonomy of self") and the foundations of general principles of criminal liability (by limiting its applicability to manifestation of the actor's "autonomy of self").[23]

If the U.S. Supreme Court were to embark on an autonomy-based project of constitutionalizing criminal law, it would not be alone. The Canadian Supreme Court and the German Constitutional Court have undertaken more or less ambitious efforts to develop a constitutional law of crime and punishment, each based more or less explicitly on the concept of personal autonomy (with the Canadian court taking the more ambitious and explicit route). Both courts have rejected invitations to rein in legislative discretion in the special part of criminal law by limiting the legislature's power to criminalize to violations of, or at least threats to, a person's autonomy, in the guise of either a constitutional "harm principle" (in Canada)[24] or a constitutional *"Rechtsgut* principle" (in Germany).[25] Nonetheless, both courts have accepted the relevance, and even the sufficiency (if not the necessity), of (actual or threatened) autonomy infringement for the question of criminalization.

Both courts also have been more willing to assign autonomy a central, if not the central, role in the constitutional analysis of the criminal law's general part. The Canadian Court, in particular, has developed – often in explicit deviation from the U.S. Supreme Court's hesitance in this area – a fairly extensive autonomy-based jurisprudence on the constitutional foundations of the prerequisites for criminal liability, including a general *mens rea* requirement,[26] specific *mens rea* requirements for particular offenses,[27] and the availability (and definition) of certain defenses.[28] The German Constitutional Court has been less expansive and explicit in its review of the constitutional foundations of the general part of criminal law, relying heavily on the "guilt principle" (*Schuldprinzip*), which tends to be traced to a concept of the person as autonomous, which is said to figure prominently not only in German constitutional law, but also in German criminal law.[29] Constitutionalization of criminal law, however, is no panacea; it certainly is no end in itself. In both countries, the constitutionalized version of a norm may contract its scope or dull its bite, at worst, and add nothing more than a layer of constitutional fairy dust. In Canada, for instance, it has been argued that traditional common law rules on attempt may be more demanding than those constitutionally required.[30] Similarly, in Germany, the Constitutional Court has been criticized (even from within) for its rejection of a norm developed over decades by German criminal law science (the *Rechtsgut* principle) in favor of a far more flexible, and deferential, approach to the constitutional analysis of criminal provisions.[31]

More generally, it has been argued that an aggressive judicial constitutionalization project may not only interfere with legislative discretion in particular cases, but stunt more systematic criminal law reform. For instance, in Canada, the failure of comprehensive criminal code reform has been attributed to the Canadian Supreme Court's campaign to constitutionalize the general part of criminal law, which after an initial period of exuberant expansion became mired in doctrinal specifics and eventually faced internal resistance (not unlike the trajectory of the constitutionalization of criminal *procedure* in the U.S. Supreme Court). The effort remains unfinished in breadth and depth, in the face of indications that the Court has lost its taste for constitutional reform, the legislature's recodification effort having long since been abandoned.

In Germany, the constitutionalization of principles of criminal law often amounts to little more than an assertion of putative, if not actual, constitutional roots.[32] The guilt principle, for instance, tends simply – and rather unhelpfully – to be declared to derive from the so-called *Rechtsstaat* (rule of law) principle in art. 20(3) Basic Law, which provides that "the legislature shall be bound by the constitutional order, the executive and the judiciary by law (*Gesetz*) and justice (*Recht*)."

An inquiry into constitutional foundations is only useful, and in fact necessary, if it forms part of a continuous critical analysis of the legitimacy of state punishment in all of its manifestations, substantive, procedural, or inflictive, that is, if it contributes to posing, and addressing, the challenge of legitimating the state's penal interference with the very rights of the very constituents upon the protection of which its legitimacy rests. In the United States, this critical analysis has yet to occur in earnest. Unless and until it does, attempts to bring the constitution to bear on American criminal justice will be both groundless and pointless.

Notes

1. This chapter focuses on the federal constitution. I suspect that the discussion also applies to state constitutions, which – one might think – would have provided an occasion to consider the need to reconceptualize state penality equal, and even superior, to the federal constitution.
2. See generally MARKUS D. DUBBER, THE POLICE POWER: PATRIARCHY AND THE FOUNDATIONS OF AMERICAN GOVERNMENT (2005); THE NEW POLICE SCIENCE: THE POLICE POWER IN DOMESTIC AND INTERNATIONAL GOVERNANCE (Markus D. Dubber & Mariana Valverde, eds., 2006).
3. See ARTHUR P. SCOTT, CRIMINAL LAW IN COLONIAL VIRGINIA 202 (1930) (discussing an eighteenth-century missive from the King to his Virginia colony: "[A]t the time, the Slave is the Master's Property he is likewise the King's Subject, and ... the King may lawfully bring to Tryal all Persons here, without exception, who shall be suspected to have destroyed the Life of his Subject.").
4. See generally Markus D. Dubber, *"An Extraordinarily Beautiful Document": Jefferson's Bill for Proportioning Crimes and Punishments and the Challenge of Republican Punishment*, in MODERN HISTORIES OF CRIME AND PUNISHMENT 115 (Markus D. Dubber & Lindsay Farmer, eds., 2007).
5. THOMAS JEFFERSON, AUTOBIOGRAPHY 37 (1821), available at http://etext.virginia.edu/toc/modeng/public/JefAuto.html (last visited Apr. 25, 2013).
6. See 2 THE PAPERS OF THOMAS JEFFERSON 504 (Julian P. Boyd et al., eds., 1950).
7. Scott, supra note 3, at 161–2.
8. JEFFERSON, AUTOBIOGRAPHY, supra note 5, at 39.
9. See 2 PAPERS OF THOMAS JEFFERSON, supra note 6, at 316.
10. See 1 DUMAS MALONE, JEFFERSON AND HIS TIME 269–70 (1948).
11. On the origins of some procedural provisions, see WILLIAM J. CUDDIHY, THE FOURTH AMENDMENT: ORIGINS AND ORIGINAL MEANING 602–1791 (2009); LEONARD LEVY, ORIGINS OF THE FIFTH AMENDMENT: THE RIGHT AGAINST SELF-INCRIMINATION (1968). See also THE PRIVILEGE AGAINST SELF-INCRIMINATION: ITS ORIGINS AND DEVELOPMENT (R. M. Helmholz et al., eds., 1997).
12. See Anthony F. Granucci, *Nor Cruel and Unusual Punishments Inflicted: The Original Meaning*, 57 CAL. L. REV. 839 (1969). On the policial origins of prohibition of "cruel and unusual" punishment as a marginal constraint on the otherwise unlimited disciplinary authority of householders and quasi-householders (military superiors, ship captains, teachers, wardens, etc.), see Markus D. Dubber, *Miscarriage of Justice as Misnomer*, in MAKING SENSE OF MISCARRIAGES OF JUSTICE 281 (Austin Sarat & Charles Ogletree eds., 2008).
13. WILLIAM ROSCOE, OBSERVATIONS ON PENAL JURISPRUDENCE AND THE REFORMATION OF CRIMINALS 176–7 (1819); see generally Phila. Soc'y for Alleviating the Miseries of Pub. Prisons, *Constitution of the Philadelphia Society for alleviating the Miseries of Public Prisons*, in REFORM OF CRIMINAL LAW IN PENNSYLVANIA: SELECTED ENQUIRIES, 1787–1819 105 (William Bradford, William Roscoe & Benjamin Rush 1972).
14. Michael Meranze, *The Penitential Ideal in Late Eighteenth-Century Philadelphia*, 108 PA. MAG. HIST. & BIOGRAPHY 431, 442(1984) (quoting Pennsylvania Gazette, Sept. 26, 1787).

15 *Ruffin v. Commonwealth*, 62 Va. 790 (1871).
16 As English judges and commentators periodically recognize. See, e.g., *R. v. Tolson* (1889) 23 Q.B.D. 168 (Stephen, J.); Jeremy Horder, *Two Histories and Four Hidden Principles of Mens Rea*, 113 L. Q. REV. 95 (1997).
17 Jerome Michael & Herbert Wechsler, *A Rationale of the Law of Homicide I & II*, 37 COLUM. L. REV. 701 & 1261 (1937); see also Herbert Wechsler, *The Challenge of a Model Penal Code*, 65 HARV. L. REV. 1097 (1952); see generally MARKUS D. DUBBER, CRIMINAL LAW: MODEL PENAL CODE (2002).
18 AMERICAN PSYCHIATRIC ASSOCIATION, DIAGNOSTIC AND STATISTICAL MANUAL: MENTAL DISORDERS (DSM I) (1952).
19 See Henry M. Hart, Jr., *The Aims of the Criminal Law*, 23 L. & CONTEMP. PROBS. 401 (1958). For more recent examples, see WILLIAM J. STUNTZ, THE COLLAPSE OF AMERICAN CRIMINAL JUSTICE (2011); Markus D. Dubber, *Toward a Constitutional Law of Crime and Punishment*, 55 HASTINGS L. J. 509 (2004) [hereinafter Dubbber, *Toward a Constitutional Law*].
20 See *Patterson v. New York*, 432 U.S. 197 (1977).
21 *Morissette v. United States*, 342 U.S. 246 (1952); cf. *R. v. Tolson*, 23 Q.B.D. 168 (1889) (rebuttable common law presumption of mens rea requirement).
22 *Lawrence v. Texas*, 539 U.S. 558, 562 (2003).
23 An illustrative outline of this approach appears in Dubber, *Toward a Constitutional Law*, supra note 19; for earlier reflections along similar lines, see David A. J. Richards, *Human Rights and the Moral Foundations of the Substantive Criminal Law*, 13 GA. L. REV. 1395 (1979).
24 *R. v. Malmo-Levine*, (2003) 3 S.C.R. 571.
25 24 BVerfGE 120, 224 (Feb. 26, 2008); see Markus D. Dubber, *Policing Morality: Constitutional Law and the Criminalization of Incest*, 61 U. TORONTO L. J. *(Special Issue)* 737 (2011) (special issue on constitutionalism and the criminal law).
26 *Re B.C. Motor Vehicle Act*, [1985] 2 S.C.R. 486.
27 *R. v. Vaillancourt*, (1987) 2 S.C.R. 636; *R. v. Martineau*, (1990) 2 S.C.R. 633 (murder).
28 *R. v. Daviault*, (1994) 3 S.C.R. 63 (intoxication); *R. v. Ruzic*, (2001) 1 S.C.R. 687 (duress).
29 See Markus D. Dubber, *Theories of Crime and Punishment in German Criminal Law*, 53 AM. J. COMP. L. 679 (2006).
30 Kent Roach, *Mind the Gap: Canada's Different Criminal and Constitutional Standards of Fault*, 61 U. TORONTO L.J. 545 (2011).
31 See the remarkable dissent by Judge Hassemer, not coincidentally a distinguished professor of criminal law, in the Incest Case. 24 BVerfGE 120, 224, at paras. 73 ff.
32 For extensive critiques of these assertions, see IVO APPEL, VERFASSUNG UND STRAFE: ZU DEN VERFASSUNGSRECHTLICHEN GRENZEN STAATLICHEN STRAFENS (1998); OTTO LAGODNY, STRAFRECHT VOR DEN SCHRANKEN DER GRUNDRECHTE: DIE ERMÄCHTIGUNG ZUM STRAFRECHTLICHEN VORWURF IM LICHTE DER GRUNDRECHTSDOGMATIK DARGESTELLT AM BEISPIEL DER VORFELDKRIMINALISIERUNG (1996).

PART II

RACE AND CRIMINAL PROCEDURE

3

The Challenges of "Quality of Life" Policing for the Fourth Amendment

Susan A. Bandes

In New York City in the last several years, record numbers of people, overwhelmingly nonwhite, have been stopped and frisked by police. In 2009, nearly 600,000 people were stopped,[1] 84 percent of them black or Latino.[2] In 2010, the number of people stopped exceeded the 600,000 mark, and 87 percent of those stopped were black or Latino.[3] Although frisks are authorized only to investigate a reasonable suspicion that a suspect is armed, only very rarely did those stops and frisks lead to discovery of a weapon.[4] Only a small minority led to an arrest or summons.[5] Even among those arrested, a minuscule number actually went to trial, where the legality of the police conduct could be tested.[6] In short, under the current Fourth Amendment framework, most of that police activity was never subjected to any judicial scrutiny, either before or after it occurred, to determine whether it was legally authorized or legally carried out.

In its 1968 decision in *Terry v. Ohio*[7] the Supreme Court made it clear that stops and frisks are governed by the Fourth Amendment and adopted constitutional criteria specifying when these intrusions are permissible and how they should be conducted. The Court set out to rein in the unguided discretion exercised by police in their encounters with the citizenry; a discretion that led to abuse of power, harassment, and discrimination based on race, ethnicity, and other pernicious factors. In order to impose limits on this vast category of police conduct, the Court sought not only to articulate rules for when and how police could stop and frisk the citizenry, but, crucially, to ensure that police compliance with these rules was reviewable in the courts. Even at the time, the Court recognized that its approach had limitations. It recognized that stop and frisk activity eludes judicial review when no weapon or contraband is found and no arrest is made. As it has turned out, stop and frisk and other street-level encounters between police and citizens have become increasingly insulated from court supervision, both for the reason the Court recognized and for other reasons it did not foresee.

The current Fourth Amendment structure took shape in the Warren Court and still reflects many of the concerns of that era, for better or worse (and to complicate matters, it has for many years since been interpreted by courts hostile to the aims of the Warren Court). The Warren Court decisions reflected the need to impose federal constitutional standards on local law enforcement agencies, to expose street level police citizen encounters to judicial review, and to create an enforceable remedy for illegal police conduct. They also reflected the Court's view of the relative competence of various institutions. The Warren Court put tremendous faith in the courts to supervise police conduct. Or to put the point less positively, the Warren Court evinced little faith in nonjudicial institutions to regulate the police. It relied on the courts to issue warrants predicated on probable cause before the conduct occurred, and to review searches and seizures after the fact. Its main remedy for violations of the Fourth Amendment was the exclusionary rule, which requires the exclusion of illegally obtained evidence at trial and therefore can operate only if the suspect is arrested and the government seeks to introduce evidence in his criminal trial.

As we head toward 2020, we have a policing regime in which, in certain neighborhoods, policing is a pervasive influence on the quality of everyday life. It affects where people can go, and when, and with whom, and how they are treated as they traverse their neighborhoods. It funnels people into the criminal justice system at an early age, often for acts that attract no police attention elsewhere, ratcheting up the consequences against them with each minor infraction. The Fourth Amendment framework currently in use to control police discretion is not up to the task of regulating this sort of regime. It requires some serious rethinking – both about how the courts can be brought back into the equation, and about what other institutions besides the courts should be doing to protect Fourth Amendment rights.

There are several problems with the current judicial framework for regulating police-citizen interactions, some already evident when the Warren Court decided *Terry v Ohio*,[8] others created by *Terry*,[9] and many exacerbated by later developments. One basic problem is that on the whole, the Supreme Court's Fourth Amendment jurisprudence is atomistic. That is, it works one case at a time, trying to resolve individual disputes between law enforcement and individual suspects. It asks, "did police act unconstitutionally *in this case?*"[10]

This individualized focus has turned out to be highly problematic. First of all, it is poorly suited to identifying and addressing *shared harms*, such as the effects of aggressive policing regimes on the quality of life of entire neighborhoods, or the injuries inflicted when the burden of police intrusion falls most heavily on certain racial or ethnic or economic groups, or the widespread (albeit relatively minor) intrusions authorized by the increasing number of so-called special needs searches that require no individualized suspicion of wrongdoing. Second, the atomistic focus is poorly suited to addressing shared *causes of harm*. Fourth Amendment jurisprudence has yet to grapple with policing as an institution, or with the complex web of institutions that affect policing and are affected by it.[11] The *Terry* Court referred to "certain elements of the police community" that might harass minority groups.[12] The implication is that there are always a few rogue cops, bad apples, who will flout the rules. Yet the current problem of aggressive policing of minority groups and the neighborhoods in which they reside cannot be laid at the doorstep of a few bad cops. Most of the impetus for these regimes originates in legislative or administrative initiatives, not decisions by individual cops. And even when the impetus for problematic policing can be traced to "certain elements of the police community," the problem can rarely be addressed individually – it requires, at minimum, a broader focus on the culture and incentives of the department, and more likely a focus on the priorities of the police community and the community more broadly.[13] That is, the problem of police culture and police incentives is systemwide and must be addressed systemically. The courts, left to their own devices, cannot achieve this sort of reform.

The Warren Court placed its trust in the court system to regulate police conduct. This regulation is meant to occur primarily through prior approval of searches and seizures via the issuance of warrants and after-the-fact review of searches and seizures through motions to suppress illegal evidence at criminal trials. One major problem with this framework, as the *Terry* Court understood, is that it cannot work when police have no intention or likelihood of introducing evidence in court. The Court in 1968 observed: "The wholesale harassment by certain elements of the police community of which minority groups frequently complain will not be stopped by the exclusion of any evidence from any criminal trial....Under our decision, courts still retain their traditional responsibility to guard against police conduct which is overbearing or harassing."[14] The Court suggested that other remedies might be necessary to supplement the exclusionary rule,[15] and indeed the ability to sue law enforcement agents and agencies under civil rights statutes began a brief but dramatic expansion during the Warren Court era.[16]

I will return shortly to the most powerful remedial points contained in that quote – first, that courts have an affirmative duty to guard against police harassment, and, second, that there is room for other remedies not to replace the exclusionary rule, but to supplement it where it falls short. But, first, it is important to understand why the problem that *Terry* foresaw, but entirely underestimated, has become such a threat to the Fourth Amendment's ability to limit police illegality. Certain changes in the law enforcement landscape over the past forty years have rendered the *Terry* approach to judicial regulation increasingly ineffectual and irrelevant. I will discuss two such developments, overcriminalization, and aggressive so-called quality of life[17] policing in low-income minority neighborhoods, and will make brief mention of a third: the increasing use of "special needs" searches.

1. OVERCRIMINALIZATION

The first major change that has undermined the *Terry* approach and helped create an ineffectual Fourth Amendment is the vast expansion in the use of criminal law to regulate minor infractions. The most important task of the criminal justice system is to separate the guilty from the innocent. The most important task of the Fourth Amendment is to ensure that the government intrudes on individual privacy and liberty when, and only when, it has reason to think criminal activity is afoot. But the broader the net of criminalization of everyday conduct, the less the probable cause threshold acts as a brake on police power or on the abuse of police discretion. If we are all violating *some* traffic law or municipal ordinance, probable cause is no longer a meaningful limit. For that matter, neither is innocence, since we are, most of us, guilty of some infraction – and just lucky the criminal law is not enforced uniformly and equally.

For an example that could affect most of us, consider automobile searches incident to arrest. Anyone who drives a car is likely to be violating some traffic law. Police often assert that they can follow a car for five seconds and find some vehicular violation (failure to signal a lane change,[18] straddling lanes,[19] mud flaps too low,[20] vehicle sticker too high,[21] broken taillight,[22] traveling one or more miles above the speed limit,[23] driving too slowly,[24] improper u-turn,[25] and careless driving,[26] to name a few.) That means, essentially, that the police can arrest any driver on probable cause. The Court has declined to use most of the tools at its disposal for hemming in this discretion. In a case involving a custodial arrest[27] for failure to use a seat belt, the Court declined to require the adoption of rules limiting the types of crimes and infractions that can lead to a custodial arrest, leaving open the possibility of custodial arrest for a simple traffic citation.[28] The Court has declined to use the Fourth Amendment to inquire into whether police are using minor traffic arrests and citations as pretexts for pulling people over to conduct investigations for other reasons that cannot be legally justified or are flat-out unjustifiable.[29]

Evidence gathered in Fourteenth Amendment class action suits or pursuant to Justice Department pattern and practice consent decrees shows that in traffic stop cases, police exercise their discretion by singling out minority motorists in vast disproportion to their numbers. For example, a study of traffic stops on the New Jersey Turnpike found that 73.2 percent of motorists stopped and arrested were black, although only 13.5 percent of cars on the road had a black driver or passenger, and although data showed that blacks and whites violated the traffic laws at almost exactly the same rate.[30] A study of traffic stops by the Maryland State Police on Interstate 95 found that although the percentages of blacks and whites violating the traffic code were virtually identical, and although only 17.5 percent of those violating the traffic code were black, more than 72 percent of those stopped and searched were black, and more than 80 percent were members of a racial minority.[31]

Of course, automobiles are highly regulated and operated in public, so their vulnerability to police intrusion is not surprising. However, overcriminalization is not confined to vehicle rules; it turns out to pose similar problems for those simply living their lives in certain neighborhoods. The additional factor here is that the singling out of these neighborhoods is governmentally sanctioned as part of programs of aggressive order-maintenance policing. This kind of policing regime targets open containers, public drunkenness, loitering in groups, graffiti, disorderly conduct, and other low-level infractions.[32] It is based on "broken windows theory," which posits that if police concentrate on petty "quality of life" offenses in neighborhoods that are at risk for social disorder, they will decrease fear and increase respect for law in the community, and that a decrease in serious crime will follow.[33] The assumptions underlying broken windows theory have been called into serious question. For one, it is highly controversial whether a causal link exists between addressing low-level offenses and decreasing serious crime.[34] For another, even if the link exists, it does not follow that *aggressive* treatment of low-level offenses will have the desired effect, and indeed broken windows theory began as a theory about the desirable effects of cooperative community policing.[35] Yet in its current incarnation, it is an aggressive tactic, and one that targets exclusively low-income, minority neighborhoods.[36]

Rules governing mobility, the use of space, the zone of privacy, and the quality of life differ markedly in certain neighborhoods, where police are empowered (or perceive themselves to be empowered) to control comings and goings and activities that are beyond their purview elsewhere. As former Bronx assistant public defender David Feige notes, "reality, as many poor people eventually understand it, is that between rules about truancy, trespass, loitering, disorderly conduct, and dog walking, most any adventure can wind up getting you a summons. And that's if you're lucky."[37] A record of low-level arrests (with escalating consequences) in some neighborhoods becomes a rite of passage, not a reliable means of identifying habitual criminals.

For example, for those who live in low-income housing projects, visiting a friend or relative in another project may constitute trespass. Trespass usually requires some showing that the visitor is unwelcome, but when it comes to public housing, the mere fact of being on the property may establish a prima facie or even unreviewable case. Public housing no-trespass rules tend to grant enormous discretion to officials to determine whom to bar. As one author observed, "given free rein to stop any nonresident at any time in order to ascertain whether she is listed in the no-trespass log, police may make pretextual stops or engage in racial profiling. Indeed, during the first five years of a no-trespass regime promulgated by the Dayton Municipal Housing Authority, 2,310 individuals were barred, eighty-nine percent of who were male, and most, if not all, were black."[38] In most such programs, those who return to visit the housing project after having been given a warning or placed on a no-trespass list are arrested. Maybe the arrestee can ultimately show that she was an invited guest and not a trespasser, but that involves going to court, finding a sitter for children, taking time off from work, more time in the event of a continuance or three. For most people, this sort of time commitment, with its attendant costs, including a possible loss of livelihood, is simply not a viable option.

David Feige describes one resident of a poor primarily black neighborhood in the Bronx who was arrested for walking a friend's dog while not carrying the dog's vaccination papers on him. Feige describes, in harrowing detail, the man's efforts to contest the charges, and why he eventually came to believe that he had no choice but to plead guilty to a crime he had not committed.[39] Feige describes clients arrested for drinking a beer on their own front stoop, while he himself would drink a nice bottle of wine in Central Park with no legal consequences.[40] As these sorts of cases illustrate, probable cause to arrest is plentiful, albeit for crimes for which most of us would never imagine being arrested.

Thus in these sorts of cases probable cause does not act as an effective filter between those who are justly suspected of crime and those who are not – perversely, it acts as a kind of rubber stamp authorization for police to search and seize people at will, and at their discretion. Moreover, the warrant requirement affords no protection in these cases, because automobile stops, arrests in public, and *Terry* stops are all exempt from the need for a warrant.[41]

2. STOP AND FRISK AND THE LIMITS OF THE EXCLUSIONARY RULE

Just as before-the-fact probable cause and warrant requirements are ineffectual in these cases, so is the Fourth Amendment's primary after-the-fact remedy. Standard Fourth Amendment doctrine has one main tool for reshaping future police incentives: exclusion of illegal evidence at trial. Yet for the arrestee, in the vast majority of cases there will be no trial, and thus no opportunity to contest the evidence. Cases are overwhelmingly dismissed at an early stage, and a vanishingly small number go to trial. In New York City, for example, only 0.2 percent of misdemeanor and violation cases are ever tried.[42] Even a quickly dismissed charge exacts a heavy toll on the suspect, including "being taken into custody, handcuffed, transported, booked, often strip-searched, and jailed overnight."[43] And these are just some of the tangible costs; less tangible costs include stigma, loss of dignity, and erosion of trust.[44] A steady regime of such encounters exacts a heavy toll on a community.[45]

To compound the problem, much aggressive order-maintenance policing is not aimed toward generating arrests. In each of the last several years, New York City police have stopped and frisked well over half a million people, more than five times the number of felony arrests, and more than double the number of misdemeanor arrests.[46] The program is aimed at removing weapons from the street (though whether it succeeds in doing so is hotly contested),[47] at improvement in quality of life, or, seen in another light, at routine harassment and social control. In a recent series of interviews of people who had been stopped by New York police, one recurring theme was that young black and Latino men in certain neighborhoods are repeatedly commanded to explain why they are walking in their own neighborhoods, standing in front of their own homes, or walking in their own hallways.[48]

Stop and frisk requires a lower standard of suspicion than arrest: reasonable suspicion rather than probable cause. Police may conduct a stop if they have a reasonable suspicion that crime may be afoot. They may conduct a frisk based on reasonable suspicion that the suspect is armed and presently dangerous. Typical reasons articulated for a stop or a frisk include "furtive movements," "inappropriate attire for the season," "wearing clothes commonly used in a crime," and a "suspicious bulge."[49] Many of the stop and frisk criteria are highly malleable and, as some have argued, highly vulnerable to the effects of bias – both conscious and subconscious.[50] As Professor Randall Kennedy explains, even a well-intentioned police officer may interpret a movement by a black man as particularly furtive or threatening because of his preexisting fears about "the criminality or potential for criminality of African-Americans."[51]

Moreover, there is evidence that minority suspects are subjected to a disproportionate amount of force, including more frequent handcuffing and other such use of restraint,[52] and are too frequently subjected to disrespectful language and epithets.[53] An additional limitation of the current *Terry* approach is that it does not focus on such issues. It concentrates on *whether* a stop or frisk is justified, but not, except in the most formal sense, on *how* a stop or frisk is carried out.[54] Concerns about harassment, abuse of power, and discrimination cannot be adequately addressed without attention to how police conduct themselves during these encounters.

The *Terry* Court meant to regulate stop and frisk behavior by requiring that police possess objective and articulable reasons for stopping and frisking suspects, reasons that could be reviewed in a court of law. But when illegal police behavior is not aimed at obtaining a conviction, or when there is no real possibility that a court will ever review the constitutional basis of a stop and frisk or an arrest, exclusion of evidence becomes an irrelevant remedy, and illegal police behavior remains unchecked.

This is no diatribe against the exclusionary rule. The exclusionary rule, increasingly under attack by the Supreme Court, has long played a crucial role in implementing compliance with the Fourth Amendment.[55] It is puzzling that so many arguments about the limitations of the rule take an either-or form. The argument goes: the rule does not do enough, so we ought to get rid of it entirely (or undercut it fatally, as the Roberts Court seems poised to do).[56] Rather, we should take a clear-eyed look at the rule's benefits as well as its limitations and shore it up and supplement it in the areas in which it falls short.

3. THE NEED FOR A BROADER INSTITUTIONAL RESPONSE TO SYSTEMIC POLICE ILLEGALITY

But before turning to the question of solutions, it is important to note that there are two forces at work in Fourth Amendment doctrine that in some respects overlap and in other respects pull in different directions. One is the failure to control police discretion, leading to the increasing danger of abuse of discretion, including the singling out of suspects based on race, poverty, and ethnicity. Overcriminalization, the expansion of stop and frisk, and the Court's refusal to use the tools at its disposal to control pretext searches or impose limits on custodial arrest all help create the conditions for police abuse of discretion. The other is a trend toward what we might call "spreading the misery": the increasing use of special needs or administrative searches subjecting increasing numbers of people to investigative intrusions based on prior administrative authorization. These special needs searches, at least in theory, impose on all of us without regard to race, ethnicity, or economic class. Airport searches, drug testing of schools or workplaces, drivers' license or sobriety checkpoints – these intrude on the privacy of large numbers of people and can be effectuated in most cases with no suspicion at all, as long as they are conducted pursuant to a prior administrative plan, and as long as their primary purpose is not criminal investigation.[57]

The hope expressed by some scholars is that if the misery is spread widely enough across the political and economic spectrum, the democratic process will constrain it.[58] Intrusive pat-downs at airports, for example, have led to a spirited dialogue,[59] one that includes the voices of U.S. senators and others with the power to influence policy.[60] But this sort of dialogue is unlikely to generate sufficiently broad outrage or wield sufficient influence when the misery is concentrated in certain neighborhoods or among certain groups, inevitably those with little political clout or access. As one New York legislator recently summed up the dynamics of the debate over statutory limits on stop and frisk, "There is an ethnic divide on who's being stopped and frisked, and there is an ethnic divide on who's fighting against the policy."[61] The current Fourth Amendment framework, for all its limitations, was premised on an understanding that courts play an indispensable role in supervising police conduct and in protecting the rights of the unpopular and the marginalized. The political process is generally least responsive to those groups hardest hit by police illegality.

4. THOUGHTS ON SOLUTIONS

Thus the Court must continue to play a role, and there is plenty of room for judicial improvement. The language from the *Terry* opinion mentioned previously, referring to an affirmative judicial obligation to guard against police harassment, sounds sadly quaint. Fourth Amendment doctrine has not generally been animated by the notion of a judicial responsibility to guard against police misconduct. It is enough to recall the *Whren* case,[62] in which the Court set up a kind of shell game for claims of racial disparity in policing. It said, essentially, you have looked under the wrong shell; we decline to interpret the Fourth Amendment reasonableness clause to prohibit pretextual searches; your remedy lies with the Fourteenth Amendment. At the same time it has created daunting barriers to disparate impact claims under the Fourteenth Amendment.[63] The remedial gap is even further widened by the erection of increasingly high judicial barriers to civil rights suits, both against individual police officers and against law enforcement agencies.[64] The message seems to be that if broad swaths of lawless police conduct fall through the cracks between doctrines, the Court has neither the obligation nor the power to address this remedial gap.

A more muscular Fourth Amendment reasonableness clause could be used to limit pretextual searches and seizures, to insist on a nexus between the type of crime for which an arrest is made and the scope of the accompanying search incident to arrest, and to oversee not only when stops and frisks occur, but with how much force and how much respect for dignity they are effectuated. The Court could improve its ability to guard against patterns of police harassment by lowering the barriers it has created to standing for injunctive relief and municipal liability under 42 U.S.C. § 1983. It should also revisit its Fourteenth Amendment jurisprudence, in particular the intent requirement that insulates so much discriminatory conduct. But realistically, there is little reason to believe that this Court will take those steps by the year 2020.

Moreover, most of the problems discussed in this chapter are largely legislative and administrative creations. Rolling back statutorily authorized overcriminalization is not a judicial task. It requires legislative action and the political will to accomplish it. Large-scale reform of police priorities and tactics (such as aggressive order-maintenance policing) is unlikely to occur through the courts or without substantial participation by a variety of legislative and administrative entities. Under 1994 legislation, the Department of Justice has made important strides in bringing pattern and practice suits to obtain injunctive relief against local law enforcement agencies for misconduct such as excessive force or racially discriminatory stops.[65] This is one important model for expanding law's investigative and enforcement power. But federal oversight cannot take the place of state and local initiatives addressing decriminalization, policing priorities and tactics, and a range of other issues.

Likewise, police culture needs to be reformed. Departments need to adopt best practices to guide them at the investigative stages. Departments need to track patterns of misconduct; to address resistance to civilian complaints; to improve screening, training, and monitoring of police, including training that addresses unconscious bias; and to create incentives to good policing, not merely to racking up stops, arrests, and convictions.

There is no road map for approaching the most daunting challenge of all. Structural and cultural change is unlikely to occur without political will, and the lack of political will is the recurring hurdle to reform of police practices. It is rarely politically advantageous to back police reform or to be perceived as "siding against the police," especially when aggressive police tactics are confined to the neighborhoods where the politically powerless reside.[66] Elected state court judges know this,[67] and even some federal judges have learned it to their detriment.[68] Municipal officials are aware of it too, preferring to pay out millions of dollars of settlement money each year for police misconduct rather than institute reform.[69]

Thus I am less hopeful than others about the power of the political process. But to paraphrase Winston Churchill, the democratic process is the worst option we have, except for all the others. The balance between liberty and security is best safeguarded by an ongoing dialogue about what intrusions we should be forced to accept in a free and open society. Perhaps the key word in the previous sentence is "we." Debate about what intrusions ought to be borne in the name of public safety must take account of racial, ethnic, and empathic divides in experience and understanding about the effects of police power and discretion. Our best option is to ensure the dialogue is inclusive, informed, and vigorous.

Notes

1   576,394 people were stopped and 326,369 were frisked. NYPD Stop-and-Frisk Statistics 2009 and 2010, Ctr. for Constitutional Rights, available at https://ccrjustice.org/files/CCR-Stop-and-Frisk-Fact-Sheet-2010.pdf (last visited Apr. 30, 2013).
2   Blacks and Latinos comprise 26% and 27% of the NYC population, respectively. *Id.*
3   *Id.* In 2002, when numbers of stops were first tallied, 9,837 were stopped and 52,803 were frisked. *Id.*
4   In 2009 and 2010, fewer than 2.5% of stops led to contraband and only 1.25% led to weapons. NYCLU Fact Sheet on Stop and Frisk Practices, N.Y. Civ. Liberties Union, available at http://nyclu.org/issues/racial-justice/stop-and-frisk-practices (last visited Apr. 30, 2013).
5   12% in 2009 and 14% in 2010. *Id.* This pattern of activity has been the subject of a series of class action suits challenging the NYPD's policy of conducting stops and frisks without reasonable suspicion of criminal activity in violation of the Fourth Amendment. See *Daniels v. City of New York*, No. 99 Civ. 1695, 2001 WL 228091 (S.D.N.Y. March 8, 2001); *Floyd v. City of New York*, 739 F. Supp. 2d 376 (S.D.N.Y. June 25, 2010); *Floyd v. City of New York*, 283 F.R.D. 153 (S.D.N.Y. May 16, 2012) (upholding class certification and finding "the stop an frisk ethos" to be "hierarchical, unified, and systemic.")
6   "Only 0.2% of misdemeanor and violation cases are ever tried in New York City." K. Babe Howell, *Broken Lives from Broken Windows: The Hidden Costs of Aggressive Order-Maintenance Policing*, 33 N.Y.U. Rev. L. & Soc. Change 271, 300 (2009).
7   *Terry v. Ohio*, 392 U.S. 1 (1968).
8   *Id.*
9   For example, *Terry* opened the door to the growing trend toward exempting police conduct from the warrant and probable cause requirements and evaluating it solely on whether it is reasonable; a trend that has led to the rapidly growing category of "special needs searches." See infra notes 57–61 and accompanying text.
10 This is somewhat of an oversimplification. For example the exclusionary rule is aimed more broadly at general deterrence of future police conduct. Susan A. Bandes, *The Roberts Court and the Future of the Exclusionary Rule*, Am. Constitution Soc'y for Law & Pol'y, April 2009, available at http://www.acslaw.org/files/Bandes%20Issue%20Brief.pdf (last visited Apr. 30, 2013).
11 For excellent discussions of policing as an institution, see Rachel Harmon, *The Problem of Policing*, 110 Mich. L. Rev. 761 (2012); see also Eric J. Miller, *Putting the Practice into Theory*, 7 Ohio St. J. Crim. L. 31 (2009).

12 *Terry*, 392 U.S. at 14.
13 Susan Bandes, *Patterns of Injustice: Police Brutality in the Courts*, 47 BUFF. L. REV. 1275 (1999).
14 *Terry*, 392 U.S. at 14–15.
15 *Id.* at 15.
16 See, e.g., *Monroe v. Pape*, 365 U.S. 161 (1961) (holding police officers suable under Sec. 1983 civil rights act if acting under color of state law, even if they acted in violation of state law). The expansion continued during the subsequent Burger Court, which held that municipal agencies like police departments could be sued for their unconstitutional policies, *Monell v. Dep't of Soc. Serv.*, 436 U.S. 658 (1978), and that municipal agencies could not claim immunity from suit, *Owen v. City of Independence*, 445 U.S. 622 (1980).
17 Howell, supra note 6.
18 See, e.g., OR. REV. STAT. § 811.400 (2001).
19 See, e.g., COLO. REV. STAT. § 42-4-1007 (1994).
20 See, e.g., MINN. STAT. § 169.733 (2005).
21 See, e.g,. ME. REV. STAT. ANN. TIT. 29, § 2082 (1995).
22 IOWA CODE § 321.388 (1985).
23 See, e.g., NEB. REV. STAT. § 60-682.01 (2009).
24 NJSA Point Schedule, STATE OF N.J. MOTOR VEHICLE COMM'N http://www.state.nj.us/mvc/Violations/penalties_pointSchedule.htm (accessed Sept. 2, 2012).
25 *Id.*
26 *Id.*
27 That is, an arrest in which the suspect is taken into custody rather than released and permitted to pay a ticket or show up in court at a later date. Once police make a custodial arrest they are also permitted a full-body search of the arrestee and, in some circumstances, a search of the entire passenger compartment of his car, including the glove compartment and the contents of any containers in the car. *New York v. Belton*, 453 U.S. 454 (1981); *Arizona v. Gant*, 556 U.S. 332 (2009).
28 *Atwater v. City of Lago Vista*, 532 U.S. 318, 354–55 (2001). See also *Virginia v. Moore*, 553 U.S. 164 (2008) (holding that even where a state law limits the types of violations that can give rise to a custodial arrest, those limits are overridden by the Fourth Amendment, which sets no such limits). However, the Court recently placed some welcome limits on the ability of police to search a car incident to arrest of a driver or passenger. *Gant*, 556 U.S. at 1723-4.
29 *Whren v. United States*, 517 U.S. 806, 819 (1996).
30 David A. Harris, *The Stories, the Statistics, and the Law: Why "Driving while Black" Matters*, 84 MINN. L. REV. 265, 277–9 (1999).
31 *Id.* at 280–1.
32 Howell, supra note 6, at 273.
33 *Id.* at 276 (citing James Q. Wilson & George L. Kelling, *Broken Windows: The Police and Neighborhood Safety*, ATLANTIC MONTHLY, Mar. 1982, at 29, 34).
34 Jeffrey Fagan & Garth Davies, *Street Stops and Broken Windows: Terry, Race, and Disorder in New York City*, 28 FORDHAM URB. L.J. 457, 465–7 (2000).
35 *Id.* at 470–3.
36 *Id.* at 476–7.

37 DAVID FEIGE, INDEFENSIBLE: ONE LAWYER'S JOURNEY INTO THE INFERNO OF AMERICAN JUSTICE 127 (2006).
38 Elena Goldstein, *Kept Out: Responding to Public Housing No-Trespass Policies*, 38 HARV. C.R.-C.L. L. REV. 215, 217 (2003). In, *Ligon v. City of New York* (12 Civ. 2274, S.D.N.Y., January 8, 2013), one of the companion suits to the Floyd case (supra note 5), the federal district court recently held unconstitutional the NYPD's practice of routinely stopping people without suspicion in front of public housing residential buildings in the Bronx in order to enforce rules against trespassing.
39 *Id.* at 127–33.
40 *Id.* at 127.
41 *Chambers v. Maroney*, 399 U.S. 42 (1970) (granting broad power to search cars on probable cause without the need for a warrant); *United States v. Robinson*, 414 U.S. 218 (1973) (holding search incident to custodial arrest in a public place requires no warrant); *Terry v. Ohio*, 392 U.S. 1 (1968) (holding stop and frisk activity exempt from the warrant clause).
42 Howell, supra note 6, at 312 n.12 (citing Steven Zeidman, *Policing the Police: The Role of the Courts and the Prosecution*, 32 FORDHAM URB. L.J. 315, 321 n. 35 [2005]).
43 Fagan & Davies, supra note 34, at 476.
44 Thus one counterproductive byproduct of aggressive policing may be the loss of community goodwill and an increasing unwillingness to cooperate with law enforcement. See, e.g., Wendy Ruderman, *Rude or Polite, New York Police Leave Raw Feelings in Stops*, N.Y. TIMES, June 27, 2012, at A21. See generally Tom Tyler, *The Psychology of Legitimacy: A Relational Perspective on Voluntary Deference to Authorities*, 1 PERSONALITY AND SOC. PSYCHOL. REV. 323 (1997).
45 Of course the consequences of a conviction, even for a minor crime, are far greater. See generally Howell, supra note 6.
46 See supra note 1.
47 Howell, supra note 6, at 289.
48 Ruderman, supra note 44, at A21.
49 See Report Under New York City Administrative Code Chapter 1 Title 14, Section 14–150, New York City Police Department Stop Question and Frisk Activity for the period April 1, 2011 to June 30, 2011.
50 See L. Song Richardson, *Arrest Efficiency and the Fourth Amendment*, 95 MINN. L. REV. 2035 (2011).
51 RANDALL KENNEDY, RACE, CRIME, AND THE LAW 154 (1997).
52 See *Stop and Frisk Facts*, N.Y. CIV. LIBERTIES UNION, http://www.nyclu.org/node/1598 (accessed Sept. 2, 2012).
53 See, e.g., Ruderman, supra note 44 (describing use of epithets and rude language during stop and frisk encounters).
54 See, e.g., *Illinois v. Caballes*, 543 U.S. 405 (2005) (holding that the introduction of a narcotics detection dog to sniff for drugs during a routine traffic stop did not violate *Terry* because it did not extend the duration of the stop).
55 See Bandes, *The Roberts Court and the Future of the Exclusionary Rule*, supra note 10.
56 *Id.*

57 See generally Eve Brensike Primus, *Disentangling Administrative Searches*, 111 COLUM. L. REV. 254 (2011).
58 Christopher Slobogin, *Government Dragnets*, 73 LAW & CONTEMP. PROBS. 107 (2010); William Stuntz, *Implicit Bargains, Government Power, and the Fourth Amendment*, 44 STAN. L. REV. 553 (1992).
59 See, e.g., Susan Stellin, *Pat-Downs at Airports Prompt Complaints*, N.Y. TIMES, Nov. 18, 2010.
60 See, e.g., *Even U.S. Senators Complain about Airport Patdowns*, AIRWISE (Nov. 18, 2010), http://news.airwise.com/story/view/1290121754.html (last visited Apr. 30, 2013). One bill in the Texas legislature sought to criminalize intrusive TSA pat-downs. Douglas Stanglin, *Bill to Criminalize Intrusive TSA Pat-Downs Dies in Texas House*, USA TODAY, June 29, 2011, available at http://content.usatoday.com/communities/ondeadline/post/2011/06/bill-to-criminalize-intrusive-tsa-pat-downs-dies-in-texas-house/1#.T2yWXmGPV2B (last visited Apr. 30, 2013).
61 John Eligon, *Fighting Police Stops, and Hitting Racial Divide*, N.Y. TIMES, Mar. 23, 2012, at A1 (citing State Senator and retired police captain Eric L. Adams).
62 *Whren v. United States*, 517 U.S. 806 (1996).
63 See, e.g., *McCleskey v. Kemp*. 481 U.S.306 (1987); *Washington v. Davis*, 426 U.S. 229 (1976).
64 See, e.g., *City of Los Angeles v. Lyons*, 461 U.S. 95 (1983) (creating high barriers to standing in injunctive suits); Board of the County Comm'rs of *Bryan County v. Brown*, 520 U.S. 397 (1997) (creating high barriers to municipal liability); *Briscoe v. Lahue*, 460 U.S. 325 (granting police officers broad immunity from suit).
65 Crime Control Act of 1994, 42 U.S.C. § 14141.
66 A recent poll of New York City voters found that 59% of white voters but only 27% of black voters approve the current stop and frisk regime. Eligon, supra note 61, at A3.
67 See *Republican Party of Minn. v. White*, 536 U.S. 765, 788 (2002) (O'Connor, J., concurring).
68 Bandes, *Patterns of Injustice*, supra note 13, at 1323 (discussing federal judge Harold Baer and the reaction to his opinion in *United States v. Bayless*, 913 F. Supp. 232 (S.D.N.Y. 1996), vacated, 921 F. Supp. 211 (S.D.N.Y. 1996)).
69 *Id.* at 1337.

4

Implicit Racial Bias and the Fourth Amendment

L. Song Richardson

1. INTRODUCTION

In recent years, legal scholars have utilized the science of implicit social cognition[1] to reveal how unconscious biases affect perceptions, behaviors, and judgments. This science combines the lessons of social psychology, cognitive psychology, and cognitive neuroscience to examine mental processes that occur outside conscious awareness and that operate without conscious control. Employing this science, scholars have critiqued legal doctrine and challenged courts to take accurate theories of human behavior into account or to explain their failure to do so.

The lessons of implicit social cognition can contribute much to the understanding of police behavior, especially as it relates to hit rates or "arrest efficiency" – the rates at which police find evidence of criminal activity when they conduct a stop and frisk. Empirical evidence consistently demonstrates that the police disproportionately stop and frisk nonwhites, although stops and searches of whites are often more successful in yielding evidence of criminal activity. While economists and criminal process scholars both suggest that arrest inefficiency is due to conscious racial bias, the science reveals that unconscious biases may also contribute. Taking account of the science of implicit social cognition is important to the study of Fourth Amendment jurisprudence and policing. The failure to recognize the effects of implicit bias has resulted in a Fourth Amendment jurisprudence that unintentionally exacerbates the effects of implicit bias on police behavior. Changes to Fourth Amendment doctrine as well as structural changes within police departments are necessary steps to protect privacy against arbitrary government intrusion more effectively.

This chapter is adapted from L. Song Richardson, *Arrest Efficiency and the Fourth Amendment*, 95 MINN. L. REV. 2035 (2011). Extensive citations supporting the arguments made here are available in the original version.

2. OVERVIEW OF IMPLICIT BIASES AND THEIR BEHAVIORAL EFFECTS

Research in the field of implicit social cognition repeatedly demonstrates that individuals of all races have implicit biases against blacks. These take the form of unconscious stereotypes and prejudices that might conflict with a person's consciously and genuinely held thoughts and feelings. However, once activated, these biases can negatively and unconsciously influence judgments of and behaviors toward blacks in ways that a person is unaware of and largely unable to control. The unconscious stereotype consists of the cultural stereotype of blacks, especially young men, as violent, hostile, aggressive, and dangerous. In the policing context, these unconscious stereotypes can cause an officer who harbors no conscious racial animosity and who rejects using race as a proxy for criminality unintentionally to judge and treat individuals differently solely on the basis of their racial appearance. Some behavioral effects of implicit bias are discussed next.

a. Increased Scrutiny

Researchers consistently find that blacks, especially young black men, capture attention before whites do. This occurs unconsciously and automatically. Scientists attribute this type of unconscious racial profiling to the fact that people have automatic and rapid threat reactions toward black men. Indeed, brain scans demonstrate that people show more activation of the amygdala, a portion of the brain associated with fear, when viewing faces of black men versus white men.

Conscious racial attitudes do not predict this so-called attentional bias. Rather, the only predictor of how quickly an individual's attention is unconsciously drawn to blacks is the strength of the perceiver's implicit association between blacks and danger. Those for whom the implicit black-danger association is highly accessible are quicker to pay attention to black faces than white faces. Those for whom the danger stereotype is not as accessible do not demonstrate attentional bias.[2]

b. Biased Evaluations

For more than sixty years, social psychologists have demonstrated that black men are stereotyped as violent, criminal, and dangerous. These cultural stereotypes affect the evaluation of behaviors performed by blacks. This was powerfully demonstrated in a study that required participants to rate an ambiguous physical contact between two people.³ Researchers had subjects watch a video of two men engaged in a discussion that grew increasingly heated. The subjects were unaware that the men were actors following a script. Instead, they were told that they were observing a discussion occurring in another room. Researchers asked the subjects to rate the behavior of the two men at various points during the discussion. Eventually, one man pushed the other and the subjects had the option of rating the contact as horsing around, dramatic, aggressive, or violent. Researchers manipulated the race of the pusher and the victim to test whether race would affect the subjects' perceptions.

Remarkably, the actor's race significantly influenced how subjects evaluated the contact. When the victim was white and the person initiating the physical contact was black, 75 percent of the subjects interpreted the shove as violent. However, when the victim was black and the pusher was white, only 17 percent of the subjects labeled the contact as violent. Forty-two percent of the subjects rated the white perpetrator as horsing around or being dramatic. Finally, when the two actors were black, the perpetrator's behavior was rated as more aggressive than when the two individuals were white – 69 percent versus 13 percent. The researchers concluded that negative stereotypes associating blacks with violence explained why the subjects evaluated ambiguous behaviors as more aggressive when performed by a black actor as opposed to a white actor. The presence of a black individual automatically brought negative black stereotypes such as violence to the forefront of the subject's memory, making the trait more available for use in evaluating ambiguous behavior.

Other studies support the finding that individuals evaluate blacks more negatively than whites engaged in identical behavior. In one study, black and white school age children rated an ambiguous bump in the hallway as more aggressive when performed by a black actor rather than a white actor.[4] In another, subjects evaluated the same facial expression as more hostile on a black face than on a white face.[5] In a third study using buttons labeled "shoot" and "don't shoot" as a weapon's trigger, the unconscious activation of black stereotypes caused individuals more quickly to shoot a potentially hostile black than a potentially hostile white.[6]

c. Biased Treatment and Behavioral Confirmation

Negative stereotypes and unfavorable attitudes toward blacks can cause individuals to treat them differently than nonstereotyped group members. One experiment demonstrating this involved white subjects interviewing "job applicants."[7] Researchers trained the applicants to respond to interview questions in a standard format so that any differences in the treatment they received from the interviewer would be attributable to race. The results demonstrated that white interviewers treated black and white job applicants differently. With black applicants, the interviewer maintained greater physical distance, made more speech errors, and ended the interview sooner than with white applicants. Researchers concluded that these differences resulted from the negative stereotypical beliefs about the black job applicants held by the interviewers.

This interview study did not specifically test whether implicit bias caused the negative treatment of blacks. However, more recent experiments make this connection. In one, researchers asked participants to complete a tedious computer task consisting of 130 trials.[8] Before each trial, the participants were shown photos of either black or white faces subliminally (below the level of conscious awareness). On the 130th trial, as planned, the computer program crashed and researchers told the participants that they would have to begin the entire task from the beginning.

Researchers videotaped the participants' reactions and coded them for hostility. The results demonstrated that subjects primed with photos of black faces reacted with more hostility to the news than those primed with photos of white faces. This occurred, the researchers concluded, because those primed with black faces automatically activated negative black stereotypes that then affected their behavior. Surprisingly, subjects acted more aggressively after the black-face prime regardless of whether they had consciously negative attitudes toward blacks. Importantly, this study does not suggest that individuals will inevitably respond with aggression whenever black stereotype activation occurs. Rather, stereotype activation can cause aggressive behavior in situations where aggression is one possible appropriate response.

Receiving negative treatment can cause individuals to respond in kind. This is known as the self-fulfilling prophecy or behavioral confirmation effect. Numerous researchers note that the originators of negative behavior will likely be completely unaware of the role their own behavior played in triggering the negative response. Hence, the behavioral confirmation effect "provide[s] a powerful mechanism by which stereotypes and prejudicial behavior are maintained" since "the perceiver interprets the target's behavior in line with the expectancy and encodes yet another instance of stereotype-consistent behavior."[9]

3. EXAMINING THE *Terry v. Ohio* DOCTRINE

On the basis of the science, it is reasonable to conclude that implicit biases can cause the police to target, stop, and search blacks more often than similarly situated whites. Police attention may be drawn to black individuals in general, and to young black men in particular, regardless of whether these individuals are engaged in suspicious behavior. Once officers' attention is captured, automatic stereotype activation can cause them to interpret behavior as aggressive, violent, or suspicious even if identical behavior performed by a white individual would not be so interpreted. When officers approach the individual to confirm or dispel their suspicions, implicit biases can cause officers to behave aggressively without realizing it. The confronted individual may respond in kind, fulfilling officers' beliefs that the individual is suspicious and aggressive. This entire series of events, triggered not by conscious racial animus but by implicit racial biases, will likely lead officers to conduct a frisk. All the while, officers will be unaware that the behavioral effects of their implicit bias triggered the entire chain of events. In the end, officers may stop and frisk black individuals, whom they would not have deemed suspicious if they had been white, not because of bigotry or conscious considerations of race, but because of implicit cognitions.

Although the scientific evidence has much to contribute to understandings of police decision making and judgment, judges continue to employ commonsense, intuitive theories of human behavior in crafting Fourth Amendment legal standards. As a result, the Court's stop-and-frisk jurisprudence not only fails to achieve the appropriate balance between privacy and security, but also exacerbates the effects of implicit bias on behavior, leading to arrest inefficiencies.

For instance, in *Terry v. Ohio*,[10] Officer McFadden was on the lookout for shoplifters and pickpockets in the middle of the afternoon in downtown Cleveland. At some point, he noticed Terry and Chilton standing on a street corner. McFadden could not articulate "precisely what first drew his eye to them."[11] They just "didn't look right," he testified, even though they were dressed in topcoats, customary attire at the time.[12] "To be truthful," he admitted, "I just didn't like them."[13] Both Terry and Chilton were black.

McFadden watched the two men for ten minutes as they took turns walking down the street, looking into a store window, and returning. Their behavior led McFadden to suspect that the two were casing a store in preparation for a daytime robbery. Without probable cause, McFadden grabbed Terry, spun him around, frisked him, and found a concealed weapon.

The issue before the Court was whether the Fourth Amendment permitted officers to seize and frisk individuals in the absence of probable cause. The Court answered the question in the affirmative. It held that reasonable suspicion, and not the traditional probable cause standard, authorized officers to detain individuals for questioning and to conduct a limited search for weapons. In order to justify what is colloquially known as a "stop and frisk," the reasonable suspicion test requires an officer "to point to specific and articulable facts which ... leads him reasonably to conclude in light of his experience that criminal activity may be afoot" or that the individual with whom he is interacting is armed and dangerous.[14]

Through the reasonable suspicion standard, the Court attempted a delicate balance, granting police the discretion to stop and frisk suspicious individuals while attempting to protect individuals from unjustified encroachments upon their liberty. In keeping with its goal of cabining police discretion and simultaneously allowing the police to act on their suspicions in appropriate cases, the Court prohibited officers from acting on their "inchoate and unparticularized suspicion[s] or hunch[es]," including racial hunches.[15] Instead, "in justifying the particular intrusion the police officer must be able to point to specific and articulable facts."[16] "Anything less," the Court cautioned, "would invite intrusions upon constitutionally guaranteed rights based on nothing more substantial than inarticulate hunches, a result this Court has consistently refused to sanction."[17]

The *Terry* decision contains implicit behavioral theories of police judgment and decision making that do not withstand empirical scrutiny when implicit biases are considered. As a result, the reasonable suspicion standard is not up to the task of preventing intrusions based upon nothing more than hunches. Rather, the test may facilitate policing that inadequately protects liberty while failing to further effective law enforcement. These flawed behavioral assumptions are considered next.

a. Interpretation of Ambiguous Behavior

In *Terry*, the Court constructed a test that allows officers to stop and frisk an individual on the basis of their interpretation of the individual's ambiguous behavior. The test requires officers to justify stops and frisks by articulating the facts that led them to feel suspicious, and then courts review those facts for reasonableness. This articulation requirement represents the Court's attempt to cabin officer discretion by prohibiting stops and frisks based upon hunches.

The behavioral assumption underlying the reasonable suspicion test is that well-intentioned officers are capable of interpreting identical behavior similarly, regardless of the race of the individual they are observing. While this behavioral assumption is intuitively appealing, it does not withstand scientific scrutiny. Unconscious stereotype activation in the presence of black individuals may cause officers to interpret their ambiguous behaviors as suspicious, aggressive, and dangerous while similar behaviors engaged in by whites would be unnoticed. Upon feeling suspicious, an officer can easily articulate the specific facts that he believes led him to feel suspicious without realizing that his initial feelings of suspicion may have been caused by the operation of implicit racial bias.

b. Officer Experience

When determining whether an officer's stop and frisk is justified by reasonable suspicion, the *Terry* Court wrote that "due weight must be given ... to the specific reasonable inferences which [an officer] is entitled to draw from the facts in light of his experience."[18] This deference is justified by the belief that an experienced officer can "draw[] inferences and make[] deductions [from facts] ... that might well elude an untrained person."[19] The behavioral assumption is that officers, on the basis of their experiences, are better than civilians at distinguishing innocent from guilty conduct. However, the nature of their jobs may lead officers to perform no better than civilians when it comes to differentiating criminal from noncriminal activity. In fact, they perhaps may perform even worse in situations where nonwhites are involved for two reasons.

First, thinking about crime can trigger unconscious thoughts about blacks, which in turn activate negative black stereotypes. In one study, researchers found that the connection between blacks and crime has become so entrenched and ubiquitous that not only does seeing a black individual bring negative racial stereotypes to mind unconsciously, but simply thinking about crime triggers implicit thoughts about blacks in police officers and civilians alike.[20] The researchers concluded that "[n]ot only are Blacks thought of as criminal, but also crime is thought of as Black."[21] Since officers are constantly on the lookout for criminal activity, they likely are steeped in unconscious black stereotypes that influence their judgments and behaviors. Once activated, these implicit stereotypes can cause officers unconsciously to pay more attention to Blacks than to Whites and to interpret the ambiguous behaviors of blacks as suspicious and criminal.

Second, police often view blacks in environments that are urban and poor. Officers working in urban environments exhibit higher levels of implicit bias than those who do not.[22] And research confirms that perceptions of disorder increase when communities are majority black instead of majority white, even when the neighborhoods are otherwise similarly situated.[23] Thus, an officer patrolling a poor urban majority-black neighborhood is more prone to judge ambiguous behaviors as suspicious, causing him to stop more individuals who are innocent.

In sum, officers' experiences do not necessarily make them better able to distinguish guilty from innocent conduct. The Court's assumption that officers are better than civilians at distinguishing guilty from innocent conduct may not withstand scientific scrutiny when nonwhites are involved.

c. Race Salience

The Supreme Court has established that race can be relevant to determining whether a reasonable suspicion of criminality exists so long as it is not the sole factor.[24] Not surprisingly then, police officers sometimes rely upon race to justify *Terry* seizures. However, when courts allow officers to utilize race to overcome shortcomings in demonstrating reasonable suspicion, they assume that officers accurately remember their experiences and, thus, can make sound correlations between race and criminality. The empirical evidence on memories and illusory correlations should lead courts to be more cautious.

Stereotypes about black criminality can affect memories about contacts with blacks. This can occur because people are more likely to encode events into memory that are consistent with their preexisting beliefs and expectations. Because of both implicit and conscious biases, officers are likely to have better memories of individuals who confirm their suspicions of criminality than of those who do not. Then, flawed memories can cause officers to see correlations between blacks and crime that do not exist and to miss correlations between behavior and crime that actually do exist. These illusory correlations between race and criminality can "persist even in the face of data in which these correlations are nonexistent,"[25] because people unintentionally search their memories for evidence that confirms an existing hypothesis rather than engaging in a balanced search for evidence that either confirms or refutes it. Thus, officers' correlations between race and criminality may say more about their preexisting stereotypes than about the accuracy of their beliefs.

4. PRELIMINARY THOUGHTS ON DOCTRINAL REFORMS

The failure to be realistic about police decision making and judgment has pernicious effects on policing and privacy. Fourth Amendment jurisprudence is primarily concerned with prohibiting arbitrary invasions of privacy by the government. In constructing the doctrine to protect against arbitrary invasions, the Court made inaccurate behavioral assumptions about police decision making that actually undermine this core value. This leads to policing that fails to protect equally the privacy rights of all individuals regardless of their race. To realize the normative goal of the Fourth Amendment, courts should take accurate understandings of decision making into account rather than basing their legal standards on assumptions that are empirically unsupportable. Some tentative proposals for *Terry* reform that will serve both law enforcement and privacy interests by taking the empirical evidence about human behavior and decision making seriously are discussed next.

a. Return to Probable Cause

The reasonable suspicion test fails to prevent the police from acting on racial hunches. By allowing officers to act on their interpretation of ambiguous behavior, the test underprotects the privacy rights of nonwhites; they will be stopped and frisked more often than similarly situated whites, not because they are acting more suspiciously, but because implicit biases likely will affect how police interpret and react to their behavior.

One solution is to return to the probable cause standard as the sole justification for stops and frisks. Probable cause is a tougher standard than reasonable suspicion. The probable cause standard would require officers to gather more information and to observe more unambiguous behavior before seizing individuals. The science demonstrates that individuation (i.e., compiling more information about an individual) can reduce the effects of implicit cognitions on behavior, resulting in stops and searches that are more accurate.

Data from the Maryland State Police provide some evidence that requiring officers to have probable cause before acting increases accuracy. The data demonstrate that when officers conducted searches based upon probable cause, their hit rates were 53 percent. However, when officers asked individuals for consent to conduct a search, likely because they did not have probable cause, their hit rates dropped to 22 percent.[26]

One potential problem with this approach is that it is unlikely that courts would actually implement it. Additionally, even if it was implemented, courts might dilute the probable cause standard to such an extent that it would operate much as the reasonable suspicion test currently does. A final problem is that the probable cause standard is not necessarily immune from the effects of implicit bias. Although the standard is theoretically more difficult to meet than the reasonable suspicion test, the standard is "non-technical," "fluid," and based upon "common-sense."[27] Consequently, the standard still requires officers to evaluate ambiguous behavior unless they catch an individual red-handed.

b. No Automatic Deference

Currently, courts defer to officer judgments of criminality in determining whether a reasonable suspicion exists without requiring empirical evidence to support either the officer's ability to make sound conclusions or the validity of the evidence the officer used to make his judgment.[28] Rather, courts rely upon the officer's "common sense conclusions about human behavior."[29] However, the science demonstrates that an officer's commonsense conclusions are likely unconsciously influenced by the race of the person being observed.

Thus, a court's blind deference to officer judgments may underprotect the liberty of nonwhites and facilitate inefficient policing.

In order to reduce the effects of implicit bias on policing, courts should not defer automatically to officer judgments of criminality. At the very least, courts should require officers to provide empirical support for their inferences before giving those inferences any weight in the reasonable suspicion calculus. This empirical support could be in the form of individual officer "hit rates." For instance, officers could be required to provide specific information that out of "X" number of stops based upon criteria "Y," this officer's percentage of productive stops and frisks is "Z." Providing this evidence avoids the problem of relying upon the accuracy of an officer's memories of his experiences.

However, aggregate hit rates alone should be insufficient to justify a *Terry* stop because this would undermine the notion of individualized suspicion that is at the core of the Fourth Amendment. For instance, even if an officer demonstrated a hit rate of 30 percent for finding contraband when he stopped young white men, with close-cropped hair, wearing baggy pants, and living in high-income areas, this information alone should not entitle officers to stop all young white men who meet this description with impunity. Rather, additional evidence to support the officer's inference that the particular individual stopped is likely engaged in criminal activity should be required. Thus, aggregate hit-rate data alone should not be a sufficient basis for finding a stop and frisk reasonable.

The important point here is that courts should not defer to officer judgments about when an individual's actions denote criminality in the absence of any evidence of the particular officer's ability to make these judgments. When courts determine whether a reasonable suspicion exists, they should base their judgments, in part, on some form of empirically validated evidence rather than relying upon an officer's personal experiences or commonsense conclusions, which the science demonstrates are often incorrect. Since unproductive stops will affect an officer's aggregate hit rates, requiring officers to provide empirical evidence will likely create incentives for them to think carefully about the criteria they use before conducting *Terry* stops. To the extent that this motivates officers to individuate, it will decrease the effects of implicit bias on police behavior.

c. *No Reliance on Race or Race Proxies*

Some courts currently allow officers to rely on race and proxies for race (such as consideration of high-crime neighborhoods) to justify *Terry* seizures. Courts assume that these considerations help officers ferret out criminal behavior.

However, the science demonstrates that consideration of race and race proxies may make officers less, not more, accurate.

By countenancing consideration of race to infer criminality, courts exacerbate implicit biases by solidifying the association between race and crime. First, purposefully focusing officer attention on blacks and their criminal stereotype makes negative stereotypes salient and thus more available for use in judging behavior. This predisposes officers to interpret ambiguous behaviors as more suspicious than they might otherwise.

While solidifying the association between race and crime occurs even when race is not consciously highlighted, focusing attention on the race-crime association exacerbates it. Thus, race salience encourages police encounters with blacks. It draws police attention to blacks with the assumption that they are involved in criminal activity. The unconscious activation of negative racial stereotypes, then, may cause officers to interpret ambiguous behavior as suspicious.

Second, by making race salient, the doctrine encourages officers to approach black individuals with the expectation of finding evidence of criminal activity. Conscious affirmation and practice of racial stereotypes facilitate the creation of automatic and unconscious associations. The automatic activation of negative stereotypes then has behavioral effects, leading to increased scrutiny, negative evaluations of ambiguous behaviors, and negative treatment. Thus, conscious consideration of race can exacerbate the behavioral effects of implicit bias, negatively affecting nonwhites.

In order to protect individuals from the arbitrary policing caused by the operation of implicit bias, courts should decouple the association between race and crime. Courts can accomplish this by refusing to consider race and proxies for race in deciding whether the police acted reasonably in conducting a stop and frisk. In fact, courts should go further and clearly state that race is irrelevant to a determination of whether a *Terry* seizure is justified. By making this change, the doctrine can play an important normative role, potentially influencing an officer's beliefs about the appropriate uses of race in policing. At the very least, if the refusal to consider race and race proxies makes it more difficult for officers to establish reasonable suspicion, officers will likely be more accurate in the stops they conduct.

5. STRUCTURAL REFORMS

Reducing the behavioral effects of implicit bias in proactive policing will take more than doctrinal fixes. This section concentrates on structural changes within the institution of the police for reducing the effects of implicit bias on their behavior. Since implicit biases are malleable, police departments may be able to implement strategies to moderate their effects.

a. Review of Existing Practices

Police departments should identify practices and procedures that have the potential to exacerbate implicit biases and then consider whether they can and should be changed. One easily implemented change is to eliminate the use of training videos that portray racial minorities as perpetrators. This type of video likely strengthens implicit biases by reinforcing the race-criminal stereotype. Likewise, training simulations and similar practices should be conducted in ways that do not bolster racial stereotypes.

Departments also should reconsider the techniques they employ to reduce racial profiling. Studies demonstrate that making race salient increases activation of implicit stereotypes, even when individuals are instructed to *avoid* using racial stereotypes in their judgments. This phenomenon is known as the "rebound effect" and demonstrates that attempts to suppress thoughts can make those thoughts "become hyperaccessible once people relax their efforts at suppression or become preoccupied with other tasks."[30] This rebound effect can explain why consciously trying to avoid considerations of race can lead to greater use of racial stereotypes.

An important reason to avoid training officers to consider race in making judgments of criminality is its obvious effect of increasing the association between race and crime. It also encourages officers to categorize individuals by race consciously, a practice that can increase automatic stereotype activation. The science demonstrates that giving individuals a goal that encourages individuation rather than racial categorization may reduce activation of implicit stereotypes. Another reason to avoid connecting race with criminality is that encouraging the race-crime connection can create a community that supports racial stereotyping. The motivation to conform one's beliefs to those of the in-group affects implicit stereotypes.

Another area of concern is police deployment patterns. Black neighborhoods are simultaneously underpoliced and overpoliced. They are underpoliced when it comes to police responses to calls reporting criminal activity. Yet, these neighborhoods are overpoliced when it comes to proactive policing. Deploying officers to majority-black neighborhoods to engage in proactive policing does not seem to affect police responsiveness to citizen complaints. Studies show that implicit biases increase when individuals view blacks in contexts that trigger negative stereotypes, such as in poor urban neighborhoods. Hence, departments should consider whether it is better to refrain from deploying officers to these neighborhoods solely to engage in proactive policing when doing so both strengthens implicit biases and does not significantly increase community safety.

b. Debiasing Strategies

There are a number of specific debiasing strategies that may increase arrest efficiency by reducing or negating the effects of implicit biases. The suggestions offered here are based upon techniques that have shown promise in the research context. However, the question of how to translate laboratory findings into real life policing is complicated. Thus, the goal here is simply to highlight the need to think about reducing the effects of implicit bias on officer behavior and to identify ways of doing so. The proposals are divided into four general categories: increasing awareness, training, hiring, and incentivizing positive interactions.

i. Increasing Awareness

The possibility for moderating or overcoming implicit biases is at its highest when individuals are aware of the potential for bias and for controlling it. One way to increase officer awareness is to teach both police recruits and current officers about the results of research into the behavioral effects of implicit bias that may affect their interactions with citizens. At the police academy, a class on the science of implicit bias could be added to the curriculum. In police precincts, periodic classes that would be mandatory for officers assigned to proactive patrols units could be held.

Another way to increase awareness is to educate officers about hit-rate data. Explaining that implicit biases, rather than conscious racial animus, can account for the data may reduce defensiveness. Discussing the data can also facilitate a frank discussion about officer beliefs that racial disparities in seizures and frisks exist because of differential crime rates among ethnic groups. The idea is not to force officers to take problack attitudes, but to point out that in the proactive policing context, the hit-rate data demonstrate that their assumptions may be incorrect, and their preconceived notions may create a self-fulfilling prophecy. Importantly, the tenor of this discussion should not be accusatory or critical. Rather, the attitude should be one of collaboration and teamwork to increase the success rates of stops and searches.

A final idea for increasing awareness is to have recruits and officers take the Implicit Association Test (IAT). Introduced in 1998, the IAT is the most widely used mechanism for revealing the existence of implicit attitudes and stereotypes. The test has produced consistent results demonstrating that implicit biases are "pervasive," are unrelated to conscious beliefs, and "predict behavior."[31] The IAT will be easy to administer because it is available online. Officers should be assured that taking the IAT is solely for educational purposes and that their results will remain confidential.

ii. Training

A 2007 study involving police officers provides intriguing evidence that extensive training of officers to individuate may reduce the effects of implicit stereotyping. This study tested experimental shooter-bias situations in which individuals mistakenly shot unarmed blacks and mistakenly failed to shoot armed whites as a result of implicit social cognitions. In this study, researchers found that officers as well as civilians activated negative black stereotypes upon viewing black individuals. As a result, both officers and civilians were quicker to shoot an unarmed black than an unarmed white.

However, officers performed much better than civilians did. Officers were better able to exercise control over their automatic stereotypes and performed much better than civilians when making decisions whether to shoot. The researchers tentatively suggested that their training and experience "may allow officers to more effectively exert executive control in the shoot/don't-shoot task, essentially overriding response tendencies that stem from racial stereotypes."[32]

An earlier shooter-bias study involving police officers found that, after repeated exposure to pairings where race and having a weapon were unrelated, they exhibited reduced shooter bias relative to initial trials. Other studies similarly demonstrate that repeatedly pairing race with a nonstereotypical trait resulted in reduced implicit race bias. Importantly, then, it appears that training can reduce implicit biases. Field exercises or simulations where officers are trained to dissociate race from criminality may capitalize on the effectiveness of training to reduce the behavioral effects of implicit bias.

In another study, researchers found that it was possible to reduce the effects of implicit biases on behavior by asking individuals to develop a strategy for what they would do or think when they encounter a stereotyped group member. In the study, researchers asked subjects to "firmly commit" themselves to thinking "safe" each time they saw a black face.[33] Remarkably, subjects who committed themselves to this "counterstereotypic ... intention" reduced the effects of automatic stereotyping on their ability to differentiate weapons from innocuous objects accurately. This method holds the intriguing possibility that simply asking police officers to commit themselves to thinking, "If I see a black individual, I will think 'innocent'" or some other appropriate counterstereotypic intent may reduce the effects of implicit bias on their behavior toward blacks. For example, officers might commit themselves to thinking, "If I see a black individual that I believe is acting suspiciously, I will first consider whether I would have viewed the same actions as suspicious if the individual were white" before conducting a *Terry* seizure. This idea builds from Professor Cynthia Lee's race-switching jury instruction that would ask jurors whether they would feel the same way about a homicide if the defendant were white and the victim were black.[34] Other techniques that have worked in the lab to reduce the automatic activation of stereotypes include extensive practice denouncing stereotypes or affirming counterstereotypes, and the use of mental imagery.

Training officers to focus their attention on goals that encourage individuation may reduce implicit bias. How this is accomplished will be important. Asking officers to gather more evidence of suspicious behavior prior to engaging in a stop and frisk may actually cause officers to interpret the target's behavior as more suspicious than they otherwise would because of the activation of implicit stereotypes. Instead, it may be more effective to ask officers in the field to determine whether the actions they observe are consistent with innocence. This formulation will focus attention away from criminality and guilt.

iii. Hiring

An individual's cohort, both in his or her personal life and at the workplace, may be important in reducing implicit biases.[35] For instance, one study found that an officer who reported more positive personal contacts with blacks was less likely to have negative beliefs about the criminality and violence of blacks. Furthermore, positive personal contacts were the "only significant predictor" of a reduction in shooter bias.[36]

This has implications for job interview questions. Perhaps potential hires should be asked to describe positive personal experiences they have had with nonwhites. Certainly, such questions are job-related to the extent that such contacts may affect officer assessments of nonwhite suspects. If potential officers have had no experience or no positive experience with blacks, for example, departments should consider this factor in hiring. If hired, this officer might require additional training or perhaps should not be deployed to black neighborhoods.

Additionally, there is evidence that exposure to counterstereotypic group members, especially over the long term, reduces implicit biases. Not only does this provide support for asking officers about their personal contacts with nonwhites, but it also supports increasing the diversity of police departments. Furthermore, increasing diversity will decrease implicit biases both by providing more opportunities for officers to work in cooperative relationships with peers of different races and by changing the social norms and attitudes of departments. Similarly, promoting nonwhites to positions of authority may also be important because it may affect patrol officers' implicit biases.

iv. Incentivizing Positive Interactions

Efforts should be made to involve officers in positive interactions with members of the communities they police. One study involving police officers demonstrated that those who had had negative contacts with blacks reported higher levels of negative expectations of blacks, including about their propensity for violence and criminality, than those who had had positive experiences. Increasing the proportion of positive contacts between the community and the police – especially among those officers who will be patrolling those neighborhoods – will be important to minimize the stereotypical connection between blacks and criminality. Departments should create incentives to encourage officers to engage in positive experiences with community members. These interactions should include opportunities for working together in ways that reduce status differences because this encourages individuals to make judgments that are less reliant on stereotypes.

6. CONCLUSION

The failure of judges to account for the effects of implicit bias on police behavior and decision making has resulted in a Fourth Amendment legal regime that unintentionally strengthens the effects of implicit bias on police behavior. This chapter argues that courts should take the science of implicit social cognition into account and attempt to construct legal doctrine in a manner that more effectively protects privacy against arbitrary government intrusion. Considering the science also provides a framework for engaging police departments in efforts to uncover institutional structures and practices that may hinder effective policing and for thinking creatively about institutional solutions.

Notes

1. Jerry Kang, et al., *Implicit Bias in the Courtroom*, 59 UCLA L. REV. 1124, 1129 n. 10 (forthcoming 2012) ("Implicit social cognition (ISC) is a field of psychology that examines the mental processes that affect social judgments but operate without conscious awareness or conscious control.") (citations omitted).
2. Jennifer L. Eberhardt et al., *Seeing Black: Race, Crime, and Visual Processing*, J. PERSONALITY & SOC. PSYCHOL. 876 (2004); Nicole C. Donders et al., *Danger Stereotypes Predict Racially Biased Attentional Allocation*, 44 J. EXPERIMENTAL SOC. PSYCHOL. 1328, 1332 (2008).

3 Birt L. Duncan, *Differential Social Perception and Attribution of Intergroup Violence: Testing the Lower Limits of Stereotyping of Blacks*, 34 J. PERSONALITY & SOC. PSYCHOL. 590, 591 (1976).
4 Andrew H. Sager & Janet W. Schofield, *Racial and Behavioral Cues in Black and White Children's Perceptions of Ambiguously Aggressive Acts*, 39 J. PERSONALITY & SOC. PSYCHOL. 590 (1980).
5 Kurt Hugenberg & Galen V. Bodenhausen, *Ambiguity in Social Categorization: The Role of Prejudice and Facial Affect in Race Categorization*, 15 PSYCHOL. SCI. 342, 342–5 (2004). See also Kurt Hugenberg & Galen V. Bodenhausen, *Facing Prejudice: Implicit Prejudice and the Perception of Facial Threat*, 14 PSYCHOL. SCI. 640 (2003) (demonstrating that implicit bias scores predicted how long it took White participants to judge when a hostile expression on a Black face became non-hostile).
6 Joshua Correll et al., *The Police Officer's Dilemma: Using Ethnicity to Disambiguate Potentially Threatening Individuals*, 83 J. PERSONALITY & SOC. PSYCHOL. 1314 (2002); B. Kieth Payne, *Weapon Bias: Split-Second Decisions and Unintended Stereotyping*, 15 CURRENT DIRECTIONS IN PSYCHOL. Sci. 287 (2006) (noting that split-second decisions limit individual ability to control for racial bias caused by racial stereotypes).
7 Carl O. Word et al., *The Nonverbal Mediation of Self-fulfilling Prophecies in Interracial Interaction*, 10 J. EXPERIMENTAL SOC. PSYCHOL. 109 (1974).
8 John A. Bargh et al., *Automaticity of Social Behavior: Direct Effects of Trait Construct and Stereotype Activation on Action*, 71 J. PERSONALITY & SOC. PSYCHOL. 230 (1996).
9 *Id.*
10 392 U.S. 1 (1968)
11 *Id.* at 5.
12 *Id.*
13 *Id.*
14 *Id.* at 21, 30, 31.
15 *Id.* at 27.
16 *Id.* at 21.
17 *Id.* at 22.
18 *Id.* at 27.
19 *U.S. v. Cortez*, 499 U.S. 411, 418 (1981).
20 Jennifer L. Eberhardt et al., *Seeing Black: Race, Crime, and Visual Processing*, 87 J. PERSONALITY & SOC. PSYCHOL. 876 (2004).
21 Id. at 883.
22 Joshua Correll et al., *Across the Thin Blue Line: Police Officers and Racial Bias in the Decision to Shoot*, 92 J. PERSONALITY & SOC. PSYCHOL. 1006 (2007).
23 Robert J. Sampson & Stephen W. Raudenbush, *Seeing Disorder: Neighborhood Stigma and the Social Construction of "Broken Windows,"* 67 SOC. PSYCHOL. Q. 319 (2004).
24 See, e.g., *U.S. v. Brignoni-Ponce*, 422 U.S. 873, 885–7 (1975), *U.S. v. Martinez-Fuerte*, 428 U.S. 543, 563 (1976).
25 ZIVA KUNDA, SOCIAL COGNITION: MAKING SENSE OF PEOPLE 128 (1999).

26 Samuel R. Gross & Katherine Y. Barnes, *Road Work: Racial Profiling and Drug Interdiction on the Highway*, 101 MICH. L. REV. 651, 692 (2002) (citation omitted).
27 *Illinois v. Gates*, 462 U.S. 213 (1982).
28 For more detailed discussions of this proposal, see L. Song Richardson, *Police Efficiency and the Fourth Amendment*, 87 IND. L. J. 1143 (2012).
29 *U.S. v. Cortez*, 499 U.S. 411, 418 (1981).
30 Ziva Kunda & Lisa Sinclair, *Motivated Reasoning with Stereotypes: Activation, Application, and Inhibition*, 10 PSYCHOL. INQUIRY 12, 20 (1999) (citation omitted).
31 Jerry Kang & Kristin Lane, *A Future History of Implicit Social Cognition and the Law* 8, available at http://ssrn.com/abstract=1458678 (2009) (last visited Apr. 28, 2013).
32 Joshua Correll et al., *Across the Thin Blue Line: Police Officers and Racial Bias in the Decision to Shoot*, 92 J. PERSONALITY & SOC. PSYCHOL. 1006 (2007).
33 Brandon D. Stewart & B. Kevin Payne, *Bringing Automatic Stereotyping Under Control: Implementation Intentions as Efficient Means of Thought Control*, 34 PERSONALITY AND SOC. PSYCHOL. BULL. 1332, 1334–6 (2008).
34 CYNTHIA LEE, MURDER AND THE REASONABLE MAN: PASSION AND FEAR IN THE CRIMINAL COURTROOM 224 (2003).
35 For an extended discussion about why hiring decisions are important, see L. Song Richardson, *Cognitive Bias, Police Character and the Fourth Amendment*, 44 ARIZ. ST. L.J. 267 (2012).
36 B. Michelle Peruche & E. Ashby Plant, *The Correlates of Law Enforcement Officers' Automatic and Controlled Race-Based Responses to Criminal Suspects*, 28 BASIC & APPLIED SOC. PSYCHOL. 193, 197 (2006).

Part III

POLICING AND PRIVACY

5

The Exclusionary Rule

Its Effect on Innocence and Guilt

Tonja Jacobi

The exclusionary rule is the principal constitutional remedy for police violations of Fourth Amendment rights. It prevents juries from considering relevant evidence, so as to deter future police misconduct. The Supreme Court acknowledges that preventing admission of potentially determinative evidence will allow some guilty defendants to go free, but it justifies the rule on the ground that no other remedy properly deters police abuse, harassment, or other misconduct. But this assumes two quite questionable facts. First, it assumes that the rule does actually effectively deter, despite the fact that there are still many incentives for police to engage in illegal evidence-gathering mechanisms: to get contraband off the street, to discourage crime by policing aggressively, to maintain arrest statistics, or to legally use illegally gained evidence in other ways, such as against coconspirators. Second, the Court's analysis also assumes that the effect of the rule will only be to set some guilty people free, and not to convict some innocent people. Many scholars, judges, and lawyers have debated whether the exclusionary rule effectively deters police misconduct, but everyone has assumed that the second claim is obvious, since the exclusionary rule only excludes inculpatory evidence, not exculpatory evidence. This chapter outlines a different concern with the exclusionary rule: that it sets the guilty free at the expense of convicting innocent defendants.[1]

The theory of the exclusionary rule is that judges can prevent evidence from ever reaching the jury, but there is strong evidence that this is not how the trial process works in practice. Jurors make inferences about excluded evidence from admitted evidence and trial procedure. For instance, if there are obvious holes in the prosecution's case, such as key evidence that is missing, jurors might reasonably infer that other evidence was found but not allowed to be introduced at trial. Extensive social science evidence shows that when jurors figure out that evidence is being withheld from them, they will alter their deliberative process to work around rules they do not like. And the exclusionary rule is definitely one of those rules – it is highly unpopular among the populace. So when jurors deduce – or simply assume – the operation of the exclusionary rule, they will take their assumptions about the missing evidence into account. Since only inculpatory evidence is ever excluded under the rule, this means they will discount the prosecution's burden of proof – and the defendant's right to reasonable doubt – by an estimate of the effect of the rule.

It would be bad enough if jurors were, in lieu of seeing the actual evidence, simply substituting their potentially inaccurate assessments of evidence they are inferring exists but has been kept from them; but the inaccuracy inherent in this process will actually mean that defendants who have not had the exclusionary rule exercised in their favor will be systematically penalized. Jurors will assume the rule's operation, even when there is none. Exclusion of tainted evidence does not simply return defendants to the position they would have been in but for the illegal search. Rather, the exclusionary rule benefits defendants most likely to be guilty at the expense of the actually innocent – the exclusionary rule actually *decreases* the chance of finding a reasonable doubt for those defendants most likely to be innocent.

The well-worn debate over the exclusionary rule is framed in terms of the extent we should be willing to allow the guilty to go free so as to interpret the rights of accused criminals expansively.[2] However, wrongly convicting the innocent is not part of that deal. The proverbial ten guilty men are not meant to be set free for their own sake, but rather so that the one innocent person goes free. This chapter establishes that by instituting constitutional protections for actually guilty criminal suspects, the exclusionary rule creates a higher burden of proof for actually innocent defendants. As such, the vast literature justifying or criticizing the exclusionary rule for the extent to which it treads the correct balance for guilty suspects misses the most vital point. The rule undermines the foundation of the criminal justice system, in sorting innocent and guilty defendants.

There are four steps in how jurors process information, which this chapter outlines in turn. The first is juror resistance – jurors resist having information concealed from them; they make inferences from silence, drawing implications about what evidence is missing, and respond to instructions not to consider evidence by giving the evidence even greater weight. The second is juror error – jurors will substitute inaccurate assumptions when they are not given accurate information. The third is juror antipathy – jurors will be most resistant to those rules that they personally oppose. The fourth is the end product, a "perverse screening" effect – the result will be the reversal of the differentiation the criminal justice process would otherwise make between innocent and guilty defendants, with innocent defendants more likely to be convicted and guilty defendants less likely to be convicted.

Finally, these problems manifest themselves not only among jurors, but also among judges. At the trial stage, judges engage in the same resistance that jurors display, through manipulating their fact finding. Appellate judges also display resistance to the rule, and this is even more problematic: in attempting to mitigate the adverse effects of the exclusionary rule, higher court judges twist and subvert the secondary doctrines in this area of law. For instance, certain searches are recategorized as nonsearches, to avoid the rule's operation and its unattractive outcomes. These jurisprudential distortions further undermine innocence-guilt screening. In order to overcome both the direct harms of the exclusionary rule and these secondary manifestations, I propose that future rules should be structured to promote differentiation between guilty and innocent defendants. The ultimate purpose of the criminal justice system, and the approach that is most likely to achieve justice with minimal intrusions on the constitutional rights that the Fourth Amendment is designed to protect, is to differentiate between guilty and innocent defendants. As such, ancillary rules should be assessed in those terms.

1. JUROR RESISTANCE

The exclusionary rule only works if trial courts can effectively control what information juries receive. But that process of control itself provides information to the jury. Even though court rules attempt to ensure that evidence is excluded before it reaches the jury, there will often still be evidence that exclusion has occurred: even without hints such as continued objections or whispered conferences between judges and attorneys, there will be holes in prosecutors' cases that suggest evidence is missing. Studies have established that jurors gain information about the criminal justice system from popular television shows and media reports, and this affects their assessments of guilt. When information is excluded, the story is not going to be complete, but it is the jurors' job to make sense of the case before them, to fill in the blanks in that incomplete story, something they are strongly motivated to do correctly. They draw inferences from gaps in the evidence, they receive and interpret cues throughout the course of the trial, and they introduce their own prejudices and assumptions, including assumptions about the operation of the legal process and the operation of the exclusionary rule.

There is strong evidence in both the civil and criminal contexts that jurors make inferences from silence, that is, from the absence of evidence. This effect has been found in all manner of studies: controlled mock juror studies, surveys of actual jurors, and observation of actual jurors' process of deliberation. In each, researchers found that jurors make frequent references to topics that are forbidden for them to consider. For instance, observation of actual jurors in civil suits showed they discuss insurance in 85 percent of deliberations and attorney's fees in 83 percent of cases, though both topics are explicitly forbidden. Both considerations also had a clear impact on the verdict in some cases.[3]

When it comes to making inferences about whether evidence of the crime was found by police during a search, jurors similarly draw their own interpretations of ambiguous and missing evidence. If jurors know that a search is successful, that knowledge makes them more likely to interpret other testimony in a manner that favors the police.[4] Even when jurors have not seen the evidence, they are subject to a number of triggers that are likely to activate their general expectations about the operation of the exclusionary rule. The most obvious triggers are steering of witnesses away from particular topics or hushed sidebar conversations. However, another pervasive trigger is a prosecution narrative that does not quite make sense. For example, in a murder trial without a murder weapon when neither side mentions a search of the defendant's home, it stands to reason that a search was conducted but its proceeds excluded. It does not make sense that the police would not search the defendant's home if they could not otherwise locate the murder weapon, or that the defense would fail to mention that a search was conducted and no murder weapon was found.[5] Therefore, jurors seeking to determine the defendant's actual guilt or innocence, and primed with a basic awareness of the exclusionary rule's existence, may rationally infer that the weapon was found in the defendant's possession but excluded (but they make errors in this assessment, as discussed later).

It is practically impossible for jurors to follow instructions not to consider nonadmissible evidence. The proverbial instruction not to think about elephants only emphasizes the relevance of elephants. Empirical studies have repeatedly shown that judges' instructions do not in fact restrict jurors' consideration of the prohibited evidence: inadmissible evidence impacts verdicts in the direction of the content of that evidence that is meant to be ignored – by as much as a 40 percent change in the probability of conviction.[6] Jurors appear to retaliate against judicial instructions by giving the evidence *more* consideration than they would have if no instructions had been given, and the more strongly worded the judicial instructions are, the more this effect occurs.

This is because the notion of excluding evidence is inherently contradictory: "Information is withheld from jurors to prevent it from adversely affecting their decisions, yet [exclusion] is effective only if jurors desist from speculation and inference – and given the lack of clarity on many complex legal issues and jurors' natural tendencies to make sense of these complexities, both speculation and inference are likely."[7] As such, exclusion is futile when jurors can be expected to come to trial with knowledge that will lead them to speculate about information being withheld from them, as research on criminal exclusion suggests they do.

Worse yet, an inference of exercise of the exclusionary rule can also taint subsequent evidence of innocence at trial. One study found that taped telephone confession evidence not only was considered incriminating at the time when the evidence was given (as tested on a handheld dial response measurement device), it also altered the way jurors perceived subsequent evidence.[8] Of particular note, jurors for whom the evidence was inadmissible because of the exclusionary rule interpreted subsequent evidence as considerably more incriminating.

Juror resistance to the mandate to ignore evidence or not make inferences from the absence of evidence arises in various forms: jurors expressly consider excluded evidence when forming their verdicts, attach increased weight to other similar evidence, and further rely on that evidence when instructed not to do so. In addition, as the following section shows, the extent of this resistance varies with their preexisting attitudes and biases.

2. JUROR ANTIPATHY

The extent that jurors do cooperate with the prohibition on considering excluded evidence depends on juror idiosyncrasy – particularly, whether the rationale for exclusion aligns with their own sense of propriety or whether it accords with their sense of the integrity of the investigative process and the reliability of evidence.

This conclusion is supported by a study by Professors Saul M. Kassin and Samuel R. Sommers that compared jurors' reactions to two rulings of admissibility of a taped telephone confession, excluded either because the tape was illegally obtained or because the tape was of poor quality.[9] In the latter group, jurors largely followed the instruction to disregard the evidence, convicting at the same rate as a control group that had not seen the evidence at all. But in the former group, they did not. In fact, the group that was meant to ignore the evidence because it was inadmissible by virtue of the exclusionary rule convicted the defendant at the same rate as those who were explicitly allowed to consider the evidence – and at considerably higher rates than those who were instructed to disregard the evidence because of its unreliable quality. This shows not only that jurors selectively consider evidence they are meant to ignore, but also that they show particular reluctance to ignore evidence excluded on the basis of the exclusionary rule. Such a result has important implications for the exclusionary rule, suggesting that the extent of resistance to the rule will reflect individual biases.

The cause of these differences appears to be that jurors have different preconceptions of the inherent fairness of using different types of evidence. Similar effects have been found with other forms of evidence: just as with the unreliable tape, jurors show a strong inclination to comply with the duty not to make inferences from hearsay testimony, since that too tends to be unreliable. But they display the opposite response, a strong inclination to rely on evidence, when that evidence is suggestive of guilt without having an unreliable foundation. Like evidence excluded because of improper police procedures, prior conviction evidence is indicative of guilt, given high rates of recidivism among offenders. And just as jurors showed particularly resilient partiality to inferences regarding evidence excluded only because of the means by which it was obtained, multiple studies have shown that jurors will willingly consider evidence of, and make inferences from, prior conviction evidence.

These results are unsurprising given that numerous polls have shown that jurors are actively opposed to rules of the criminal justice system that are seen to give unfair advantage to guilty suspects. Public attitudes to criminal justice generally tend strongly toward preferences for greater criminal sanctions. In testing attitudes toward the severity of criminal courts in a person's local area, studies have asked people, "In general, do you think the courts in this area deal too harshly or not harshly enough?" Between 1985 and 2002, a large majority always responded, "not harshly enough." The percentage of those responding "too harshly" was always in the single digits. Those responding "about right" ranged from 8 to 18 percent.[10] These figures vary surprisingly little when broken down by demographic characteristics; there is always a solid majority in the "not harshly enough" category, regardless of sex, race, age, education, income, occupation, region, religion, or politics of the respondent.

As for the exclusionary rule itself, there is "an instinctive and deep-seated hostility to the exclusionary rule," and "the perception that the rule sets the guilty free undermines public confidence in our system of justice."[11] The overwhelming majority of Americans think more needs to be done, and that it should be the top priority of reform objectives, to make sure that punishments fit the crimes.[12] The exclusionary rule is seen as a means by which criminals "get off on technicalities" and is viewed as contrary to this populist goal. The effect is that "as an empirical matter, the rule probably does more damage to public respect for the courts than virtually any other single judicial mechanism, because it makes courts look oblivious to violations of the criminal law and involves prosecutors, defense attorneys and judges in charade trials in which they all know the defendant is guilty."[13]

This attitude is further reflected in public support for police, which contrasts with the dim view of judges. Whereas 58 percent of people believe police and law enforcement are doing an excellent or good job, in contrast, only 37 percent feel the same way about judges. The single most popular reason given for this negative assessment of judges is flaws in the criminal justice system, particularly "loopholes that allow criminals to 'get off,'" which account for 18 percent of those expressing dissatisfaction with judges.[14] Criminal punishment is perceived as being overly lenient, and a strong cause of this excess lenience is lack of fit between crime and punishment, in particular allowing criminals to avoid appropriate sanction through technical prodefendant rules like the exclusionary rule. These attitudes exacerbate juror resistance to ignoring excluded evidence.

So in summary, it is well established that jurors commonly ignore instructions to exclude; that even where they do follow exclusion instructions, they will only do so in some circumstances that accord with their own sense of justice rather than judicial instructions; and that instructions to ignore evidence commonly backfire, leading jurors to rely even more heavily on that evidence than they otherwise would have. Given the unpopularity of the exclusionary rule, the evidence that juror resistance is exacerbated by juror antipathy renders jurors especially likely to consider any evidence they infer has been excluded under the rule. Overall, this suggests that exclusion instructions are more likely than not to be ignored, and excluded evidence will shape verdicts. The next two sections explore *how* those inferences from excluded evidence will shape verdicts.

3. JUROR ERROR

Like Sherlock Holmes, jurors will make inferences from the "dog that did not bark"; however, unlike the fictional master detective, jurors will often make the wrong inferences. As discussed, there will be many triggers that suggest that the exclusionary rule has been exercised, but many of these triggers will in fact be false. Jurors' inclinations to consider inferences stemming from the exclusionary rule can result in both inaccuracy and bias; this section considers the former, the next section the latter.

When the exclusionary rule is exercised, the result may be that obvious holes are created in the prosecution's case. The victim was shot and there was evidence of gun residue on the defendant's hands, but no gun was ever admitted into evidence – one possible inference from that information is that the gun was seized in contravention of the Fourth Amendment and excluded. At other times, however, those holes in the prosecution's case may arise because the prosecutor does not in fact have all of the information about the crime — that is, the case may be incomplete even without the operation of the exclusionary rule. The police may simply have never found the gun used to shoot the victim, rather than having found the gun in the defendant's possession and its being subsequently excluded. Cues that exclusion has operated do not invariably stem from actual exercises of exclusion. Gaps in the evidence may manifest, for instance, because the prosecution witness proved to be unreliable. Since prosecutors are subject to significant resource constraints, they may also push ahead with a prosecution in the hope that all of the dots will connect by the end of the trial, or else that the jury will be willing to overlook some deficiencies in the case. The problem is that the existence of the exclusionary rule may create an impression that evidence has been excluded even where the rule has not in fact operated. This misinformation can be extremely harmful.

The foregoing evidence showed that jurors will adjust their expectations of guilt, and so their probable verdicts, on the basis of excluded and absent evidence, but jurors will not always be accurate when adjusting their assessments of guilt on the basis of inferences of excluded information. Typically, jurors know about the existence of the exclusionary rule but cannot know with any certainty whether it has operated in a given case, versus when natural holes have arisen in the prosecutor's case. As such, they will only have impressions of whether the rule has operated in any case. Jurors will base their expectations of guilt on the information that they have been presented with, along with their inferences of whether additional evidence exists but has been excluded by the rule. Because the exclusionary rule only works in favor of the defense, these estimates of whether the exclusionary rule has operated, and consequent reestimates of the defendant's guilt, will only shift in one direction: in favor of the prosecution. As such, jurors will adjust their beliefs in a way that effectively reduces the burden of proof that the prosecution ordinarily has to bear.

For instance, in a case where jurors hear that evidence implicating the defendant was found in his office, but no mention is ever made of a search of his home, jurors may estimate that the odds that the exclusionary rule has operated to exclude evidence found in the home are high. Without other evidence, this inference may not take the jurors very far, but if there is considerable other evidence — gunshot residue, bloodied clothing, and so on — but the gun was never found, jurors might feel confident in dismissing the doubt that the missing piece of evidence otherwise might create; whereas if there were no exclusionary rule, that missing gun could constitute reasonable doubt.

If jurors do infer that the exclusionary rule operated to some extent, and they recalculate their expectations of the defendant's guilt accordingly, that inference will translate into giving the prosecutor a discount in her burden of proof. Say jurors estimate that, given the other evidence found and the lack of a search producing the gun, the odds that the gun was found but excluded are fifty-fifty, then they would give the defendant only half of the benefit of the doubt over whether he had the gun.

Even if jurors are unsure whether the exclusionary rule operated, there is considerable evidence that people are generally overconfident of their ability to make such assessments. But even if juror estimates are right, the outcome will be wrong. Even assuming that an estimate is perfectly accurate, the conclusion that follows will nonetheless be inaccurate. For example, if jurors estimate that the odds that the exclusionary rule has been exercised are fifty-fifty, in the actual case where the gun was excluded, they will be underestimating the operation of the rule by 50 percent, and where it was not excluded, they will be overestimating by 50 percent. If the defendant did in fact have the gun and it was excluded from admission as evidence, the jurors will have only assumed away half of the benefit of the exclusionary rule to the defendant – they will still give the defendant half of the benefit of the doubt. And in the case where the defendant did not have the gun and it simply was never found, the defendant will not receive the benefit of the doubt that he otherwise would have – he will effectively be penalized for the prosecution's failure to find the murder weapon. The exercise of the exclusionary rule is an either/or outcome, but the jurors' best estimate of the probability that the rule has been exercised is necessarily a fraction. So by necessity, the jury will have overestimated the effect of the exclusionary rule half of the time and underestimated it in the other half.

Juror resistance and antipathy mean that jurors will be filling in gaps in prosecutors' cases with potentially inadmissible evidence; juror error means this process of gap filling increases the inaccuracy of the criminal justice system. The next section shows that gap filling also introduces a bias against innocent defendants.

4. PERVERSE SCREENING

For defendants for whom the exclusionary rule has been exercised, juror resistance and juror antipathy to the rule will mean that much of the intended protective effect of the exclusionary rule will be undermined. Nonetheless, these defendants will still receive some benefit from the rule – juror inaccuracy will mean they will never mitigate the full inculpatory effect that excluded evidence would have had were it admitted (unless jurors are massively overestimating how common operation of the rule is). The real harm occurs when we consider the effect on defendants for whom the exclusionary rule has *not* in fact been exercised. They will be penalized by the very existence of the rule. Instead of their being given the benefit of the doubt, that doubt will be reduced, as before, but with a foundationally different effect. There will be no direct benefit from exclusion, since nothing is excluded, and at the same time jurors will nonetheless reduce the prosecutor's burden, out of the same estimation that the exclusionary rule has been exercised. Whereas without the exclusionary rule these defendants would have the full benefit of the doubt, with the rule jurors will often wrongly conclude that these defendants probably have benefited from exclusion and thus penalize them for the wrongs that the police have done to others. These defendants will be worse off than if the exclusionary rule did not exist.

Worse yet, the fact that the absence of evidence can be seen as a trigger means that jurors could actually take a weak prosecution case as implying the operation of the exclusionary rule. Then, the very feebleness of the prosecution's case would increase the discount of the prosecutor's burden. Ironically, the more stringent the exclusionary rule is understood to be, the greater the discount to the prosecutor's burden. This is because the more that the exclusionary rule operates automatically to translate any minor technical breach by the police into an evidentiary exclusion, the more likely jurors are to assume it will have operated in any given case, and the more likely they are to reduce the prosecution's burden of proof.

It is possible that the distribution between the two groups of defendants – those for whom the exclusionary rule has been exercised and those for whom it has not – could be random, with some defendants gaining a benefit from the exclusionary rule (a positive benefit even when discounted) at the cost of other defendants. But the more likely outcome is that the guilty will benefit at the cost of the innocent. The rule necessarily operates where there is evidence to be excluded – and only applies to inculpatory evidence. That the probability of guilt will increase with each additional piece of inculpatory evidence is axiomatic to the criminal justice system. Since Fourth Amendment exclusions do not raise reliability concerns (unlike, for instance, coerced confessions excluded under the Fifth Amendment), then logic dictates that any exclusion of evidence under the Fourth Amendment is more likely to benefit guilty rather than innocent defendants. In fact, the Supreme Court has implicitly recognized this relationship in its repeated acknowledgment that the cost of the exclusionary rule is to let guilty criminals go free.

There are two forms of empirical evidence that are strongly suggestive that it will be guilty defendants who benefit most from the exclusionary rule. First, there is evidence that it is overwhelmingly reoffenders who successfully exercise the exclusionary rule at the trial stage. Second, there is evidence that those who do successfully exercise the exclusionary rule subsequently reoffend. When these two findings are combined with evidence of the relationship between prior offenses and conviction rates, these data confirm that actually guilty defendants are most likely to benefit from the exclusionary rule. Defendants who exercise the exclusionary rule are very commonly subsequently rearrested; they are also overwhelmingly those with prior records, and having a prior record is the best predictor of a guilty verdict, whether or not the jury knows of those prior crimes. As such, there is strong empirical evidence that those who benefit from the exclusionary rule are those most likely to be actually guilty. So guilty defendants are being encouraged to make use of the exclusionary rule, while innocent defendants are being denied their full benefit of the doubt.

The usual solution to adverse selection problems of this kind is to create "screening" – structuring incentives so as to encourage innocent defendants to exercise their full rights, leading to self-revelation of innocence or guilt. However, what the exclusionary rule does is create *perverse screening*, whereby the opposite result is achieved: guilty defendants are encouraged to exercise their full exclusionary rule rights, making it more difficult for juries to differentiate between innocent and guilty defendants, and at the same time innocent defendants are effectively hampered in exercising their full rights.

This means that those who benefit from the exclusionary rule are primarily actually guilty, but they do not gain that benefit at the cost of police and society more generally, as the Supreme Court claims. Rather, guilty defendants gain that benefit at the cost of the actually innocent. The actually innocent have their entitlement to the benefit of the doubt considerably diminished by the exercise of the exclusionary rule, without any correlative benefit.

This undermines the claim that the costs of the exclusionary rule are the costs of the Fourth Amendment itself. In fact, the exclusionary rule does not simply undo a constitutional violation; rather, it just shifts the burden for that violation from one defendant to another. That shift occurs by increasing the burden at the judicial stage onto the actually innocent.

5. JUDICIAL DISTORTION OF THE EXCLUSIONARY RULE

Recent jurisprudence has seen the Supreme Court developing numerous exceptions to the exclusionary rule, a process that has arguably steadily eroded Fourth Amendment protections over time. But this is not simply a result of an ideological turn of the Court against criminal defendants; rather, the exclusionary rule itself is responsible for much of this doctrinal development. The problem is that the rule was developed as an automatic and binary mechanism whereby evidence is admitted or not admitted, depending on the violation of a fixed constitutional line, regardless of the substantive unfairness to the defendant or the probative value of the evidence. This engendered the unpopularity of the rule, which in turn causes it to be underenforced, not only by jurors but also by judges. Like jurors, judges respond to the inherent overreach of exclusion and attempt to mitigate its effects in two ways: through avoidance and contraction. That is, trial court judges display similar resistance to jurors and avoid applying the rule in criminal cases, and higher court judges also display resistance, which leads to contraction of the doctrinal substance of associated rules, as they attempt to minimize the effects of exclusion. As a consequence, judges both make errors and increase perverse screening by confusing signals of guilt.

The unpopularity of the exclusionary rule and the view of a majority of citizens that the courts are "too easy" on criminals mean that at the trial level, judges may be reluctant to apply the exclusionary rule in criminal cases. For elected judges, there are obvious electoral incentives to avoid appearing to let criminals off on technicalities. But more generally, judges are uncomfortable applying the rule, particularly for minor violations of police procedure, and especially in the case of more serious crimes. For instance, judges themselves report knowingly accepting police perjury as truthful to avoid applying the exclusionary rule.[15] Judges are reluctant to free, or be seen to free, seemingly guilty defendants, so they manipulate the jurisprudence so as to avoid exclusion.

The second way that judges mitigate the effect of the exclusionary rule is through the formation of law. Numerous cases in various areas of constitutional criminal law have developed rules that strain the definitions of searches and seizures. For instance, individualized close examination by a trained narcotics dog was not considered a search,[16] and a person is not seized by police when questioned without reasonable suspicion within the cramped confines of a bus that he did not feel free to leave.[17] These rules constitute doctrinal distortions that arise out of higher court judicial attempts to narrow the application of the exclusionary rule. Such attempts to mitigate the ill effects of the exclusionary rule create confused jurisprudence, which will necessarily result in unfair outcomes.

So the exclusionary rule causes distortion of the facts, which is problematic because it fails to recognize or remedy violations of individual defendants' Fourth Amendment rights; its effect on doctrine is worse, as this causes a ratchet effect, whereby future violations are even less likely to be dealt with.

Since much of this jurisprudential manipulation appears to be driven by a desire to avoid the cost of "letting the criminal go free," a better, more direct way to achieve that goal is to embrace rules that aid screening between innocent and guilty defendants and forgo rules that blur those categories. This may sound obvious, as it is the role of the criminal justice system to sort the innocent from the guilty, but in fact numerous doctrines do the opposite, and this extends beyond the Fourth Amendment search and seizure examples described. For instance, threatening a suspect at gunpoint does not violate the Fifth Amendment,[18] despite the fact that it is likely to induce confessions by innocent as well as guilty suspects; yet words or actions stated by the police that are likely to elicit an incriminating response from the suspect when counsel is not present do violate the Sixth Amendment, even when they are only likely to elicit a confession from a guilty suspect.[19] Both of these rules undermine differentiation between innocent and guilty defendants – in the first case by incentivizing innocent defendants to confess, in the latter by discouraging guilty defendants from confessing.[20]

It is not enough to address the extensively debated question of whether the exclusionary rule should be kept or abolished; either way, we will be left with numerous doctrines that undermine guilt-innocence screening, that have been developed as part of judicial attempts to avoid the application of the exclusionary rule. I propose that a core criterion in assessing whether constitutional criminal procedure doctrines should be embraced or rejected is whether they create ideal or perverse screening, of the type described. This will complement rather than replace other criteria, such as the level of intrusion or greater protection given for a search of a home. It will not entirely eradicate the cost to innocent defendants of the exclusionary rule, but it will provide some means of assessing the secondary doctrinal components of the surrounding law and provide a mechanism for reforming the most harmful effects of the exclusionary rule.

Notes

1. This chapter is based on an article that provides greater detail, including citation information, and that also more formally proves the effects described here. See Tonja Jacobi, *The Law and Economics of the Exclusionary Rule*, 87 NOTRE DAME L. REV. 585 (2012).
2. See *Mapp v. Ohio*, 367 U.S. 643, 659 (1961) ("The criminal goes free, if he must, but it is the law that sets him free. Nothing can destroy a government more quickly than its failure to observe its own laws, or worse, its disregard of the charter of its own existence."). Other disagreements about the exclusionary rule include whether it is more harmful to the truth-seeking function of the court system to exclude pertinent evidence, or to have the courts tainted by using illegally gained evidence.
3. Shari Seidman Diamond & Neil Vidmar, *Jury Room Ruminations on Forbidden Topics*, 87 VA. L. REV. 1857, 1894 (2001).
4. Jonathan D. Casper et al., *Juror Decision Making, Attitudes, and the Hindsight Bias*, 13 LAW & HUM. BEHAV. 291, 306 (1989).
5. Defendants cannot claim that no evidence was found if the evidence was actually found and excluded. FED. R. EVID. 403. While this does mean it is theoretically possible that jurors can infer the operation of the exclusionary rule from the reasons given or not given for that absence of evidence, this will only mitigate the problem described here to the extent that it undermines the rule itself, rather than combating the perverse effect of the rule.

6 See Nancy Steblay et al., *The Impact on Juror Verdicts of Judicial Instruction to Disregard Inadmissible Evidence: A Meta-Analysis*, 30 LAW & HUM. BEHAV. 469, 476 (2006).
7 Edith Greene et al., *'Shouldn't We Consider...?': Jury Discussions of Forbidden Topics and Effects on Damage Awards*, 14 PSYCHOL. PUB. POL'Y & L. 194, 199 (2008).
8 Saul M. Kassin & Samuel R. Sommers, *Inadmissible Testimony, Instructions to Disregard, and the Jury: Substantive Versus Procedural Considerations*, 23 PERSONALITY & SOC. PSYCHOL. BULL. 1046, 1049–50 (1997). A similar result was found by Kurt A. Carlson & J. Edward Russo, *Biased Interpretation of Evidence by Mock Jurors*, 7 J. EXPERIMENTAL PSYCHOL.: APPLIED 91, 91 (2001).
9 Kassin & Sommers, supra note 7, at 1048.
10 U.S. DEP'T OF JUSTICE, SOURCEBOOK OF CRIMINAL JUSTICE STATISTICS 140–1 tbl. 2.47 (Ann L. Pastore et al., eds., 2003), available at http://www.albany.edu/sourcebook/toc.html (citing NAT'L OP. RES. CTR., GENERAL SOCIAL SURVEYS 1972–2002 (reporting years 1985 to 2002)) (last visited Apr. 29, 2013). Similarly large majorities – between 63% and 67% – responded that courts do not deal harshly enough with criminals, in biennial surveys between 2002 and 2008. NAT'L DATA PROGRAM FOR THE SOC. SCI., GENERAL SOCIAL SURVEY 1972–2008. This is a decline from the 1980s and 1990s, when those numbers never dropped below 70% in any category.
11 L. Timothy Perrin et al., *If It's Broken, Fix It: Moving Beyond the Exclusionary Rule: A New and Extensive Empirical Study of the Exclusionary Rule and a Call for a Civil Administrative Remedy to Partially Replace the Rule*, 83 IOWA L. REV. 669, 672 (1998).
12 NAT'L CTR. FOR STATE COURTS, THE NCSC SENTENCING ATTITUDES SURVEY 38 (2006).
13 Christopher Slobogin, *Why Liberals Should Chuck the Exclusionary Rule*, 1999 U. ILL. L. REV. 363, 436–7; Akhil Reed Amar, *Fourth Amendment First Principles*, 107 HARV. L. REV. 757, 793 (1994); Lawrence Crocker, *Can the Exclusionary Rule Be Saved?* 84 J. CRIM. L. & CRIMINOLOGY 310, 311 (1993) ("[The exclusionary rule] is attacked as one of the chief technical loopholes through which walk the guilty on their way out of the courthouse to continue their depredations."). This led to its negative position in public opinion, long before that view was reflected by the Court. *Id.*
14 NAT'L CTR. FOR STATE COURTS, supra note 11, at 16.
15 See Myron W. Orfield, Jr., *Deterrence, Perjury and the Heater Factor: An Exclusionary Rule in the Chicago Criminal Courts*, 63 U. COLO. L. REV. 75, 118 (1992). Orfield conducted interviews in which 58% of judges admitted being "biased in favor of the prosecution and less likely than they should be to disbelieve police testimony" in big cases. ID.
16 *United States v. Place*, 462 U.S. 696 (1983); although a dog sniff conducted on the curtilage of a home now constitutes a search. See Florida v. Jardines, 569 U.S. ___ (2013).
17 *Florida v. Bostick*, 388 U.S. 218 (1967).
18 See *Chavez v. Martinez*, 538 U.S. 760 (2003).
19 See *Brewer v. Williams*, 430 U.S. 387 (1977).
20 The application of this proposal to the Fifth and Sixth Amendments is explored in more detail in a work in progress by the author.

6

Consent, Dignity, and the Failure of Scattershot Policing

Janice Nadler

1. INTRODUCTION

Law enforcement officers often work under conditions that afford them a great deal of individual discretion about how to exercise their power to police. In this chapter, I explore how Fourth Amendment doctrine, as formulated by the U.S. Supreme Court, and as interpreted and applied by lower courts, influences law enforcement policy and individual officers' exercise of this discretion. It does so not only by articulating specific rules for conduct, but by expressing opinions and values about the power relationships between law enforcement officers and those they police. I argue that the Court's Fourth Amendment jurisprudence has encouraged the aggressive targeting of large numbers of people for stops and searches, the vast majority of whom are innocent of any crime. Many of these searches are premised on the highly questionable notion that the individuals targeted have freely consented to a search of their persons, vehicles, or belongings. The result is a set of law enforcement practices that maximize unpleasant and frightening encounters between civilians and police; the vast majority of these encounters uncover no crime, yet collectively they are gradually cultivating a popular attitude of fear and resentment, rather than a willingness to cooperate with legal authorities. In order to repair what is now an atmosphere of bitterness and distrust toward the police in some communities, law enforcement agencies and officers should follow the lead of the handful of state supreme courts that have limited the ability to conduct consent searches on a scattershot and arbitrary basis. I conclude that rather than leveraging their broad discretion into a fishing expedition for criminal activity based on little or no reasonable suspicion, law enforcement agencies should leverage the cooperation of ordinary people who share their aim to reduce crime and build safer communities.

2. LEGAL RULES AND LAW ENFORCEMENT PRACTICES

Legal rules and law enforcement practices respond to and shape each other. Police departments seeking to make contraband arrests, for example, can increase the volume of arrests by using to their advantage legal rules governing when they can stop individuals, search property, and enter places. When investigating a specific crime, law enforcement agencies can acquire a suspect's statement by leveraging legal rules about waiver of rights to remain silent and to have counsel present. Ever mindful of what the legal rules require and prohibit, law enforcement agencies develop policies, train officers, and institute practices that comply with the rules (or at least permit a plausible claim of compliance) and simultaneously satisfy institutional goals regarding making arrests and gathering evidence. The legal rules are themselves derived in large part from Supreme Court decisions and lower and state court decisions interpreting the standards articulated by the Court. At the same time, the Supreme Court examines existing law enforcement practice in each case that comes before it and uses that practice as a starting point for the decision it makes about the reasonableness of the practice in question.

Broadly speaking, the Court's interpretation of what the Fourth Amendment requires and permits is what shapes the circumstances under which police stop citizens and conduct searches. Similarly, Fifth Amendment jurisprudence shapes police practices in the interrogation room. I will argue in this chapter that as a matter of current practice, the Court tends to take the perspective of law enforcement, and so the rules of engagement created by the Court are sometimes based on highly questionable assumptions about what citizens in these situations believe and understand. The result is a jurisprudence of stops, searches, and confessions that imagines a marketplace of free exchange between police officers and citizens, in which the police officer invites the citizen to participate in a search or to offer a statement, and the citizen mulls the offer as a customer would mull the opportunity to purchase a Persian rug. The reality as experienced by citizens is quite different, as I will discuss in detail.

3. THE JURISPRUDENCE OF CONSENT AND WAIVER

When a suspect makes an incriminating statement to police, or when a citizen grants permission to an officer to search her car, the court reviews the circumstances of the statement or the grant of consent to search to ensure it was voluntarily made. Judges understand that police rely heavily on the consensual encounter technique to discover evidence of ordinary criminal wrongdoing, and that police rely heavily on incriminating statements made by suspects accused of serious crimes. At the same time these police-citizen interactions pose challenges to the boundaries of the Fourth and Fifth Amendments. When is a street encounter between an officer and a citizen a consensual one, and when does it rise to the level of a seizure under the Fourth Amendment? When is an individual's grant of permission for an officer to search his bag voluntary and when is it mere acquiescence to legitimate authority? When is a suspect's statement a knowing and voluntary waiver of his right to remain silent under the Fifth Amendment, and when is it a result of submission to the pressures of custodial interrogation?

The lower courts analyze these issues every day, and the Supreme Court has formulated a set of standards to assist lower courts and law enforcement agencies in delineating where voluntary action ends and compulsion begins. The Court has held that police requests to stop and talk or to search persons or bags or vehicles are not coercive per se for purposes of the Fourth Amendment. And the Court has held that government interrogation of a suspect in custody is inherently coercive, but that coercion is dispelled as a matter of law when the suspect is advised of her right to remain silent and her right to have counsel present. There are now large bodies of law governing when a seizure occurs, when a consent search is voluntary, and when an incriminating statement is made voluntarily. But in an effort to guide law enforcement in the continual process of bumping up against the boundaries of the Bill of Rights, the Court has decided to disregard a basic social truth: as a general matter, when law enforcement officers make a request, people feel enormous pressure to say yes. When a police officer asks to please see a driver's license and registration during a traffic stop, the driver does not deliberate about whether to grant or decline this request – she understands that "no" is not an option. When an officer approaches a pedestrian walking down the sidewalk and says, "I have a few questions to ask you," most people do not think they would feel free to leave or say no to the officer; this commonsense truth is actually supported by empirical evidence.[1] Survey evidence similarly supports the notion that when an officer approaches a bus passenger to ask questions, most people do not think they would feel free to refuse.[2] Law enforcement officers generally have authority over citizens, and citizens in turn feel compelled to submit to that authority, even when, as in the sidewalk and bus scenarios just mentioned, they have a legal right to refuse.[3] In the words of Richard Uviller, a police request for consent "however gently phrased, is likely to be taken by even the toughest citizen as a command. Refusal of requested 'permission' is thought by most of us to risk unpleasant, though unknown, consequences."[4]

The commonsense wisdom that it is best to submit to police requests is a matter of perceptions of power and social authority, not a matter of information and the logic of legal rules. Even when people are explicitly told they have a right to refuse to comply with the officer's request, many still feel compelled to do so, because of the inherent authority of the officer making the request. Thus, Ohio motorists stopped on the interstate consented to have their vehicles searched at the same rate regardless of whether or not the officer advised them of their right to refuse consent.[5] Indeed, even the now-famous *Miranda* warnings, in which suspects are advised of their right to remain silent and to have an attorney present, apparently have had very little, if any, influence on the rate at which suspects decide to talk to the police.[6] In the station house, suspects sometimes feel enormous pressure to talk, despite having heard the *Miranda* warnings. Many succumb to these pressures. Some succumb even when they are innocent, and the confession they give is false.

In all of the situations just discussed, the lawfulness of the officer's act of stopping, or searching, or obtaining a statement from the citizen turns on the question of whether the citizen voluntarily assented to the stop or search or confession. Even though citizens sometimes feel enormous pressure to assent, judges often do not recognize these pressures, instead focusing on the propriety of the officers' conduct. By ignoring the situational pressures inherent in almost any police-citizen encounter, judges systematically deny the reality experienced by ordinary citizens and the social meaning underlying the law enforcement request to stop, to search, or to confess. Judges who systematically ignore the compulsion inherent in these police-citizen encounters thereby construct a collective legal myth of autonomy and free choice that provides support for the proliferation of the police practice of approaching and searching innocent people in large numbers. Depending on the nature of the threat at hand, the social and political costs of law enforcement officers' approaching, questioning, and searching citizens might or might not be worthwhile. But the U.S. Supreme Court has declined to engage in any serious analysis of this question and instead has accorded a great deal of deference to the government's claim that a reasonable person in the situation would not have felt restricted in his freedom of movement or his ability to refuse the officer's request. Implicit in these deferential judgments, however, are unrealistic assumptions about how ordinary people perceive their freedom to resist when a law enforcement officer seeks their cooperation and compliance. I explore these assumptions in more detail in the next section.

4. BUS SWEEPS AND THE LANGUAGE OF CONSENT

When police officers ask someone whether they can take a look in their bags or in their car, there are two key legal issues that the reviewing court must decide: 1) whether the consent to search was voluntarily given, and 2) whether the person who consented to the search was unlawfully seized at the time consent was given. Both questions require the judge to decide, under the totality of the circumstances, whether a reasonable person would have felt free to refuse or to walk away. To decide the consent question, courts examine, among other things, the manner in which the police requested consent to search. Following the lead of the Supreme Court, lower courts examine whether the police spoke to the citizen in a polite manner, and whether the police asked for permission in the form of a question. In so doing, courts often analyze the encounter in question as if the conversation that took place has a fixed meaning that can be readily gleaned without reference to the context.

Yet it is implausible to conclude, as the Court does, that the language of the exchange itself dispels inferences of coercion. Consider the following example. In *United States v. Drayton*,[7] three police officers boarded a Greyhound bus during a scheduled stopover. The driver had collected all of the passengers' tickets and gone into the terminal to complete paperwork. On the bus, one police officer knelt backward in the driver's seat; one police officer stood at the back of the bus, where he could see everyone; and one officer began questioning passengers about their destinations and their bags. As he asked questions, the officer stood over the seated passengers and leaned down toward them, placing his face twelve to eighteen inches from theirs. He held up his badge and explained that he was conducting a drug interdiction and said that he would like their cooperation. He then asked for permission to search their bags.

During oral argument in the case, Justice Scalia made clear his view that the police officer was merely making a request, and the words the officer used would "counteract" contextual cues suggesting compulsion. Specifically, Justice Scalia asked, "Why ... is it that the most immediate expression of the police officer does not counteract whatever other indications of compulsion might exist under the circumstances?... There's a policeman in the front of the bus. Who cares? He ... has made it very clear that he's asking for your permission."[8] To answer Justice Scalia's rhetorical question, the bus passengers are the ones who care, because they could not help but notice the following: the driver and tickets were absent; one police officer was now in the driver's seat; the police had effectively commandeered the bus. The bus was apparently going nowhere until the police got what they wanted, which, in their own words, was the passengers' "cooperation" in their drug interdiction mission. But Justice Scalia and the majority in *Drayton* appeared to see the matter differently – interestingly, they seemed to take the perspective of the officer, who was, after all, just trying to follow the law. The officer's act of asking permission "counteract[s] ... other indications of compulsion."[9] According to this view, the authority of armed police officers fades away when they merely follow the rules of the game show *Jeopardy* and express their desire to search in the form of a question.

It is only through the prism of the officer's perspective, then, that the Court could sensibly declare that when an armed police officer approaches and asks to search, "the presence of a holstered firearm ... is unlikely to contribute to the coerciveness of the encounter absent active brandishing of the weapon."[10] Rather, for judges viewing the encounter from the perspective of the police, the polite tone of voice used by the officers gives rise to the inference that the citizen was free to decline to talk to the officers or to decline the request to search. Indeed, the Court has not only approved but actually lionized the exchange that takes place between police and citizens in consent searches:

> In a society based on law, the concept of agreement and consent should be given a weight and dignity of its own. Police officers act in full accord with the law when they ask citizens for consent. It reinforces the rule of law for the citizen to advise the police of his or her wishes and for the police to act in reliance on that understanding. When this exchange takes place, it dispels inferences of coercion.[11]

5. WORKING AROUND THE U.S. SUPREME COURT'S UNREALISTIC NOTION OF CONSENT

Ever since *Drayton*, lower courts interpreting the federal Constitution have had no choice but to follow the lead of the Supreme Court. In doing so, those courts routinely and mechanically point to the police officer's polite tone of voice as a key basis for finding that the defendant voluntarily consented to being searched. In one recent case, the police pulled over a car and arrested the driver for driving without a license.[12] The officer then asked the passenger whether he had any drugs, and asked, "Well, do you mind if I check?" The passenger did not answer and did not gesture. The officer ordered the passenger out of the car. The passenger complied, placing his hands in the air. The police officer then searched the passenger and found drugs. Incredibly, the court held that the passenger had consented voluntarily to the search by raising his hands in the air. Apparently, when the officer uttered the magic words "Well, do you mind if I check?" this rendered the remainder of the encounter voluntary.

Although lower courts applying the Fourth Amendment have little choice but routinely to find consent searches voluntary under the tightly constrained precedent that the Supreme Court has constructed, state courts are free to interpret their own state constitutions to require a higher level of scrutiny of consent searches, and a few have done so.[13] For example, some states have held that the prosecution must prove that the person consenting knew that she had a choice in the matter.[14] Further, in some jurisdictions, a police officer making a traffic stop is prohibited from requesting consent to search unless he or she has a "reasonable and articulable suspicion" to believe that a crime is occurring.[15] The Supreme Court of Hawaii has gone further and applies a similar "reasonable suspicion" standard for requesting consent during any police encounter, not just traffic stops.[16]

It is interesting to compare the perspective-taking strategy of the few state courts that have interpreted their state constitutions as granting broader protections regarding consent searches with the perspective-taking strategy of the U.S. Supreme Court. The Supreme Court routinely takes the perspective of law enforcement officers and has made it very clear that the considerations about social authority and pragmatic implicature are to be ignored in consent search cases, no matter how compelling those considerations might be. Instead, it has signaled to lower courts that when police phrase their goal in the form of a question and speak in a polite tone of voice, that is a request that as a matter of law can be freely refused, regardless of whether the context of the conversation suggests otherwise. This, after all, is the most we can expect law enforcement officers to do to minimize the coercive nature of the encounter.

On the other hand, the few state courts that provide broader protection under state constitutional law tend to take the perspective of the citizen, rather than the officer. Where the U.S. Supreme Court asks whether the officer has used a polite tone of voice and phrased utterances in the form of a question, these group of state courts instead recognize and describe the subjective experience of being targeted by the government. The New Jersey Supreme Court, for example, begins with the observation that because it is nearly impossible to drive without eventually unwittingly committing some infraction of the vehicle code, virtually anyone driving can be stopped and asked for consent to search. To the New Jersey court, this in itself presents a policy problem, because "treating all citizens like criminals in order to catch the malefactors among us represents an unwise policy choice, an outlook favoring crime prevention over all of our other values."[17] The New Jersey court was concerned that the exercise of broad police discretion would "invite intrusions upon constitutionally guaranteed rights based on nothing more substantial than inarticulate hunches."[18] The New Jersey court then boldly proclaimed the truth that the U.S. Supreme Court has steadfastly denied: "Many persons, perhaps most, would view the request of a police officer to make a search as having the force of law."[19] By interpreting their own state constitutions as requiring more than what the U.S. Supreme Court takes the Fourth Amendment to require, these state courts have rebalanced the scale of the costs and benefits of consent searches.

6. CUSTODIAL INTERROGATION AND VOLUNTARY WAIVER

Like the Fourth Amendment inquiry about whether the citizen's consent to search was made voluntarily, the Fifth Amendment inquiry about a suspect's decision to make an incriminating statement also inquires about voluntariness. However, unlike the consent search analysis, which examines all of the surrounding circumstances of each individual case, the *Miranda* standard for voluntariness first asks whether the suspect was in custody and being interrogated at the time he made the incriminating statement. If he was, then before taking a statement the officers must first dispel the coercive atmosphere of custodial interrogation by advising the suspect of his rights. In the majority opinion in the *Miranda* case,[20] the Court took the perspective of the suspect and recognized that there are fixed features of the custodial interrogation context that threaten to overbear a suspect's will. By looking at the situation of custodial interrogation through the eyes of the suspect, the Court recognized that the informal pressure to speak during custodial police questioning could rise to the level of compulsion under the Fifth Amendment.

In recent years, the Court has narrowed the reach of *Miranda* to some extent, by circumscribing the conditions under which the warning requirement has been violated. Recently, in *Howes v. Fields*, the Court was faced with the question of whether a suspect was in custody when he was interrogated while he was an inmate in jail.[21] The suspect was serving a forty-five-day sentence for disorderly conduct when he was escorted by a corrections officer to a room in another part of the building and interrogated about a sex crime by armed sheriff's deputies for five to seven hours, until about 2:00 a.m. The suspect was told in the beginning of the interview that he could leave and return to his cell whenever he wanted. Several hours later in the interview, he told deputies several times that he no longer wanted to talk to them, but they did not return him to his cell in response to these requests. Because the officers never gave the suspect his *Miranda* warnings, the question of whether he was in custody at the time he made a statement was crucial – if there was no custody, then there was no requirement for warnings. The Court ultimately concluded that the suspect was not in custody, because a reasonable person in his situation would feel at liberty to terminate the interview and leave.

The conclusion and reasoning in *Fields* are remarkably analogous to the conclusion and reasoning in Fourth Amendment consent search and seizure cases. In the Fourth Amendment cases, the Court identifies as the crucial question whether a reasonable person in the same situation as the citizen would feel free to terminate the police encounter or refuse the request to search, and the answer is almost always yes. In its Fifth Amendment analysis in *Fields*, the Court identified the same issue as key for making the determination of whether the suspect was in custody – would a reasonable person in the suspect's situation feel free to terminate the interview and leave? Like the Court's analysis in *Drayton*, the reasoning in the *Fields* opinion has an air of unreality.[22] More than once, the suspect told his interrogators that he did not wish to speak with them anymore, but this request was never heeded. Yet, the Court found that a reasonable person in his situation would feel free to terminate the interview. Once again, the Court relies on questionable assumptions about what citizens in police encounters perceive about their freedom to extricate themselves from the situation.

7. THE COST TO INNOCENT PEOPLE SUBJECT TO "CONSENT" SEARCHES

In Fourth Amendment cases involving consent searches and seizures, and in Fifth Amendment cases involving statements offered during custodial interrogation, the Court has insisted upon building a set of standards based upon unrealistic assumptions about human psychology. The standards constructed guide law enforcement practices, not only because of the specific rules of police conduct inherent in these standards, but also because of the values expressed by the standards and their underlying rationale. Law enforcement practices that evolve from Supreme Court decisions about constitutional criminal procedure have consequences that reach beyond the individual cases that the Court decides. Criminal procedure case law creates incentives that encourage specific law enforcement practices. In this section, I explore some of the costs of the law enforcement practices that have evolved in response to the Supreme Court's Fourth Amendment jurisprudence.

Consent searches are now a routine method of crime control in many localities, where suspicionless searches of large numbers of people have become common. Police departments and other law enforcement agencies provide training for their officers on obtaining consent, using tactics similar to the training that salespeople receive in inducing customers to buy things they do not want. Consent searches require no justification: they may be done pursuant to an officer's hunch, or for no reason at all. In some places, officers have adopted a practice of requesting consent to search during every traffic stop.[23] Because of unsystematic or nonexistent record keeping, it is very difficult to estimate the frequency of consent searches accurately. One estimate concludes that more than 90 percent of warrantless police searches are consent searches.[24] But the underlying number of searches is unknown, though the number is likely to be increasing, especially since the September 11 terrorist attacks. In a single Florida city, the local police have routinized bus sweeps, assigning a special squad of officers to conduct daily consent searches on intercity buses making stopovers at the bus station. In a typical year, the officers board and search buses containing more than twenty-six thousand passengers, all of whom become potential search targets.[25] In another Florida city, one police officer testified that he had personally conducted consent searches of more than three thousand bags just in the previous nine months. In Ohio, one officer testified that in the past year he made 786 requests to search motorists whom he had stopped for routine traffic violations.

The policy and practice of conducting scattershot consent searches ought to be permitted only if the costs are justified. The costs are arguably high, however, because the vast majority of people subjected to consent searches are innocent of any crime.[26] For those innocent people subject to consent searches, there are psychological costs. The scattershot approach to consent searches directly affects many thousands of innocent people every year who possess no illegal drugs or guns and are not engaged in illegal activity. Yet they find themselves in a position where a police officer has approached them and wants them to submit to a search. In the view of the Supreme Court, this involves a simple yes/no decision, and the only issue is one about information. The Court has struggled with questions like Do most people have enough information about the legal rules to know whether they are free to decline the officer's request? If they do not, should it be the officer's job to provide it to them? Or would we prefer to encourage people to gather this information on their own? In the Court's collective mind, the citizen is imagined as a dispassionate legal analyst, using information about standards for probable cause and reasonable suspicion. The citizen concludes that she has a choice and then communicates her preference to the officer. But in reality, social interactions are not merely questions of deductive logic, and the problem does not primarily involve information. The citizen who has been stopped by an officer of the law is now involved in a social interaction with a person who possesses a great deal of power over her. To be sure, as a strategic interaction it is governed by law and logic, but as a social interaction it is also governed by principles of pragmatics and social authority, as well as emotional arousal.[27]

Taking the sole perspective of the law enforcement officer has blinded the Court to seeing the ways in which scattershot consent searches, as social interactions, can be costly. Yet, some of these costs are not difficult to discern. For example, the New Jersey Supreme Court has engaged in an explicit weighing of the costs and benefits of suspicionless consent searches. Among the costs it identified is subjecting "travelers on our State highways ... to the harassment, embarrassment, and inconvenience of an automobile search following a routine traffic stop."[28] As another example from Ohio, a survey of citizens stopped and searched on highways revealed that a large majority felt negatively about the experience.[29] Here are some examples of individuals' reactions to consent searches, expressed sometimes months or even years later:

> I don't know if you ever had your house broken into or ripped off ... [it's] an empty feeling, like you're nothing.
> It was embarrassing. It pissed me off ... they just treat you like a criminal and you ain't done nothing.... I think about it every time I see a cop.
> I feel really violated. I felt like my rights had been infringed upon. I feel really bitter about the whole thing.
> I don't trust [the police] anymore. I've lost all trust in them.[30]

When routine police practice involves rummaging through the vehicles and personal belongings of innocent motorists, repeated hundreds and thousands of times, it leaves in its wake a flood of shaken people, whose sense of personal security is shattered.

8. CONSENT SEARCHES IN THE CONTEXT OF OTHER LAW ENFORCEMENT PRACTICES

These routinized requests for consent searches, in conjunction with permissive rules about traffic stops, custodial arrests, and strip searches, paint a disturbing picture of police power. To illustrate this claim, consider the following. The Supreme Court has declared that the police can stop any vehicle using a pretextual justification such as a cracked taillight or failure to use a turn signal in order to follow up on a hunch or just to have a look at the car and its occupants.[31] The officer's motivation for making the traffic stop is legally irrelevant, so long as the officer can point to a violation of a traffic regulation observed at the time of the stop. Because traffic regulations are so numerous, and because at times, safe driving entails the violation of one or more traffic regulations (such as exceeding the speed limit to keep pace with the flow of traffic), the practical upshot is that nearly any driver can be stopped by police at nearly any time, on the basis of a hunch or worse.

Having ordered a vehicle to stop, and in the absence of probable cause or at least reasonable suspicion of a crime (other than the traffic violation), the police are not permitted to accomplish much through physical force. But they are permitted to ask questions unrelated to the traffic violation without having to inform the motorist that she is now free to leave, even if the motorist is under the impression that the questioning is part of the initial traffic stop.[32] The motorist is motivated to minimize the time involved in the stop and so is eager to show the officer that there are no grounds to suspect criminal activity. The officer leverages this motivation by asking the motorist whether he has anything illegal in the car and immediately follows up with "Then you don't mind if I take a look?" This tactic leverages the constitutional rules of criminal procedure. First, the police are free to pose any questions they want, and they do not need individualized suspicion to ask for permission to search.[33] Second, once a person consents to be stopped or to be searched, the Fourth Amendment does not apply.[34]

When asked by police for consent to search their vehicle, most drivers agree, oftentimes because they feel they have no choice.[35] If any contraband is found in the car, such as a pipe containing marijuana residue, the officers can arrest occupants of the vehicle.[36] Even if no contraband is found, the Supreme Court has declared that the police can make a custodial arrest anyway, so long as they can find some type of offense punishable by a fine, such as driving without a seat belt.[37] Once someone is arrested, the Supreme Court has declared that the government can strip search the citizen, no matter what the circumstances of the arrest or how minor the offense charged.[38] Thus, even if a person is arrested for failing to pay a fine, he can be held for days, transferred to multiple holding jails, and subjected to multiple nude strip searches, involving a supervised delousing shower and inspection of the genitals and bodily orifices.[39]

Nor is this frightening chain of events limited to contacts that are initiated in traffic stops. At first glance, government stops of pedestrians would seem more difficult because law enforcement does not have at its disposal the complex vehicle and traffic codes from which it can cherry-pick suspected violations. The Supreme Court has declared that law enforcement can indeed stop and frisk individuals, but only if the officer has articulable reasons to suspect that criminal activity is afoot.[40] Under this standard, it would seem unlikely that police could stop and frisk pedestrians at will; nonetheless, this practice is now common and the frequency of these stops is increasing, at least in some places. In New York City, for example, the police department's own records reveal their officers stopping and frisking of close to 700,000 individuals in a single recent year, and the number has increased every year for the past several years.[41] New York Police Department policy requires officers to record the reasons for each stop and frisk they make. Critics charge that police officers use thin pretexts for conducting warrantless, consentless searches on a massive scale. Police department records arguably bear this out: the two most frequent justifications for stops and frisks, noted in about half the stops, are 1) the citizen's making "furtive movements" and 2) the citizen's being present in a "high-crime area."[42] More than 80 percent of those stopped are black or Latino, and these residents are more likely to be stopped than whites both because most stops occur in black/Latino neighborhoods regardless of crime rates, and because even in white neighborhoods, black and Latino residents are more likely to be stopped than whites. Despite this extraordinarily high volume of stops and frisks, arrests take place in only about 5 percent of all documented stops. Similar practices have been documented in other U.S. cities.[43]

9. THE FOURTH AMENDMENT, SECURITY, AND DIGNITY

The extent to which lower courts will sanction these stop and frisk practices is not yet known. In light of the values that the U.S. Supreme Court has expressed in the context of its consent jurisprudence, it is perhaps not surprising that police departments have taken the scattershot approach to consent searches one step further and simply dispensed with the fiction of asking for consent to search. Law enforcement agencies are no longer hampered by the U.S. Supreme Court's former concern that citizens be treated with dignity and respect by government agents. More than four decades ago in *Terry v. Ohio*, the case that initially authorized the brief detention and frisking of citizens upon a showing of reasonable suspicion of criminal activity, the Court sent a clear message to law enforcement:

> It is simply fantastic to urge that [a stop and frisk] performed in public by a policeman while the citizen stands helpless, perhaps facing a wall with his hands raised, is a "petty indignity." It is a serious intrusion upon the sanctity of the person, which may inflict great indignity and arouse strong resentment, and it is not to be undertaken lightly.[44]

A lot has happened since *Terry*, and the current Court does not seem to embrace these concerns about dignity. Even more fundamentally, the Court is not focused on protecting the security of the people against the government. The text of the Fourth Amendment protects "the right of the people to be secure in their persons, houses, papers and effects, against unreasonable searches and seizures." The scattershot approach to policing poses serious costs on the ability of the people to feel secure from arbitrary intrusions by the state. When people who are not engaging in criminal activity have reason to worry that a walk down the street or a drive to the grocery store will end with being stopped, searched, and perhaps even arrested and strip searched, then "the right of the people to be secure in their persons, houses, papers and effects, against unreasonable searches and seizures" has been eroded to the point of being unrecognizable. The volume and frequency of scattershot stops and searches create a profound harm to the security of the people as a whole. As Jed Rubenfeld has argued, "Freedom requires that people be able to live their personal lives without a pervasive, cringing fear of the state ... produced by the justified apprehension that their personal lives are subject at any moment to be violated and indeed taken from them if they become suspicious in the eyes of governmental authorities."[45]

10. FROM FEAR TO COOPERATION

The practice of widespread, scattershot stops and searches derives from an assumption that effective policing is based on using the most intrusive tools available within the boundaries of the law. Adopting the perspective of law enforcement, the U.S. Supreme Court has expressed approval for intrusive tactics, by employing assumptions about human behavior that conflict with both common sense and empirical research. There is reason to think, however, that intrusive, scattershot policing does not serve well the government's interests in the long run. In order to deter crime, the police need the cooperation of the community members it polices.[46] People obey the law to the extent that they view legal actors and institutions as legitimate,[47] and they care a great deal about the extent to which law enforcement officers exercise their authority fairly and respectfully.[48] If community members perceive their police as treating people unfairly and disrespectfully, they will not be motivated to go forward to report crime, they will be more likely to believe that the police are engaging in illegitimate tactics like racial profiling, and they may even be more likely to engage in criminal activity themselves.[49]

Instead of looking to formal law to define the boundaries of everyday police practices, law enforcement agencies would do well to take the perspective of the citizens whom they police, just as the supreme courts of New Jersey and Hawaii and a handful of other state supreme courts have in interpreting their state constitutions. Instead of simply examining the officers' actions and words from the officers' perspective, these courts have taken seriously the idea that it is a mistake to treat all citizens like criminals in the hope of getting "lucky" and finding some evidence of criminal wrongdoing. The scattershot approach to law enforcement turns citizens against the police, because stops and searches are in fact serious governmental intrusions that often leave the individual feeling violated, degraded, and resentful. Ultimately, scattershot policing is counterproductive: it yields little evidence of criminal activity, and its costs to legitimacy and compliance are potentially devastating.

Notes

1. David K. Kessler, *Free to Leave – An Empirical Look at the Fourth Amendment's Seizure Standard*, 99 J. CRIM. L. & CRIMINOLOGY 51 (2009).
2. *Id.*
3. The subjective experience of compulsion to comply with law enforcement holds even for those who are aware of their legal right to refuse, *Id.* at 78, and for people from relatively privileged socio-economic backgrounds, *Id.* at 80 n.159.
4. RICHARD UVILLER, TEMPERED ZEAL 81 (1988).
5. Illya Lichtenberg, *Miranda in Ohio: The Effects of Robinette on the Voluntary Waiver of Fourth Amendment Rights*, 44 HOW. L.J. 349 (2000). In this study for part of the period in question, police were not required to advise motorists of their right to refuse consent, and for part of the period, police were required to so advise. The rate of consent during both periods was about 90%.
6. Stephen J. Schulhofer, *Reconsidering Miranda*, 54 U. CHI. L. REV. 435, 436 (1987) ("[T]he view that MIRANDA posed no barrier to effective law enforcement [has] become widely accepted, not only by academics but also by such prominent law enforcement officials as Los Angeles District Attorney Evelle Younger and Kansas City police chief [later FBI director] Clarence Kelly.").
7. 536 U.S. 194 (2002).
8. Official Transcript of Oral Argument at 46, *United States v. Drayton* (2002), 2002 U.S. Trans. LEXIS 37 at *46.
9. *Id.*
10. *Drayton*, 536 U.S. at 204.
11. *Id.* at 207.
12. *People v. Tupper*, 2009 Cal. App. Unpub. LEXIS 4908 (Cal. App. June 17, 2009).
13. These states include Alaska, Hawaii, Minnesota, New Jersey, and possibly Wyoming. See *Brown v. State*, 182 P.3d 624 (Alaska Ct. App. 2008); *State v. Quino*, 74 Haw. 161 (1992); *State v. Fort*, 660 N.W.2d 415, 416 (Minn.2003); *State v. Carty*, 170 N.J. 632 (2002); *O'Boyle v. State*, 117 P.3d 401, 411 (Wyo.2005).
14. See *Carty*, 170 N.J. at 639.
15. See, e.g., *id.* at 632.
16. *Quino*, 74 Haw. 161.
17. *Carty*, 170 N.J. at 641.
18. *Id.* (quoting *Terry v. Ohio*, 392 U.S. 1 (1968)).
19. *Id.* at 644.
20. *Miranda v. Arizona*, 384 U.S. 436 (1966).
21. *Howes v. Fields*, 132 S. Ct. 1181 (2002).
22. See *United States v. Drayton*, 536 U.S. 194, 208 (2002) (Souter, J., dissenting).
23. *Ohio v. Robinette*, 519 U.S. 33, 40 (1996); *Harris v. State* 994 S.W.2d 927, 932 n.1 (Tex. Crim. App. 1999).
24. Ric Simmons, *Not Voluntary but Still Reasonable: A New Paradigm for Understanding the Consent Searches Doctrine*, 80 IND. L.J. 773 (2005).
25. Janice Nadler, *No Need to Shout: Bus Sweeps and the Psychology of Coercion*, 2002 SUP. CT. REV. 153, 210.
26. Statistics are difficult to come by and are quite scattered. The Sheriff in one Florida county arrested 55 of the 507 motorists subjected to consent searches over

a three year period. Jeff Brazil & Steve Berry, *Color of Driver Is Key to Stops in I-95 Video*, ORLANDO SENTINEL TRIB., Aug. 23, 1992, at A1 Relatedly, New York City police arrest about 5% of pedestrians of recorded stops and frisks. If they stop individuals without filling out a report, then the 5% figure is an underestimate.

27 Janice Nadler & J. D. Trout, *The Language of Consent in Police Encounters*, in OXFORD HANDBOOK OF LANGUAGE AND LAW 326–39 (L. Solan & P. Tiersma, eds., 2012).
28 *State v. Carty*, 170 N.J. 632, 646 (2002).
29 Illya D. Lichtenberg, *Voluntary Consent or Obedience to Authority: An Inquiry into the "Consensual" Police-Citizen Encounter*, 1999 (unpublished Ph.D. dissertation) (on file with author).
30 See *id.* at 283, 285, 288 (subject numbers 11091, 12731, 14735, and 15494).
31 *Whren v. United States*, 517 U.S. 806 (1996).
32 *Ohio v. Robinette*, 519 U.S. 33 (1996).
33 *Florida v. Rodriguez*, 469 U.S. 1, 5–6 (1984).
34 *Id.*
35 Lichtenberg, supra note 29.
36 *Atwater v. Lago Vista*, 532 U.S. 318 (2001).
37 *Id.*
38 *Florence v. Bd. of Chosen Freeholders of Burlington*, 132 S. Ct. 1510 (2012).
39 *Id.*
40 *Terry v. Ohio*, 392 U.S. 1 (1968).
41 Michael Powell, *Former Skeptic Now Embraces Divisive Tactic*, N.Y. TIMES, Apr. 9, 2012. The actual number is likely to be higher, assuming that police make additional stops and frisks that they fail to document.
42 Al Baker, *New York Minorities More Likely To Be Frisked*, N.Y. TIMES, May 12, 2010.
43 *Id.*; Allison Steele, *Philly Stop-and-Frisk Policy Gets Court Supervision*, PHILA. INQUIRER, June 22, 2011.
44 *Terry*, 392 U.S. at 16–17.
45 Jed Rubenfeld, *The End of Privacy*, 61 STAN. L. REV. 101 (2008).
46 TOM R. TYLER & YUEN J. HUO, TRUST IN THE LAW: ENCOURAGING PUBLIC COOPERATION WITH THE POLICE AND COURTS (2002).
47 TOM R. TYLER, WHY PEOPLE OBEY THE LAW (1st ed., 1990).
48 Tom R. Tyler & Jeffrey Fagan, *Legitimacy and Cooperation: Why Do People Help the Police Fight Crime in Their Communities?* 6 OHIO ST. J. CRIM. L. 231 (2008); Aziz Z. Huq, Tom R. Tyler & Stephen J. Schulhofer, *Why Does the Public Cooperate with Law Enforcement? The Influence of the Purposes and Targets of Policing*, 17 PSYCHOL., PUB. POL'Y, & L. X 419–50 (2011).
49 Janice Nadler, Flouting the Law, 83 TEX. L. REV. 1399 (2005).

7

Neurotechnologies at the Intersection of Criminal Procedure and Constitutional Law

Amanda C. Pustilnik

The last realm of privacy is your mind. This will invade that.
— CEO of Veritas Scientific Corporation, describing his company's mind-reading helmet.[1]

1. INTRODUCTION

The rapid development of neurotechnologies poses novel constitutional issues for criminal procedure, among other areas of law.[2] These technologies can identify directly from brain waves whether a person is familiar with a stimulus such as a face or a weapon, can model blood flow in the brain to indicate whether a person is lying, and can even interfere with brain processes themselves via high-powered magnets to cause a person to be less likely to lie to an investigator. By obtaining information directly from a subject's involuntary physiological responses, investigators could use such "neuroassay" technologies to make an end run around the Fifth Amendment privilege against compelled, self-incriminating speech. Neuroassays complicate, as well, the question of what constitutes a Fourth Amendment "search" and "seizure." Yet, jurisprudence under both amendments stumbles on a conceptually limited distinction between body and mind, physical and informational. Such a distinction can no longer stand, as brain processes and emanations sit at the juncture of these categories.

This chapter first explains why neurotechnologies may be useful in criminal investigations and describes key neurotechnologies actually in use or under development. It then analyzes the implications of these technologies under the Fourth and Fifth Amendments. Building on work by other law and neuroscience scholars, it offers a framework for Fourth and Fifth Amendment analysis that aims to avoid current doctrine's false dualism.

In its existing Fifth Amendment jurisprudence, the Supreme Court has emphasized distinctions between bodily samples and communicative acts or statements, privileging only the latter as "testimonial." This dichotomy between bodily facts and communicative acts is collapsed by direct access to neural processes, the physical substrate of thought and speech. This chapter suggests that Fifth Amendment jurisprudence ought to dispense with tests predicated on this problematic dichotomy. Instead, drawing on other strands of Supreme Court reasoning, it proposes that the Fifth Amendment inquiry should focus on whether law enforcement elicited or "evoked" the self-incriminating information. This allows for a principled distinction between two sets of physical products: those whose information content is independent of law enforcement inquiry, like blood-alcohol level or hair color, which are presumptively not privileged, and those that communicate mental contents evoked by law enforcement, which presumptively would be privileged.

Fourth Amendment jurisprudence, too, trips on distinctions between searches of bodily and nonbodily private spaces. The Court has correlated the degree of protection against compelled bodily searches with the degree of the search's physical invasiveness. Yet, brain searches via neuroassay show invasiveness to be a poor benchmark. Brain waves can be detected from outside the skull; yet, information from a brain search may be equivalent to the content of private conversations or documents, which receive high Fourth Amendment protection. Normatively and culturally, the mind is an archetypal space of privacy, making searches of the brain more like searches of the home than like the noninvasive taking of other physical samples, such as fingernail clippings. This chapter suggests that brain searches should be conceived of not as noninvasive physical searches but as searches of private information within a space of presumed privacy.

The speed with which neurotechnologies are developing makes it perilous to predict how they may shape future legal practices. Some concerns of today might be obviated tomorrow by the failure of current technologies or the invention of new ones. But this uncertainty also makes the predictive enterprise important: exploring potential influences of neuroscience on criminal law now allows us to set a course thoughtfully toward the law's possible futures.

2. COGNITIVE NEUROSCIENCE AND NEUROTECHNOLOGIES

Cognitive neuroscience is a subfield of neuroscience that studies how the brain operationalizes thinking, feeling, and behaving.[3] To measure or infer the activity of neurons in the brain, researchers most commonly use direct and indirect electrophysiological measurement, like electroencephalography (EEG),[4] and neuroimaging, like magnetic resonance imaging (MRI).[5] Researchers also increasingly use a third, more recent mode of investigation, transcranial magnetic stimulation (TMS).[6]

In the specialized cognitive neuroscience subfield of "mind reading" and "lie detection," investigators make use of all three modes, EEG, MRI, and TMS. These technologies aim to reduce uncertainty around whether an individual possesses any relevant knowledge, what that knowledge might be, and whether the individual is being honest in his or her representations to investigators. This section briefly describes the most promising current neuroassay[7] technologies.

a. Assaying Knowledge: Concealed Information Tests

Several neurotechnologies assay the subject's mind for particular experiences, items of knowledge, and emotions. These assay techniques aim to detect experiential traces encoded in the subject's brain. The longest-studied and most well-validated brain-based information-seeking technique is the concealed information test, or CIT.[8] The CIT presents subjects with familiar and unfamiliar stimuli and uses EEG to measure the subject's brain's responses to the stimuli. The test is based on the "well established ... principle" that the brain produces a brain wave known as the P300 in response to familiar stimuli only.[9] An investigator presents the subject with a series of related words or images,[10] and within that set will be one word or image that ought to stand out to the subject because of what he or she knows or has experienced – the so-called oddball or probe stimulus.[11] The P300 response is not perfect, but in controlled laboratory tests it is very good: it correctly detects "lies" between 74 and 80 percent of the time. These are strong results, but false negatives and false positives occur in a meaningful number of tests.[12] Researchers are working to combine the P300 with other physiological measures.[13]

An example illustrates how the test works. Suppose a victim was bludgeoned to death with the *Bluebook*. An investigator might expose a suspect to a class of words related to legal research, including the probe "Bluebook." If our suspect bludgeoned the victim, he ought to find the probe term more familiar and salient than, say, "pin cite," eliciting a P300 wave. Yet, if he emits a P300, that does not prove he is the killer. He might be in the midst of Bluebooking an article or Bluebook-phobic from a journal competition. The test proves familiarity plus salience, not guilt per se. Although the P300 is outside conscious control, it still turns on the person's mental life – what is important to him and how that may vary in different contexts.[14]

A corporation called VERITAS is developing a CIT helmet for mass memory screening. The company is producing helmets for use by the U.S. military in field investigations, so that large groups of people can be screened quickly to determine whether they recognize the faces of individuals of interest. The helmet shows images of interest, for example, the face of a terrorism suspect, to the subject within the helmet. A P300 response indicates that the subject likely is familiar with the person he has just seen. While the current planned use for these helmets is in field investigations in conflict areas, the technology could be deployed domestically.

b. Assaying Veracity: fMRI Lie Detection

Brain-based lie detection techniques primarily rely upon functional magnetic resonance imaging (fMRI).[15] The general theory behind fMRI-based lie detection is that it is more cognitively demanding for a subject to utter an intentionally false statement than a statement he believes to be true.[16] The dominant model of how lies come about posits that when a subject is asked a question, the subject's brain automatically produces what it has stored as the correct response.[17] To utter a false response, the subject must override the initial response and fabricate the falsehood in its place.[18] Since lying takes more mental activity than truth telling, a lie should be slower to produce and require the brain to work harder. The time factor can be measured as response latency,[19] while the additional cognitive work should result in heightened blood to the working areas in order to satisfy their metabolic demand.

The heightened blood flow to involved regions should produce a distinct color map on an fMRI. The areas that most commonly become active in deception tasks include the anterior cingulate cortex, orbitofrontal cortex, inferior frontal cortex, and parts of the temporal lobe.[20] Researchers thus must look at fMRIs for patterns involving numerous brain regions to infer indicators of deception. There is no universal "tell" within the brain for all kinds of lying and deception – or if there is, researchers have not discovered it. For this reason, scientists[21] and members of the legal community[22] have questioned whether fMRI lie detection is reliable enough to merit being admissible or available in courtroom and commercial contexts.[23]

fMRI lie detection has advantages and drawbacks relative to CITs. fMRI protocols discern more generally whether the subject is uttering truthful statements, without requiring precise, advance knowledge on the part of the investigator about the details of the target event. Conversely, unlike CIT, an fMRI examination "requires a high level of subject compliance," as the subject must lie still in the scanner and willingly respond to questions.[24]

c. Shifting Preferences: TMS Changes Subjects' Responses

Before a person has had a chance to answer a question, the neurotechnology known as transcranial magnetic stimulation (TMS)[25] could shift his or her preferences about whether to tell the truth – and perhaps whether to respond at all. While several historical and contemporary technologies aim at lie detection, this is the first neurotechnology that may be useful for *lie prevention*.

A recent study by Inga Karton and Talis Bachmann measured the impact of magnetic stimulation on a particular brain region, the dorsolateral prefrontal cortex (DLPFC),[26] on whether subjects told the truth or a lie.[27] Subjects in the experiment were offered the choice to respond truthfully or falsely at will to investigators' questions about the color of a shape they had seen. Researchers found that TMS to the right lobe of the DLPFC caused subjects to be somewhat more likely to tell the truth; TMS to the left DLPFC caused subjects to be somewhat more likely to lie.[28]

The single study, which must be repeated by other investigators, suggests that TMS on certain brain regions may act to shift preferences about whether to lie – changing mental processes and acting on what we think of as the core free will exercises of choosing between alternatives. If TMS changes a person's mental processes so that he or she makes different subjective determinations about whether to tell the truth or to speak at all, then the state would not just be finding existing facts – it would be causally interfering with mental processes that are at the core of personhood.

3. TO SPEAK OR NOT TO SPEAK? THAT IS NO LONGER THE QUESTION

Neurotechnologies that allow investigators to obtain information by bypassing an individual's voluntary speech or other forms of voluntary communication impinge on several constitutional protections, notably the Fourth Amendment protection against unreasonable search and seizure and the Fifth Amendment privilege against self-incrimination. This part explores the interrelated constitutional interests that arise when the state seeks to perform neuroassays on subjects.

Whether and under what circumstances the state could compel individuals to submit to neuroassays under existing Fourth and Fifth Amendment jurisprudence depends on how neuroassays and the brain products they detect are characterized. Brain waves and fMRI patterns have a dual nature as physical traces and as information products. Whether courts construe their physical sample–like properties or their information product–like properties to predominate would lead to different degrees of protection under each regime. Predicting how courts may deal with neuroassays under the Fourth and Fifth Amendments turns on the extent to which courts can find a suitable analogy between brain processes and existing categories of protected or unprotected materials. Are brain waves like breath, a mere spontaneous physical emanation? Are memory traces like documents in a file drawer, the static, physical embodiment of predetermined information? If so, the neural products detected by neuroassays look unlike testimony and unlike anything in which one would have an expectation of privacy. But if memory traces and emotional responses are brought into being – evoked, authored – in response to the neuroassay itself, then they look more like testimony or like documents authored by the subject, categories that receive high degrees of constitutional protection.

How courts construe the physical aspects of mental processes may turn in part on the biology of memory. Memory is associative and reconstructive.[29] It is a process, not a thing. Although our memories feel unitary, they are virtual objects that exist in diffuse brain regions and must be reassembled upon recall.[30] This aspect of memory would argue for the testimonylike or authorshiplike view, rather than documents-in-a-file-drawer view. Query, however, whether courts will be comfortable having these rights turn on the contingencies of the biology of memory – or, indeed, on the contingencies of the state of the science. Advancing neuroassay technologies may glean more information from smaller and smaller amounts of neural data, making memory's authorlike and associative nature moot and putting on infirm ground any constitutional conclusions that rested on the science of memory. Courts may fairly determine that constitutional values transcend the particular mechanisms by which various neural responses arise and instead ground their analyses in principles like the sanctity of a sphere of mental privacy.[31]

a. Self-Incrimination via Evoked Mental Contents under the Fifth Amendment

The Fifth Amendment's privilege against self-incrimination allows a person to refuse to make any statements or engage in communicative conduct that could place him or her in criminal jeopardy.[32] The Supreme Court has repeatedly described the Fifth Amendment as being rooted in the framers' rejection of "historical practices, such as ecclesiastical inquisitions and the proceedings of the Star Chamber, 'which placed a premium on compelling subjects of the investigation to admit guilt from their own lips.'"[33] On this view, the privilege protects the individual from the excesses of state power; similarly, it may protect the state from itself by pretermitting its inclinations to extract confessions through harsh means. While scholars continue to debate the purposes behind the Fifth Amendment, there is some consensus around the "excuse" model:[34] that the privilege provides the suspect with an excuse to avoid the "cruel trilemma of self-accusation, perjury or contempt" he would face were he compelled to testify against himself.[35] Relatively recently, in *Pennsylvania v. Muniz*, the Supreme Court appeared to emphasize the value of protecting mental privacy itself.[36] The Court concluded in *Muniz* that the purpose of the privilege is "'served when the privilege is asserted to spare the accused from having to ... share his thoughts and beliefs with the Government,'"[37] because it is "the attempt to force [the accused] 'to *disclose the contents of his own mind*'" that the privilege protects against.[38]

The core case that establishes the modern contours of the privilege, the case that permits the state to compel bodily-product-as-chemicals but not bodily-product-as-expression-of-mental-state-or-knowledge, is *Schmerber v. California*.[39] Police found Armando Schmerber and his friend after Schmerber wrecked his car. The officer transported him to a hospital for treatment; having smelled alcohol on Schmerber, the officer requested that a doctor take a blood sample that would show whether Schmerber had been driving with a blood-alcohol content higher than the legal limit. Schmerber refused the blood draw, so the officer instructed the doctor to take his blood against his will. Schmerber challenged the blood draw, arguing that it constituted an unreasonable search and seizure and the impermissible compulsion of self-incriminating evidence in violation of the Fourth and Fifth Amendments respectively.[40]

The Court held as to the Fifth Amendment challenge that "the privilege protects an accused only from being compelled to testify against himself, or otherwise provide the State with evidence of a testimonial or communicative nature."[41] The "withdrawal of blood and use of the analysis ... did not involve compulsion to these ends."[42] The Court reasoned that bodily substances, unlike thoughts and decisions, are not an individual's to control in the first place: the drunk driver's breath or blood reveals his degree of intoxication independent of his choices and beyond the reach of his perjury. Access to blood or other physical products like breath or saliva thus would not place the individual in the "cruel trilemma of self-accusation, perjury or contempt."[43] A defendant on the stand contemplating how to answer a prosecutor's question would face that painful choice; a blood sample, which simply shows what it shows, does not. So holding, *Schmerber* established a physical/verbal divide: physical evidence may be compelled by the state under the Fifth Amendment,[44] but verbal statements and utterances may not be compelled because they are "communicative" or "testimonial" in ways that violate the Fifth Amendment's protection against causing one to be a "witness" against oneself.

Schmerber's deceptively simple, bright-line test has some appeal and suffices in many cases dealing with traditional bodily products like blood and traditional compelled verbal statements like forced confessions. Yet, in light of neurotechnologies that can detect and translate the physical correlates of thoughts, the line between a physical fact and a thought or feeling becomes faint, if not meaningless.[45] Indeed, the materialist view is that all thoughts and feelings are subserved by physical brain states. Even Descartes, the exemplar of mind/body dualism, recognized that the physical brain produced mental states and behaviors.

One approach to *Schmerber*'s conundrum may be found in another drunk driver case, *Pennsylvania v. Muniz*.[46] This case helps clarify the physical/verbal or physical-verbal-mental problem because it involves a party's challenge to each kind of evidence. In *Muniz*, a drunk driver moved to suppress on Fifth Amendment grounds the following evidence: his poor physical performance on field sobriety tests on the road and in custody, his spontaneous statements about his own drunkenness while he performed the sobriety tests, and his confused verbal responses to police questioning once he was in custody. In particular, Muniz could not provide police with the date and year of his sixth birthday.[47] All of these facts and statements, including his stumbling response to the birthday question, were introduced at his trial.[48]

The Court held that Muniz's motor indicia of drunkenness and his spontaneous admissions of the same could be used against him, but that the content of his garbled verbal responses to questions that the police asked him once he was in custody[49] could not.[50] His verbal response to custodial questioning constituted communications against his penal interests, regardless of the fact that his responses, like his statement that he could not figure out his birth date, did not substantively constitute inculpatory admissions.[51]

Drawing on *Schmerber*, the *Muniz* Court distinguished between preexisting physical facts that the police may merely discover – like blood alcohol content – and those that the police, through their questioning, "evoke."[52] "Evoke" can mean to elicit or call forth that which is preexisting (e.g., to "evoke evil spirits").[53] "Evoke" can also mean "re-create imaginatively."[54] Evocation, like provocation, causes the subject to create a novel response. We might say that a novel's textured prose evoked in the reader's mind a vision of the alien planet. This is evocation in the sense of creating anew because the reader could not previously have had thoughts or memories about a fictional world she is encountering for the first time. We might also say that a person's criticism evoked her partner's anger. In this sense, evocation straddles the preexisting and the novel: the partner surely has felt anger at other times and has the general capacity to feel anger, but this instance of anger has been created in response to or brought about by the prompting of the criticism.

The police questioning in *Muniz*, which required the suspect to formulate novel responses, created or brought about or "evoked" that which would not have existed but for the question. Put simply, if the police had not asked Muniz about his birthday and year, his blood alcohol still would have showed what it showed, but, absent the question, Muniz would not have engaged in the new mental work of creating a reply to the birthday question. The reply to the question, then, was novel mental content that the police evoked (caused to be created), while the blood sample was an independent and preexisting physical fact.

Muniz's emphasis on the Fifth Amendment's protection of "evoked" mental responses provides a basis for transcending *Schmerber*'s problematic physical/verbal divide and making principled Fifth Amendment distinctions among numerous categories of responses. *Muniz* points to a distinction between two sets of physical signs: (1) the nonprivileged set of physical signs that does not reveal evoked mental contents and (2) the privileged set of physical signs that does.[55] Breath, bodily fluids, finger- and iris-prints, imaging (x-ray, CT, or MRI) of body and brain for their *structural* features, and fingernail and hair clippings, among other kinds of evidence, fall into the first set of physical signs. These signs may yield legally relevant information, like DNA or evidence of intoxication, or they may help to confirm aspects of the suspect's identity.[56] But such information is not "evoked" (it exists independent of investigators' inquiry) and it does not express "contents of [the] mind."[57]

Construing the Fifth Amendment to protect evoked mental responses allows for clear and consistent distinctions between all of the categories of evidence at issue in *Muniz* – and at large in the world. The static chemical composition of bodily substances neither is evoked nor reveals mental contents and so is not privileged. Motor activity, like a field sobriety test, indicates the general state of the brain but does not evoke or show the presence or absence of particular mental content. Verbal *or* physical evoked evidence that reveals mental "contents"[58] or "knowledge"[59] should be subject to the privilege and evaluated for voluntariness. Yet not all verbal utterances merit protection: A verbal utterance could reveal no mental content, as when a person with Tourette's syndrome yells out a meaningless phrase. Conversely, the body can express the contents of the mind, as through brain wave emanations and functional activation patterns. If the Fifth Amendment protects against the "compelled" "evocation" of the "contents of [the] mind,"[60] then whether the subject conveys that content through speech or through speech's precursor, brain waves, should be a matter of indifference.

b. Individual and Mass Brain Searching under the Fourth Amendment

The Fourth Amendment protects "the right of the people to be secure in their persons, houses, papers, and effects, against unreasonable searches and seizures."[61] The Fourth Amendment applies broadly to all searches and seizures, whether of the suspect him- or herself, the alleged victim, witnesses, or other third parties. Unlike the Fifth Amendment, its protections apply without regard to whether the material sought by the state tends to incriminate its source. It is not a blanket protection against undesired intrusions; rather it protects "against official intrusions up to the point where the community's need for evidence" rises to the level of "probable cause" to believe that the search will yield evidence of a crime.[62] Once probable cause has been established, "it is ordinarily justifiable for the community to demand that the individual give up some part of his interest in privacy and security to advance the community's vital interests in law enforcement."[63]

The Fourth Amendment protection attaches where "a person [has] exhibited an actual (subjective) expectation of privacy and ... the expectation [is] one that society is prepared to recognize as 'reasonable.'"[64] Physical or informational products that people expose to public view, like their facial features or voice, or publish, like public social media updates or documents, lack any expectation of privacy. In matters people do not make public, a privacy expectation may attach. Case law and cultural norms support the conclusion that people have a reasonable expectation of privacy and security in their physical bodies, in the contents of and in their actions within private spaces like the home, and in their unexpressed or unpublished thoughts and reflections.

Neuroassays sit at the juncture of these three categories of searches of the body, private spaces, and thoughts. Spontaneous physical emanations of the brain may be analogous to breath or blood. The mind, housed within the cranium, might be a sphere of cherished and presumptive privacy like the home.[65] And the information content of the brain – particularly evoked thoughts, as discussed in the preceding section – may be analogous or partially homologous to private thoughts committed to a diary. The first part of this section will explore the implications of the physical-spatial-informational distinction in the context of Fourth Amendment jurisprudence. This is the "how" of Fourth Amendment neuroassay problems: *how* should neuroassays be characterized – as searches of the body, of a privileged private space, or of authored information?

This section will then turn from the "how" to the "who": the degree to which the Fourth Amendment applies to neuroassays may depend upon *who* is subject to search. If a reasonable expectation of privacy depends in part on what "society is prepared to recognize as 'reasonable,'"[66] then outcomes may turn on the ways in which social expectations of privacy and criminal procedures vary as to different categories of individuals – from suspect, to key witness, to general member of the population.

i. Bodily Searches and Samples

The threshold for a "reasonable" bodily intrusion under the Fourth Amendment is the presence of probable cause and either a warrant or a warrant exception like exigent circumstances.[67] After the threshold requirement is met, the reasonableness inquiry turns to the type of procedure, its degree of intrusiveness, and the manner in which it is performed.[68] Courts evaluate the permissibility of bodily searches and sampling along a continuum of invasiveness, with the least protection accorded to the least invasive procedures.

In *Schmerber*, the defendant challenged the state's compelled, warrantless extraction of his boozy blood on the Fourth Amendment ground that the blood draw constituted an unconstitutional search and seizure.[69] The Court concurred with Schmerber that the state's compelled extraction of blood falls within the Fourth Amendment's purview both because it is a "search" and because "the integrity of an individual's person is a cherished value of our society."[70] Indeed, where "intrusions into the human body are concerned," as with intrusions into the home, a warrant is required.[71] However, the Court rejected Schmerber's argument that the state's failure to obtain a warrant rendered the blood draw unconstitutional. Alcohol in a person's bloodstream decreases rapidly, and, therefore, the physical facts of the case presented "exigent circumstances" that relieved the state of its obligation to obtain a warrant.[72]

In approving the warrantless seizure of blood under exigent circumstances, the Court held out the prospect that constitutional considerations might narrowly limit or even fully bar other bodily intrusions by the state. While the Constitution "does not forbid ... *minor* intrusions into an individual's body under stringently limited circumstances," the Court observed, this small grant of authority "in no way indicates that [the Constitution] permits more substantial intrusions, or intrusions under other conditions."[73]

This prediction cashed out in *Winston v. Lee*.[74] In *Winston*, the state of Virginia sought and received a warrant to compel a suspect, Rudolph Lee, to have a bullet surgically removed from beneath his collarbone, on the basis of its assertion that it had probable cause to believe the bullet would link Lee to a crime.[75] The Court granted *certiorari* "to consider whether a State may, consistently with the Fourth Amendment, compel a suspect to undergo surgery of this kind in a search for evidence of a crime."[76] The Court concluded that the state could not compel Lee to have surgery under general anesthesia, which involved a risk of permanent injury or death, to remove a bullet under circumstances where the state already had ample evidence to link Lee to the crime. Even where probable cause is present, the Court held, and even where the search is "likely to produce evidence of a crime," a "compelled surgical intrusion into an individual's body for evidence, ... implicates expectations of privacy and security of such magnitude that the intrusion may be 'unreasonable.'"[77]

This holding protected Lee from compelled surgery and fulfilled *Schmerber's* prediction that some bodily intrusions may be so great that probable cause and a warrant do not suffice to compel them. But the case actually establishes a weak and uncertain rule: *Winston* does not identify when a person may be secure in his body from surgical intrusion by the state. It instead defaults to a "case-by-case" balancing test "in which the individual's interest in privacy and security are weighed against society's interests in conducting the procedure."[78] In Lee's particular case, the Court found the risk of death from general anesthesia to be unreasonable to procure marginal evidence in an attempted robbery case where the state already had enough other evidence to convict. But it did not find the intrusion to be unreasonable per se as shocking to the conscience or treading on inviolable rights against bodily intrusion by the state. It is impossible to say how *Winston* might have come out had it involved a less risky procedure or a greater need for the evidence.

Winston and *Schmerber* together create uncertainty about the permissible bounds of the state's intrusion upon the body: if probable cause is present, if the public's need for the evidence is great, and if the physical risk to the suspect is slight, there currently is no defined Fourth Amendment limit on the state's power to intrude physically into the suspect. To the extent these cases establish limits, such limits primarily relate to the risk of bodily harm: *Schmerber* emphasizes that the blood draw was permissible because it was physically nearly without risk; *Winston* emphasizes that Lee had to be spared surgery because of the physical risk.

This harm-focused standard provides very little guidance in the context of state intrusions via neuroassay. fMRI and EEG-based CIT tests are less physically invasive than even a blood test and involve negligible risk of physical harm.[79] Given the low degree of physical discomfort and inconvenience, the state likely would need to make only a traditional showing of probable cause. Indeed, in physical sample cases where the sample is obtained noninvasively – as with saliva samples – courts have split on whether the state's compulsion of such samples even requires a warrant.[80]

Although this potentially low degree of protection comports with the physical nonintrusiveness of the test, it belies the nature of the thing: who among us would value our thoughts equally to our fingernail clippings just because both can be obtained without risk or pain? Looking at brain emanations as physical samples apart from their informational content and apart from the extent to which mental privacy allows us to constitute our identities is so impoverished as to be false. Fortunately, cases involving bodily samples are not the only precedents that may apply to brain searches; precedents developed for spatial and informational searches also may apply to neuroassays.

ii. Spatial and Informational Fourth Amendment Protections

Brain waves and thought processes are not tangible physical products, like DNA or blood, and neuroassay techniques do not physically intrude inside the body as a blood draw or surgery does. More robust analogies for neuroassay, then, may come from Fourth Amendment jurisprudence dealing with the detection of intangible information, protection of the traditionally private spaces like the home, and the authorship of information. *Katz v. United States*[81] and *Kyllo v. United States*[82] together show the heightened privacy interest that the Court has recognized under the Fourth Amendment in intangible information products that people generate in traditionally private spaces. Emphasizing the nonbodily, information-content aspects of the neural products detected by neuroassay may result in a higher degree of protection against such searches than emphasizing their brain-based, physical aspects. This mirrors the possible Fifth Amendment treatment of neuroassays, where construing the substrates detected by neuroassays as evoked mental contents rather than as bodily products (physical samples) results in a higher degree of protection.[83]

In *Katz v. United States*, the Court held that a listening device placed outside a phone booth constituted a "search" even though the device did not intrude into the phone booth. The Court reasoned that "what [a person] seeks to preserve as private, even in an area accessible to the public, may be constitutionally protected," while what he "knowingly exposes to the public, even in his own home ... is not a subject of Fourth Amendment protection."[84] Thus, "the Fourth Amendment protects people, not places."[85]

Yet, place matters: in his concurrence, Justice Harlan noted that determining the degree of protection the Fourth Amendment affords to people "requires reference to a 'place.'"[86] This is because the rule requires not only that a person have kept the materials in question actually private but that society recognize his expectation of privacy as "reasonable."[87] Society's conventions about whether an expectation of privacy is reasonable have much to do with place; "thus a man's home is, for most purposes, a place where he expects privacy."[88]

The Court strengthened the union between private information and private space in *Kyllo v. United States*. In *Kyllo*, the Court held that the state of California violated Danny Lee Kyllo's Fourth Amendment rights when, without a warrant, it used a fairly crude thermal imaging technology to discern heat patterns emanating from Kyllo's home. The thermal detection system did not reveal specific, private activities; rather, it produced thermal readings, which the system converted into pictures of relative heat, from which investigators could make inferences about activities within the home.[89] The heat images, the United States argued, did not constitute information in which Kyllo had any reasonable expectation of privacy because they revealed no intimate details and because the information was so indistinct that it had meaning only based on later inferences by investigators. The Court rejected both contentions. Emphasizing the special expectations of privacy around the home, it asserted that "in the home, ... *all* details are intimate details, because the entire area is held safe from prying government eyes."[90] Indeed, "the interior of [the] home[] [is] the prototypical ... area of protected privacy."[91]

The Court then rejected the contention that thermal imaging did not constitute a search because the patterns and blobs that were its output took on meaning only through investigators' inferences. Criticizing "the dissent's extraordinary assertion that anything learned through 'an inference' cannot be a search," the majority noted that technological searches frequently produce data that need analysis, "*i.e.*, the making of inferences."[92] Moreover, because the expectation of privacy in the home is so high, "the Fourth Amendment's protection of the home has never been tied to measurement of the quality or quantity of information obtained."[93]

Kyllo and *Katz* together suggest the ongoing power of place, of a spatial seclusion interest, in informing the expectations of privacy that a society recognizes as reasonable. The spatial analogy applies powerfully to neuroassays that invade the ultimate private space of mind. fMRI, which peers directly into the private space of the brain, and EEG, which detects its emanations, are much like the listening and thermal imaging technologies at issue in *Katz* and *Kyllo* that detected without invasion the content subjects secluded in private spaces. The idea of the mind *as* a house has deep roots in Western thought and literature. This powerful metaphor recurs through religious and philosophical writings, as when Saint Augustine refers to his memory as a "great harbour";[94] through poetry, as when Joseph Beaumont and Emily Dickinson speak of the "house of the mind"[95] and its "corridors";[96] through to popular culture, as when Sherlock Holmes says in *The Hound of the Baskervilles* that to solve the crime he must retreat to his "mind palace."[97]

Kyllo's thermal imaging of heat from the home makes an excellent analogy with EEG detection of brain waves that emanate from the mind. Electrical brain waves, like thermal signatures from an occupied home, are automatically and continuously produced as long as a person is alive and a home is not abandoned. Yet we maintain an expectation of privacy in both of these forms of physical information, in part because they are invisible and undetectable absent special technology. Such technologies may produce only thermal patterns or, in the case of EEG, jagged lines, but the need for decoding does not make the raw information itself unprotected by the Fourth Amendment.[98] Nor is it of significance for constitutional purposes if the information obtained reveals little of "intimate" interest.[99] *Kyllo* thus may suggest that people have a reasonable expectation of privacy in the information that they automatically generate, and that may be covertly detectable, but that they do not broadcast or otherwise expose to the public gaze.[100]

A distinct way of conceptualizing the neural products evoked and detected by neuroassay as informational products for Fourth Amendment purposes is to construe them as "authored works." Leveraging the frameworks of intellectual property law, Professor Nita Farahany applies the concept of a secrecy right in authored works to the search and collection of brain waves and neural response patterns.[101] She notes that while courts have relied on the common law property interest of seclusion to determine whether a Fourth Amendment interest has been violated during a search,[102] they often also have implicitly relied on the interest of secrecy drawn from intellectual property law.[103] A standard that explicitly uses this intellectual property secrecy interest in conjunction with the traditional Fourth Amendment seclusion interest would provide a clearer basis for the existing heightened protection of novel information and would extend logically to protect authored mental phenomena.[104]

iii. Mass Brain Searches: What Is the Privacy of Crowds?

Beyond the traditional Fourth Amendment domains of search and seizure, neuroassays may be useful as a substitute for more traditional methods of questioning witnesses. It also may enable mass searches of groups and crowds. Returning to *Schmerber*, consider the information that investigators could obtain about whether Schmerber was drunk from Schmerber's friend and from all the people who happened to be in the same bar as Schmerber on the night in question. Police could subject all of them to a session in the CIT helmet to assay whether their brains recorded relevant information. Would Schmerber's friend and all the bystanders have any Fourth Amendment grounds on which to resist an on-the-spot brain scan? As with the issues considered previously, this potential use of neuroassays sits at the intersection of verbal questioning and compelled physical samples. It also sits at the procedural intersection of investigations that may be conducted by grand jury subpoena and those that must be conducted pursuant to a warrant or a recognized warrant exception, like exigent circumstances.

The example of Schmberer's friend helps isolate the issue of subpoena versus warrant in the context of neuroassaying nonsuspects. Suppose that police seek to question Schmerber's friend about the events preceding Schmerber's arrest for drunk driving, and suppose further that the friend, having had no legal duty to prevent Schmerber from driving drunk, has no Fifth Amendment privilege relative to these questions. In a world without neuroassays, the friend can decline to speak with investigators. If he were to decline, investigators could seek a grand jury subpoena or its equivalent pursuant to which he would be compelled to appear and answer questions – although he could appear and claim he had no recollection, which would end the matter.[105]

Matters change once neuroassays are introduced. A prosecutor could seek a grand jury subpoena to compel him to undergo neuroassays that may reveal the events of that night. If a subpoena were to issue, could Schmerber's friend move to quash by claiming that the neuroassay constitutes an unreasonable search under the Fourth Amendment? Or could the state search the friend's brain on the basis of the much slighter showing that supports a subpoena than that which supports a warrant?

To the extent that neuroassays are construed as bodily intrusions, the field is particularly undeveloped. No Supreme Court case has addressed the compulsion of physical samples from nonsuspects; indeed, a state rarely has cause to compel a physical sample from a nonsuspect. Neuroassays, however, present a case where the physical traces stored in one person's body may powerfully incriminate another person. Schmerber's friend's blood could not have proven whether Schmerber was intoxicated. But Schmerber's friend's memories could show whether he saw Schmerber drinking or whether he believed Schmerber was drunk as he drove away in his car.

Courts have split on the degree of intrusion into the subject's body, privacy expectations, and dignitary interests that renders a subpoena inadequate to compel the intrusion. In one case, *In re Grand Jury Proceedings Involving Vickers*, the respondents to a grand jury subpoena challenged the subpoena's request for saliva samples, arguing that such a search and seizure required a warrant.[106] The court declined to quash the subpoena, reasoning that a cheek swab does not go "beneath the skin"[107] and involves "no risk of physical pain, injury, or embarrassment."[108] It held that the state may compel such a physical sample by subpoena as long as it is "relevant" to an investigation and "could be probative" in furthering the investigation, a fairly minimal standard.[109] Conversely, in another saliva-by-subpoena case, *United States v. Nicolosi*, the court quashed a prosecutor's (non-grand jury) subpoena, holding that the Fourth Amendment requires a warrant or probable cause plus exigent circumstances before the state may compel such an intrusion.[110] *Nicolosi* describes a saliva sample as "a search within the skin, if not literally beneath it" and emphasized the private medical information that the state could discern from the sample.[111]

The single case to consider the issue as to blood samples held that a grand jury subpoena does not suffice to compel the physical sample. In *In re Grand Jury Proceedings (T.S.)*, a subpoena respondent moved to quash a grand jury subpoena compelling his blood sample. Considering "whether a grand jury subpoena, rather than a warrant," can be used to obtain a blood samples, the court considered the intrusion under the skin and the privacy interests one has in the medical information that can be obtained from blood; separately, it emphasized the inadequacy of the subpoena process in light of the warrant requirements for blood samples set forth in *Schmerber*.[112] T.S. quashed the subpoena and concluded that "the warrantless search and seizure" of a blood sample "should be subject to the same standards as any warrantless search," which are "'probable cause ... and exigent circumstances justifying the search.'"[113] The court instructed that a warrant should only issue if the state's need for the evidence "is greater than the extent to which the blood test poses a risk of harm to T.S. and infringes his dignitary interests in privacy."[114]

Neuroassays do not require an invasion beneath the skin in the sense of puncturing or cutting and pose no risk of physical harm to the subject. Thus a court might follow the reasoning of *Vickers* to hold that the state can, without a warrant, compel an individual to undergo a neuroassay. Alternatively, a court might conclude that neuroassays are "a search *within* the skin, if not literally beneath it,"[115] implicating the individual's privacy interests and requiring the Fourth Amendment balancing of reasonable expectations of privacy against the state's need for the information.

No case yet has dealt with mass physical intrusions into bystanders or their mass detention for compelled questioning, as would be the case if police sought to put the CIT helmet on everyone in Schmerber's bar. Ordinarily, mere bystanders' expectations of privacy and security in their person against state intrusion would be quite high. Police do question bystanders for relevant information, but while there is no legal right to lie about a crime, there is also no affirmative duty to speak up. By custom if not by law, there may be a higher expectation within society that mere bystanders will be free of unanticipated neural intrusion by the state than there is relative to suspects or key witnesses.

Yet, the high expectation of privacy might be defeated by the potentially low intrusiveness of the search and, under some circumstances, exigent need for the information. The degree of intrusion would be low if the neuroassay could do the barest of scans: a binary yes–no test as to whether the subject saw Schmerber that night. Such a test would be brief and would not intrude on the private reflections or feelings of the subject. Perhaps the helmet either would not collect ancillary mental information or could automatically shield certain information from the operator. Further tilting the balance in favor of mass, on-the-spot brain searches, the state might plead, as with Schmerber's blood, exigent circumstances: the memories might not decay rapidly like alcohol in the bloodstream, but the bystanders themselves might disperse, never to be seen again. These hypotheticals are merely speculative but point to the need to develop reasoned Fourth Amendment positions relative to nontraditional subjects of a nontraditional kind of search.

Collateral information gleaned via neuroassay might heighten the privacy interest of Schmerber's friend and the people in Schmerber's bar, further arguing for the protection of the warrant process. A subject's neuroassay might incidentally show that he suffers from a medical or psychiatric condition, or is likely to develop one, or has some markers of negative personality traits like psychopathy. The investigating authority could store such information and use it in future investigations or fail to keep it sufficiently private. Such sensitive information implicates strong privacy interests, as it could lead to adverse social, financial, and employment consequences. Judicial balancing would need to take place to ensure that the state's need for the information outweighs the witness's – and society's – interest in the mental and neurological privacy of the common citizen.

4. CONCLUSION

The house of thought and memory has no doors yet may be more searchable than a dwelling. The mind has no mouth but can be made to speak against us. This is because U.S. constitutional law has yet to grapple with the informational content of what we keep private within our bodies. Instead, it has emphasized the grosser aspects of bodily intrusions, limiting the state's right to collect information from our bodies largely on the basis of risks of physical pain and injury from those intrusions.

Law enforcement's use of neuroassays will require reexamining the relationship among physical, informational, and spatial intrusions. Going forward, the Court may choose to develop jurisprudence around neuroassay and other sophisticated forms of informational monitoring that draw less on cases like *Schmerber* and *Winston*, which emphasize risk and pain, and more on cases like *Muniz*, which emphasizes the protection of mental contents. Perhaps even more instructive is the *Katz* and *Kyllo* line of cases dealing with intrusions into spaces that carry an expectation of privacy. These cases conclude that using high technology to detect emanations from a private space is equivalent to searching within it. This conclusion as to houses and phone booths maps exactly onto the case of neuroassays, where high technologies detect the emanations and internal processes of an otherwise completely secluded space. This relationship between private structures and private bodily spaces goes beyond analogy: property in one's body fundamentally anchors rights in real property in Anglo-American political history.[116]

Neuroassays will force courts to think more deeply, too, about ordinary predetermined biological information versus information that the state's search itself brings into being. The DNA in one's cells or the alcohol content of a person's blood exists independently of the tests that measure it. When the state samples these, it finds preexisting facts just as when it finds traditional physical evidence in a person's cabinets or drawers. Such preexisting and independent facts are due Fourth Amendment protection depending upon the invasiveness of the search and society's expectation of privacy in the body and in the information that the bodily samples encode. When such a search finds independent, preexisting biological facts about the brain, like its size, structure, or regional rates of glucose metabolism, these may be due a similar or higher degree of protection as these features may reveal even more sensitive information than a person's genetic code.

But when a search goes beyond finding facts about the brain and detects information encoded within the brain – even information as binary and bare as whether a mental room is empty or contains a package – the matter changes: that search treads into the private details held within an archetypal space of seclusion. As invasive as such a search would be, neuroassays go further than merely detecting information encoded in the brain: they incite the brain to assemble new information in response to questionlike prompts. These evoked responses are like testimony, or like a compilation document that the state causes the subject to create from his or her preexisting data. The brain creates its responses to these prompts preconsciously. But in circumventing not just the subject's volition but the subject's very *capacity* for volition, these tests impose the truest possible compulsion, as if words could be pulled like a rope from a subject's throat or the hand automated to write its confession. This is the ultimate aim of every Star Chamber: To compel reliable self-accusation. That these brain-based techniques are bloodless and painless should be a matter of indifference, unless the great and deep proscription against these reviled practices reduces to no more than squeamishness about blood. Precisely because they are both bloodless and effective, neuroassays will challenge the meaning of core constitutional protections – as well as our fidelity to them.

Notes

1. Celia Gorman, *The Mind-Reading Machine*, IEEE SPECTRUM (July 2012), http://spectrum.ieee.org/biomedical/diagnostics/the-mindreading-machine (quoting CEO of Veritas Scientific Corporation describing his company's mind-reading helmet) (last visited Apr. 28, 2013).
2. Numerous scholars have written on the potential implications of neuroscience on various branches of law and on basic legal concepts. See, e.g., Joshua Greene & Jonathan Cohen, *For the Law, Neuroscience Changes Nothing and Everything*, 359 PHIL. TRANSACTIONS ROYAL SOC'Y BIOLOGICAL SCI. 1775 (2004); Robert M. Sapolsky, *The Frontal Cortex and the Criminal Justice System*, 359 PHIL. TRANSACTIONS ROYAL SOC'Y BIOLOGICAL SCI. 1787 (2004); Henry T. Greely, *Prediction, Litigation, Privacy and Property: Some Possible Legal and Social Implications of Advances in Neuroscience*, in NEUROSCIENCE AND THE LAW: BRAIN, MIND, AND THE SCALES OF JUSTICE 114 (Brent Garland, ed., 2004). But see Stephen J. Morse, *Neuroscience and the Future of Personhood and Responsibility*, in CONSTITUTION 3.0: FREEDOM AND TECHNOLOGICAL CHANGE 113 (Jeffrey Rosen & Benjamin Wittes, eds., 2011) (arguing traditional legal conceptions of personhood and responsibility will not fundamentally be changed by any developments in neuroscience).
3. See generally MICHAEL GAZZANIGA, RICHARD B. IVRY & GEORGE R. MANGUN, COGNITIVE NEUROSCIENCE: THE BIOLOGY OF THE MIND (3d ed., 2008).
4. O. Carter Snead, *Neuroimaging and the "Complexity" of Capital Punishment*, 82 N.Y.U. L. REV. 1265, 1280–90 (2007).
5. *Id.*
6. Rather than measuring or imaging activity within the brain, TMS uses electromagnets to temporarily and selectively disable targeted brain regions. Researchers then can make inferences about the function of the temporarily disabled region by seeing how subjects are affected by the stimulation. See, e.g., Tracy Hampton, *Magnetism on the Brain: Researchers Probe Transcranial Magnetic Stimulation*, 293 JAMA 1713 (2005).
7. I use the term "neuroassay" to encompass technologies that assay the brain for its information content and to distinguish such technologies from the many other neurotechnologies that provide different kinds of information about the brain. For example, CT scans and MRIs provide information about a brain (its size, shape, and physical integrity) but do not reveal anything about the information content encoded within that brain.
8. Gershon Ben-Shakhar & Eitan Elaad, *The Guilty Knowledge Test (GKT) as an Application of Psychophysiology: Future Prospects and Obstacles*, in HANDBOOK OF POLYGRAPH TESTING 87 (Murray Klein, ed., 2002).
9. See Samuel Sutton et al., *Information Delivery and the Sensory Evoked Potential*, 155 SCIENCE 1436 (1967) (a foundational article describing the P300 response). For an overview, see MEMORY DETECTION: THEORY AND APPLICATION OF THE CONCEALED INFORMATION TEST (Bruno Verschuere et al., eds., 2011).
10. Editorial, *Forensic Neuroscience on Trial*, 4 NATURE NEUROSCIENCE 1 (2001).
11. J. Peter Rosenfeld, *Event-Related Potentials in the Detection of Deception, Malingering, and False Memories*, in HANDBOOK OF POLYGRAPH TESTING, supra note 8 at 265.

12 Vahid Abootalebi, Mohammed Hassan Moradi & Mohammad Ali Khalizadeh, *A Comparison of Methods for ERP Assessment in a P300-based GKT*, 62 INT'L J. PSYCHOPHYSIOLOGY 309 (2006); David Carmel et al., *Estimating the Validity of the Guilty Knowledge Test from Simulated Experiments: The External Validity of Mock Crime Studies*, 9 J. EXPERIMENTAL PSYCHOL.: APPLIED 261 (2003).

13 See Xiaoqing Hu & J. Peter Rosenfeld, *Combining the P300-complex Trial-Based Concealed Information Test and the Reaction Time-Based Autobiographical Implicit Association Test in Concealed Memory Detection*, 49 PSYCHOPHYSIOLOGY 1090 (2012).

14 Galit Nahari & Gershon Ben-Shakhar, *Psychophysiological and Behavioral Measures for Detecting Concealed Information: The Role of Memory for Crime Details*, 48 PSYCHOPHYSIOLOGY 733 (2011) (showing "informed innocents," aware of the same crime details as "guilty" subjects but for different reasons, showed P300 responses equivalent to "guilty" participants in a mock-crime study).

15 For an excellent overview of fMRI-based lie detection technologies, and their protocols and limits, see Francis X. Shen & Owen D. Jones, *Brain Scans as Evidence: Truths, Proofs, Lies, and Lessons*, 62 MERCER L. REV. 861 (2011).

16 D. D. Langleben et al., *Brain Activity During Simulated Deception: An Event-Related Functional Magnetic Resonance Study*, 15 NEUROIMAGE 727, 731 (2002) ("We speculate that this increase in activation reflects additional effort needed to 'overcome' the inhibited true response.").

17 Id.; see also, e.g., Sean A. Spence et al., *A Cognitive Neurobiological Account of Deception: Evidence from Functional Neuroimaging*, 359 PHIL. TRANSACTIONS ROYAL SOC'Y BIOLOGICAL SCI. 1755, 1757 (2004) ("[W]e may posit that in the normal situation the liar is called upon to do at least two things simultaneously. He must construct a new item of information (the lie) while also withholding a factual item (the truth) ….").

18 Spence et al., supra note 17.

19 See, e.g., Martin R. Sheridan et al., *Reaction Times and Deception – the Lying Constant*, 2 INT'L J. PSYCHOL. STUD. 41, 46 (2010) (asserting "lying adds a constant delay to true responses, and can be reliably distinguished from true responses in terms of average RT [response time]").

20 See F. Andrew Kozel et al., *Detecting Deception Using Functional Magnetic Resonance Imaging*, 58 BIOLOGICAL PSYCHIATRY 605, 608 (2005); Tatia M. C. Lee, *Lie Detection by Functional Magnetic Resonance Imaging*, 15 HUM. BRAIN MAPPING 157, 161 (2002).

21 Greg Miller, *fMRI Lie Detection Fails a Legal Test*, 328 Science 1336, 1337 (2010) ("[Martha] Farah, like many neuroscientists, is deeply skeptical about using fMRI lie detection in legal cases, and she says she went into the hearing thinking there was no chance the judge would allow it as evidence.").

22 *United States v. Semrau*, No. 07–10074 MI/P, 2010 WL 6845092 (W.D. TN June 1, 2010) (amended report and recommendation) (holding fMRI lie detection evidence inadmissible under the *Daubert* test).

23 Kevin A. Johnson et al., *The Neuroscience of Functional Magnetic Resonance Imaging fMRI for Deception Detection*, 7 AM. J. BIOETHICS 58, 60 (2007).

24 Id. at 59.

25 See supra note 7 and accompanying text.

26 This brain region is involved in decision-making, self-control, emotional intelligence, risk-seeking, and a host of other important behaviors. See, e.g., THE HUMAN FRONTAL LOBES: FUNCTIONS AND DISORDERS 355 (Bruce L. Miller & Jeffrey L. Cummings, eds., 2007).

27 Inga Karton & Talis Bachmann, *Effect of Prefrontal Transcranial Magnetic Stimulation on Spontaneous Truth-Telling*, 225 BEHAV. BRAIN RES. 209 (2011).

28 The effect size was small but statistically significant. rDLPFC stimulation and lDLPFC stimulation increased truth-telling and false reporting, respectively, by about five percent relative to controls. *Id.* at 209.

29 Eric R. Kandel et al., *The Past, the Future, and the Biology of Memory Storage*, 354 PHIL. TRANSACTIONS ROYAL SOC'Y BIOLOGICAL SCI. 2027, 2031–32 (1999) (describing involvement of numerous brain regions in reconstructing and experiencing a single memory and describing cases that defeated the earlier view that memory is localized to one brain region).

30 *Id.*

31 Michael S. Pardo argues for this position in *Neuroscience Evidence, Legal Culture, and Criminal Procedure*, 33 AM. J. CRIM. L. 301 (2006).

32 U.S. CONST. amend. V ("No person ... shall be compelled in any criminal case to be a witness against himself").

33 *Andresen v. Maryland*, 427 U.S. 463 (1976) (quoting *Michigan v. Tucker*, 417 U.S. 433, 440 (1974)); see also *Couch v. United States*, 409 U.S. 322, 327 (1974) (describing Fifth Amendment as the bulwark against "any 'recurrence of the Inquisition and the Star Chamber, even if not in their stark brutality'") (quoting *Ullmann v. United States*, 350 U.S. 422, 428 (1956)).

34 William J. Stuntz, *Self-Incrimination and Excuse*, 88 COLUM. L. REV. 1277, 1277 (1988); see also Nita A. Farahany, *Incriminating Thoughts*, 64 STAN. L. REV. 351, 364–66 (2012) (discussing excuse model).

35 *Murphy v. Waterfront Comm'n*, 378 U.S. 52, 55 (1964). The *Murphy* Court also spoke of "our respect for the inviolability of the human personality ...." ID. (internal quotations and citations omitted). The "human personality" view of the Fifth Amendment has, however, fallen out of favor academically and with the Court. See, e.g., *United States v. Balsys*, 524 U.S. 666, 691 (1998).

36 *Pennsylvania v. Muniz*, 496 U.S. 582, 595 (1990).

37 *Id.* (quoting *Doe v. United States*, 487 U.S. 201, 213 (1988)).

38 *Id.* (quoting *Curcio v. United States*, 354 US 118, 128 (1957) (emphasis added)).

39 *Schmerber v. California*, 384 U.S. 757, 761 (1966).

40 Brief for Petitioner, *Schmerber v. California*, 384 U.S. 757 (1966), 1966 WL 100527 at *3-*4.

41 *Schmerber*, 384 U.S. at 761.

42 *Id.*

43 *Murphy v. Waterfront Comm'n*, 378 U.S. 52, 55 (1964).

44 See Part 3.b (explaining the State's right to physical evidence is limited by the Fourth Amendment).

45 Farahany, supra note 34, at 355. Several scholars have explored the relationship between neurotechnologies and the Fifth Amendment, splitting along *Schmerber*'s lines to conclude that such evidence would be "physical and unprivileged or testimonial and privileged." See *id.* at 355 n. 11 (gathering articles).

46   496 U.S. 582.
47   *Id.* at 585–6.
48   *Id.* at 587.
49   The police failed to advise Muniz of his right to remain silent. *Id.* at 585–86.
50   See *id.* at 590–600.
51   See *id.* at 592–600.
52   See *id.* at 613 (Marshall, J., concurring in part and dissenting in part).
53   *Evoke*, in MERRIAM-WEBSTER'S COLLEGIATE DICTIONARY (11th ed., 2008).
54   *Id.*
55   This set of categories is but one potential replacement for SCHMERBER's physical/verbal dichotomy. Professor Nita Farahany has proposed as an alternative a "spectrum that spans identifying, automatic, memorialized, and uttered evidence," which emphasizes the critical distinctions between evoked and unevoked information. See Farahany, supra note 34, at 400.
56   Physical characteristics that are merely identifying, like voice, handwriting, evidence of injuries, tattoos and the like are not protected under the Fifth Amendment. See *United States v. Dionisio*, 410 U.S. 1, 7 (1973) (holding suspects could be compelled to provide voice samples "solely to measure the physical properties of [the speakers'] voices, not for [their] ... communicative content"); *Gilbert v. California*, 388 U.S. 263, 266–7 (1967) (holding suspect could be compelled to provide handwriting sample for identification purposes only).
57   See supra notes 39–40, 54 and accompanying text.
58   *Pennsylvania v. Muniz*, 496 U.S. 582, 595 (1990) (stating the Fifth Amendment protects a person from being forced to disclose the "'contents of his own mind'") (quoting *Curcio v. United States*, 354 U.S. 118, 128 (1957)).
59   *Id.* at 591–2 (discussing the protection of "knowledge").
60   See supra notes 34–5, 39–40, 54 and accompanying text.
61   U.S. CONST. amend. IV.
62   *Winston v. Lee*, 470 U.S. 753, 759 (1985).
63   *Id.* at 759.
64   *Katz v. United States*, 389 U.S. 347, 361 (1967) (Harlan, J., concurring).
65   Discussed infra notes 79–80. Searches of the body additionally could be construed as trespasses in light of the Court's renewed emphasis on physical trespass in *United States v. Jones*, 132 S. Ct. 945 (2012). The Court has not looked to trespass in its canonical bodily search cases but perhaps may do so in future cases if *Jones* prefigures a general turn toward trespass as the touchstone for Fourth Amendment jurisprudence. Trespass has some superficial appeal in bodily search cases but would create paradoxes in the context of neuroassays and other technological searches that detect internal information. A trespass standard would provide more protection for a cheek swab than for some kinds of brain scans. It would lead to significant differences in Fourth Amendment protection among functionally indistinguishable forms of brain scans based on slight differences in their underlying technologies.
66   *Katz*, 389 U.S. at 361 (Harlan, J., concurring).
67   *Schmerber v. California*, 384 U.S. 757, 770 (1966) ("Search warrants are ordinarily required for searches of dwellings, and absent an emergency, no less could be required where intrusions into the human body are concerned."); see also

Hammer v. Gross, 884 F.2d 1200, 1204–05 (9th Cir. 1989), *vacated on other grounds*, 932 F.2d 842 (9th Cir. 1992); *United States v. Berry*, 866 F.2d 887 (6th Cir. 1989).
68 *Schmerber*, 384 U.S. at 772.
69 See supra note 40 and accompanying text.
70 *Schmerber*, 384 U.S. at 772.
71 *Id.* at 769–70.
72 *Id.* at 770–71.
73 *Id.* at 772 (emphasis added).
74 470 U.S. 753.
75 *Lee v. Winston*, 717 F.2d 888 (4th Cir. 1983).
76 *Winston*, 470 U.S. at 758.
77 *Id.* at 759.
78 *Id.* at 760.
79 EEG and fMRI carry no risk of harm in themselves. A subject conceivably could suffer from claustrophobia or other discomfort while being examined in an MRI machine or CIT helmet.
80 See Part 3.b.iii, principally discussing *United States v. Nicolosi*, 885 F. Supp. 50 (E.D. N.Y. 1995) (holding a warrant to be required to compel defendants to produce saliva sample; prosecutor's non-grand jury subpoena invalidated as insufficient) and In re *Grand Jury Proceedings Involving Vickers*, 38 F. Supp. 2d 159 (D. N.H. 1998) (holding grand jury subpoena sufficient to compel production of saliva).
81 389 U.S. 347.
82 533 U.S. 27.
83 SEE Part 3.a.
84 *Katz v. United States*, 389 U.S. 347, 351 (1967) (citations omitted).
85 *Id.*
86 *Id.* at 361 (Harlan, J., concurring).
87 *Id.*
88 *Id.*
89 *Kyllo v. United States*, 533 U.S. 27, 34–41 (2001).
90 *Id.* at 37.
91 *Id.* at 34.
92 *Id.* at 36 ("[W]here the police 'inferred' from the activation of a beeper that a certain can of ether was in the home.") (citing *United States v. Karo*, 468 U.S. 705 (1984)).
93 *Id.* at 37.
94 AURELIUS AUGUSTINUS, THE CONFESSIONS OF ST. AUGUSTINE 174 (Edward B. Pusey trans., 1909).
95 Joseph Beaumont, *The House of the Mind*, in LYRA SACRA: A BOOK OF RELIGIOUS VERSE 174 (H. C. Beeching, ed., 1895).
96 Emily Dickinson, *One Need Not Be a Chamber to Be Haunted*, in THE COMPLETE POEMS OF EMILY DICKINSON (1924).
97 "The Hounds of Baskerville," *Sherlock*, dir. Paul McGuigan, perf. Benedict Cumberbatch, Martin Freeman, Rupert Graves (BBC television broadcast 2012) (based on A CONAN DOYLE, THE HOUND OF THE BASKERVILLES (1902)).

98   See *Kyllo*, 533 U.S. at 36 (rejecting the argument that a search that obtains only raw information from which investigators must make inferences is not subject to the Fourth Amendment).
99   *Id.* at 37 (stating that, relative to searches of the home, "*all* details are intimate details, because the entire area is held safe from prying government eyes").
100 *Id.* at 34–41.
101 Nita A. Farahany, *Searching Secrets*, 160 U. Pa. L. Rev. 1239, 1241 (2012).
102 *Id.* at 1243.
103 An author's discretion to limit the audience and exposure of an original work is part of the secrecy interest protected by copyright law. Id. at 1261, 1293 (citing Richard A. Posner, The Economics of Justice 268–76 (1981)).
104 Farahany, supra note 101, at 1304.
105 "[A] subpoena to appear before a grand jury is not a 'seizure' [of the person] in the Fourth Amendment sense, even though that summons may be inconvenient or burdensome." *United States v. Dionisio*, 410 U.S. 1, 9 (1973) (citations omitted).
106 38 F. Supp. 2d 159.
107 *Id.* at 167.
108 *Id.*
109 *Id.*
110 885 F. Supp. 50 (E.D. N.Y. 1995).
111 *Id.* at 56.
112 *In re* Grand Jury Proceedings (T.S.), 816 F. Supp. 1196, 1205 (W.D. KY 1993).
113 *Id.* at 1200 (quoting United States v. Berry, 866 F.2d 887, 891 (1989)) (citing *Chambers v. Maroney*, 399 U.S. 42, 51 (1970)).
114 *Id.* at 1206.
115 *Nicolosi*, 885 F. Supp. at 56 (emphasis added).
116 The relationship between property in one's own body and all other property rights is put most famously by John Locke in his Two Treatises of Government (1689):
Though the Earth...be common to all Men, yet every Man has a Property in his own Person. This no Body has any Right to but himself. The Labour of his Body, and the Work of his Hands, we may say, are properly his. Whatsoever then he removes out of the State that Nature hath provided, and left it in, he hath mixed his Labour with, and joyned to it something that is his own, and thereby makes it his Property ..., that excludes the common right of other Men. (Book II, ¶ 27.)

Part IV

TECHNOLOGY AND THE SURVEILLANCE SOCIETY

8

Information and Social Control

Wayne A. Logan

Human societies have long desired to render criminal risk more knowable. While this need was initially met by overt means, such as by the physical branding or mutilation of offenders,[1] in time more bureaucratic, information-based technologies came to predominate.[2] Today, consistent with our increasingly data-driven culture[3] and the need of governments to wean themselves from expensive brick and mortar corrections options, information is assuming unparalleled importance in social control.

The shift is perhaps most evident in the handling of probationers and parolees, who constitute the lion's share of individuals under active correctional supervision,[4] with governments making increased use of electronic mentoring technologies.[5] Yet information also plays a lynchpin role with individuals "off-paper" (i.e., not subject to active probation or parole conditions), who have paid their penal debt to society.

Perhaps the most prominent example of the latter application is found in government treatment of the hundreds of thousands of individuals for whom a past conviction triggers ongoing supervision as a result of registration and community notification (RCN) laws, now in effect nationwide. With RCN, individuals are required, under threat of punishment, to provide and update identifying data (e.g., home/work/school addresses, vehicle information, and physical characteristics such as tattoos or facial hair) to government authorities, for a minimum of ten years and often for their lifetimes. The information is then put to two uses. First, it is maintained by police to allow for the monitoring of registrants and to instill in them the sense that they are being watched, in the hope of deterring possible criminal misconduct. Second, it is provided to the public at large (and worldwide, via the Internet), to augment surveillance and provide community members with information to take self-protective measures vis-à-vis registrants.

This chapter uses RCN as a case study to highlight the central role that information now plays in the nation's social control apparatus. After providing a brief overview of RCN's history, the chapter examines its critically important impact on prevailing understandings of privacy and public safety, and its role in paving the way for continued, and perhaps even greater, resort to information-based social control methodologies in the years to come.

1. ORIGINS AND STAYING POWER

The idea of requiring ex-convicts to register with authorities first took root in the United States in the early 1930s, when Los Angeles, California, and surrounding localities, anxious over the nation's increasingly mobile and anonymous population, mandated that individuals convicted of a variety of offenses provide police with information, including conviction history and home address.[6] While registration enjoyed sporadic use in ensuing years,[7] in the 1990s it experienced a massive resurgence in popularity, this time as a result of state (not local) laws focusing mainly on convicted sex offenders (versus offenders more generally).

At the same time, renewed interest in registration was complemented by a new information-based social control strategy: community notification. In 1990, lawmakers in Washington State, responding to public outrage over news of the brutal sexual assault of a young boy by a convicted sex offender who resided in the community with the knowledge of police, yet not community members, agreed to allow registrant information to be made publicly available. While registration afforded police real-time identifying information on registrants, community notification provided such information to members of the public, allowing them to augment the monitoring of registrants and take self-protective measures.

The developments in Washington State prompted legislative activity elsewhere, perhaps most notably in New Jersey, in the wake of the July 1994 rape and murder of seven-year-old Megan Kanka by a convicted sex offender who lived nearby. Again, while local police were aware of the assailant's history, his neighbors reportedly were not. Voicing a sentiment that would come to define RCN laws, Megan's mother, Maureen Kanka, asserted that "if [she and her family] had known there was a pedophile living on our street, [Megan] would be alive today."[8]

Political interest in RCN among the states, meanwhile, did not go unnoticed by the federal government. In 1994, the Jacob Wetterling Act, named after an eleven-year-old Minnesota boy who disappeared five years earlier, was signed into law by President Bill Clinton. The Wetterling Act required registration of persons convicted of specified sexual offenses, pressuring states without registration to enact laws under threat of losing a portion of their general criminal justice funding if they did not. The Wetterling Act authorized but did not require that states utilize community notification, a stance that was to change two years later with the federal Megan's Law, which mandated community notification among the states, again under threat of lost government funds.

In response to federal pressure, by 1998 the few outlier states came into conformity, accounting for the current nationwide network of registries, made publicly available at a minimum on the Internet and possibly disseminated by means of in-person community meetings or distributed handbills.[9] RCN remains enormously popular with the public and politicians alike.[10] That this is so is curious, given the paucity of evidence of its public safety efficacy[11] and, indeed, concern that it might actually promote recidivism, based on its adverse effect on registrants, including vigilantism, social ostracism, and difficulties in securing and retaining employment,[12] stressors known to hinder crime desistance.[13]

2. A RECONFIGURED SOCIAL CONTROL MODEL

RCN, for better or worse, has afforded a new social control model, one consisting of three components. The first involves registrants themselves, who under pain of threatened punishment must provide identifying information to government authorities and confirm the continued accuracy of such information at prescribed intervals, making them complicit in their own surveillance. The second involves society at large. Unlike in the past, when community members were expected to be passive beneficiaries of the government's public safety efforts, today they are expected to be active consumers and users of convict information, itself no longer subject to government monopoly. They do so on the basis of both the assertion that they are morally entitled to it to protect loved ones, and the perceived public safety failure of government, making disclosure a practical necessity.[14]

Finally, with dissemination of registry information and the devolution of public safety responsibility to the public at large, government has been relieved of its historic exclusive public safety responsibility.[15] Registrants, governments, and community members now serve as "coproducers" of public safety,[16] with government serving as an information broker. While probation and parole previously entailed community monitoring of released offenders,[17] RCN radically expanded this role. Just as Americans provide tips on criminal fugitives, in response to the popular television show *America's Most Wanted* (hosted by John Walsh, who himself figured centrally in the modern push for notification), they are now expected to monitor their fellow community members under the aegis of RCN.

From a purely antipaternalist perspective, the development would appear an unalloyed good. Close examination of the policy shift, however, reveals fault lines. Perhaps most significant is the concern that the empowerment ideal of RCN remains just that – an ideal – because community members are often ignorant of registry information (a particular concern among those lacking Internet access) and even when aware fail to engage in self-protective efforts.[18] Moreover, as Professor Jonathan Simon has observed, RCN presumes that a "family has the resources to protect itself by choosing a location in which the streets are safe and a family structure that allows the kind of surveillance that Maureen [Kanka] might have been able to provide Megan had she been alerted to that particular threat."[19] As a result, rather than promoting public safety, the laws, even assuming they contain full and accurate information,[20] possibly instill a dangerous false sense of security among individuals[21] and distract from pursuit of perhaps more effective public safety measures.

At the same time, amid this reconfiguration, governments have been insulated from blame for the negative effects of RCN. They have they been absolved of moral responsibility for registrant recidivism[22] and afforded themselves formal statutory immunity from legal liability for RCN,[23] including with regard to community vigilantism. Such impunity is troubling and at odds with past sentiment voiced by the Supreme Court. In 1958, for instance, in granting a challenge to Alabama's forced disclosure of NAACP membership lists, a unanimous Court wrote:

> It is not sufficient to answer, as the State does here, that whatever repressive effect compulsory disclosures of names of petitioner's members may have on participation by Alabama citizens in petitioner's activities follows not from state action but from private [action]. The crucial factor is the interplay of government and private action, for it is only after the initial exertion of state power represented by the production order that private action takes hold.[24]

Similarly, in 1982, in invalidating an Ohio law requiring disclosure of contributors to the Socialist Workers' Party, the Supreme Court noted that there need only be a "reasonable possibility" that the compelled disclosure would subject individuals to "threats, harassment, or reprisals from either Government officials or private parties."[25]

While the foregoing cases arose in instances in which First Amendment–protected rights (such as freedom of association) were threatened, disregard for government responsibility remains problematic. Even if, as the Court has held, government has no generalized legal duty to protect individuals from harm by third parties,[26] RCN entails what Professor James Whitman has aptly called an "ugly and politically dangerous complicity between the state and the crowd."[27] "Once the state stirs up public opprobrium against an offender it cannot really control the way the public treats that offender"; dissemination of such information marks a "dangerous willingness, on the part of government, to delegate part of its enforcement power to a fickle and uncontrolled general populace."[28]

3. INFORMATIONAL PRIVACY

RCN has also recast accepted understandings of informational privacy. While from the 1930s through the 1980s the privacy debate centered on whether police alone should have access to identifying information on registrants, RCN blew apart the paradigm. Today, the public feels entitled to and demands free access to individuals' criminal history information, along with where registrants live and work and the cars they drive.[29]

On first impression, the disclosure of public information would appear to present no privacy issue whatsoever. Indeed, when the dissemination of truthful information is at issue, disclosure proponents assert, the benefits of transparency readily trump individual interest.[30] Any value in nondisclosure, as Professor Diane Zimmerman has asserted with regard to disclosure more generally, is outweighed by society's "powerful countervailing interest in exchanges of accurate information about the private lives and characters of its citizenry."[31]

From a law and economics perspective, the dissemination of ex-offender information is socially efficient: it permits individuals to make informed decisions about one another, lessening the likelihood of interpersonal evasion and misperception, which can be tantamount to fraud.[32] For example, an employer who wishes to avoid hiring an ex-offender can, with accurate criminal history information in hand, make an informed hiring decision.[33] By analogy, with accurate information on a registrant, a neighbor is empowered to take protective measures. Without such information, the thinking goes, targeted self-protection cannot occur and communities risk the socially undesirable chilling effect associated with not knowing who is a registrant. Under this view, "the problem [with dissemination practices] is not that they reveal too much, but that they reveal too little."[34]

The "more is better" argument, however defensible in principle, is problematic in this context. As Professor Daniel Solove has recognized, a central problem stems from the underlying premise that "more disclosure will generally yield more truth" and that more information ensures "more accurate judgments about others."[35] "The 'truth' about a person is much more difficult to ascertain than the truth about a product or thing. People are far more complex than products."[36] Put another way, as Professor Jeffery Rosen has written, the free market mentality risks "mistaking information for knowledge."[37]

Ultimately, the informational empowerment premise of RCN is thus more complicated than might first appear. Even if it were possible to achieve full informational awareness about an individual with an offending history, several reasons suggest that associated social detriments can outweigh the benefits.

First, RCN reflects and promotes the view that a criminal conviction should serve as a perpetual badge of dishonor. Because it is typically retroactive in its coverage, often dating back many years, RCN forces continued scrutiny and public exposure of individuals whose convictions date well into their past, even when they have long since rejoined the ranks of law-abiding society.[38] The outcome has troubling implications for a society that continues to imprison unprecedented numbers of individuals and must eventually reintegrate them. As the California Supreme Court once noted with respect to an ex-offender whose aged conviction was made public by a magazine article, "Ideally, his neighbors should recognize his present worth and forget his past life of shame. But men are not so divine as to forgive the past trespasses of others."[39] RCN creates conditions that ensure continued disdain for ex-offenders, undermining the possibility that this "divine" forgiveness will be achieved.

At the same time, the retroactive reach of registration undercuts the rational choice premise of law and economics theoreticians, noted earlier. Just as having information on a recently convicted person not likely to reoffend does not promote efficient social choices, for instance, by inspiring unwarranted protective measures, providing information on those with aged convictions and years of law-abiding behavior is inefficient. The predictive value of prior convictions, including aged ones, for future crime has always been accepted as an article of faith. Research has shown, however, that recidivism risk declines quickly over time, such that after seven years the risk of new offense among ex-offenders resembles risk of offense commission among nonoffenders.[40]

4. WHITHER (OR WITHER) THE JUDICIARY?

Despite the foregoing, the judiciary has remained largely unconcerned. Whereas in the past it was not unheard-of for courts to have difficulty with registration alone,[41] starting in the 1990s such concern evaporated. Courts had no difficulty turning back constitutional challenges against new era registration laws of more onerous nature, combined with community notification – with its far more intrusive personal consequences for registrants. State and federal courts alike regularly rejected claims sounding in equal protection, substantive and procedural due process, ex post facto, and double jeopardy.[42] They also rejected habeas corpus claims, based on the finding that registrants were not in "custody," despite the manifest burdens and negative effects of RCN.[43]

In 2003, the U.S. Supreme Court weighed in with a pair of important decisions of its own. In *Smith v. Doe*,[44] the Court held that Alaska's RCN law was regulatory in nature and hence did not qualify as punishment sufficient to implicate the Ex Post Facto Clause of the U.S. Constitution. In so doing, the Court implicitly foreclosed other claims based on bill of attainder, double jeopardy, and cruel and unusual punishment, each of which requires that a punishment be involved.[45] On the same day, the Court handed down *Connecticut Department of Public Safety v. Doe* (*CDPS*),[46] rejecting a procedural due process challenge against Connecticut's RCN law, allowing individuals to be subject to RCN solely on the basis of a prior conviction (as opposed to individualized risk assessment, the policy in several states at the time).

The two decisions are significant for more than their direct precedential effect. In tone and content they signalled the Court's distinct disinclination to engage in critical evaluation of the intent behind and effects of RCN. The *Smith* Court, for instance, in rejecting petitioners' claim that RCN constituted impermissible retroactively imposed punishment, blithely accepted the Alaska Legislature's avowed regulatory (nonpunitive) purpose – "protecting the public" by imposing restrictive measures on sex offenders – which Justice Souter fairly referred to as "naïve."[47] With respect to RCN's effects, the Court evinced a marked obliviousness to broader shifts in penology, in which information, not brick-and-mortar containment, plays a lynchpin role.

In assessing whether RCN imposed an "affirmative disability or restraint," the Court downplayed the fact that RCN both saddles individuals with ongoing reporting requirements and subjects them to constant monitoring and hardships such as loss of housing and employment. Adversities suffered by registrants were but a "collateral consequence of a valid regulation" and, despite having a "lasting and painful impact," merely flowed from dissemination of "accurate, nonprivate information" about registrants.[48] To the *Smith* Court, Alaska's online registry was like a "visit to an official archive of criminal records," simply made "more efficient, cost effective, and convenient for Alaska's citizenry."[49]

CDPS is significant for both what it did and what it did not resolve. The Court resolved a lingering question over whether governments can subject individuals to RCN solely on the basis of a prior conviction, without an individualized risk determination – holding that they can do so.[50] In so deciding, however, the Court failed to reach a key question raised by petitioners: whether RCN affects a liberty interest, based on privacy, sufficient to require procedural due process protection. Courts refusing to find a liberty interest have done so by rejecting arguments that registration and notification (1) violate registrants' right to privacy and/or (2) violate the "stigma-plus" test.

Courts rejecting the privacy-related claim conclude that publicly disseminating identifying information on registrants is permissible because the information – name, conviction records, addresses, and the like – is already public (i.e., nonsecret) as a technical matter. As the Ninth Circuit Court of Appeals concluded in one case, the information is "already fully available to the public and is not constitutionally protected."[51] Adopting a similar view, shared by other courts, a federal district court in Michigan summarily found no privacy right implicated by the "compilation and dissemination of truthful information that is already, albeit less conveniently, a matter of public record."[52] Magnifying the scope of information availability, courts have also held, does not change the constitutional analysis.[53]

Such a view, however, is wrong for several reasons. Most fundamentally, the mere fact that the information is public in a technical sense in no way resolves the constitutional question. As the Supreme Court stated in 1989 with respect to the information contained in a criminal "rap sheet," "[p]lainly there is a vast difference between the public records that might be found after a diligent search of court house files ... [and a] summary located in a single clearinghouse of information."[54] The Court dismissed what it called a "cramped notion of personal privacy," stating that "the fact that an event is not wholly private does not mean that an individual has no interest in limiting disclosure or dissemination of that information."[55] Registration and community notification, as the New Jersey Supreme Court has observed, similarly "link[] various bits of information – name, appearance, address and crime – that otherwise remain unconnected."[56] The court continued:

> However public any of those individual pieces of information may be, were it not for the Notification Law, those connections might never be made.... Those convicted of crime may have no cognizable privacy interest in the fact of their conviction, but the Notification Law, given the compilation and dissemination of information, nonetheless implicates a privacy interest. The interests in privacy may fade when the information is a matter of public record, but they are not non-existent.[57]

In practical terms, as a federal district court in New Jersey concluded, registration and notification "ensure that, rather than lying potentially dormant in a courthouse record room, a sex offender's former mischief – whether habitual or once-off – shall remain with him for life, as long as he remains a resident of New Jersey."[58]

RCN is also distinctive because of the nature of the information it deploys – home addresses in particular. The Supreme Court itself has recognized a privacy interest in one's home address, stating that "an individual's interest in controlling the dissemination of information regarding personal matters does not dissolve simply because that information may be available to the public in some form."[59] The Court emphasized that the disclosures (there, of nonunion members' home addresses to union officials) were problematic because they threatened intrusions into the home (by means of unsolicited mailings, calls, or visits), a domain "accorded special consideration in our Constitution, laws, and traditions."[60] If this concern supports a liberty interest and more searching scrutiny in the context just described, it should easily do the same with RCN, where the risk of harassment, ostracism, and vigilantism has been amply demonstrated.[61]

The reigning view of courts on the alternate method of finding a protectable liberty interest – the "stigma-plus" test[62] – is equally problematic. These decisions have been based on one of two conclusions: either that RCN does not stigmatize individuals, resulting in outright denial of a claim, or that if stigma is present, there is no additional harm to an established right sufficient to qualify as a "plus." Courts finding an absence of stigma have mainly based their conclusion on the view that stigma, if any, stemmed from the underlying conviction that triggered registration,[63] and that the information in registries is already publicly available.[64]

As discussed, however, the laws do more than merely assemble and make available identifying information. They compel the information from individuals and require that it be updated and verified (possibly at three month intervals), under constant threat of criminal punishment. The information is then provided to community members who otherwise very likely would not go to the trouble and expense of obtaining it. And, again, not just neutral information is provided; the information carries the purposeful message that targeted individuals merit fear and disdain. When the government gathers and synthesizes information in order to label one of its citizens in a derogatory manner, as the Oregon Supreme Court observed, "the interest of the person to be labelled goes beyond mere reputation.... It is an interest in knowing when the government is moving against you and why it has singled you out for special attention. It is an interest in avoiding the secret machinations of the Star Chamber."[65]

More commonly, courts have concluded that registration and notification stigmatize but do not find the requisite "plus." The Sixth Circuit Court of Appeals, for instance, presumed the existence of stigma but rejected the proffered "plus" in the form of alleged loss of and right to pursue employment. The Tennessee law challenged merely made registrants "less attractive" to employers and did not "expressly infringe[] upon [the petitioner's] ability to seek, obtain and maintain a job."[66] Another court, echoing *Smith*, concluded that while dissemination of the "truthful, public information ... may result in damage to plaintiffs' reputation, or may destabilize their employment and other community relations, such effects ... would appear to flow most directly from plaintiff's own convicted misconduct and from private citizens' reactions thereto, and only tangentially from state action."[67]

Smith and *CDPS*, along with similarly supportive case law from state and lower federal courts, ensure the continued existence of RCN. Together, the decisions signal a significant shift in judicial sensibility. In 1941, in the shadow of totalitarian oppression abroad, the Supreme Court cautioned in *Hines v. Davidowitz* that "champions of freedom for the individual have always vigorously opposed burdensome registration systems[,]" and noted historic opposition to requirements "at war with the fundamental principles of our free government, in that they would bring about unnecessary and irritating restrictions upon personal liberties of the individual."[68] Today, such words seem a quaint reminder of a distant past.

5. CONCLUSION

For reasons noted at the outset, information will play an ever more central role in American social control efforts in coming years. The discussion here has focused on one particular method, registration and community notification, which despite uncertainty over its actual public safety benefit, remains enormously popular and of late has been applied to non–sex offender populations.[69] As technology allows RCN to be combined with other information-based methods, such as global positioning systems and subdermal "chips," allowing for real-time location tracking of subjects, we should expect even further expansion in its use.

Government use of information to achieve social control ends, suffice it to say, is neither good nor bad in principle. Indeed, compared to the manifold negative consequences of physical imprisonment,[70] increased resort to any information-based, noncarceral strategy is a potential cause for optimism. Whether this is warranted, however, depends on a number of factors, including perhaps most critically a dampened American ardor to criminalize individuals, itself not yet in evidence. Until such time as this occurs, information will merely serve as a means to enable and facilitate the wide casting of the nation's correctional net, allowing for what the sociologist Stanley Cohen once termed a "hidden custody,"[71] unconstrained by the expense of brick and mortar imprisonment.

In the final analysis, RCN can serve as an instructive object lesson in the use of information-based social control. Perhaps some future assemblage of Supreme Court justices, more sensitized to the impact of government use of nominally "public" information,[72] will take a more critical view than that evidenced to date. Until such time, however, RCN and the constitutional jurisprudence condoning it will endure, providing a foundation for the continued expanded use of information as a means of social control.

Notes

1. See Peter Spierenburg, *The Body and the State: Early Modern Europe*, in THE OXFORD HISTORY OF THE PRISON 45, 48, 53 (Norval Morris & David J. Rothman eds., 1998).
2. See Wayne A. Logan, *Policing Identity*, 92 B. U. L. REV. 1561 (2012) (surveying evolution of identification technologies, including nineteenth anthropometric measurements and photography and early twentieth century fingerprinting).
3. See generally SIMSON GARFINKEL, DATABASE NATION: THE DEATH OF PRIVACY IN THE 21st CENTURY (2000).
4. See Lauren E. Glaze, *Correctional Population in the United States*, U.S. DEP'T. OF JUST. BULL., Dec. 2011, at 2, available at http://bjs.gov/content/pub/pdf/cpus10.pdf (noting that roughly 7 in 10 persons under supervision in U.S. adult correctional system are supervised in the community on the basis of probation or parole) (last visited Apr. 25, 2013).
5. See, e.g., FLA. DEP'T. OF CORR., A REPORT ON RADIO FREQUENCY (RF) MONITORING AND GLOBAL POSITIONING SATELLITE (GPS) MONITORING (Sept. 2009), available at http:www.dc.state.fl.us/pub/gbsrf/2009/index.html (last visited Apr. 28, 2013).
6. For a history of criminal registration laws, and their subsequent augmentation by community notification, see WAYNE A. LOGAN, KNOWLEDGE AS POWER: CRIMINAL REGISTRATION AND COMMUNITY NOTIFICATION LAWS IN AMERICA 20–48 (2009).
7. Registration attracted national attention in 1957 with *Lambert v. California*, 355 U.S. 225 (1957), which struck down a local registration law on due process-notice grounds but expressed no principled concern over registration itself. See *id.* at 229 (deeming registration "a law enforcement technique designed for the convenience of law enforcement agencies through which a list of the names and addresses of felons then residing in a community is compiled.").
8. *Id.*
9. For a ready access point, collecting registries from the 50 states, Territories, the District of Columbia, and participating Indian tribes, see U.S. *Dep't. of Just., Dru Sjodin National Sex Offender Public Website*, http://www.nsopw.gov/Core/Portal.aspx (last visited Sept. 6, 2010).
10. For extended discussion of how and why this is so, see Wayne A. Logan, *Megan's Laws: A Case Study in Political Stasis*, 61 SYRACUSE L. REV. 271 (2010).
11. See, e.g., Richard Tewksbury & Wesley G. Jennings, *Assessing the Impact of Sex Offender Registration and Community Notification on Sex-Offending Trajectories*, 37 CRIM. JUST. & BEHAV. 570, 572 (2010); Kristin Zgoba et al., *An Analysis of the*

Effectiveness of Community Notification and Registration: Do the Best Intentions Predict the Best Practices? 27 JUST. Q. 667, 690 (2010).

12 See generally Human Rights Watch, No Easy Answers: Sex Offender Laws in the US 86–99 (2007), available at http://www.hrw.org/sites/default/files/reports/us0907webwcover.pdf (last visited April 28, 2013).

13 See Naomi J. Freeman, *The Public Safety Impact of Community Notification Laws: Rearrest of Convicted Sex Offenders*, 58 CRIME & DELINQ. 539, 557 (2009); Jill S. Levenson & Leo P. Cotter, *The Effect of Megan's Laws on Sex Offender Reintegration*, 21 J. CONTEMP. CRIM. JUST. 49 (2005).

14 The shift was also affected by a broader change in sensibility entailed in what one commentator termed a view of the "state as 'service station'" MARGARET CANOVAN, NATIONHOOD AND POLITICAL THEORY 85–7 (1996). Here manifest by citizen-consumers with informational needs and desires that they wanted satisfied.

15 Indeed, the prospect unabashedly figured in the genesis of community notification itself, according to the police chief who spearheaded its emergence. See Jolayne Houtz, *When Do You Unmask a Sexual Predator?*, SEATTLE TIMES, Aug. 30, 1990 (quoting Mountainlake Terrace, Washington Police Chief John Turner).

16 In this sense, RCN is consistent with community policing initiatives surfacing in the 1980s. See ROY ROBERG ET AL., POLICE & SOCIETY 88 (3d ed., 2005) (noting that community policing sought to "encourage individual citizens and community groups to shoulder some responsibility" for community safety). Cf. Benjamin Wittes, *Innovation's Darker Future: Biosecurity, Technologies of Mass Empowerment, and the Constitution*, in CONSTITUTION 3.0: FREEDOM AND TECHNOLOGICAL CHANGE 214, 236 (Jeffrey Rosen & Benjamin Wittes, eds., 2011) (discussing devolution of security over biotechnology risks to non-governmental actors with expertise).

17 See Jonathan Simon, *Managing the Monstrous: Sex Offenders and the New Penology*, 4 PSYCHOL., PUB. POL'Y & L. 460 (1998).

18 See, e.g., Amy L. Anderson & Lisa L. Sample, *Public Awareness and Action Resulting from Sex Offender Community Notification Laws*, 19 CRIM. JUST. POL'Y REV. 371, 389 (2008); Victoria S. Beck & Lawrence Travis III, *Sex Offender Notification: A Cross-State Comparison*, 7 POLICE PRAC. & RES. 293 (2006).

19 Jonathan Simon, *Megan's Law: Crime and Democracy in Late Modern America*, 25 LAW & SOC. INQUIRY 1142 (2000).

20 It is well known, however, that this is not the case. See HUMAN RIGHTS WATCH, supra note 12, at 57–8 (noting common high rates of inaccuracies and missing information in registries).

21 Indeed, concern exists that registrants determined to re-offend will fulfill their criminal designs elsewhere, anonymously, in a community other than their own. See, e.g., Grant Duwe et al., *Does Residential Proximity Matter? A Geographic Analysis of Sex Offense Recidivism*, 35 CRIM. JUST. & BEHAV. 484, 500 (2008).

22 As one New Jersey resident commented in 1995, it is as if "[t]he state says 'We think he's a danger, a threat, a time bomb waiting to go off and we thought you'd like to know.' But if the state couldn't deal with him, what can I do?" Shankar Vedantam, *Sex Offender Notification Law Questioned by Experts: Offenders' Civil Rights One Issue*, TIMES-PICAYUNE (New Orleans), Sept. 17, 1995.

23 See, e.g., VT. STAT. ANN. tit. 13. § 5412 (2010) (affording government immunity for all but "gross negligence or willful misconduct").
24 *NAACP v. Alabama ex rel. v. Patterson*, 357 U.S. 449, 463 (1958).
25 *Brown v. Socialist Workers '74 Campaign Comm.*, 459 U.S. 87, 93 (1982).
26 See *DeShaney v. Winnebago City Dep't. of Soc. Serv*, 489 U.S. 189, 197 (1989).
27 James Q. Whitman, *What's Wrong with Inflicting Shame Sanctions?* 107 YALE L.J. 1055, 1059 (1998).
28 *Id.*
29 See, e.g., IDAHO CODE ANN. § 18–8302 (2010) (entitled "Sex Offender Registration and Community Right-to-Know Act").
30 See, e.g., Peter B. Edelman, *Free Press v. Privacy: Haunted by the Ghost of Justice Black*, 68 TEX. L. REV. 1195, 1224 (1990) ("[T]he immense value of truth will always outweigh the countervailing interest of an individual in nondisclosure of private information.").
31 Diane L. Zimmerman, *Requiem for a Heavyweight: A Farewell to Warren and Brandeis's Privacy Tort*, 68 CORNELL L. REV 291, 341 (1983).
32 See, e.g., RICHARD POSNER, ECONOMIC ANALYSIS OF LAW 46, 660–3 (5th ed., 1998). According to Richard Epstein, "the plea for privacy is often a plea for the right to misrepresent one's self to the rest of the world." Richard A. Epstein, *The Legal Regulation of Genetic Discrimination: Old Responses to New Technology*, 74 B.U. L. REV. 12, 74 (1994).
33 See Lior Strahilevitz, *Privacy versus Antidiscrimination*, 75 U. CHI. L. REV. 363, 365–6 (2008).
34 *Id.* at 380.
35 Daniel J. Solove, *The Virtues of Knowing Less: Justifying Privacy Protections against Disclosure*, 53 DUKE L.J. 1033, 1035 (2003).
36 *Id.*
37 JEFFREY ROSEN, THE UNWANTED GAZE: THE DESTRUCTION OF PRIVACY IN AMERICA 200 (2000).
38 See, e.g., Robert Jacobson, Note, *"Megan's Law": Reinforcing Old Patterns of Anti-Gay Harassment*, 87 GEO. L.J. 2460 (1999) (discussing experience in California where the expansive retroactive reach of the State's law (to 1944) required registration of elderly men with decades-old convictions reflecting anti-gay animus).
39 *Briscoe v. Reader's Digest Ass'n*, 483 P.2d 34, 41–2 (Cal. 1971). Forty years before, the same court avowed that "we, as right-thinking members of society, should permit [the law abiding ex-offender] to continue in the path of rectitude rather than throw him back into a life of shame or crime." *Melvin v. Reed*, 297 P.2d 91, 93 (Cal. 1931).
40 See Kevin Lapp, *Reforming the Good Moral Character Requirement for U.S. Citizenship*, 87 IND. L.J. 1571, 1627–8 (2012) (surveying studies).
41 In 1973, for instance, the California Supreme Court held that an individual needed to be advised of a registration requirement before pleading guilty because it enabled "continual police surveillance .... Although the stigma of a short jail sentence should eventually fade, the ignominious badge carried by the convicted sex offender can remain for a lifetime." *In re Birch*, 515 P.2d 12, 17 (Cal. 1973). Five years later, the California Court of Appeals opined that it "cannot be doubted" that registration "has de facto punitive aspects": registrants suffer "a multitude of

disabilities" and registration "severely limits a person's freedom of movement and places him under continuous police surveillance." *People v. Mills*, 146 Cal. Rptr. 411, 414 (Cal. Ct. App. 1978).

42 See Wayne A. Logan, *Liberty Interests in the Preventive State: Procedural Due Process and Sex Offender Community Notification Laws*, 89 J. CRIM. L. & CRIMINOLOGY 1167 (1999).

43 See Wayne A. Logan, *Federal Habeas in the Information Age*, 85 MINN. L. REV. 147 (2000).

44 538 U.S. 84 (2003).

45 Indeed, relying on *Smith*, the California Supreme Court reversed its 1983 decision invalidating registration alone as cruel and unusual punishment, concluding that "[d]evelopments since [1983] have persuaded us that [its] analysis is no longer viable." See *People v. Alva*, 92 P.3d 311, 317 (Cal. 2004).

46 538 U.S. 1 (2003).

47 *Smith*, 538 U.S. at 108–9 (Souter, J., concurring).

48 *Id.* at 99.

49 *Id.* at 100.

50 *CDPS*, 538 U.S. at 8.

51 *Russell v. Gregoire*, 124 F.3d 1079, 1094 (9th Cir. 1997).

52 *Doe v. Kelly*, 961 F. Supp. 1105, 1112 (W.D. Mich. 1997).

53 See, e.g., *Akella v. Mich. Dep't. of State Police*, 67 F. Supp. 2d 716, 729 (E.D. Mich. 1999) ("plaintiffs have cited no authority for the proposition that the magnitude of dissemination, in and of itself, is sufficient to trigger a deprivation of a liberty interest.")

54 *United States Dep't. of Justice v. Reporters' Comm. for Freedom of the Press*, 489 U.S. 749, 763 (1989).

55 *Id.* at 763, 770. More recently, a similar sentiment was voiced in *United States v. Jones*, 132 S. Ct. 945 (2012), invalidating warrantless police placement and extended tracking of a GPS tracking device on a car, where a majority of the Justices attached importance to government aggregation of otherwise publicly visible conduct (driving a car). See *id.* at 954 (Sotomayor, J., concurring); *id.* at 957 (Alito, J., concurring, joined by Ginsburg, Breyer, Kagan, J.J.)

56 *Doe v. Poritz*, 662 A.2d 367, 411 (N.J. 1995).

57 *Id.*

58 *Artway v. N.J. Attorney Gen*, 876 F. Supp. 666, 689 (D. N.J. 1995). See also *Boutin v. LaFleur*, 591 N.W.2d 711, 718 (Minn. Ct. App. 1999) ("[T]here is a distinct difference between the mere presence of such information in court documents and the active dissemination of such information.").

59 *United States Dep't. of Def. v. Fed. Labor Relations Auth.*, 51 U.S. 487, 500 (1994).

60 *Id.* at 501.

61 See HUMAN RIGHTS WATCH, supra note 12, at 86–90 (recounting instances of personal and property crimes targeting registrants over the years).

62 See *Paul v. Davis*, 424 U.S. 693 (1976).

63 See, e.g., *Doe v. Phillips*, 194 S.W.3d 833, 844 (Mo. 2006) ("[Stigma from] listing on the registry comes not from fact that [petitioners] are listed, but from their convictions of the offenses that led to their listing.").

64 See, e.g., *Meinders v. Weber*, 604 N.W.2d 248, 257 (S.D. 2000) ("The information contained in the sex offender registry is almost the same information available as a public record in the courthouse where the conviction occurred.").
65 *Noble v. Bd. of Parole and Post-Prison Supervision*, 964 P.2d 990, 995 (Or. 1998).
66 *Cutshall v. Sundquist*, 193 F.3d 466, 479, 480 (6th Cir. 1999).
67 *Doe v. Kelly*, 961 F. Supp. 1105, 1112 (W.D. Mich. 1997). A handful of courts have found the "plus" criterion satisfied. See, e.g., *Doe v. Pryor*, 61 F. Supp. 2d 1224, 1231 (M.D. Ala. 1999) (citing likely loss of employment opportunities as a result of RCN).
68 312 U.S. 52, 70–1 (1941).
69 See, e.g., Erica Goode, *States Seeking New Registries for Criminals*, N.Y. TIMES, May 20, 2011, at A1 (noting extension inter alia to homicide convicts and likening expansion to "Christmas ornaments on a tree, [added] year after year.").
70 See generally Sharon Dolovich, *Exclusion and Control in the Carceral State*, 16 BERKELEY J. CRIM. L. 259, 269–70, 277–8 (2011) (noting negative effects of incarceration on inmates, their families and their communities).
71 STANLEY COHEN, VISIONS OF SOCIAL CONTROL: CRIME, PUNISHMENT AND CLASSIFICATION 71 (1985).
72 Cf., e.g., *United States v. Jones*, 132 S. Ct. 945, 956 (2012) (Sotomayor, J., concurring) (citation omitted) (observing that "[a]wareness that the Government may be watching chills associational and expressive freedoms" and that unfettered government use of GPS technology may 'alter the relationship between citizen and government in a way that is inimical to democratic society.'").

9

Is the Fourth Amendment Relevant in a Technological Age?

Christopher Slobogin

1. INTRODUCTION

The year is 2015. Officer Jones, a New York City police officer, stops a car because it has a broken taillight. The driver of the car turns out to be a man named Ahmad Abdullah. Abdullah's license and registration check out, but he seems nervous, at least to Jones. Jones goes back to his squad car and activates his Raytheon electromagnetic pulse scanner, which can scan the car for weapons and bombs. Nothing shows up on the screen. Nonetheless, he takes down Abdullah's Vehicle Identification Number, which he hopes can facilitate tracking the car's public travels, using signals sent by the car's factory-installed transponder to New York's Intelligent Transportation System (ITS) computers.

Over the next several weeks, New York police do precisely that. They also observe Abdullah taking walks from his apartment, relying on public video cameras mounted on buildings and light poles. When cameras cannot capture his meanderings or he takes public transportation or travels in a friend's car, the police monitor him with drone cameras, powerful enough to pick up the numbers on a license plate. Police interest is piqued when they discover that he visits not only his local mosque but several other mosques around the New York area. They requisition his phone and Internet service provider records to ascertain the phone numbers and e-mail addresses of the people with whom he communicates. Through digital sources, they also obtain his bank and credit card records. For good measure, the police pay the data collection company Choicepoint for a report on all the information about Abdullah that can

---

A more elaborate version of this chapter appears in CONSTITUTION 3.0: FREEDOM AND TECHNOLOGICAL CHANGE 11–36 (Jeffrey Rosen & Benjamin Wittes eds., 2011).

be gleaned from public records and Internet sources. Finally, since Abdullah tends to leave his windows uncurtained, police set up a Star-Tron – binoculars with night vision capacity – in a building across the street from Abdullah's apartment so they can watch him through his window.

These various investigative maneuvers might lead to discovery that Abdullah is consorting with known terrorists. Or they might merely provide police with proof that Abdullah is an illegal immigrant. Then there is always the possibility that Abdullah has not committed any crime.

The important point for present purposes is that the Constitution has nothing to say about any of the police actions that take place in Abdullah's case once his car is stopped. The constitutional provision that is most likely to be implicated by the government's attempts to investigate Adbullah is the Fourth Amendment, which prohibits unreasonable searches of houses, persons, papers, and effects and further provides that, if a warrant is sought authorizing a search, it must be based on probable cause and describe with particularity the place to be searched and the person or thing to be seized. This language is the primary constitutional mechanism for regulating police investigations. The courts have held that when police engage in a search, they must usually have probable cause – about a 50 percent certainty – that the search will produce evidence of crime, and they must usually also have a warrant, issued by an independent magistrate, if there is time to get one. As construed by the U.S. Supreme Court, however, these requirements are irrelevant to many modern police practices, including all of those involved in Abdullah's case.

The Fourth Amendment's increasing irrelevance stems from the fact that the Supreme Court is mired in precedent decided in another era. Over the past two hundred years, the Fourth Amendment's guarantees have been construed largely in the context of what might be called "physical searches" – entry into a house or car, stopping and frisking a person on the street, or rifling through a person's private papers. But today, with the introduction of devices that can see through walls and clothes, monitor public thoroughfares twenty-four hours a day, and access millions of records in seconds, police are relying much more heavily on what might be called "virtual searches," investigative techniques that do not require physical access to premises, people, papers, or effects and can often be carried out covertly from far away. As Abdullah's case illustrates, this technological revolution is well on its way to altering drastically the way police go about looking for evidence of crime. To date, the Supreme Court's interpretation of the Fourth Amendment has both failed to anticipate this revolution and continued to ignore it.

2. THE SUPREME COURT'S FOURTH AMENDMENT

The Fourth Amendment's protections – warrants sworn under oath, particular descriptions of sought-after evidence, and cause requirements – are not triggered unless the government is carrying out a "search." The Supreme Court has never defined this word the way a layperson would, as an act of looking for or into something. Rather, it has looked to either property law or privacy values in fleshing out the concept.

Initially, the Court defined Fourth Amendment searches in terms of property interests. A search occurred only when government engaged in some type of trespass.[1] Thus, for instance, wiretapping a phone was not a search because the surveillance involved accessing only outside lines. By contrast, the use of a spike mike that touched the baseboard of a house did implicate the Fourth Amendment.[2]

Then, in 1967, came the Court's famous decision in *Katz v. United States*, which held that covert interception of communications counts as a Fourth Amendment search.[3] Acting without a warrant, FBI agents bugged the phone booth Charlie Katz was using to place illegal bets. The government sought to justify the absence of a warrant by arguing that a phone booth is not a "constitutionally protected area" (because it is not a house, person, paper, or effect) and that planting and listening to the bugging device on a public booth worked no trespass. Justice Black also argued, in dissent, that conversations like those intercepted in *Katz* were intangibles that "can neither be searched nor seized" and in any event did not fit into the Fourth Amendment's foursome of houses, persons, papers, and effects.[4] All of these arguments were consistent with the traditional, property-based approach to the Fourth Amendment. But the majority stated that the Fourth Amendment "protects people, not places" and concluded that "what [a person] seeks to preserve as private, even in an area accessible to the public, may be constitutionally protected."[5] Justice Harlan's concurring opinion elaborated on the latter idea by recognizing that while the Fourth Amendment's protection of people still usually "requires reference to a place," places should receive that protection if they are associated with "an expectation ... that society is prepared to recognize as 'reasonable.'"[6] It was this latter language that became the focal point for the Supreme Court's treatment of the Fourth Amendment's threshold.

Although it still defined "search" more narrowly than a layperson would, *Katz* was hailed as a long-overdue expansion of Fourth Amendment protection that was needed in an increasingly technological age. That celebration was premature. Supreme Court case law since *Katz* has pretty much limited that decision to its facts. While nonconsensual interception of the contents of one's communications over the phone or via computer remains a Fourth Amendment search, all other government efforts to obtain evidence of wrongdoing are immune from constitutional regulation unless they involve some type of physical intrusion. The Court has arrived at this intriguing result relying on four variations of the search as physical intrusion theme: the knowing exposure doctrine, the general public use doctrine, the contraband-specific doctrine, and the assumption of risk doctrine. All four doctrines have the effect of enabling the government to conduct most technologically aided, virtual searches without having to worry about the Fourth Amendment.

a. The Knowing Exposure Doctrine

Katz itself said that while conversations over a public phone can be private for Fourth Amendment purposes, "what a person knowingly exposes to the public, even in his own home or office, is not a subject of Fourth Amendment protection."[7] This notion was first applied to government monitoring of activities in public spaces. In *United States v. Knotts*, the police lost visual sighting of the defendant's car as it traveled the streets but were able to locate it eventually by using a tracking device that they had attached to an ether can the defendant had subsequently purchased and put in his car.[8] Although the police would have been unable to find the defendant without the beeper, the Court held that its use was not a Fourth Amendment search because "a person travelling in an automobile on public thoroughfares has no reasonable expectation of privacy in his movements from one place to another."[9] Thus, after *Knotts*, police could use technology to spy on public activities without worrying about the Fourth Amendment.

In three later decisions, sometimes called the "flyover cases," the Court held that the knowing exposure doctrine also sanctions suspicionless police viewing of activities on *private* property – even those that take place on the curtilage (the area immediately surrounding the premises) – so long as the police do not physically enter that area but rather view it from the air.[10] To the argument that the curtilage should be protected by the Fourth Amendment, at least when it is surrounded by a fence, the Court fancifully responded that "any member of the public" flying in navigable airspace could have seen what the police saw.[11] In one of the flyover cases, Chief Justice Burger, apparently recently returned from a trip to London, opined that even someone on a double-decker bus could have seen over the defendant's fence, thus rendering unreasonable any privacy expectation harbored by the defendant.[12]

In an important case decided in 2012, the Court declared that when the police *do* intrude onto private property, the fact that what they are after is exposed to public view is not dispositive. In *Jones v. United States*, the tracking device was placed on the defendant's car, rather than, as in *Knotts*, planted on an item that the defendant subsequently purchased.[13] That subtle property-based difference was enough for a majority of the Court to hold that use of the device to track Jones's car was a search. Recognizing the fictional nature of this distinction, five justices indicated they might even be willing to overturn *Knotts*, or at least limit it to short-term tracking. But as of now, unless a trespass is involved, the knowing exposure doctrine still stands.

The implications of the Court's stance for technological surveillance should be fairly clear. As long as the police are located on a lawful vantage point, they can use technology to spy on anything occurring in public spaces or on private property outside the home without worrying about the Fourth Amendment. Governments have been quick to recognize how significantly this rule enhances investigations in an era of technological innovation. Putting a cop on every street corner around the clock is expensive and not cost-effective. But video cameras of the type used to track Abdullah are increasingly seen as a good investment, especially since 9/11 has triggered federal funding for such projects. For instance, Chicago trains more than twenty-two hundred cameras, many equipped with zoom and night viewing capacity, on its urban populace day and night, every day of the week, some operating openly, others covertly; all of them are patched into the city's $43 million operations center.[14] Where cameras do not exist, satellite photography or drone cameras might be available.[15] The holding in *Knotts* ensures that the Fourth Amendment will not get in the way of these surveillance systems, at least if they are trained on venues outside the home and do not involve a trespass.

Similar developments are occurring with tracking technology. Today it is both technologically and economically feasible to outfit every car with a radio frequency identification device that communicates current and past routes to an ITS computer, as occurred in Abdullah's case.[16] Cell phones can be used to track anyone who has one within feet of his or her location, at least when they are turned on; in the past several years, police have made millions of requests to phone companies for help in carrying out cell phone GPS tracking.[17] Despite *Jones*, courts can hold that the Fourth Amendment has nothing to say about such programs, even when they catalog weeks of travel, so long as they do not track movements inside the home and no physical trespass is involved.[18] The flyover cases similarly make clear that tracking onto private property, short of entry into the home, does not implicate the Fourth Amendment as long as, during that process, no government agent physically intrudes on curtilage.[19]

b. The General Public Use Doctrine

One of the flyover cases also introduced the second Court doctrine limiting the definition of search – the concept of general public use. In *Dow Chemical v. EPA*, the government relied on a $22,000 mapmaking camera to spy on Dow Chemical's fenced-in business property from an airplane. The Court had no problem with this use of technology because, it astonishingly asserted, such cameras are "generally available to the public."[20] According to the majority, because ordinary citizens can obtain such cameras and use them to view open fields and curtilage from airplanes, the government's actions in *Dow Chemical* did not infringe the Fourth Amendment.

Fifteen years later, the Court appeared to rethink this idea, at least with respect to technology used to spy on a home. In *Kyllo v. United States*, it held that a thermal imaging device is not in general public use – despite the fact that it cost a mere $10,000 – and went on to hold that relying on such a device to detect heat differentials inside a house is a search.[21] In the end, however, *Kyllo* places few limitations on the use of technology to spy on the populace, for three reasons.

First, *Kyllo*'s ban on sophisticated technology applies only to viewing of the home. Thus, as already noted, government is able to use, without infringing Fourth Amendment interests, any type of technology, generally available or not, if the target is located in a public space or on curtilage that is viewed from an area outside the curtilage.

Second, *Kyllo* expanded on *Dow Chemical*'s holding by stipulating that even the home is not protected from surveillance with devices that are in "general public use." While thermal imagers may not cross that threshold, a wide array of technology is easily accessible by the public and thus can be used to peer inside the home. For instance, the lower courts have been willing to hold that police reliance on flashlights, binoculars, and zoom cameras to see inside premises does not implicate the Fourth Amendment.[22] Since telescopes can be bought at Wal-Mart for less than one hundred dollars, presumably they too fit in this category. Two courts have even held that night vision scopes of the type used in Abdullah's case are in general public use (which is not surprising, since they can be bought on eBay for less than two thousand dollars).[23]

A third reason *Kyllo* is little more than a pyrrhic victory for privacy advocates is that, in a bow to the knowing exposure doctrine, the majority in that case stated that even very sophisticated technology may be used to view activities that take place in the home if it merely duplicates what a law enforcement officer could have seen with the naked eye from a lawful vantage point.[24] That idea, taken literally, could mean that government can rely on images from public camera systems or even satellites to see through uncurtained windows without infringing Fourth Amendment interests, as long as those windows are situated near a public street or sidewalk.

c. Contraband-Specific Searches

Even those parts of the home that are curtained and walled off may not be protected from sophisticated technological surveillance if the technology is contraband specific, meaning that it detects only items that are evidence of criminal activity. The Supreme Court broached this third limiting doctrine in a case involving a drug-sniffing dog, where it concluded, as a majority of the justices later put it, that "government conduct that can reveal whether [an item is contraband] and no other arguably 'private' fact[] compromises no legitimate privacy interest."[25] As anyone who has visited an airport knows, scientists have developed "mechanical dogs" that can sniff out weapons or contraband. Most of these instruments, particularly if based on x-ray technology, are not weapon or contraband specific; they expose other items as well. But as contraband-specific surveillance devices are developed, such as the Raytheon instrument the state police officer aimed at Abdullah's car, they will allow police to cruise the streets scanning vehicles, people, and homes for illicit items without in any way infringing on Fourth Amendment interests, because that type of virtual search would reveal only contraband.[26]

d. The Assumption of Risk Doctrine

The three doctrines discussed to this point provide law enforcement officials with a wide array of options that allow technology to play an important, if not a dominant role, in their investigative pursuits, with no interference from the Fourth Amendment. The Supreme Court doctrine that most powerfully facilitates that role, however, is found in a series of cases holding that people assume the risk that information disclosed to third parties will be handed over to the government and thus cannot reasonably expect it to be private.

The two most important decisions in this regard are *Miller v. United States* and *Smith v. Maryland*. In *Miller*, the Court held that an individual "takes the risk, in revealing his affairs to another, that the information will be conveyed by that person to the government ... even if the information is revealed on the assumption that it will be used only for a limited purpose and the confidence placed in the third party will not be betrayed."[27] That reasoning might make sense when the other person is an acquaintance, who can decide for his or her own reasons to reveal a friend's secrets to others.[28] But in *Miller* the third party was a bank. The Court held that even here one assumes the risk of a breach of confidence and therefore that depositors cannot reasonably expect that information conveyed to their banks will be protected by the Fourth Amendment. In *Smith*, the Court similarly held that a person who uses the phone "voluntarily" conveys the phone number to the phone company and "assume[s] the risk that the company would reveal to police the numbers he dialed."[29] As a result of *Miller* and *Smith*, the Fourth Amendment is irrelevant when government agents obtain personal information from third-party record holders, at least when the subject of that information knows or should know that the third party maintains it.

These decisions, which occurred at the dawn of the information age in the mid-1970s, have enormous implications for law enforcement investigation today. Traditionally, gathering documentary evidence required physically traveling to the relevant repository and asking for the appropriate records or, in somewhat more modern times, arranging for a fax transmission. That has all changed in the past couple of decades. The quantity of the world's recorded data has doubled every year since the mid-1990s. Computing power necessary to store, access, and analyze data has also increased geometrically since that time, and at increasingly cheaper cost.[30] Because of *Miller* and *Smith*, government can access free and clear of Fourth Amendment constraints all of this information, as well as the other types of data the police gathered in Abdullah's case, either directly or through the many private companies that today exist for the sole purpose of collecting and organizing personal transactions.

As Abdullah's case illustrates, not only is personal information now easier to obtain, but it is also much easier to aggregate. In the old days accumulation of data from disparate sources involved considerable work. Today it can often occur at the touch of a button, with the result that private companies as well as governments now excel at creating "digital dossiers" from public and quasi-private records.[31]

The scope of the government's technologically driven data-gathering efforts is staggering. A program tellingly called REVEAL combines information from sixteen government and private databases, including those maintained by the Internal Revenue Service and the Social Security Administration.[32] MATRIX, a federally funded data accumulation system that at one time catered to a number of state law enforcement agencies, claims that it allows clients to "search tens of billions of data records on individuals and businesses in mere seconds."[33] The best-known effort in this regard originally carried the discomfiting name Total Information Awareness (TIA), later changed to Terrorism Information Awareness. The brainchild of Admiral Poindexter and the Department of Defense's Defense

Advanced Research Projects Agency, TIA was designed to access scores of information sources, including financial, travel, educational, medical, and even veterinary records, at which point terrorist profiles would help determine which individuals should receive special attention.[34] Although TIA was defunded in 2003, it continues to exist under other names and in other forms, including something called "fusion centers," which feature computer systems that "fuse" information from many different sources in an effort to assist law enforcement efforts.[35]

Total Information Awareness's original icon, a picture of an all-seeing eye surveying the globe accompanied by the maxim "Knowledge Is Power," would seem to trigger the privacy protection meant to be provided by the Fourth Amendment. But the Supreme Court's assumption of risk doctrine has apparently exempted TIA-like programs from constitutional scrutiny. As a result, government may constitutionally construct personality mosaics on each of us, for no reason or for illicit ones, as long as all of the information is held by third parties.

e. The Special Needs Doctrine

Even if, because of its scope, the Total Information Awareness program were thought to be governed by the Fourth Amendment, other Supreme Court doctrines might well permit it to continue in relatively unrestricted fashion. The most important of these doctrines is implicated, in the words of a widely cited 1985 Supreme Court opinion, "in those exceptional circumstances in which special needs, beyond the normal need for law enforcement, make the warrant and probable cause requirements impracticable."[36] Lower courts have made clear that this special needs exception readily applies to antiterrorism efforts like TIA. For instance, courts have held that checkpoints established to detect terrorists are not focused on "normal" crime. As Judge Sotomayor stated in upholding a federal program that authorized routine suspicionless searches of passengers and cars on a New York ferry system in the wake of 9/11, "Preventing or deterring large-scale terrorist attacks presents problems that are distinct from standard law enforcement needs and indeed go well beyond them."[37]

Courts have also relied on special needs analysis to uphold programs that are not investigative in nature. For instance, in holding that a government plan to force prisoners to provide DNA samples is exempt from traditional Fourth Amendment rules, the Court of Appeals for the Fourth Circuit noted that the sampling was "not trying to determine that a particular individual has engaged in some specific wrongdoing."[38] Courts could easily decide that TIA and similar programs are designed primarily to collect intelligence about terrorism or other criminal activity and thus are special needs programs that, even if denominated "searches," do not have to meet the usual Fourth Amendment requirements.

3. A TECHNOLOGICALLY SENSITIVE FOURTH AMENDMENT

If reform of the Fourth Amendment were thought to be important as a means of responding to technological developments, the most obvious first step would be to conform the definition of search to its lay meaning of looking into, over, or through something in order to find somebody or something.[39] This move would immediately encompass virtual searches within the ambit of the Fourth Amendment's protections. Camera surveillance, tracking, targeting places or people with devices (whether or not they are in general public use or contraband specific), and accessing records via computer all involve searches under this definition.

Reform could not stop there, however. Current Fourth Amendment law also usually requires probable cause for a search. If police attempts to watch a person walk down the street, follow a car on the public highway, or acquire access to court records or utility bills all required probable cause, law enforcement would come to a screeching halt. Indeed, it may have been to avoid such a disaster that most justices on the Court, including many of its liberal members, have been willing simply to declare that these investigative techniques are immune from constitutional review.[40]

But there is a compromise position, suggested by the Fourth Amendment itself. After all, the Fourth Amendment requires only that searches and seizures be "reasonable." It does not require probable cause or any other particular quantum of suspicion.

I have argued elsewhere that the Fourth Amendment's reasonableness inquiry should adhere to a proportionality principle.[41] The idea of calibrating the justification for an action by reference to its impact on the affected party permeates most other areas of the legal system.[42] For instance, at the adjudication stage the law assigns increasingly heavier burdens of proof depending on the consequences: a mere preponderance of the evidence in civil litigation, the more demanding clear and convincing evidence standard for administrative lawsuits and civil commitment, and the most onerous requirement of proof beyond a reasonable doubt when the state deprives an individual of liberty through criminal punishment. Similarly, levels of scrutiny in constitutional litigation vary depending on whether the individual right infringed by the government is "fundamental."

The proportionality principle even has found its way into the Supreme Court's Fourth Amendment case law. It provides the best explanation, for example, of why arrests require probable cause while stops require only reasonable suspicion. As the Court stated in *Terry v. Ohio*, the case that established this particular hierarchy, "There can be 'no ready test for determining reasonableness other than by balancing the need to search against the invasion which the search entails."[43] Unfortunately, the Court has applied this principle only haphazardly and, when it does apply it, inconsistently.

A more formal adoption of the proportionality principle would state that for every government action that implicates the Fourth Amendment, government must demonstrate "cause" – defined as the level of certainty that evidence of wrongdoing will be found – roughly proportionate to the intrusiveness of the search.[44] Given the history of the Fourth Amendment, the baseline rule for application of the proportionality principle would be that searches of houses and similarly intrusive actions require probable cause. But less intrusive searches and seizures could be authorized on something less. For instance, the Court is clearly correct in its intuition that police viewing of public activities is generally less invasive than police entries into houses. Short-term camera surveillance and tracking of public movements, use of binoculars to look through a picture window, or perusal of a record of an individual's food purchases would not require probable cause under proportionality reasoning.

In contrast to the Supreme Court's jurisprudence, however, only the most minimal intrusions would be exempt from Fourth Amendment regulation in a proportionality-driven regime. Thus while randomly surveying the public streets with a camera might be untouched by the Fourth Amendment, using cameras to target an individual would trigger its guarantees (albeit perhaps only in the sense that an articulable reason for the targeting would be required).[45] In further contrast to the Supreme Court's approach, proportionality reasoning dictates that law enforcement demonstrate a high degree of cause for virtual searches determined to be as invasive or nearly as invasive as entry into the home. For instance, given the high expectations of privacy associated with bank and phone records,[46] *Miller* and *Smith* would be overturned, and police would have to demonstrate reasonable suspicion or perhaps even probable cause before gaining access to such information.

At least one exception to the proportionality principle should be recognized, however. When the purpose of a search is to prevent significant, specific, and imminent danger, society's interest in protecting itself is sufficiently strong that the justification normally required by proportionality reasoning should be relaxed. This danger exception is consistent with the clear and present danger exception in First Amendment jurisprudence, as well as with *Terry v.*

Ohio, which sanctioned preventive frisks when police have reasonable suspicion, rather than probable cause, that a person they have stopped is armed.[47]

Other exceptions might be necessary, especially if the search is of a large group.[48] The important point for now is that proportionality reasoning should be the presumptive framework for Fourth Amendment analysis. The Court's Fourth Amendment jurisprudence – which, aside from the holding in *Katz* itself, is identical to the property-based regime that *Katz* supposedly discarded – opens the door wide to the extremely invasive investigative techniques that technological advances are providing the government at an increasing rate. By recognizing that some Fourth Amendment searches may take place on something less than probable cause, proportionality reasoning facilitates extension of the Fourth Amendment's protection beyond physical invasions and thus allows it to adapt to modern law enforcement.

4. CONCLUSION

Virtual searches are rapidly replacing physical searches of homes, cars, and luggage. Outdoor activities and many indoor ones as well can be caught on camera, monitored using tracking devices, or documented using computers. Yet none of this technological surveillance can be challenged under the Fourth Amendment if its target could conceivably be viewed, with the naked eye or with common technology, by a member of the public, or could be detected using a contraband-specific device, or has been voluntarily surrendered to a human or institutional third party. And even those technological investigations that are considered searches will usually survive Fourth Amendment challenge, if they can be characterized as preventive or intelligence-gathering exercises rather than efforts to solve ordinary crime.

It is time to revert to first principles. A search involves looking for something. Justification for a search of an individual targeted by the police should be proportionate to its intrusiveness except in the rare circumstances when the search is aimed at preventing specific, imminent, and significant danger. These principles will restore the Fourth Amendment to its place as the primary arbiter of how government investigates its citizens, even when those investigations rely on technology that can be used covertly and from a distance.

Notes

1   See, e.g., *Silverman v. United States*, 365 U.S. 505, 510 (1961).
2   Compare *Olmstead v. United States*, 277 U.S. 438 (1928), with *Silverman*, 365 U.S. at 509–10.
3   *Katz v. United States*, 389 U.S. 347 (1967).

4   *Id.* at 365 (Black, J., dissenting).
5   *Id.* at 351 (majority opinion).
6   *Id.* at 361 (Harlan, J., concurring).
7   *Id.* at 351 (majority opinion).
8   *United States v. Knotts*, 460 U.S. 276 (1983).
9   *Id.* at 281.
10 *Ciraolo v. California*, 476 U.S. 207 (1986); *Riley v. Florida*, 488 U.S. 445 (1989); *Dow Chemical v. United States*, 476 U.S. 227 (1986).
11 *Riley*, 488 U.S. at 446.
12 *Ciraolo*, 476 U.S. at 211.
13 *Jones v. United States*, 132 S. Ct. 935 (2012).
14 Fran Spielman, *Feds Give City $48 Million in Anti-Terrorism Funds*, CHI. SUN-TIMES, Dec. 4, 2004, at 10.
15 See, e.g., Richard M. Thompson, Drones in Domestic Surveillance Operations: Fourth Amendment Implications and Legislative Responses 2-3 (2012) (FAA predicts 30,000 drones over U.S. airspace in next twenty years).
16 See FED. TRADE COMM'N, RADIO FREQUENCY IDENTIFICATION: APPLICATIONS AND IMPLICATIONS FOR CONSUMERS (Mar. 2005): 3, 5; SMITHSONIAN NAT'L AIR AND SPACE MUSEUM, *How Does GPS Work?* (1998), www.nasm.si.edu/exhibitions/gps/work.html (last visited Apr. 29, 2013).
17 Justin Elliott, *How Easy Is It for the Police to Get GPS Data from Your Phone?* TPM MUCKRAKER, (Dec. 9, 2009, 2:13 PM), http://tpmmuckraker.talkingpointsmemo.com/2009/12/cell_phone_surveillance_unpacking_the_legal_issues.php (last visited Apr. 29, 2013).
18 See Kevin Keener, *Personal Privacy in the Face of Government Use of GPS*, 3:3 ISJLP 473 (2007) (describing cases permitting warrantless use of GPS for real-time tracking and to learn about previous travels and noting that only three jurisdictions require a warrant for either purpose). See also *In re* Application of U.S. for an Order Directing a Provider of Elec. Commc'n Serv. to Disclose Records to Gov't, 620 F.3d 304 (3d. Cir. 2010) (requiring only "specific and articulable facts" establishing that cell phone location information outside the home is "relevant" to an investigation).
19 The Court's recent decision in *Florida v. Jardines*, 133 S.Ct. 1409 (2013) reinforces this point. See note 25.
20 *Dow Chemical*, 476 U.S. at 238.
21 *Kyllo v. United States*, 533 U.S. 37, 40 (2001).
22 *State v. Vogel*, 428 N.W.2d 272, 275 (S.D. 1988) (zoom cameras); *State v. Rose*, 909 P.2d 280, 286 (Wash. 1996) (flashlights); *People v. Oynes*, 920 P.2d 880, 883 (Colo. Ct. App. 1996) (binoculars); *State v. Carter*, 790 P.2d 1152, 1155 (1990) rev'd, 848 P.2d 599 (1993) (binoculars).
23 *Baldi v. Amadon*, No. Civ. 02–3130-M, 2004 WL 725618, at *3 (D.N.H. Apr. 5, 2004); *People v. Katz*, No. 224477, 2001 WL 1012114, at *2 (Mich. App. Sept. 4, 2001).
24 *Kyllo*, 533 U.S. at 40 (concluding that if the police could have seen the details inside the home "without physical intrusion" then viewing them technologically is not a search).
25 *Jacobsen v. United States*, 466 U.S. 109, 122–3 (1984) (stating that this conclusion is "dictated" by *Place v. United States*, 462 U.S. 696 (1984), which held that a dog

sniff of luggage is not a search). Although the Court recently held that a dog sniff of a house that requires a trespass is a search, *Jardines v. Florida*, 133 S.Ct. 1409 (2013), it also strongly suggested that if the dog stays on a public sidewalk or similar lawful vantage point, even dog sniffs of homes remain unregulated by the Fourth Amendment.

26 See Paul Joseph Watson, *Fourth Amendment–Violating Mobile X-Ray Scanners Hit the Streets*, PRISONPLANT.COM (Aug. 25, 2010) www.prisonplanet.com/4th-amendment-violating-mobile-x-ray-scanners-hit-the-streets.html (last visited Apr. 29, 2013) ("[B]ackscatter x-ray vision devices mounted on trucks are already being deployed inside the United States to scan passing individuals and vehicles.").

27 *Miller v. United States*, 425 U.S. 435, 443 (1976).

28 See, e.g., *Hoffa v. United States*, 385 U.S. 293 (1966).

29 *Smith v. Maryland*, 442 U.S. 735, 744 (1979).

30 Jeffrey W. Seifert, Cong. Research Serv., RL31798, Data Mining and Homeland Security: An Overview 2, (2007), available at www.fas.org/sgp/crs/intel/RL31798.pdf (last visited Apr. 29, 2013).

31 See DANIEL SOLOVE, THE DIGITAL PERSON: TECHNOLOGY AND PRIVACY IN THE INFORMATION AGE ch. 2 (2004); Martha Neil, *Beyond Big Brother: Some Web Hosts Are Watching Your Every Keystroke*, Aba journal (Aug. 2, 2010 6:02 PM), www.abajournal.com/news/article/some_web_hosts_are_watching_your_every_keystroke/ (last visited Apr. 29, 2013) ("Web hosts are watching what you read, what you say, what you buy and where you go online, via cookies and other tracking tools that enable them to assemble – and sell – detailed profiles to other companies....").

32 Dalia Naamani-Goldman, *Anti-Terrorism Program Mines IRS' Records*, L.A. TIMES, Jan. 15, 2007, at C1.

33 See Laura K. Donohue, *Anglo-American Privacy and Surveillance*, 96 J. CRIM. L. & CRIMINOLOGY 1059, 1151 (2006).

34 Def. Advanced Research Projects Agency, U.S. Dep't of Def., Report to Congress Regarding the Terrorism Information Awareness Program 3–9 (2003).

35 The TIA program was defunded by a voice vote. See 149 CONG. REC S1379–02: 1373, 1416 (daily ed., Jan. 23, 2003). For a description of post-TIA programs, see Ellen Nakashima and Alec Klein, *Profiling Program Raises Privacy Concerns*, *Washington Post*, Feb. 28, 2007, at B1; Shane Harris, *TIA Lives On*, NATIONAL JOURNAL 66, Feb. 25, 2006; and Lillie Coney, Assoc. Dir., Electronic Privacy Info. Ctr., *Statement to the Dep't of Homeland Security Data Privacy and Integrity Advisory Comm.* 1, 4 (Sept. 19, 2007) (transcript available at www.epic.org/privacy/fusion/fusion-dhs.pdf) (last visited Apr. 29, 2013).

36 *T.L.O. v. New Jersey*, 469 U.S. 325, 353 (1985) (Blackmun, J., concurring).

37 *Cassidy v. Chertoff*, 471 U.S. 67, 82 (2d Cir. 2006).

38 *Nicholas v. Goord*, 430 F.3d 652, 668 (2005). See also *United States v. Pool*, 621 F.3d 1213 (9th Cir. 2010) *reh'g en banc granted*, 646 F.3d 659 (9th Cir. 2011) and vacated, 659 F.3d 761 (9th Cir. 2011) (upholding provision of federal Bail Reform Act requiring defendant to provide DNA sample as a condition of pretrial release).

39 Of more than passing interest is the fact that, in *Kyllo*, Justice Scalia felt prompted to note that this was also the definition of search at the time the Fourth Amendment was drafted. *Kyllo*, 533 U.S. at 32 n1.

40 See Christopher Slobogin, *The Liberal Assault on the Fourth Amendment*, 4 OHIO ST. J. CRIM. L. 603, 605–11 (2007) (making this argument).
41 Christopher Slobogin, Privacy at Risk: The New Government Surveillance and the Fourth Amendment (2007).
42 See generally Alice Ristroph, *Proportionality as a Principle of Limited Government*, 55 DUKE L.J. 263 (2005) ("Principles of proportionality put the limits into any theory of limited government.").
43 *Terry*, 392 U.S. at 21 (quoting *Camara v. Mun. Court of City & County of San Francisco*, 387 U.S. 523, 536–7 (1967).
44 References to "intrusiveness" or "invasiveness" are found throughout the Court's Fourth Amendment case law with little or no attempt at definition. I have argued that the concept should be an amalgam of empirically determined views and positive law reflecting views about privacy, autonomy, freedom of speech and association, and, most generally (following the Fourth Amendment's language), security. SLOBOGIN, PRIVACY AT RISK, supra note 41, at 23–37, 98–108. See also Christopher Slobogin, *Proportionality, Privacy, and Public Opinion: A Reply to Kerr and Swire*, 94 MINN. L. REV. 1588, 1594–608 (2010) (describing the concept of intrusiveness in detail).
45 For a more detailed description of this regime, see SLOBOGIN, PRIVACY AT RISK, supra note 41, at ch. 5.
46 See *id.* at 112, 184 (tables reporting lay perceptions of intrusiveness ranking access to bank and phone records approximately the same as search of a car).
47 See *id.* at 28. The exception would not, however, allow relaxation of justification requirements associated with investigating past crime; the intrusiveness associated with search of a house does not vary by the nature of the crime, just as the prosecution's burden of proof is not lessened simply because homicide is the charge. See Slobogin, *Proportionality*, supra note 44, at 1611–14, for elaboration of this argument.
48 See Christopher Slobogin, *Government Dragnets*, 73 J.L. & CONTEMP. PROBS. 107 (Summer, 2010).

Part V

CONFESSIONS AND *MIRANDA*

10

False Confessions and the Constitution

Problems, Possibilities, and Solutions

Richard A. Leo

1. INTRODUCTION

On November 17, 1989, police in Peekskill, New York, discovered the body of fifteen-year-old Angela Correa, who had been raped, beaten, and strangled. On the basis of a detailed profile of the alleged offender prepared by Raymond M. Pierce of the New York Police Department, as well as behavior that they perceived to be highly unusual, Peekskill Detectives Thomas McIntyre and David Levine quickly locked in on Jeffrey Deskovic, a sixteen-year-old classmate of the victim who had been late to school the day after the victim disappeared, as their exclusive suspect. They sought to build a case against him by obtaining his confession to the crime.

Between December 1989 and January 1990, the detectives questioned Deskovic eight times. Throughout these contacts, the police used what they termed *passive/active* techniques, alternating from low-key questioning to high-stress, accusatory, and confrontational interrogation in an effort to induce Deskovic to confess. On January 25, 1990, the detectives gave Deskovic three polygraph exams and interrogated him for approximately eight hours. When they were unable to obtain a confession, even after falsely telling Deskovic that he had failed the polygraph tests, the detectives became more aggressive and confrontational. According to Deskovic, Detective McIntyre told him repeatedly that all the evidence, including the polygraphs, conclusively established his guilt and threatened that if Deskovic did not confess, he would go to prison. However, Detective McIntyre promised that if he confessed, he would receive psychiatric treatment and be allowed to go home.

Deskovic finally confessed. According to Detective McIntrye, Deskovic began by describing the acts committed by the perpetrator in the third person, switching to the first person later in the narrative when he told Detective McIntyre that "I lost my temper" and hit Correa in the back of the head with a

Gatorade bottle. Although he never confessed to raping Correa, Deskovic, now crying, then said that he put his hand over Correa's mouth and "may have left it there too long." According to Deskovic, his statements were false. He was simply repeating details he had learned from the detectives during the lengthy accusatorial interrogation. "I was tired, confused, scared, hungry – I wanted to get out of there," he recalled. "I told the police what they wanted to hear, but I never got to go home. They lied to me."[1] By the end of the interrogation, Deskovic was under the table, curled up in a fetal position, sobbing uncontrollably. Deskovic was arrested for and charged with the murder and rape of Angela Correa.

Lacking DNA or any other forensic or physical evidence tying Deskovic to the crime, prosecutors relied exclusively on his confession to secure his conviction. To persuade the jury to convict Deskovic, police and prosecutors argued that Deskovic's statements were reliable because they contained details that only the true perpetrator could have known, including that there were multiple crime scenes and that the victim had written a note to a former boyfriend shortly before her death, a note that was found crumpled under her body. Police also attributed other details to Deskovic, including that Correa suffered a blow to the head, that he tore her clothes, that there was a struggle, and that he held his hand over her mouth. Throughout Deskovic's trial, police witnesses testified that they took precautions to prevent disclosing any critical crime scene facts to Deskovic.[2] Moreover, police and prosecutors relied heavily on one fact that was supposedly unknown to police prior to Deskovic's disclosure: a "Gatorade bottle" was used to strike the victim in the head. They claimed that police found a Gatorade cap during a search conducted only after Deskovic had told them about the bottle and that injuries inflicted on Correa were consistent with a "heavy bottle."[3] Deskovic was convicted of Correa's murder and sentenced to fifteen years to life.

Deskovic's conviction was affirmed on appeal, and efforts to overturn his conviction through state appellate and federal habeas proceedings failed. The state appellate court found nothing wrong with the interrogation techniques used by the police. The court concluded that the evidence against him was "overwhelming" and that his inculpatory statements were "corroborated" by physical evidence, such as autopsy findings.

In September 2006, DNA testing comparing Deskovic's blood with semen samples taken from vaginal swabs from the victim's body matched to a convicted murderer named Steven Cunningham, who soon thereafter confessed to the crime. Deskovic was officially exonerated on November 2, 2006, after serving nearly sixteen years in prison for a rape and murder he did not commit. Cunningham pled guilty to the murder and rape of Angela Correa on March 14, 2007.[4]

The Jeffrey Deskovic case is not an isolated one. Police-induced false confessions have been a leading cause of wrongful convictions throughout American history. In the last two decades, scholars have documented several hundred confessions that have been proven false to near or absolute certainty,[5] as well as many others that are probable or highly probable to be false.[6] Despite this, however, we do not know the frequency at which false confessions occur or the rate at which they lead to the wrongful conviction of the innocent. No well-founded estimates have ever been published; nor is it presently possible for social scientists to provide one.[7] Nevertheless, because most cases of disputed confessions are rarely publicized and likely to be unreported by the media, unacknowledged by police and prosecutors, and unrecognized by researchers, the documented cases of interrogation-induced false confessions almost certainly understate the true extent of the phenomenon and are thus likely to represent only the tip of a much larger problem.

Regardless of the frequency at which they occur, false confessions remain highly consequential because confession evidence itself is considered such incriminating and persuasive evidence of guilt. The former U.S. Supreme Court justice William Brennan's observation that "no other class of evidence is so profoundly prejudicial"[8] is well supported by social science research. Confessions strongly bias the perceptions and decision making of criminal justice officials and jurors alike because most people assume that a confession by its very nature must be true. Police, prosecutors, judges, jurors, and the media all tend to view confessions as self-authenticating while discounting false confessions as contrary to common sense, irrational, and self-destructive. Moreover, police-induced false confessions tend to be considered facially persuasive because they typically contain content cues that people view as indicative of truthful confessions, such as crime scene details, expressions of remorse, the confessor's alleged motives for committing the offense, other explanations of what occurred, and acknowledgments of voluntariness.[9] Confession evidence therefore tends to define the case against a defendant – as it did against Jeffrey Deskovic – and trump contradictory information and evidence of innocence.[10] Thus, if introduced against a defendant at trial, false confessions are highly likely to lead to wrongful convictions. Empirical studies of real world confessions show that 73–81 percent of false confessors whose cases go to trial are wrongfully convicted; these results are consistent with the findings of mock jury studies in the experimental psychology literature.[11]

In this chapter, I will briefly review some of the main empirical findings from more than three decades of social science research on the causes, consequences, and indicia of police-induced false confessions. I will couch this discussion in the context of the three sequential errors – misclassification, coercion, and contamination – that occur in virtually all police-induced false confessions and that combine to create the powerful, but erroneous, appearance that a false confession is true and persuasive, sometimes leading to the wrongful conviction of an innocent person. I will then briefly review the constitutional law of criminal procedure that governs the admissibility of confession evidence in American courts. I will argue that it fails both to protect suspects meaningfully against interrogation methods that cause false confessions and to prevent the use of false confession evidence against them at trial. I will briefly suggest how the law of criminal procedure can "bring reliability back in" by creating meaningful constitutional safeguards to minimize the risk that police-induced false confessions will lead to wrongful convictions. Finally, I will briefly discuss the challenges and issues going forward.

2. THE PSYCHOLOGY AND SOCIAL SCIENCE OF FALSE CONFESSIONS: THE THREE ERRORS

a. Misclassification

The first mistake that occurs in the sequence of events leading to a false confession is misclassification error, that is, when police erroneously conclude that an innocent suspect is guilty. As Deborah Davis and I have pointed out, "the path to false confession begins, as it must, when police target an innocent suspect."[12] Once specific suspects are pursued, police interviews and interrogations are thereafter guided by a working presumption of guilt, as occurred in the Jeffrey Deskovic case.

Two interrelated factors can lead police mistakenly to classify an innocent person as a guilty suspect. The first stems from poor and erroneous interrogation training. Police are taught, falsely, that they can become human lie detectors capable of distinguishing truth from deception at high rates of accuracy based on the suspect's body language, demeanor, and verbal and nonverbal "behavior symptoms."[13] This deeply ingrained police belief is both wrong and dangerous. It is wrong because it is based on inaccurate speculation that is explicitly contradicted by virtually all the published scientific research on this topic. Social scientific studies repeatedly demonstrate across a variety of contexts that people are poor human lie detectors and thus highly prone to error in their judgments about whether an individual is lying or telling the truth. The interrogator as human lie detector myth is dangerous because it can easily lead a detective to make an erroneous judgment about an innocent suspect's guilt based on little or nothing more than his body language – or, as in Jeffrey Deskovic's case, his "unusual behavior" – and then mistakenly subject him to an accusatorial interrogation that can lead to a false confession.

As empirical research has shown, the human lie detector mythology in investigative police work significantly increases detectives' confidence in the accuracy of their erroneous judgments, leading to what researchers have called the *investigator response bias* (i.e., the tendency to presume a suspect's guilt with near or complete certainty).[14] As empirical research has demonstrated, erroneous but confidently held prejudgments of deception also increase the likelihood that the investigators will subject the innocent suspect to an accusatorial interrogation in which they seek to elicit information and evidence that confirms their prejudgments of guilt and discount information and evidence that does not.

b. Coercion

i. In General

Once interrogation commences, the second and primary cause of police-induced false confessions is psychologically coercive police methods. Some interrogation techniques – like implied or explicit threats and promises – are inherently coercive; others may become cumulatively coercive if they cause a suspect to perceive that he has no meaningful choice but to comply with the interrogator's demands. Psychologically coercive interrogation techniques include some examples of the old third degree, such as deprivations of essential necessities. However, in the modern era, these techniques are rare. Instead, when today's police interrogators employ psychologically coercive techniques, they usually consist of (implied or express) promises of leniency or threats of harsher treatment, as occurred in Jeffrey Deskovic's case.[15]

More generally, the custodial environment and physical confinement of interrogation are intended to isolate and disempower the suspect. Interrogation is designed to be stressful and unpleasant, and this stress and unpleasantness increase the more intensely it proceeds and the longer it lasts. Interrogation techniques are meant to cause the suspect to perceive that his guilt has been established beyond any conceivable doubt, that no one will believe his claims of innocence, and that by continuing to deny the detectives' accusations he will only make his situation (and the ultimate outcome of the case against him) much worse. The suspect may perceive that he has no choice but to comply with the detectives' wishes because he is fatigued, is worn down, or simply sees no other way to escape an intolerably stressful experience. When a suspect perceives that he has no choice but to comply, his resulting compliance and confession are involuntary and the product of coercion.

ii. Vulnerable Suspects

Even though psychological coercion is regarded as the primary cause of police-induced false confessions, individuals differ in their ability to withstand interrogation pressure and thus in their susceptibility to making false confessions. All other factors being equal, those who are highly suggestible or compliant are more likely to make false confessions. Highly suggestible individuals tend to have poor memories, high levels of anxiety, low self-esteem, and low assertiveness – personality factors that make them more vulnerable to the pressures of interrogation. Sleep deprivation, fatigue, and drug or alcohol withdrawal heighten interrogative suggestibility. Highly compliant individuals tend to be conflict avoidant, acquiescent, and eager to please others, especially authority figures.

But highly suggestible or compliant individuals are not the only ones who tend to be unusually vulnerable to the pressures of police interrogation. People who are mentally retarded or cognitively impaired, juveniles, and mentally ill individuals are also more likely to confess falsely.[16] Jeffrey Deskovic was at a heightened risk for a false confession because he was, at the time of his interrogation, a naive sixteen-year-old boy with serious psychological difficulties – speaking to the police against the wishes of his mother – who had no prior experience with the criminal justice system.

c. Contamination

"Contamination" refers to police disclosure or leakage of nonpublic crime facts to the suspect during interrogation. The process of contaminating a suspect during interrogation may be advertent or inadvertent. In his study of the false confessions in the first 250 DNA exonerations, Brandon Garrett found that thirty-eight of forty proven false confessions involved police contamination. Perhaps not surprisingly, false confession cases tend to involve both coercion[17] and contamination.[18] If the use of coercive interrogation techniques often explains why innocent suspects were led to confess falsely in the first place, the process of contamination often explains why demonstrably false confessions appear to contain persuasive indicia of reliability (i.e., nonpublic details that were too unique to be guessed by chance).

A confession is more than an "I did it" statement. It also consists of a subsequent narrative that contextualizes and attempts to explain the "I did it" statement. The postadmission narrative (the account of how and why the suspect committed the crime) transforms a fledgling admission into a fully formed confession. The postadmission narrative is the story that is wrapped around the admission and thus makes it appear, at least on its face, to be a compelling account of the suspect's guilt. The content and rhetorical force of a suspect's postadmission narrative explain, in part, why confessions are treated as such powerful evidence of guilt and sometimes lead to the arrest, prosecution, and conviction of the innocent. The contamination of the suspect's postadmission narrative is thus the third mistake in the trilogy of police errors that cumulatively lead to the elicitation and construction of a persuasive false confession.

3. CONSTITUTIONAL LAW: WHY CRIMINAL PROCEDURE OFTEN FAILS TO PREVENT POLICE-INDUCED FALSE CONFESSIONS AND THE WRONGFUL CONVICTIONS THEY SPAWN

The law governing confessions places far too much importance on the procedural fairness of the interrogation process and far too little importance on the substantive truthfulness of the confession. The Fifth, Sixth, and Fourteenth Amendments regulate the admissibility of confession evidence. If any one of these doctrines is violated, the confession should, in theory, be excluded from evidence at trial.

According to current interpretations of the Fourteenth Amendment's due process clause, a confession is inadmissible if police interrogation methods overbear the suspect's will and thus cause him to make an "involuntary" confession. Under this standard, the voluntariness (and hence admissibility) of a confession is evaluated case by case, on the basis of the totality of the circumstances (i.e., the facts of the case, the suspect's personality characteristics, and the specific police interrogation methods). The Fourteenth Amendment's due process clause additionally permits courts to exclude as "involuntary" any confession obtained by fundamentally unfair police methods, regardless of the confession's voluntariness.[19]

According to the Sixth Amendment, a confession may be excluded from evidence if, *after* a suspect has been indicted, he is questioned outside the presence of his lawyer.[20] And, of course, the Fifth Amendment's privilege against self-incrimination permits judges to exclude confessions from evidence if police did not properly recite the *Miranda* warnings or if they did not obtain a knowing and voluntary waiver.[21] The *Miranda* warnings inform suspects that they have the right to remain silent, that anything they say can and will be used against them, that they have the right to an attorney, and that if they cannot afford an attorney, one will be appointed.

None of these doctrines currently provides much protection against the admission of unreliable or false confessions into evidence at trial. While the Fourteenth Amendment's due process test may have once focused on the reliability of a confession in determining its voluntariness, the early nexus between reliability and voluntariness has long been severed.[22] The due process test no longer concerns itself in any meaningful way with the reliability of a suspect's confession. Instead, it is interpreted as protecting a suspect from coercive and/or fundamentally unfair police questioning methods. If an unreliable confession is excluded under the due process test, it is only because the confession was judged involuntary or because police pressures were so unfair as to shock the judicial conscience. Unreliable or false confessions produced by standard interrogation methods or procedures that do not rise to the level of legal coerciveness or fundamental unfairness are admitted into evidence.

The Sixth Amendment's entirely procedural concern with postindictment questioning also offers little or no protection against the admission of false confessions, since virtually all police interrogations occur prior to indictment. Like the Fourteenth Amendment's due process test, the Sixth Amendment is concerned entirely with the procedural fairness that occurs during the *process* of interrogation but not at all with the substantive reliability of the confession that is the *outcome* of interrogation.

And so it is with *Miranda*, which is concerned only with the procedural fairness of the interrogation process – whether a suspect retains his rational and voluntary decision-making ability in the face of inherently compelling police pressures – not with the substantive truth of the interrogation outcome. While it may prevent some suspects from speaking to police, *Miranda* offers little or no protection against the elicitation of false confessions from innocent suspects or their admission into evidence.[23] This is true for at least two reasons.

First, the vast majority of suspects – at least 80–90 percent[24] – waive their *Miranda* rights and willingly submit to police interrogation. What is more important here, however, is understanding who chooses to speak to police. Those suspects least likely to give a false confession – individuals who have prior criminal records and have been hardened by their earlier exposure to police and the criminal justice system – are most likely to invoke their *Miranda* rights to terminate police questioning. Conversely, those suspects who are most likely to give false confessions – individuals who do not have criminal records and are more vulnerable to suggestion – are least likely to invoke their *Miranda* rights to terminate police questioning. Ironically, then, the minimal protection *Miranda* in theory offers against the possibility of false confessions is in practice entirely misdirected.[25]

Second, once the interrogator recites the fourfold warnings and obtains a waiver, *Miranda* is irrelevant to both the process and the outcome of the subsequent interrogation. Any protection *Miranda* might have offered a suspect typically evaporates as soon as an accusatory interrogation begins – which is exactly when a suspect is most likely to feel the inherently compelling pressures of police-dominated custodial interrogation. Once issued and waived, *Miranda* does not restrict deceptive or suggestive police tactics, manipulative interrogation strategies, hostile or overbearing questioning styles, lengthy confinement, or any of the inherently stressful conditions of modern accusatorial interrogation that may lead the innocent to confess.[26] In other words, once police issue warnings and obtain a waiver (and very few suspects subsequently invoke their *Miranda* rights after they have been waived), *Miranda* is virtually irrelevant to the problem of false confessions.[27]

It bears mentioning here that often police detectives do not need to give any *Miranda* warnings in order to interrogate criminal suspects. Because *Miranda* warnings are required only when a suspect is legally in custody (i.e., either under arrest or not free to leave), police often redefine the circumstances of questioning so that the suspect technically is not in custody. They do this by simply telling the suspect that he is not under arrest and is free to leave. In California, detectives refer to this strategy as issuing "*Beheler* warnings," named after a Supreme Court case from California that legally permits them to do so.[28] Once detectives have issued "*Beheler* warnings," they can proceed to interrogate the suspect without giving *Miranda* warnings or eliciting a *Miranda* waiver, thereby avoiding the risk that the suspect will terminate the interrogation by exercising his right to silence or counsel. Detectives sometimes issue "*Beheler* warnings" instead of *Miranda* warnings even after they have transported the suspect to the station house with the express purpose of questioning and eliciting incriminating statements from him.[29]

It is possible that *Miranda*, even when it is required, has undermined any protection the law might have otherwise offered against the admission of false confessions into evidence. For *Miranda* has de facto displaced the due process voluntariness standard as the primary test of a confession's admissibility, shifting the court's analysis from the voluntariness of a confession to the voluntariness of a *Miranda* waiver.[30] As Justice Souter noted in 2004: "Giving the warnings and getting a waiver has generally produced a virtual ticket of admissibility; maintaining that a statement is involuntary even though given after warnings and voluntary waiver of rights requires unusual stamina, and litigation over voluntariness tends to end with the finding of a valid waiver."[31] Though the *Miranda* holding is logically independent of the due process voluntariness standard, empirical research confirms Justice Souter's observation in *Missouri v. Seibert* that trial judges will almost always declare a confession voluntary if the *Miranda* procedures appear to have been properly followed.[32] To put it differently, by focusing on the proper reading and waiver of the simple *Miranda* formula, trial judges often appear to avoid the more difficult and elusive task of analyzing whether police pressures have overborne the suspect's decision-making capacity. Perhaps more importantly, by generating seemingly endless controversy (both popular and academic) about its symbolic messages and its allegedly disastrous effects on the confession and conviction rates of the guilty, *Miranda* has diverted attention from the substantive reliability of interrogation outcomes and the very real risk of wrongful convictions based on false confessions.

Regrettably, neither the Fourteenth Amendment's due process clause nor the Sixth Amendment's right to a fair trial nor the Fifth Amendment's privilege against self-incrimination nor the prophylactic *Miranda* rules offer any significant protection against the admission of false confessions. Oddly, the constitutional law of criminal procedure has no meaningful substantive safeguards in place to prevent the use of false confession evidence against innocent defendants at trial.

The more general problem is that constitutional law seems concerned only with the procedural fairness of police questioning, so much so that it currently lacks any rules to guarantee the reliability of confessions. Yet it is not uncommon for suspects – especially highly suggestible ones such as the mentally handicapped, juveniles, and individuals unusually trusting of authority[33] – to give false confessions (after waiving their *Miranda* rights) in response to police inducements that do not legally qualify as coercive or fundamentally unfair. In other words, police pressures that do not rise to the level of legal definitions of coercion or fundamental unfairness (and that are exerted after a voluntary *Miranda* waiver) may nevertheless cause innocent suspects to make false confessions.

4. THE WAY FORWARD: BRINGING RELIABILITY BACK IN

As we have seen, the constitutional law of criminal procedure does not meaningfully protect innocent defendants against the likelihood that their false confessions will be admitted into evidence at trial and lead to their wrongful conviction. Elsewhere my colleagues and I have proposed a simple change in state and federal criminal procedure law that would reduce this risk, namely, requiring that a trial judge assess both the confession's voluntariness *and its reliability* when defense attorneys challenge the validity of a disputed confession at a pretrial motion to suppress hearing.[34] In this section, I detail the basis and substance of this proposed reform.

Richard Ofshe and I have argued that the reliability of a suspect's confession can be evaluated by analyzing the fit (or lack thereof) between the descriptions in his postadmission narrative and the crime facts.[35] Courts would determine whether the suspect's postadmission narrative reveals the presence (or absence) of guilty knowledge and whether it is corroborated (or disconfirmed) by objective evidence. A suspect who committed the crime will possess personal (that is, nonpublic) knowledge about both dramatic and mundane crime facts that are known only by the perpetrator, the police, or the victim (for example, the location of the weapon, items taken during the crime, and specific aspects of the crime scene such as the color of paint on the wall or the pattern in the carpet). A suspect who did not commit the crime will not possess personal knowledge of the crime details unless the suspect has preexisting knowledge, or the police have "contaminated" the suspect through education about the crime scene facts during the interrogation process. Assuming that the suspect does not possess preexisting knowledge and has not been contaminated by police suggestion, the probative value of crime facts and details accurately provided in the suspect's postadmission narrative is directly proportionate to the likelihood that such details could have been guessed by chance.

Absent preexisting knowledge or contamination, the postadmission narratives of the guilty true confessor and innocent false confessor will look different. The guilty confessor's postadmission narrative will likely demonstrate personal knowledge of crime facts; will be able to lead police to new, missing, or derivative crime scene evidence; will be able to provide them with missing information; will be able to explain seemingly anomalous or otherwise inexplicable crime facts; and will likely be corroborated by existing objective evidence. By contrast, the innocent confessor will not be able to supply accurate crime details in a postadmission narrative unless the confessor guesses them by chance; will not be able to lead police to new, missing, or derivative evidence; will not be able to explain crime scene anomalies or other unique or unlikely aspects of the crime; and will provide a postadmission narrative that will not be corroborated by existing objective evidence. Instead, the innocent false confessor's postadmission narrative will likely be replete with guesses and errors and will either be inconsistent with or contradicted by the objective case evidence. In short, the postadmission narrative of a suspect who is confessing truthfully will tend to fit with the crime facts and objective physical evidence, whereas the postadmission narrative of an innocent suspect who is confessing falsely will not.

In many cases, analyzing the fit between a suspect's postadmission narrative and the crime facts and existing objective case evidence provides a standard against which to evaluate the statement's likely reliability. As Richard Ofshe and I have pointed out:

There are at least three indicia of reliability that can be evaluated to reach a conclusion about the trustworthiness of a confession. Does the statement (1) lead to the discovery of evidence unknown to the police? (*e.g.*, location of a missing weapon that can be proven to have been used in the crime, location of missing loot that can be proven to have been taken from the crime scene, etc.); (2) include identification of highly unusual elements of the crime that have not been made public? (*e.g.*, an unlikely method of killing, mutilation of a certain type, use of a particular device to silence the victim, etc.); or (3) include an accurate description of the mundane details of the crime which are not easily guessed and have not been reported publicly (*e.g.*, how the victim was clothed, disarray of certain furniture pieces, presence or absence of particular objects at the crime scene, etc).[36]

We have argued that courts should insist on a minimum standard of reliability, and thus independent corroboration, before admitting a confession into evidence. We have further argued that the fit analysis necessary to determine a confession's likely reliability can be properly conducted only if police have electronically recorded the interrogation in its entirety. Without this, there is no way objectively to resolve the "swearing contest" between police and the suspect over who said what during interrogation.[37]

There is little dispute that the factors identified by us should contribute to an assessment of confession evidence reliability.[38] Judges evaluating the reliability of confessions that are products of recorded interrogations should weigh three factors: (1) whether the confession contains nonpublic information that can be independently verified, would be known only by the true perpetrator or an accomplice, and cannot likely be guessed by chance; (2) whether the confession led the police to new evidence about the crime; and (3) whether the suspect's postadmission narrative fits the crime facts and other objective evidence.

Defendants will bear the burden of demonstrating unreliability but need only marshal some evidence that the confession is unreliable on the basis of the tripartite "totality of the circumstances" test outlined previously. The ultimate burden of persuasion, however, falls on the prosecution. Because the jury is the ultimate fact finder with respect to the truth or falsity of a confession, the standard for admissibility should be less than "beyond a reasonable doubt." Elsewhere my colleagues and I have proposed a "preponderance of the evidence" standard.[39]

Pretrial assessments of the reliability of the confession evidence need not lead to the kind of lengthy, contested motions sometimes seen in involuntariness hearings. In most cases, witnesses would not need to be called, the defense could submit its reasons why the confession is not reliable in its pleadings, the state could reply, and the judge could view and analyze the recorded interrogation and confession and rule on the pleadings after argument. To the extent that prosecutors must demonstrate evidence of a fit, the nonpublic facts known by the defendant and the evidence recovered as a result of the defendant's statements would allow them to do so in most cases by proffer or affidavit.

More generally, the kind of evidentiary evaluation my colleagues and I have proposed is one that trial courts do all the time to prevent unreliable or nonprobative evidence from biasing, confusing, or misleading juries.[40] Judges are routinely called upon to decide whether to admit reliable evidence. The requirement in a criminal case that the evidence presented to the jury have sufficient indicia of reliability is neither new nor novel. Had Jeffrey Deskovic's eight-hour interrogation been electronically recorded, and had such a test been in place and applied at the time, Deskovic never would have been wrongfully convicted or spent sixteen years in prison for a rape and murder he did not commit.

5. CHALLENGES FOR THE FUTURE

This chapter has been organized around the three sequential police errors – misclassification, coercion, and contamination – leading to the elicitation of false confessions that take on the appearance of persuasive evidence of guilt and that, when introduced at trial, are highly likely to lead to the wrongful conviction of the innocent. The challenges that face those seeking to reduce the prevalence of false confessions, and the wrongful convictions they sometimes cause, should in theory be easy to overcome but in practice remain entrenched. The challenges should be easy to overcome because no one – not police, prosecutors, defense attorneys, judges, or jurors – is in favor of false confessions; it is not a phenomenon for which there is a constituency. Everyone in the criminal justice system shares the goal of preventing both false confessions and wrongful convictions. Moreover, according to police training manuals and programs, the preinterrogation police investigation process is supposed to weed out, not ensnare, the innocent; and the interrogation process that follows is thus designed only for the guilty – after a case has been "thoroughly investigated" – not the innocent.[41] With such universal consensus about the goals of police investigation and interrogation, one might think that it should be relatively easy to craft and implement a solution to the problem of false confessions, especially since we now have more than three decades of empirical social scientific studies documenting and analyzing the causes, characteristics, indicia, risk factors, and consequences of interrogation-induced false confessions[42] with which to guide legal, policy, and organizational change.

But this is not so. The problem of false confessions remains difficult to overcome in practice for at least two reasons. First, American police detectives, trainers, and organizations have almost universally failed to study or learn from their mistakes. Virtually all police detectives and organizations continue to ignore the extensive body of research that shows how and why they sometimes elicit false confessions, how to recognize indicia of false and unreliable confessions, how to prevent interrogation-induced false confessions from occurring in the first place, and why they sometimes lead to the erroneous conviction of innocent men and women. Most police interrogation training manuals and programs do not address the problem of interrogation-induced false confessions; the ones that do dismiss the phenomenon as anomalous and/or falsely criticize the social science research and its implications, mischaracterizing and belittling leading scientific research as the work of "opponents of interrogation" and "false confessions theorists."

Worse still, American police interrogators persist in the very misguided beliefs and practices that lead to interrogation-induced false confessions. Consider the misclassification error. Police interrogation training firms, manuals, classes, and seminars continue to train detectives to act like human lie detectors who can identify truth and deception at high levels of accuracy by relying on "behavioral symptoms" such as gaze aversion, frozen posture, slouching, and fidgeting. However, the scientific research has repeatedly demonstrated that these commonsense behavioral cues are not diagnostic of truth or deception; that police detectives, like laypeople, are only slightly better than chance at differentiating truth tellers from liars; and that their training increases police confidence in their prejudgments of guilt, even though these prejudgments are frequently wrong.[43] Beyond their training, the myth of police interrogator as human lie detector has pervaded police interrogation culture and practice as well. The predictable result is that police investigators continue, usually with great confidence, to misclassify innocent suspects as guilty and then subject these innocent individuals to guilt-presumptive interrogations whose goal is not to "find the truth," but to build a case against them by eliciting incriminating statements that will lead to a successful prosecution.[44]

The misclassifications created by the myth and practice of police interrogator as human lie detector may seem to be the most innocent of the three errors leading to false confession, but they are in fact the most consequential because misclassification occurs earlier in the investigative process and thus is typically a predicate for both the coercion and contamination errors. With respect to psychological coercion, here too police interrogation manuals, trainers, and detectives are tone deaf to the social science research and its implications for police practice and interrogation reform. There is simply no agreement between American police investigators (including the interrogation training industry) and the social science research community about what constitutes psychological coercion and what interrogation practices increase the risk of eliciting false and unreliable confessions. For example, numerous researchers have identified techniques such as deception, minimization, and inducements that implicitly communicate promises and threats as situational risk factors for inducing false confessions.[45] Yet police interrogation training manuals continue to teach these techniques, and police detectives continue to use them. It is clear that police trainers and detectives will only accept an interrogation method as coercive or problematic if the judgment is that of an appellate court, not the scientific research community. Again, the predictable result is that police investigators continue to use psychologically coercive interrogation methods and elicit false confessions from the innocent, as the social science research has repeatedly demonstrated.

There is, however, agreement between the police interrogation training industry and the social science research community on the significance of the contamination error. Police detectives are trained that there is no legitimate investigative purpose for leaking or disclosing nonpublic crime details (that are not likely guessed by chance) during interrogation, but instead that detectives should question in a nonleading manner that will allow suspects to provide such details independently, thus verifying the accuracy of any incriminating statements. In practice, however, police interrogations leading to false confessions – such as what occurred in the Jeffrey Deskovic case – have repeatedly been shown to contain nonpublic crime facts that could not have been guessed by chance and that, instead, were learned from police interrogators. Scholars refer to such nonpublic details (suggested by the police, repeated by the suspect, and then incorporated into his confession) as "misleading specialized knowledge."[46] The problem with misleading specialized knowledge is that it creates the illusion of corroboration[47] – or what in other contexts has also been referred to as "pseudocorroboration"[48] or "corroboration inflation"[49] – because police and prosecutors assert that the nonpublic details in the suspect's confession originated with the suspect and thus betray guilty knowledge, even though the suspect is merely parroting back details that were fed to him by his interrogator(s). In these cases, the interrogating detectives seem to remain unaware – both pre and post exoneration – that they contaminated their innocent suspects with misleading specialized knowledge that contributed to the wrongful conviction. Because of the disconnect between the police investigation community and the social science research, once again there has been little attempt by police trainers, managers, and detectives to study their mistakes and to learn how to minimize and prevent contamination.

From all of this, it has become clear that the problem of police-induced false confessions is not going to be solved by police trainers, detectives, or the police interrogation training industry. The will and leadership to solve this problem – that is, minimizing, reducing, and preventing false confessions born of police misclassification, coercion, and contamination – must proceed from institutions extrinsic to policing.

The political institution that traditionally has overseen police interrogation practices, of course, is the United States Supreme Court. This is the second reason that the problem of false confessions remains difficult to overcome in practice. As we have seen, American constitutional case law regulates only interrogation procedures, not the substance of confession evidence. Perversely, in American constitutional law, it does not matter whether confession evidence is false or unreliable for it to be admitted into evidence against a defendant at trial. It only matters whether the process used to elicit the confessions complies with certain warning and waiver requirements (if applicable) and contemporary understandings of fair procedure. The historical legal safeguard against the admissibility of unreliable confessions – the Fourteenth Amendment due process voluntariness test – has effectively evaporated. As the Supreme Court stated in *Colorado v. Connelly*: "The aim of the requirement of due process is not to exclude presumptively false evidence, but to prevent fundamental unfairness in the use of evidence, whether true or false."[50] Whether a defendant's allegedly false confession should be constitutionally admissible, according to the Court, "is a matter to be governed by the evidentiary laws of the forum, and not by the Due Process Clause of the Fourteenth Amendment."[51] *Colorado v. Connelly* was decided in 1986, only three years before the innocence revolution in American criminal justice that began with the first DNA exoneration in 1989, almost a quarter of a century ago. Since 1989, hundreds of exonerations (with and without the use of DNA) have been documented, and many of these were caused in part or whole by police-induced false confessions.[52] In order to catch up with the times, the United States Supreme Court needs to reinterpret the Fourteenth Amendment as independently allowing courts to exclude unreliable confession evidence on due process grounds alone and/or to create a different doctrinal mechanism for courts to exclude false confession evidence prior to trial. Otherwise, as we know now with absolute certainty, the false confessions that American police interrogators continue to elicit will, in some number of cases, continue to lead to the wrongful conviction and incarceration of innocent men and women across the United States.

Notes

1 Fernanda Santos, *Vindicated by DNA, but a Lost Man on the Outside*, N.Y. TIMES, Nov. 25, 2007, at A11.
2 Brandon Garrett, *The Substance of False Confessions*, 62 STAN. L. REV. 1051 (2010).
3 *Id.*
4 Leslie Snyder, Peter McQuillan, William Murphy & Richard Joselson, *Report on the Conviction of Jeffrey Deskovic* (June 2007), available at http://www.westchesterda.net/Jeffrey%20Deskovic%20Comm%20Rpt.pdf (last visited Jul. 5, 2012).
5 Steven Drizin & Richard A. Leo, *The Problem of False Confessions in the Post-DNA World*, 82 N.C. L. REV. 891 (2004); RICHARD A. LEO, POLICE INTERROGATION AND AMERICAN JUSTICE (2008) [hereinafter LEO, INTERROGATION].
6 Richard A. Leo & Richard Ofshe, *The Consequences of False Confessions: Deprivations of Liberty and Miscarriages of Justice in the Age of Psychological Interrogation*, 88 J. CRIM. LAW & CRIMINOLOGY 429 (1998) [hereinafter Leo, Consequences]; LEO, INTERROGATION supra note 5.
7 LEO, INTERROGATION, supra note 5.
8 *Colorado v. Connelly*, 479 U.S. 157, 182 (1986).
9 LEO, INTERROGATION, supra note 5.
10 Leo, *Consequences*, supra note 6; Saul Kassin, *Why Confessions Trump Innocence*, 67 AM. PSYCHOLOG. 431 (2012) [hereinafter Kassin, *Trump*]
11 Leo, *Consequences*, supra note 6; Drizin, supra note 5; LEO, INTERROGATION, supra note 5.
12 Deborah Davis & Richard A. Leo, *Strategies for Preventing False Confessions and Their Consequences*, in PRACTICAL PSYCHOLOGY FOR FORENSIC INVESTIGATIONS AND PROSECUTIONS 121, 123–4 (Mark Kebbell & Graham Davies, eds., 2006).
13 FRED INBAU, JOHN REID, JOSEPH BUCKLEY & BRIAN JAYNE, CRIMINAL INTERROGATION AND CONFESSIONS (5th ed., 2013).
14 Christian Meissner & S. M. Kassin, *"You're Guilty, So Just Confess!" Cognitive and Confirmational Biases in the Interrogation Room*, in INTERROGATIONS, CONFESSIONS AND ENTRAPMENT 85 (G. D. Lassiter, ed., 2004).
15 LEO, INTERROGATION, supra note 5.
16 Saul Kassin, Steven Drizin, Thomas Grisso, Gisli Gudjohnsson, Richard A. Leo & Allison Redlich, *Police-Induced Confessions: Risk Factors and Recommendations*, 34 LAW & HUM. BEH. 3 (2010) [hereinafter Kassin, *Police-Induced Confessions*].
17 Drizin, supra note 5.
18 Garrett, supra note 2.
19 GEORGE C. THOMAS & RICHARD A. LEO, CONFESSIONS OF GUILT: FROM TORTURE TO MIRANDA AND BEYOND (2012).
20 *Massiah v. United States*, 377 U.S. 201 (1964).
21 *Miranda v. Arizona*, 384 U.S. 436 (1966).
22 THOMAS & LEO, supra note 19.
23 Steven Duke, *Does* Miranda *Protect the Innocent or the Guilty?* 10 CHAP. L. REV. 551 (2007).
24 BARRY FELD, KIDS, COPS AND CONFESSIONS: INSIDE THE INTERROGATION ROOM (2012).

25 William Stuntz, Miranda's *Mistake*, 99 MICH. L. REV. 975 (2001).
26 LEO, INTERROGATION, supra note 5.
27 Richard A. Leo, *Questioning the Relevance of* Miranda *in the Twenty-First Century*, 99 MICH. L. REV. 1000 (2001).
28 *California v. Beheler*, 463 U.S. 1121 (1983).
29 LEO, INTERROGATION, supra note 5.
30 THOMAS & LEO, supra note 19.
31 *Missouri v. Seibert*, 542 U.S. 600, 608–9 (2004).
32 Richard A. Leo, Miranda *and the Problem of False Confessions*, In THE MIRANDA DEBATE: LAW, JUSTICE AND POLICING 271 (Richard A. Leo & George C. Thomas III, eds., 1998); LEO, INTERROGATION, supra note 5.
33 G. H. GUDJONSSON, THE PSYCHOLOGY OF INTERROGATIONS AND CONFESSIONS HANDBOOK (2003).
34 Richard A. Leo, Steven Drizin, Peter Neufeld, Brad Hall & Amy Vatner, *Bringing Reliability Back In: False Confessions and Legal Safeguards in the Twenty-First Century*, 2006 WIS. L REV. 479 [hereinafter Leo, *Reliability*].
35 Richard Ofshe & Richard A. Leo, *The Decision to Confess Falsely: Rational Choice and Irrational Action*, 74 DENV. U. L. REV. 979 (1997).
36 Richard A. Leo & Richard Ofshe, *The Consequences of False Confessions: Deprivations of Liberty and Miscarriages of Justice in the Age of Psychological Interrogation*, 88 J. CRIM. LAW & CRIMINOLOGY 429, 438–9 (1998).
37 Ofshe, supra note 35.
38 *Id.*
39 Leo, *Reliability*, supra note 34.
40 *Id.*
41 INBAU, supra note 13.
42 Kassin, *Police-Induced Confessions*, supra note 16.
43 *Id.*
44 LEO, INTERROGATION, supra note 5.
45 Kassin, *Police-Induced Confessions*, supra note 16; Ofshe, supra note 35.
46 GUDJONSSON, supra note 33; LEO, INTERROGATION, supra note 5; Garrett, supra note 2.
47 LEO, INTERROGATION, supra note 5.
48 DAN SIMON, IN DOUBT: THE PSYCHOLOGY OF THE CRIMINAL JUSTICE PROCESS (2012).
49 Kassin, *Trump*, supra note 10.
50 479 U.S. 157, 167 (1986).
51 *Id.*
52 SAMUEL R. GROSS & MICHAEL SHAFFER, EXONERATIONS IN THE UNITED STATES, 1989–2012 REPORT BY THE NATIONAL REGISTRY OF EXONERATIONS (June 2012), available at http://www.law.umich.edu/special/exoneration/Documents/exonerations_us_1989_2012_full_report.pdf (last visited Mar. 31, 2013).

11

The Foggy Future of *Miranda*

Emily Hughes

Any police television show on any given night will almost invariably include a police officer telling a suspect the familiar refrain: "You have the right to remain silent. Anything you say can and will be used against you in a court of law. You have the right to an attorney. If you cannot afford an attorney, one will be provided for you."[1] While knowledge of the *Miranda* warnings[2] is nearly ubiquitous, what happens when officers fail to administer *Miranda* warnings is not as well understood.

Before the Supreme Court decided *Miranda* in 1966, the Court evaluated the admissibility of suspects' confessions by using a voluntariness test.[3] Guided by the assumption that coerced confessions are inherently untrustworthy, the Court held that a confession must be voluntary in order to be admitted into evidence.[4] The two constitutional bases for this requirement were the Fifth Amendment right against self-incrimination and the due process clause of the Fourteenth Amendment.[5] Initially, courts relied almost exclusively on the due process clause, but after the Supreme Court held that the Fifth Amendment's self-incrimination clause is incorporated in the due process clause of the Fourteenth Amendment and thus applies to the states,[6] courts began to rely more heavily on the Fifth Amendment when evaluating the admissibility of suspects' confessions.[7]

To discuss the future of *Miranda*, this chapter begins by clarifying the contours of where *Miranda* is now. The first section introduces a case, *Missouri v. Seibert*, as an example of a specific situation in which *Miranda* played a key role in a police officer's interrogation tactics. The chapter then spins the facts from *Seibert* into seven different scenarios in order to explore ways in which *Miranda* does – and does not – guide police officers' strategic decisions of how to obtain confessions from suspects. Following this discussion, the chapter concludes by looking into the future to hypothesize where *Miranda* may be headed.

1. MISSOURI V. SEIBERT

Patrice Seibert's son, Jonathon, had cerebral palsy. After Seibert found Jonathon's dead body lying in his bed on February 12, 1997, Seibert woke her other two sons, told them their brother had died in his sleep, and expressed concern that she would be charged with neglect.[8]

In response, her teenage sons devised a plan. Together with two friends, Seibert's sons decided they would set the family's mobile home on fire in order to burn Jonathon's body. They would also leave Donald Rector, a mentally ill teenager living with them, inside the mobile home in order "to avoid any appearance that Jonathon had been unattended."[9]

With the plan in place, her sons bought a five-gallon can of gasoline and Seibert left the mobile home. Her son Darian and his friend Damian Roper then poured gasoline throughout the home and set it on fire. Darian and Damian were accidentally trapped in the blaze and sustained burns. Donald died.[10]

Five days later, after Darian had been transferred to a hospital burn unit, police officers investigating the case suspected the fire had been deliberately set. They also suspected Patrice Seibert. The officers waited until 3:00 a.m. to go to Darian's hospital room. As expected, they found Patrice Seibert asleep by Darian's side. They roused Seibert, placed her under arrest, and drove her to the police station for questioning.[11]

Before the officers had even arrived at the hospital, *Miranda* was heavy on the mind of the investigating officer. Officer Hanrahan specifically told the arresting officer not to give Seibert her *Miranda* warnings when he arrested her.[12] As Officer Hanrahan later testified, this choice was deliberate. He wanted to interrogate Seibert without giving her *Miranda* warnings in order to elicit a confession from her, then give her *Miranda* warnings and hope that she would repeat her confession after the warnings.

Officer Hanrahan knew that any pre-*Miranda* confession would be inadmissible as substantive evidence in a trial against Seibert. Officer Hanrahan's interrogation training, however, led him to believe that if a suspect continued to talk after receiving *Miranda* warnings, the post-*Miranda* statement would be admissible.[13]

Officer Hanrahan's strategy worked as planned. After Seibert confessed to her knowledge of the arson in her pre-*Miranda* first-stage interrogation, which lasted somewhere between thirty and forty minutes, Officer Hanrahan gave her a twenty-minute cigarette and coffee break. He then resumed the interrogation by giving Seibert *Miranda* warnings and having her sign a written waiver of rights form. With the signed waiver in hand, Hanrahan began the post-*Miranda* second-stage questioning. Seibert then repeated her knowledge of the planned arson and her expectation that Donald was to die.[14] This second stage lasted eighteen minutes from the time Hanrahan turned on a tape recorder to the time he turned it off. After Hanrahan obtained the second-stage post-*Miranda* confession, he took Seibert to jail and charged her with first-degree murder.[15]

Prior to trial, Seibert moved to suppress her confession, arguing that the police violated her rights by failing to give her *Miranda* warnings before commencing the interrogation. In denying her motion, the trial court explained that Seibert's statement was admissible because the prosecution was only using the part of the statement obtained "after she was advised of her *Miranda* rights."[16]

At trial, the jury heard Seibert's post-*Miranda* tape-recorded confession and convicted her of second-degree murder. The United States Supreme Court eventually granted certiorari. In a fractured plurality decision, the Supreme Court held that the prosecution improperly used Seibert's confession against her and reversed for a new trial.[17]

2. SEVEN SCENARIOS

This chapter uses Patrice Seibert's interrogation as a prism through which to discuss the future of *Miranda*. In contrast to Professor Richard A. Leo's chapter analyzing the factors that contribute to false confessions, this chapter discusses confessions that are assumed to detail the suspect's role in the crime accurately and that are obtained *before* a suspect is indicted.

Prior to indictment, courts look to the Fifth Amendment's privilege against self-incrimination to decide whether to exclude a true confession that the police obtained without either giving *Miranda* warnings or obtaining a knowing and voluntary waiver.[18] The Fifth Amendment guarantees that "[no] person ... shall be *compelled* in any criminal case to be a witness against himself."[19] As a result, if a court concludes that a confession is "compelled" or "coerced" rather than "voluntary" – that is, that the confession was obtained against the will of the person rather than freely given[20] – it will exclude the statement in the prosecution's case in chief. However, if the confession is not coerced, even "the most damning admissions" do not violate the Fifth Amendment privilege.[21]

In *Miranda*, the Supreme Court presumed that interrogating a suspect in custody is inherently coercive. Because custodial interrogation is inherently coercive, when a suspect makes statements to police while s/he is in custody, those statements are inadmissible unless the police first give the suspect *Miranda* warnings and the suspect waives those rights.[22] *Miranda* warnings thereby safeguard a suspect's constitutional right against self-incrimination.

In one way, the Supreme Court's decision in *Seibert* resolved the question of whether a confession obtained through the two-step process in *Seibert* is admissible against the defendant at trial: it is not. In another way, *Seibert* highlights the murkiness that muddles the Supreme Court's *Miranda* doctrine. The failure to give *Miranda* warnings does not, in and of itself, violate any constitutional right of the suspect. What matters is the context in which the *Miranda* warnings are *not* given, as well as what the prosecution seeks to do with information it obtains in the absence of *Miranda* warnings. To showcase this, I will next discuss seven different situations in which police do not give *Miranda* warnings in order to demonstrate how slight alterations of the facts in Seibert's case impact the outcome.

a. Scenario One: No Warnings, No Confession

First, consider Scenario One. The police arrest Seibert and take her to jail, but Seibert says nothing to the police. In this situation, it makes no difference that the police did not administer *Miranda* warnings because there is no statement to use against her in court. The prosecutor's case in chief during trial would therefore turn on the circumstantial evidence the police collected. Unlike Seibert's actual trial, where Seibert's second-stage confession was integral to the prosecution's case, here, the fact that the police did not administer *Miranda* warnings is entirely irrelevant.

This scenario is the baseline of what happens in the absence of *Miranda* warnings. The general public may mistakenly believe that a police officer's failure to administer *Miranda* warnings means that the suspect automatically "wins" at trial. In reality, nothing of the kind happens. Even if the police have not given *Miranda* warnings, the suspect will not automatically "win" so long as the suspect has said nothing. When the police do not give *Miranda* warnings and a suspect chooses to talk, however, different results ensue, depending on the context in which the discussion happens. The second scenario explores one such situation.

b. Scenario Two: No Warnings, Confession to Undercover Officers

Now consider Scenario Two. Assume undercover officers sit next to Seibert in the hospital cafeteria and casually tell her that they had seen police officers walking down the hallway looking for somebody named Patrice Seibert. Also assume that Seibert did not know they were actually police. In this scenario, if Seibert says something incriminating to the undercover officers, her statement would be admissible against her at trial.

Seibert's incriminating statements to undercover officers would be admissible because *Miranda* warnings are not required if a suspect does not know that the undercover officers are actually police.[23] This is because the question of whether "coercion" exists is determined from the suspect's perspective.[24] Interrogation of individuals in a police-dominated atmosphere generates "inherently compelling pressures which work to undermine the individual's will to resist and to compel him to speak where he would not otherwise do so freely."[25] In contrast, the Court has determined that the key components of a police-dominated atmosphere and compulsion are missing when a suspect speaks to an undercover police officer.[26]

Scenario Two highlights the Court's observation that "*Miranda* was not meant to protect suspects from boasting about their criminal activities" in front of persons they do not know to be police officers.[27] It is also important to note that in Scenario Two, Seibert is in the hospital cafeteria when she speaks with the undercover police officers, so she is presumably free to leave the undercover officers sitting at the cafeteria table if she decides she does not want to talk with them. In this way, the scenario is neither "custodial" nor "police-dominated" interrogation.

c. Scenario Three: Questioned about Arson While in Prison for Different Crime

Suppose that instead of approaching Seibert as undercover officers in a hospital cafeteria, the police arrest Seibert for something entirely unrelated to the arson-murder, such as for theft from her employer. Now assume the following: Seibert is convicted of that theft and sentenced to prison. While she is serving time in prison on the theft charge, the police begin to suspect her of participating in the arson-murder that took place at her home. A prison guard takes her from her prison cell to a conference room within the prison, where she is questioned by two police officers who are investigating the arson-murder. At no time during the questioning in the conference room do the uniformed police officers give Seibert *Miranda* warnings or tell her that she does not have to talk with them. The police officers do, however, tell Seibert that she is free to leave and return to her cell at any time. Seibert tells officers that she does not want to talk but does not ask to return to her cell. Despite the fact that she said she did not want to talk further, officers question her for five hours.

The Supreme Court has held that a suspect in this type of situation is "not in custody within the meaning of *Miranda*" so even though the police did not administer *Miranda* warnings, the suspect's confession is admissible during the prosecutor's case in chief.[28] Three justices vigorously disagreed with this finding, urging the Court to train its analysis on whether the suspect was "subjected to 'incommunicado interrogation ... in a police-dominated atmosphere.'"[29] Nonetheless, the Court placed great weight on the fact that the suspect was told he was free to end the questioning and return to his cell and was therefore not "in custody."[30]

Both Scenario Two and Scenario Three show the importance of being "in custody" and in a "police-dominated atmosphere" for *Miranda* purposes. When either custody or police interrogation is missing, the failure to receive *Miranda* warnings does not result in suppression of any statements made.

d. Scenario Four: No Warnings, Custodial Confession

Scenario Four represents the most classic understanding of how *Miranda* operates. As in Scenario One, assume the police arrest Seibert and fail to give her *Miranda* warnings. This time, however, assume the police take Seibert to an interrogation room in the police station rather than booking her and taking her to a jail cell. Once in the interrogation room, police question her.

In this situation, which is what actually happened in *Seibert*, she is "in custody" because she is not free to leave. Thus, any statements Seibert made while the police interrogated her without first administering *Miranda* warnings are inadmissible against her in court. Remember that Officer Hanrahan testified he was aware of this consequence during the first stage of Seibert's actual interrogation.[31]

The reason Seibert's pre-*Miranda* statements are inadmissible is that the self-incrimination clause of the Fifth Amendment protects suspects from having statements that are not voluntarily given used against them in court. This means it was not the failure to give *Miranda* warnings that made her pre-*Miranda* statements inadmissible. Rather, because *Miranda* warnings were not given, a court will assume that the statements Seibert made during the custodial interrogation were involuntary, and involuntary statements cannot be used against a defendant during the prosecution's case in chief.[32]

Because Seibert was not given *Miranda* warnings during the first part of her confession, the prosecutor could not call Officer Hanrahan to the witness stand and ask Officer Hanrahan to testify about Seibert's pre-*Miranda* confession. Similarly, if this part of her confession had been tape recorded, the prosecutor could not have played the tape recording of Seibert's confession for the jury. Indeed, when the trial court admitted into evidence Seibert's post-*Miranda* statements, the trial court clarified that the prosecution was only using the part of the statement that was made "after [Seibert] was advised of her *Miranda* rights."[33] This was because if a person is not given *Miranda* warnings and she confesses during custodial interrogation, her statements cannot be used against her as substantive evidence at trial. This much of Seibert's case was clear to both the trial court and the United States Supreme Court.

What was less clear was whether Seibert's second-stage confession was admissible. After all, the police had administered *Miranda* warnings before Seibert made the second confession. Despite this fact, the Supreme Court found that the second-stage confession was inadmissible.

No matter what the Supreme Court intended to say as its rationale for finding the second-stage confession inadmissible in *Seibert*, scholars and courts have disagreed about what the Court meant. One complication is that *Seibert* was a plurality decision in which one of the justices' concurring votes, Justice Kennedy, provided a rationale that no other justice joined. Kennedy focused on the subjective bad faith of the officers – analyzing the "deliberate" and "intentional" strategy of undermining *Miranda*. Typically the view of the justice concurring in the judgment on the narrowest grounds sets the rule that courts are supposed to follow,[34] but scholars debate which ground was in fact the narrowest in *Seibert*.

My own colleague, Professor James J. Tomkovicz, takes the view that Justice Kennedy's approach is controlling. According to Tomkovicz, "The *only* instances in which Justice Kennedy would deem the warnings ineffective are those in which *deliberate, uncured* failures to warn yield successive statements *related to* the initial statement."[35] Tomkovicz further clarifies that "if the violation is not intentional, if curative steps are taken, or if the content of the successive confession is sufficiently unrelated to the content of the initial confession," then *Miranda* warnings given midway through the interrogation are presumptively effective.[36]

On the other side of the debate are scholars such as Professor Charles D. Weisselberg, who maintains that "there is doubt whether Justice Kennedy's concurrence could be characterized as 'narrower' since it is premised upon the officer's intent, a position expressly rejected by seven or more justices."[37] According to Weisselberg, the rationale explaining why Seibert's second-stage confession was inadmissible was not that Officer Hanrahan had deliberately set out to obtain a confession without first giving *Miranda* warnings. Instead of this intent-based rationale, Weisselberg believes that the controlling rationale is an objective test that examines whether the *Miranda* warnings Seibert received before the second-stage interrogation were "effective in advising [her] that [she] [had] a real choice about whether to give a statement."[38]

In addition to analyzing the Court's reasoning, Weisselberg examined how the federal circuits and states are implementing *Seibert*. He found that "at least six federal circuits follow Justice Kennedy's view and ask whether the violation was deliberate," while "[f]ive circuits either apply both tests, combine aspects of the two, or have declined to decide which controls."[39] As far as the state courts are concerned, some states apply the objective test, one state focuses on the officer's intent, and other states have developed mixed tests that draw from both.[40]

Seibert highlights confusion within the supposedly bright-line contours of *Miranda*. Even though Officer Hanrahan admitted he used a two-stage interrogation technique in order to elicit Seibert's confession before administering *Miranda* warnings, the splintered Supreme Court could not agree on what to do. Four justices found the post-*Miranda* confession inadmissible by using a largely objective test, one justice found the post-*Miranda* confession inadmissible by examining the deliberate intent of the officer, and four justices in dissent would have found the confession admissible.[41] The next scenario highlights yet another way in which the contours of *Miranda* are less clear than they first appear.

e. Scenario Five: Warnings Interrupted by Suspect, Voluntary Confession in Which Suspect Discloses Location of Physical Evidence

Assume in Scenario Five that on the way to the station for questioning, the arresting officer begins to give Seibert her *Miranda* warnings but gets no further than telling her that she has the right to remain silent. At this point, Seibert interrupts the officer by saying she is aware of her rights, so the officer does not finish giving Seibert her *Miranda* warnings. Instead, the officer begins questioning Seibert, asking her where the gas can is located. If Seibert tells the officer that she helped start the fire and hid the gas can in a dumpster, Seibert's admitted involvement in the arson-murder would be inadmissible in the prosecution's case in chief. The reason is that she gave the statement in the absence of complete *Miranda* warnings, while she was in custody, and while she was interrogated by people she knew to be police officers.

Importantly, however, even though the *statement* would be inadmissible, the officer can use the *information* Seibert provided to find the gas can and test it for fingerprints. Nothing in *Miranda* stops the officer from giving the gas can and fingerprint analysis to the prosecutor to use as evidence against Seibert during the prosecution's case in chief. This means that the prosecutor can call the police officer to the witness stand, hand him the gas can, and ask him to explain to the jury where he found it. The prosecutor can also call the fingerprint examiner to the stand to testify that the examiner found Seibert's prints on the gas can. What the prosecutor cannot do is ask either the officer or the fingerprint examiner to testify about whether Seibert admitted her role in the crime.

The reason for this distinction is that the Supreme Court has drawn a line between physical evidence obtained as a result of a suspect's unwarned but voluntary statement and the actual statement itself. The Court has explained that the *Miranda* rule "protects against violations of the Self-Incrimination Clause, which, in turn, is not implicated by the introduction at trial of physical evidence resulting from voluntary statements."[42] Because the gas can and fingerprints on the gas can are physical evidence, the prosecution can use the gas can and fingerprints against Seibert during its case in chief, even though it could not use Seibert's statement admitting her role in the crime during its case in chief.

With this distinction between physical evidence and confessions in mind, consider Scenario Six.

f. Scenario Six: No Warnings, Interrogated Confession, and Defendant Testifies at Trial

This fact pattern assumes that Seibert confesses to the crime in a pre-*Miranda* custodial interrogation. What is new about this scenario is its assumption that Seibert decides to testify in her own defense at trial. During her testimony, assume Seibert says she did not know about the planned arson-murder.

In such a situation, the prosecutor can confront Seibert with her pre-*Miranda* confession during cross-examination in order to raise questions about Seibert's credibility. This means that the prosecutor can read directly from Seibert's pre-*Miranda* confession and compare it to Seibert's testimony on the witness stand. By pointing out inconsistencies between Seibert's confession and Seibert's trial testimony, the prosecutor can use Seibert's pre-*Miranda* confession to argue to the jury that Seibert was lying on the witness stand. The prosecutor can argue that the jury should not trust Seibert's testimony on the witness stand because that version of events was different from the one she gave to the police earlier.[43]

While the prosecutor can highlight inconsistencies between past and current statements in this way, the prosecutor cannot use the pre-*Miranda* confession for the truth of the matter asserted. In other words, the prosecutor cannot tell the jury to rely on the confession as direct evidence that Seibert is guilty of the crime simply because Seibert admitted she was guilty. The defense will request, and the trial court will undoubtedly give, a limiting instruction to the jury that the confession is impeachment evidence and is not to be evaluated for the "truth" of what Seibert said in it. Despite the good intentions of warning the jury not to use the confession as evidence that Seibert did indeed know about the planned arson-murder, such limiting instructions are fraught with peril because telling jurors to ignore the fact that a defendant confessed to a crime is difficult to do.[44]

Nonetheless, the Supreme Court has held that the use of pre-*Miranda* confessions to impeach a defendant who testifies at trial is constitutional.[45] As the Court has explained, the "shield provided by *Miranda* cannot be perverted into a license to use perjury by way of a defense, free from the risk of confrontation with prior inconsistent utterances."[46] Because the Court allows prosecutors to impeach defendants with their pre-*Miranda* confessions, defendants may decide not to testify at trial for fear that the prosecutor will attempt to cross-examine them by pointing out inconsistencies in their pre-*Miranda* statements.[47]

In this way, a defendant's Fifth Amendment right to decide whether or not to testify at trial intersects with *Miranda*'s protections of the defendant's Fifth Amendment right against self-incrimination. A defendant's choice to testify at trial means that the defendant loses the *Miranda* protection that prevented the jury from hearing the defendant's pre-*Miranda* statement. Although this situation trades one aspect of Fifth Amendment protection for another, the Supreme Court has endorsed the trade-off.

The final scenario highlights yet another situation in which the Supreme Court is willing to forgo the shield *Miranda* provides.

g. Scenario Seven: No Warnings, Public Safety Exception

For this final scenario, assume that Seibert's mobile home is burning and that police and firefighters respond to the emergency. Assume further that as the firefighters are trying to put out the fire, Seibert arrives home and expresses shock that her home is burning. The police nonetheless suspect Seibert, and when they smell gasoline on her hands, they believe that gasoline may have been used to start the fire. In this scenario, it would be natural for the police to worry that the gas can is still near the home, where it has the potential to explode, hurting or killing the firefighters and possibly igniting nearby homes. So, without administering *Miranda* warnings, the police ask Seibert where the gas can is located and then use her information to find it.

The Supreme Court has found such a confession to be a "public safety" exception to *Miranda*.[48] This means that even though the police did not give Seibert *Miranda* warnings before asking her where the gas can was located, the prosecutors can still use Seibert's statement against her in court. Her statement would be admissible because the police officer's question was necessary to secure the safety of police and firefighters, as well as the safety of the public at large.[49]

The reason the Supreme Court allows such statements to be used against defendants is that the Court is confident that police officers "can and will distinguish almost instinctively between questions necessary to secure their own safety or the safety of the public and questions designed solely to elicit testimonial evidence from a suspect."[50] Even though the Court is confident that police officers can make such distinctions, the Court has admitted that this "public safety" exception clouds the clarity of Miranda.[51]

Having outlined both subtle and striking differences among the preceding seven scenarios, the final section of this chapter reflects on what these contrasting scenarios may portend for the future of Miranda.

3. LOOKING TOWARD THE FUTURE

The scenarios described earlier show the foggy landscape of what happens in the absence of Miranda warnings. Statements given in the absence of Miranda warnings can be used against the suspect in a variety of ways. When the Supreme Court decided Seibert, it made clear that courts must suppress statements given through the kind of two-stage interrogation Officer Hanrahan employed. That much of Seibert is clear. What is less clear is the rationale lower courts should employ when applying Seibert to future cases, as well as what the future itself holds for Miranda.

No one can be certain exactly where Miranda is headed. In the coming years, the Supreme Court could overrule Miranda expressly, although few scholars believe the Court would do that. As Professor Yale Kamisar explained when discussing possible reasons why Chief Justice Rehnquist voted to uphold the constitutionality of Miranda, "[w]hy erase all this case law when Miranda ha[s] been so weakened by various limitations and qualifications that the police [a]re now able to live with it fairly comfortably?"[52] Following Kamisar's rationale, the Court might allow Miranda to wane by constantly chipping away at its reach until it no longer reaches anything at all.

The Court could also take the opposite tack by breathing new life into Miranda. Chief Justice Rehnquist did just that in Dickerson v. United States.[53] Although the Court decided Dickerson in 2000, Congress had passed the statute at issue in Dickerson a mere two years after Miranda. Under the statute, 18 U.S.C. § 3501, federal judges were supposed to admit voluntary statements of criminal defendants, even if such statements were made during custodial interrogation without the police first administering Miranda warnings.[54] In an opinion that took many people by surprise, because of both who authored it as well as what it said, Chief Justice Rehnquist held that Miranda was a constitutional decision that may not be overruled by an act of Congress.[55] The Court could have taken the legs out from under Miranda by upholding the constitutionality of the statute. By upholding Miranda's constitutionality, the Court breathed new life into Miranda.

In a similar way, Justice Sotomayor recently authored *J.D.B. v. North Carolina*, which held that "a child's age properly informs the *Miranda* custody analysis."[56] J.D.B. was only thirteen years old when he was questioned by police. In remanding the case with instructions to take the child's age into account when determining whether or not the child was "in custody" when he was interrogated by several people, including a uniformed police officer, Justice Sotomayor emphasized that the "benefit of the objective custody analysis is that it is designed to give clear guidance to the police."[57] Sotomayor also explained that by "limiting analysis to the objective circumstances of the interrogation, and asking how a reasonable person in the suspect's position would understand his freedom to terminate questioning and leave," the Court adopts an objective test that "avoids burdening police with the task of anticipating the idiosyncrasies of every individual suspect and divining how those particular traits affect each person's subjective state of mind."[58]

J.D.B. stressed the importance of an objective custody analysis in order to give "clear guidance to the police." In so doing, *J D.B.* showed how clear the Court can be when it wants to be. *J.D.B.* set forth a bright-line rule that a child's age properly informs the *Miranda* custody analysis, whereas *Seibert* has led to federal and state courts' implementing a variety of different rules.

Indeed, rather than establishing a bright-line rule, Professor Barry Friedman has asserted that *Seibert* is an example of stealth overruling.[59] Despite whatever life *Dickerson* may have breathed into *Miranda*, Friedman is more skeptical. He asserts that the public thinks *Miranda* is alive and well, when in reality, public officials and the courts believe they can violate *Miranda* with impunity.[60] Friedman explains that before cases such as *Seibert*, "police officers read *Miranda* warnings every time they bumped into a suspect."[61] In the wake of *Seibert*, Friedman asserts that the "police seem to be increasing their use of 'softening up' techniques."[62]

Friedman also observes that interesting testimony is taking place in cases where the prosecution is trying to introduce a physical object located through a pre-*Miranda* statement. For example, in cases in which locating a defendant's drugs or guns is all that the prosecution needs to obtain a conviction, Friedman observes that the police have incentive to skip giving *Miranda* warnings entirely.[63] Friedman also notes that during oral arguments before the Supreme Court, the Department of Justice admitted that the Drug Enforcement Agency "does not seek explicit waivers of *Miranda* rights, thereby allowing agents to question suspects in the face of silence."[64]

Professor Joelle Anne Moreno shares a similar perspective, asserting that *Seibert* sends a message to judges to ignore *Miranda* violations whenever police act in good faith or take curative measures.[65] As a result, Moreno believes that *Seibert* encourages police to lie about whether their failure to administer *Miranda* warnings rested on a good faith or a bad faith intent.[66] Indeed, had Officer Hanrahan not explained his two-step interrogation technique so forthrightly, the facts behind Seibert's two confessions may never have come to light.

Whether police actually do lie is, of course, difficult to ascertain. Officer Hanrahan believed his two-step interrogation technique comported with *Miranda*'s mandate and explained exactly what he did. Officer Hanrahan was trained that the only risk was the gamble inherent within the technique itself. The fact that *Seibert* might have chosen to invoke her rights and refuse to repeat her confession after receiving her *Miranda* warnings was a risk he was willing to take. What Officer Hanrahan could not anticipate – what was not evident until the Supreme Court decided *Seibert*, however muddled the Court's reasoning remains – was that the Court was not willing to allow that particular roll of the dice.

As we look to the future of *Miranda*, what remains important – and what will only continue to grow in importance as police hone their investigative techniques – is the degree to which the Supreme Court, the state supreme courts, and the trial and appellate courts protect suspects' constitutional due process and self-incrimination rights. So long as the lighthouse guiding the courts continues to be stalwart protection of suspects' constitutional rights, that constitutional beacon will navigate courts through whatever fog may lie ahead.

Notes

1. See generally *California v. Prysock*, 453 U.S. 355 (1981) (noting that the *Miranda* rights do not have to be read in any particular order, and they do not have to precisely match the language of *Miranda* so long as they are adequately and fully conveyed).
2. *Miranda v. Arizona*, 384 U.S. 436, 444–5 (1966).
3. *Dickerson v. United States*, 530 U.S. 428, 432–6 (2000) (providing a "brief historical account of the law governing the admission of confessions).
4. *Id.* at 433.
5. *Id.* at 433.
6. *Malloy v. Hogan*, 378 U.S. 1 (1964).
7. *Dickerson*, 530 U.S. at 434.
8. *Missouri v. Seibert*, 542 U.S. 600, 604 (2003).
9. *Id.*
10. *Id.* at 604–5.
11. *Id.*
12. *Id.*
13. *Id.* at 604–6; *Missouri v. Seibert*, 542 U.S. 600 (2003) (Joint Appendix, Transcript of Suppression Proceedings, Cross-Examination of Officer Richard Hanrahan by Defense Attorney Beth Davis-Kerry):[Defense Attorney Davis-Kerry]: [S]o the first part is a deliberate decision on your part not to provide her with *Miranda* rights

until after you get the information you're seeking and that's when you decide to give her the *Miranda* rights and make a tape recording.[Rolla City Police Officer Richard Hanrahan]: The way you characterize it isn't quite the way I was trained. Basically, you're rolling the dice. You're doing a first stage [interrogation without providing *Miranda* rights] where you understand that if you're told something ... you can't use what you were told.... We were fully aware of that. We went forward with the second stage, read *Miranda*, and she repeated the items she had told us.

14 *Seibert*, 542 U.S. at 604–6.
15 *Id.*
16 *Missouri v. Seibert*, 542 U.S. 600 (Suppression hearing at *20).
17 *Seibert*, 542 U.S. at 604–6.
18 Richard Leo's chapter in this volume discusses these issues in greater detail.
19 *Miranda v. Arizona*, 384 U.S. 436 (1966) (emphasis added) (citing U.S. CONST. amend. V).
20 *United States v. Washington*, 431 U.S. 181, 187 (1977).
21 *Id.* at 187.
22 *Miranda*, 384 U.S. at 458 (emphasis added).
23 *Illinois v. Perkins*, 496 U.S. 292, 296 (1990).
24 *Rhode Island v. Innis*, 446 U.S. 291, 301 (1980).
25 *Miranda v. Arizona*, 384 U.S. 436, 467 (1966).
26 *Perkins*, 496 U.S. at 296.
27 *Id.* at 298.
28 *Howes v. Fields*, 132 S.Ct. 1181, 1194 (2012).
29 *Id.* at 1194 (Ginsburg, J., dissenting, joined by Justices Breyer and Sotomayor).
30 *Id.* at 1193–4 (majority opinion).
31 *Seibert*, 542 U.S. 600 (Joint Appendix, Transcript of Suppression Proceedings, Cross-Examination of Officer Richard Hanrahan by Defense Attorney Beth Davis-Kerry).
32 *United States v. Patane*, 542 U.S. 630, 639 (2004) ("To protect against [the] danger that 'the possibility of coercion inherent in custodial interrogation' might cause 'a suspect's privilege against self-incrimination... [to] be violated,' the *Miranda* rule creates a presumption of coercion, in the absence of specific warnings, that is generally irrebuttbable for purposes of the prosecution's case in chief.").
33 *Seibert*, 542 U.S. 600 (Suppression hearing at *20).
34 *Marks v. United States*, 430 U.S. 188, 193 (1977).
35 James J. Tomkovicz, *Saving Massiah from Elstad: The Admissibility of Successive Confessions Following Deprivations of Counsel*, 15 WM. & MARY BILL RTS. J. 711, 735–6 (2007) (emphasis in original).
36 *Id.* at 736.
37 Charles D. Weisselberg, *Mourning Miranda*, 96 CAL. L. REV. 1519, 1551 (2008).
38 *Id.* at 1550.
39 *Id.*
40 *Id.* at 1551–2.
41 *Id.* at 1550.
42 *United States v. Patane*, 542 U.S. 630, 633 (2004).
43 *Harris v. New York*, 401 U.S. 222, 226 (1971).

44 See, generally, Dan Simon, *More Problems with Criminal Trials: The Limited Effectiveness of Legal Mechanisms*, 75 LAW & CONTEMP. PROB. 167, 179 (2012) (noting that "Courts have long been skeptical about the effectiveness of curative instructions," while also observing that "[u]nder the stewardship of Chief Justices Burger, Rehnquist, and Roberts, the Court has shown no hesitation in asserting that juries can and will disregard inadmissible evidence when instructed to do so").
45 *Harris*, 401 U.S. at 226.
46 *Id.*
47 *Id.* at 231 (Brennan, J., dissenting).
48 *New York v. Quarles*, 467 U.S. 649, 651 (1984).
49 *Id.* at 657–8.
50 *Id.* at 658–9.
51 *Id.* at 658.
52 Yale Kamisar, *On the Fortieth Anniversary of the Miranda Case: Why We Needed It, How We Got It – and What Happened to It*, 5 OHIO ST. J. CRIM. L. 163, 201 (2007) (discussing *Dickerson v. United States*).
53 *Dickerson v. United States*, 530 U.S. 428 (2000).
54 For a discussion of *Dickerson*, see Yale Kamisar, Miranda *After* Dickerson: *The Future of Confession Law: Forward: From Miranda to § 3501 to Dickerson to* ..., 99 MICH. L. REV. 879 (2001).
55 *Id.* at 432.
56 *J.D.B. v. North Carolina*, 131 S.Ct. 2394, 2399 (2011).
57 *Id.* at 2402 (quoting *Yarborough v. Alvarado*, 541 U.S. 652, 654 (2004)).
58 *Id.* at 2402.
59 Barry Friedman, *The Wages of Stealth Overruling (with Particular Attention to* Miranda v. Arizona*)*, 99 GEO. L.J. 1 (2010).
60 *Id.* at 22.
61 *Id.* at 44–5.
62 *Id.* at 51.
63 *Id.* at 51 n. 297.
64 *Id.*
65 Joelle Anne Moreno, *Faith-Based* Miranda? *Why the New* Missouri v. Seibert *"Bad Faith" Test Is a Terrible Idea*, 47 ARIZ. L. REV. 395, 398 (2005).
66 *Id.* at 415–16.

Part VI

CONVICTION, SENTENCING, AND INCARCERATION

12

Collateral Consequences of Criminal Conviction

Gabriel J. Chin

1. INTRODUCTION

Constitutional criminal law and procedure have been shockingly misaligned with what is really at stake in the criminal justice system. One incongruity is that most criminal charges are resolved by dismissals or plea bargains, yet the Court has spent most of its efforts developing rules of constitutional criminal procedure for increasingly rare trials.[1] It is not that trials are insignificant, just that plea bargains, practically, are much more important.

The Court's jurisprudence is similarly off-target with regard to punishment. The Court recognizes fines and imprisonment, the traditional elements of a sentence, as punishment, and subjects them to constitutional regulation. But most people convicted of crimes, even of felonies, are not sentenced to prison and are quickly back in society. For this majority, the most severe and long-lasting effect of conviction is not imprisonment or fine; rather, it is being subjected to collateral consequences, including the actual or potential loss of civil rights, parental rights, public benefits, employment opportunities, and other aspects of legal status.

However, as described in Part 2, the Court has held that collateral consequences are not punishment. Accordingly, they are largely constitutionally unregulated. They may be imposed without notice from the court at plea or sentence. With the exception of deportation, most courts hold that defense counsel generally has no duty to warn clients about the collateral consequences they will face. Also, legislatures may create new consequences and impose them on people convicted long ago. And collateral consequences are not considered with other effects of the criminal judgment to ensure proportionality and consistency at sentencing. The net effect is that a person may be sentenced

This chapter is based on Gabriel J. Chin, *The New Civil Death: Rethinking Punishment in the Era of Mass Conviction*, 160 U. PENN. L. REV. 1789 (2012).

to unsupervised probation for a misdemeanor, yet be surprised to find that she loses her job, home, family, or right to vote because of the conviction. What is most important in most cases is somehow constitutionally irrelevant.

Part 3 offers some ways forward as the Court considers how the Constitution should accommodate the criminal justice system we actually have. First, in two older cases, *Weems v. United States*[2] and *Trop v. Dulles*,[3] the Supreme Court held that a criminal consequence substantially impairing a person's legal status was punishment. The Court should revisit *Weems* and *Trop* and recognize that systematic subjection to collateral consequences is constitutional punishment.

In addition, in *Padilla v. Kentucky*,[4] the Supreme Court held in 2010 that even if deportation was not technically punishment, its severe and pervasive effects meant that the Constitution regulated its imposition in criminal prosecutions. Even if the Court adheres to its view that collateral consequences are not punishment, the loss of status accompanying criminal conviction is momentous enough that the due process protection announced in *Padilla* should apply more broadly.

2. COLLATERAL CONSEQUENCES AND THE CONSTITUTION

a. The Nature of Collateral Consequences

A person convicted of a criminal offense has a "shattered character"[5] and therefore "customarily suffers the loss of substantial rights."[6] In addition to felony convictions, "[a] wide range of civil disabilities may result from misdemeanor convictions."[7] Every conviction works a permanent change in status, because these disabilities "carry through life."[8] Citizens may lose civil rights:[9] "A convicted criminal may be disenfranchised, lose the right to hold office, be barred from entering certain professions, be subject to impeachment when testifying as a witness, be disqualified from serving as a juror, and may be subject to divorce"[10] and may lose the right to keep and bear arms.[11] For noncitizens, conviction may lead to deportation.[12]

The effects of the loss of status are particularly profound given the many areas of life subject to governmental regulation. Conviction potentially affects many aspects of family relations, including, for example, the ability to adopt, be a foster parent, or retain custody of one's own children.[13] Conviction can make one ineligible for public employment, such as in the military and law enforcement.[14] It can preclude private employment, including working in regulated industries,[15] with government contractors,[16] or in fields requiring a security clearance.

Conviction can also restrict one's ability to hold a government contract, to obtain government licenses and permits, or to collect a vested public pension.[17] Some convicted persons lose the right to drive a car.[18] Persons convicted of sex offenses usually have to register, may be excluded from living in particular areas, and are even subject to postincarceration civil confinement.[19]

Collateral consequences are in some ways more burdensome than ever before. First, extinction of equal legal status affects a wider range of interests than it did in past decades, when there were fewer public benefits to lose.[20] In addition, there once were many more businesses and professions for which one needed no license, permit, or ability to obtain a government contract.[21]

The disabilities are also stickier. While collateral consequences can be mitigated through pardon and other forms of legal relief,[22] pardon was once a more realistic hope for convicted persons than it is now.[23] Moreover, while historically disabilities applied only in the state of conviction,[24] a conviction in one jurisdiction generally has effects across the entire country.[25]

b. Mass Conviction, Not (Just) Mass Incarceration

Although the growth in the incarcerated population has been dramatic in recent decades, collateral consequences are important because most convicted persons are not sentenced to prison. There are approximately 1.1 million new state felony convictions in a typical year,[26] and some multiple of that in misdemeanor convictions.[27] In addition, there are approximately 80,000 federal convictions annually, most of which are felonies.[28] Most defendants convicted of felonies are not sentenced to state prison – about 60 percent receive probation only or probation with local jail time.[29] Even more defendants convicted of misdemeanors avoid incarceration.[30] While many people are sentenced to prison, and even though sentence length has increased in recent decades, the average term is now less than five years.[31] Accordingly, it is likely that the vast majority even of those sentenced to prison will spend most of their lives in free society.

Those convicted but not incarcerated are typically sentenced to probation. Six and a half million people were on probation at some point during 2009,[32] three times the number in prison or jail.[33] At the broadest level of generality, approximately sixty-five million adults have a criminal record of some kind, although some of those involve arrests not leading to conviction.[34] Accordingly, the size of the offender population is not just the two million in custody; it also includes the more than six million in the control of the criminal justice system who are not in custody plus the tens of millions who have a record but are not in prison or jail or on probation or parole.

The "incarceration" part of the phrase "mass incarceration" implies that actual confinement is the most important feature of the system. However, as legally and socially significant as a term in prison is, for most people convicted of crimes, collateral consequences will generate the most significant effects.

Escaping incarceration hardly means that a person with a conviction is not subject to other legal consequences as a result of her conviction.[35] Criminal records are increasingly available to all branches of the government and to the public through computer databases, thus making collateral consequences more susceptible to ready enforcement.[36]

Loss of legal status is more important, ironically, for relatively less serious crimes. If a person is sentenced to twenty-five years imprisonment at hard labor, it likely matters little that she will be ineligible to get a license as a chiropractor when she is released. But to a person sentenced to unsupervised probation and a $250 fine for a minor offense, losing her city job or being unable to teach, care for the elderly, live in public housing, or be a foster parent to a relative can be disastrous. "In many cases the most important part" of the conviction,[37] in terms of both social policy and the legal effect, lies in the collateral consequences.

Several factors make the importance of collateral consequences likely to grow over time. One driver is the increasing cost of incarceration, which is encouraging legislatures across the country to consider more economical alternatives. Accordingly, a greater percentage of people charged with crimes may well wind up on probation or sentenced to shorter terms of incarceration; collateral consequences will be a greater part of the effect of the conviction. Further, legislatures are likely to continue to search for ways to promote public safety at lower cost than incarceration or other more intensive forms of supervision. Pressured to pass laws without spending money, policy makers may find that collateral consequences offer an attractive alternative.

Pointing in the other direction is the fact that recent statistics suggest that the correctional population is stable or even declining slightly.[38] But even if these trends hold over time, that does not necessarily mean that the importance of collateral consequences will diminish. Today, those roughly fifty and older did not spend their entire youths, when the rate of criminality is highest, in the era of mass conviction. Therefore, those in late middle age and older will have disproportionately lower rates of conviction, and thus exposure to collateral consequences, than the younger population. Unless rates of conviction dramatically decline, the overall share of the population with criminal convictions will continue to increase, as a larger percentage of Americans will have grown up when criminal prosecution was a broadly used tool.

c. Collateral Consequences as Unrestrained by the Constitution

Courts have imposed few limits on creation and implementation of collateral consequences. They are generally regarded as nonpunitive. Accordingly, they are not evaluated for overall proportionality in light of the other aspects of the sentence;[39] nor is there significant scrutiny for reasonableness. In addition, existing collateral consequences may be imposed without warning, and new ones may be created and imposed after a sentence has been fully served.

i. Individual Collateral Consequences as Regulatory Measures

Kennedy v. Mendoza-Martinez establishes the test for determining whether a sanction is criminal punishment or civil regulation.[40] The test employs seven[41] nonexclusive,[42] unweighted factors, filtered through a rule that only the "clearest proof" will overcome a legislative claim that a measure is civil.[43] Of course, the outcome of any seven-factor, nonexclusive test is indeterminate, and the key cases have been decided by very close votes.

The result is that a state may subject convicted persons to harsh treatment. While it is unconstitutional if the state acts in such a fashion for "punitive" purposes, that treatment is entirely permissible if the underlying reason is to protect public safety or to promote some other aspect of the public interest. But virtually no examination of the actual motivation of the legislature is permitted. Obviously, a test putting so much weight on formal categorization will uphold many measures that are in fact motivated by a desire to punish; Wayne Logan has written that "the *Mendoza-Martinez* factors over the years have been applied in a highly selective and ultimately inconsistent manner."[44] The scholar Paul W. Tappan, who served as chair of the U.S. Board of Parole and was associate reporter on the Model Penal Code, wrote that calling collateral consequences "civil" may seem "unimportant to the offender: he may well consider these losses to be a part of the vindictive punishments that society exacts. And, in fact, they do appear very frequently to reflect retributive sentiments rather than any real need for community protection."[45]

Even if they do not rise to the level of "punishment," restrictions on people with convictions must nevertheless be rational under the equal protection clause.[46] However, rational basis review performed by courts in this context is far from exacting.[47] For example, courts have found denials of public benefits to people with convictions to be "rational" because such restrictions save taxpayer money;[48] "the felon classification bears a rational relationship to the legitimate state purpose of assuring that only responsible citizens receive state aid."[49] The Supreme Court has found denial or burdening the exercise of civil rights to be unobjectionable in many circumstances, including deportation for noncitizens[50] and deprivation of a citizen's right to vote,[51] hold public office,[52] serve on a jury,[53] testify,[54] and possess firearms.[55] It has approved prohibitions on occupational licenses[56] and on private employment where there is a public interest.[57] It has upheld denial of public benefits[58] and special restrictions, such as registration[59] and incarceration[60] of sex offenders.

ii. Innovative Collateral Consequences

Because collateral consequences are not, strictly speaking, punishment, existing limitations may be imposed retroactively on people not subject to them at the time of conviction. In addition, states are free to create new restrictions in previously unregulated areas. Thus, if rational basis review is taken seriously, then it appears that a truly unfortunate and spectacular range of potential discriminations may be visited long after the fact on those convicted of crime.

It would seem that virtually all denials of public benefits or services are rational because such benefits direct scarce resources to the most deserving. The federal government could, apparently, deny applications for Social Security, Medicare, and Medicaid from some or all people with felony convictions[61] – because "conservation of funds constitutes a rational basis on which to deny assistance to convicted felons and sex offenders."[62] In the absence of some positive federal law to the contrary, states apparently could deny people with convictions access to public hospitals, higher education, and state benefit programs for the same reason.

Courts could find virtually all employment and licensing restrictions rational, as long as the job or occupation is one for which honesty, integrity, and moral character are relevant, for "it is not open to doubt that the commission of crime – the violation of the penal laws of a state – has some relation to the question of character."[63] It is hard to imagine a job so insignificant and inconsequential that it could be done as well by a person of bad character as by someone who was hardworking and honest. Because public employment is both a public benefit and a public trust, perhaps all restrictions in that area are rational.

Registration requirements, which originated outside the sex offender context,[64] are now returning to their roots, with more jurisdictions requiring the registration of people with records involving nonsex crimes.[65] Although *Lambert v. California* held that a particular person with a conviction could not be held liable for nonregistration on the basis of the facts of that case,[66] the Court did not hint that criminal registration might be unconstitutional in general.[67]

One novel restriction is the limitation on the residence and movement of people convicted of sex offenses. The North Carolina Supreme Court held that people with criminal records can be denied access to public parks.[68] Although some residential restrictions have been struck down on state law grounds,[69] including under state ex post facto clauses,[70] many courts considering the question have held that these restrictions are not ex post facto punishments, but instead reasonable regulations[71] – even if they mean that for practical purposes a person cannot legally live anywhere in a particular city.[72] If residence restrictions are rational and not punishment as applied to sex offenders, then there is a strong argument that they are also rational and not punishment for those convicted of other crimes. If children and others should be protected from sex offenders, then surely it is rational that they be protected from drug offenders, those who committed violent offenses or offenses with high possibilities of violence such as burglary, or, for that matter, from serial quality-of-life misdemeanants.[73]

iii. No Right to Notice at Plea or Sentence

Because collateral consequences have traditionally been understood as civil and nonpunitive, a defendant has not been constitutionally entitled to notice of existing restrictions from the court before pleading guilty or to advice about the restrictions from defense counsel when considering how to proceed in the case.[74] Deportation is, at the moment, the important exception. In March 2010 in *Padilla v. Kentucky*, seven justices voted that the Sixth Amendment required defense counsel to advise clients about the possibility that a guilty plea would lead to deportation.[75] Some lower courts have applied the advice requirement of *Padilla* to other collateral consequences,[76] but the Supreme Court itself has not yet indicated how broadly *Padilla* will apply. As a general matter, people plead guilty to relatively minor offenses with relatively small punishments having no idea of what could happen to them, other than the possibility of deportation. Or, they plead guilty because they do know what will happen and they can live with it, but years later, the legislature adds additional collateral consequences (possibly including, of course, deportation) to an old conviction.

In sum, particularly in cases where the traditional forms of punishment are relatively light, collateral consequences will be one of the major effects of the criminal judgment. Yet, under the law as it now exists, it is not clear that the defendant has a right to be advised of the most important legal effects of the decision to enter a plea agreement.

3. CONSTITUTIONALIZING COLLATERAL CONSEQUENCES

The rights of those convicted of crime are now subject to limitation, revision, and restriction, apparently for life. Even after release from prison, they no longer hold vested status as equals; their privileges and position in society are held at sufferance.

One way to understand the current situation of convicted persons is to recognize that the ancient punishment of civil death has been revived. Civil death was a common law consequence of conviction of felony in England and was adopted by statute in some U.S. states. Because the penalty for felony was death, upon a final judgment, the individual was treated as if deceased; he lost legal status and his affairs were wrapped up. This made sense when there was likely to be only a short period between sentence of death and death. But civil death as an institution faded in the United States and in England as felonies not punishable by death developed; it made no sense to have large numbers of people in society who had no rights.

Civil death was understood as a punishment at common law in England and the United States. It would make sense to recognize that what happens to people convicted of crimes in the United States is a form of civil death; if the Constitution requires due process with regard to imposition of a small fine or a day in jail, surely it should also be concerned with the permanent loss of equal status in society.

There is precedent for the Court's consideration of these kinds of harms. In *Weems v. United States*[77] and *Trop v. Dulles*,[78] the Court found near-total destruction of a person's legal status in society to be cruel and unusual punishment under the Eighth Amendment.

Weems originated in the Philippines, which was then a U.S. territory. The Court invalidated the *cadena temporal*, a punishment whereby, for a period of years, the person sentenced would be imprisoned and perform hard labor for the state.[79] In addition to the hard labor, those sentenced to *cadena temporal* would thereafter suffer "accessory penalties,"[80] namely, "civil interdiction,"[81] "perpetual absolute disqualification,"[82] and "subjection to surveillance during life."[83] The Court regarded these penalties, clearly recognizable as versions of modern collateral consequences, as harsh:

> His prison bars and chains are removed, it is true, after twelve years, but he goes from them to a perpetual limitation of his liberty. He is forever kept under the shadow of his crime, forever kept within voice and view of the criminal magistrate, not being able to change his domicil without giving notice to the "authority immediately in charge of his surveillance," and without permission in writing. He may not seek, even in other scenes and among other people, to retrieve his fall from rectitude. Even that hope is taken from him and he is subject to tormenting regulations that, if not so tangible as iron bars and stone walls, oppress as much by their continuity, and deprive of essential liberty.[84]

The Court was also concerned about the portion of the sentence involving painful labor,[85] and it is difficult to identify precisely what about the nature and degree of *cadena temporal* made it unconstitutional. Nevertheless, the "accessory penalties" were a basis,[86] perhaps the most important basis, for the Court's ruling.[87]

A half-century later in *Trop v. Dulles*, five justices found another "accessory penalty" – expatriation or denationalization of a United States citizen – to be cruel and unusual because it destroyed legal personality.[88] They ruled that Congress had no power to punish a U.S. citizen with denationalization for desertion in time of war.[89] The citizen could be executed, they determined, but deprivation of citizenship was cruel and unusual.[90]

By imposing denationalization as punishment, the plurality explained:

> There may be involved no physical mistreatment, no primitive torture. There is instead the total destruction of the individual's status in organized society. It is a form of punishment more primitive than torture, for it destroys for the individual the political existence that was centuries in the development.... In short, the expatriate has lost the right to have rights.[91]

Uncertainty based on the possibility of future discrimination was the key feature making "this punishment ... offensive to cardinal principles for which the Constitution stands."[92] Justice Brennan's opinion, providing the necessary fifth vote, also found the uncertainty created by the status to be critical.[93]

In addition, even if something is not punishment, *strictissimi juris*, it may be within the scope of the criminal provisions of the Bill of Rights. *Padilla v. Kentucky* held that defendants were entitled to be warned by their lawyers about the possibility of deportation because, although not criminal,[94] deportation followed conviction automatically,[95] had a "close connection to the criminal process,"[96] and was severe.[97] *Padilla* required advice about a particular collateral consequence – deportation. But deportation has systematic effects on status. It does not merely affect employment, or residence, or family relationships; instead, it "may result also in loss of both property and life; or of all that makes life worth living."[98] Deportation is simultaneously a specific collateral consequence and a systematic destruction of status.

The loss of status that accompanies criminal conviction is in this way like deportation. It follows conviction automatically, it has a close connection to the criminal process, and it is severe. It carries with it a systematic loss of legal status. Therefore, even if subjection to collateral consequences is not punishment, under the rationale of *Padilla*, it should nevertheless be subject to constitutional regulation.

4. CONCLUSION

In the future, courts, policy makers, and scholars addressing criminal law and the Constitution will have to resolve the mismatch between what is at stake in criminal cases and existing constitutional doctrine. Those convicted of crimes, even minor ones, may face a devastating network of impairments of their employment opportunities, civil rights, and other aspects of status. Even those who never spend a day in jail may face this burden. Accordingly, collateral consequences are an important effect, for many the most important effect, of criminal conviction.

Notwithstanding the importance of collateral consequences, in one major line of decisions, the Supreme Court has held that collateral consequences are, constitutionally, irrelevant to the criminal process. Looking at individual collateral consequences in isolation, the Supreme Court has held that they are not punishment and has placed little substantive or procedural restriction on their imposition.

However, in another line of cases, exemplified by *Padilla*, *Weems*, and *Trop*, the Supreme Court has held that systematic destruction of status as a result of criminal conviction is constitutionally significant. These cases indicate that loss of status not only may be punishment, but may be cruel and unusual punishment. The two lines of cases have not been in dialogue with each other.

Reconciling these two bodies of law, accommodating collateral consequences in constitutional criminal law is a critical task if the criminal justice system is to operate consistently with the spirit of due process. It is also a difficult one because of the legitimate concerns of both parties. Simple fairness gives people pleading guilty a right to understand the sanctions the law will impose on them. Yet, judicial hesitation to add procedural requirements to valid guilty pleas is not necessarily irrational or malicious. Courts (and prosecutors) have a strong interest in ensuring that guilty pleas are stable and reliable. Adding warnings, no matter how richly warranted, adds to the risk that a guilty plea will later be subject to challenge. A just solution requires respect for the interests of defendants in fairness of pleas, and of courts and prosecutors in the finality of pleas.

Recognizing the different roles of counsel and the court may be helpful. Defense counsel have a duty under the Sixth Amendment to negotiate the best possible plea to provide competent legal advice about its terms. Courts have an obligation to ensure basic fairness before accepting a guilty plea but cannot know all of a defendant's concerns (because of such matters as attorney client privilege) and cannot advise the defendant about what to do (because the court is obligated to be neutral). Structurally, counsel can provide more detailed and specific information to clients than can courts.

One approach, advanced by the Uniform Collateral Consequences of Conviction Act,[99] would require the court to offer a general warning that a conviction will make a person subject to consequences, but not a warning of every individual consequence. This would be consistent with the idea that convicted persons suffer a general impairment of legal personality and loss of status, a modern form of civil death. As Chief Justice Warren explained, "Conviction of a felony imposes a *status* upon a person which not only makes him vulnerable to future sanctions through new civil disability statutes, but which also seriously affects his reputation and economic opportunities."[100] Making a person, formerly a free and equal citizen, susceptible to a regime of regulation imposed on criminals is a form of punishment or at least is constitutionally significant.[101] On this theory, they should also be informed by the court of other specific collateral consequences, such as deportation or civil commitment, that, standing alone, are of great magnitude and change their legal status.

On the other hand, this approach would accept that specific collateral consequences of less comprehensive effect are not inevitably punishment and need not be specifically mentioned by the court. The general judicial warning that a guilty plea may result in a person's losing employment opportunities, public benefits, and civil rights necessarily constitutes a warning that a person might lose, say, her plumber's license, and her right to vote. The law would not require the impracticable, nearly impossible, task of a judicial warning to each person pleading guilty of each of the hundreds or thousands of collateral consequences to which the person will be subject. On the other hand, defense counsel would be in a position to spend some time addressing the particular consequences that may be important to the client.

Other approaches and mechanisms are possible, of course. But however it is done, people are entitled to know the truth about what will happen to them before they plead guilty to a crime. This important principle is one that a just Constitution should recognize.

Notes

1. See, e.g., Stephanos Bibas, *Regulating the Plea-Bargaining Market: From Caveat Emptor to Consumer Protection*, 99 CAL. L. REV. 1117 (2011).
2. 217 U.S. 349 (1910).
3. 356 U.S. 86 (1958).
4. 130 U.S. 1473 (2010).
5. *Chaunt v. United States*, 364 U.S. 350, 358 (1960) (Clark, J., dissenting).
6. *Estep v. United States*, 327 U.S. 114, 122 (1946); see also DANIELS V. UNITED STATES, 532 U.S. 374, 379 (2001); MARGARET COLGATE LOVE, JENNY ROBERTS & CECELIA KLINGELE, THE COLLATERAL CONSEQUENCES OF CRIMINAL CONVICTIONS: LAW, POLICY AND PRACTICE (2013). There are also informal, private market and psychological consequences of conviction. While important and burdensome, they are not at issue here, where the focus is exclusively consequences imposed by law.
7. See *Argersinger v. Hamlin*, 407 U.S. 25, 48 n.11 (1972) (Powell, J., concurring) (listing such civil disabilities as "forfeiture of public office, disqualification from a

licensed profession, and loss of pension rights" (citations omitted)); *Baldwin v. New York*, 399 U.S. 66, 69 n.8 (1970) ("Both the convicted felon and the convicted misdemeanant may be prevented under New York law from engaging in a wide variety of occupations."); Jenny Roberts, *Why Misdemeanors Matter: Defining Effective Advocacy in the Lower Courts*, 45 U.C. DAVIS L. REV. 277, 297–303 (2011) (listing collateral consequences of misdemeanors, including deportation for noncitizens, sex-offender registration, and eviction from public housing). Misdemeanor convictions can also lead to disenfranchisement. E.g., *Richardson v. Ramirez*, 418 U.S. 24, 76 n.24 (1974) (Marshall, J., dissenting) ("Even a jaywalking or traffic conviction could conceivably lead to disenfranchisement, since § 2 [of the Fourteenth Amendment] does not differentiate between felonies and misdemeanors.").
8 *Fiswick v. United States*, 329 U.S. 211, 222 (1946).
9 See Legal Action Ctr., *After Prison: Roadblocks to Reentry* (2004), available at http://www.lac.org/roadblocks-to-reentry/upload/lacreport/LAC_PrintReport.pdf (last visited Apr. 30, 2013) (discussing the legal barriers facing individuals following a criminal conviction).
10 *North Carolina v. Rice*, 404 U.S. 244, 247 n.1 (1971) (citations omitted).
11 See *District of Columbia v. Heller*, 554 U.S. 570, 626 (2008) (noting that "nothing in our opinion should be taken to cast doubt on longstanding prohibitions on the possession of firearms by felons").
12 See *Mahler v. Eby*, 264 U.S. 32, 39 (1924) ("It is well settled that deportation, while it may be burdensome and severe for the alien, is not a punishment.").
13 McGregor Smyth, *From "Collateral" to "Integral": The Seismic Evolution of Padilla v. Kentucky and Its Impact on Penalties beyond Deportation*, 54 HOW. L.J. 795, 825 (2011) ("Certain charges and convictions result in the loss of custody of a child or irrevocable termination of parental rights.").
14 See, e.g., 10 U.S.C. § 504(a) (2006) (restricting enlistment of people with convictions); Fla. Stat. Ann. § 943.13(4) (West 2009) (prohibiting employment as law enforcement officers of those convicted of felonies and certain misdemeanors).
15 See, e.g., *DiCola v. FDA*, 77 F.3d 504, 507–8 (D.C. Cir. 1996) (upholding lifetime debarment from the pharmaceutical industry based on criminal conviction) (citations omitted).
16 For example, 46 U.S.C. § 70105 prohibits people with certain convictions from obtaining a federal identification card allowing access to secure transportation areas. Failure to obtain a card could preclude employment necessitating entry into such an area.
17 See, e.g., *Commonwealth v. Abraham*, 996 A.2d 1090, 1095 (Pa. Super. Ct. 2010) (holding that counsel must "warn his client of the loss of pension as a consequence to pleading guilty"), rev'd, 62 A.3d 343 (Pa. 2012).
18 See 23 U.S.C. § 159.
19 See infra notes 60–1.
20 Charles A. Reich, *The New Property*, 73 YALE L.J. 733, 734–7 (1964).
21 See, e.g., *Goldberg v. Kelly*, 397 U.S. 254, 262 n.8 (1970) ("Society today is built around entitlement.... Many of the most important of these entitlements now flow from government....") (alteration omitted) (quoting Charles A. Reich, *Individual Rights and Social Welfare: The Emerging Legal Issues*, 74 YALE L.J. 1245, 1255 (1965)).

22 See Margaret Colgate Love, Relief from the Collateral Consequences of a Criminal Conviction: A State by State Resource Guide (2006).
23 See Margaret Colgate Love, *The Twilight of the Pardon Power*, 100 J. Crim. L. & Criminology 1169, 1181–2 (2010) ("[I]n most years between 1900 and 1936, more than half of the thousands of petitions filed were sent forward to the White House with a favorable official recommendation. At the White House, the president usually approved cases recommended favorably ... and sometimes was more inclined to leniency.") (footnote omitted); *id.* at 1192 (noting that during the administrations of Presidents Kennedy through Carter, pardon grant rates ranged from thirty to forty percent); see also Love, Relief from the Collateral Consequences supra note 22, at 18–38 (discussing pardon practices in the states).
24 See *Huntington v. Attrill*, 146 U.S. 657, 673 (1892).
25 See, e.g., Fla. Stat. Ann. § 790.23(1)(e) (West 2009) (denying firearms to those convicted in other states).
26 E.g., Sean Rosenmerkel et al., Bureau of Justice Statistics, NCJ 226846, *Felony Sentences in State Courts, 2006 – Statistical Tables* 1 (2009), available at http://bjs.ojp.usdoj.gov/content/pub/pdf/fssc06st.pdf (last visited Apr. 30, 2013).
27 Systematic misdemeanor statistics are not readily available, but it is clear that misdemeanor convictions are more common than felony convictions. See Kamala D. Harris, *Cal. Dep't of Justice, Crime in California* 2010, at 16 (2011), available at http://ag.ca.gov/cjsc/publications/candd/cd10/preface.pdf (last visited Apr. 30, 2013) (reporting nearly 1.4 million arrests in California in 2010, of which 448,552 were for felonies and the remainder for misdemeanors or status offenses); Nat'l Ctr. for State Courts, *Examining The Work of State Courts: An Analysis of 2008 State Court Caseloads* 47 (2010), available at http://www.courtstatistics.org/other-pages/~/media/microsites/files/csp/ewsc-2008-online.ashx (last visited Apr. 30, 2013) (reporting that misdemeanors comprised seventy-nine percent of the criminal caseload in a 2008 study of eleven state courts); Lynn Langton & Donald J. Farole, Jr., Bureau of Justice Statistics, NCJ 228538, *Public Defender Offices, 2007 – Statistical Tables* 12 tbl.5a (2010), available at http://bjs.ojp.usdoj.gov/content/pub/pdf/pdo07st.pdf (last visited Apr. 30, 2013) (reporting that public defenders surveyed were assigned a total of 378,400 felony and 575,770 misdemeanor cases in 2007); N.Y. St. Division Crim. Just. Services, 2006–10 *Disposition of Adult Arrests*, http://criminaljustice.state.ny.us/crimnet/ojsa/dispos/nys.pdf (last visited Apr. 30, 2013) (reporting that in 2010, there were 546,416 adult arrests, leading to 35,597 felony convictions, and 286,131 convictions for misdemeanors or lesser offenses); Alexandra Natapoff, *Misdemeanors*, 85 S. Cal. L. Rev. 1313, 1320 & n.25 (2012) (estimating 10.5 million nontraffic misdemeanors annually) (citing Nat'l Ass'n of Criminal Def. Lawyers, Minor Crimes, Massive Waste: The Terrible Toll of America's Broken Misdemeanor Court 11 (2009)).
28 See Mark Motivans, *Federal Justice Statistics, 2008 – Statistical Tables*, Bureau Just. Stat., tbl.5.1 (Nov. 2010), http://bjs.ojp.usdoj.gov/content/pub/html/fjsst/2008/tables/fjso8st501.pdf (last visited Apr. 30, 2013) (reporting 82,823 federal convictions in the year ending September 30, 2008, of which 75,832 were felonies).
29 Rosenmerkel et al., supra note 26, at 4 tbl.1.2.
30 See, e.g., 2006–10 *Disposition of Adult Arrests*, supra note 27, at 5 (reporting that between 2006 and 2010, between 18% and 19.8% of those arrested for misdemeanors

were sentenced to prison or jail, while another 0.9% to 1% were sentenced to jail plus probation).
31 State prison sentences averaged 59 months. Rosenmerkel et al., supra note 26, at 6 tbl.1.3. Federal sentences averaged just over five years. *Federal Justice Statistics, 2008 – Statistical Tables*, supra note 28, tbl.5.2.
32 Lauren E. Glaze & Thomas P Bonczar, Bureau of Justice Statistics, NCJ 231674, *Probation and Parole in the United States, 2009*, at 3 tbl.2 (2010), available at http://bjs.ojp.usdoj.gov/content/pub/pdf/ppus09.pdf (last visited Apr. 30, 2013).
33 *Id.*
34 Michelle Natividad Rodriguez & Maurice Emsellem, Nat'l Emp't Law Project, *65 Million "Need Not Apply": The Case for Reforming Criminal Background Checks for Employment* 27 n.2 (2011), available at http://www.nelp.org/page/-/65_Million_Need_Not_Apply.pdf (last visited Apr. 30, 2013); see also Robert Brame et al., *Cumulative Prevalence of Arrest From Ages 8 to 23 in a National Sample*, 129 PEDIATRICS 21, 25 (2012) (reporting the results of a study showing that 30% of surveyed twenty-three-year-olds had been arrested, compared to 22% that had been arrested in a similar 1965 study).
35 See JEFF MANZA & CHRISTOPHER UGGEN, LOCKED OUT: FELON DISENFRANCHISEMENT AND AMERICAN DEMOCRACY 70 (2006) ("While some felons go to prison ... many others serve time in jail or on probation in their communities.... [A]t least some states disenfranchise misdemeanants as well."); see also, e.g., Nora v. Demleitner, *Preventing Internal Exile: The Need for Restrictions on Collateral Sentencing Consequences*, 11 STAN. L. & POL'Y REV. 153, 154 (1999) ("Despite their innocuous name, for many convicted offenders, and especially those who never serve any prison time, these 'collateral' consequences 'are ... the most persistent punishments that are inflicted for [their] crime.'") (alteration in original) (quoting Velmer S. Burton, Jr. et al., *The Collateral Consequences of a Felony Conviction: A National Study of State Statutes*, FED. PROBATION, Sept. 1987, at 52).
36 James Jacobs & Tamara Crepet, *The Expanding Scope, Use, and Availability of Criminal Records*, 11 N.Y.U. J. LEGIS. & PUB. POL'Y 177, 179–80 (2007).
37 *Sutton v. McIlhany*, 1 Ohio Dec. Reprint 235, 236 (C.P. Huron County 1848).
38 Lauren E. Glaze, Bureau of Justice Statistics, NCJ 236319, *Correctional Population in the United States*, 1 fig.1 (2010), available at http://bjs.gov/content/pub/pdf/cpus10.pdf (last visited Apr. 30, 2013)
39 See, e.g., Juliet Stumpf, *Fitting Punishment*, 66 WASH. & LEE L. REV. 1683, 1684–9 (2009) (discussing a lack of proportionality in immigration law as compared to criminal punishments).
40 372 U.S. 144, 168 (1963).
41 See *id.* at 168–9 (listing the seven factors).
42 See *United States v. Ward*, 448 U.S. 242, 249 (1980) (holding that the factors may overlap, and that not all need be present in every case).
43 E.g., *Seling v. Young*, 531 U.S. 250, 261 (2001).
44 Wayne A. Logan, *The Ex Post Facto Clause and the Jurisprudence of Punishment*, 35 AM. CRIM. L. REV. 1261, 1282 (1998).
45 Paul W. Tappan, *The Legal Rights of Prisoners*, 293 ANNALS AM. ACAD. POL. & SOC. SCI. 99, 109 (1954).

46 See *Marshall v. United States*, 414 U.S. 417, 430 (1974) (upholding the exclusion from a rehabilitation program of persons with more than one felony conviction).
47 See generally Miriam J. Aukerman, *The Somewhat Suspect Class: Towards a Constitutional Framework for Evaluating Occupational Restrictions Affecting People with Criminal Records*, 7 J.L. SOC'Y 18, 27–51 (2005) (analyzing case law on criminal record-based occupational restrictions).
48 *Houston v. Williams*, 547 F.3d 1357, 1364 (11th Cir. 2008).
49 *Carbonaro v. Reeher*, 392 F. Supp. 753, 760 (E.D. Pa. 1975).
50 *Galvan v. Press*, 347 U.S. 522, 529 (1954).
51 *Richardson v. Ramirez*, 418 U.S. 24, 54–5 (1974).
52 See *Baldwin v. New York*, 399 U.S. 66, 69 n.8 (1970) (noting that in New York, "the convicted felon is deprived of certain civil rights, including the right ... to hold public office"); Andrea Steinacker, Note, *The Prisoner's Campaign: Felony Disenfranchisement Laws and the Right to Hold Public Office*, 2003 BYU L. REV. 801, 800–8 (reviewing state positions on restrictions on former felons' right to hold public office).
53 See generally Brian C. Kalt, *The Exclusion of Felons from Jury Service*, 53 AM. U. L. REV. 65 (2003).
54 E.g., Fed. R. Evid. 609.
55 See *District of Columbia v. Heller*, 554 U.S. 570, 626 (2008).
56 *Hawker v. New York*, 170 U.S. 189, 196 (1898).
57 See *De Veau v. Braisted*, 363 U.S. 144, 160 (1960) (waterfront union office).
58 See *Flemming v. Nestor*, 363 U.S. 603, 612 (1960) (Social Security benefits).
59 *Smith v. Doe*, 538 U.S. 84, 105–6 (2003).
60 *Kansas v. Hendricks*, 521 U.S. 346, 371 (1997).
61 For example, 21 U.S.C. § 862(b) allows state and federal sentencing judges to deny federal benefits to those convicted of drug possession offenses.
62 *Houston v. Williams*, 547 F.3d 1357, 1364 (11th Cir. 2008).
63 *Barsky v. Bd. of Regents of Univ. of N.Y.*, 111 N.E.2d 222, 226 (N.Y. 1953) (quoting *Hawker v. New York*, 170 U.S. 189, 196 (1898)), aff'd, 347 U.S. 442 (1954).
64 See WAYNE LOGAN, KNOWLEDGE AS POWER: CRIMINAL REGISTRATION AND COMMUNITY NOTIFICATION LAWS IN AMERICA 20–48 (2009).
65 See ID. at 73–4.
66 See 355 U.S. 225, 229–30 (1957).
67 See *id.* at 229 ("Registration laws are common and their range is wide.").
68 See *Standley v. Town of Woodfin*, 661 S.E.2d 728, 729 (N.C. 2008).
69 See, e.g., *Fross v. Cnty. of Allegheny*, 20 A.3d 1193, 1207 (Pa. 2011).
70 See Wayne Logan, *Populism and Punishment: Sex Offender Registration and Community Notification in the Courts*, CRIM. JUST., Spring 2011, at 37, 39–40.
71 See generally Marjorie A. Shields, Annotation, *Validity of Statutes Imposing Residency Restrictions on Registered Sex Offenders*, 25 A.L.R. 6th 227, 305–16 (2007).
72 See Catherine L. Carpenter & Amy E. Beverlin, *The Evolution of Unconstitutionality in Sex Offender Registration Laws*, 63 HASTINGS L.J. 1071, 1080–1 (2012) (providing examples of sex offenders forced to leave their homes to comply with residency requirements).
73 Cf. *Village of Belle Terre v. Boraas*, 416 U.S. 1, 7–9 (1974) (upholding as rational a ban on two unrelated persons living in a single housing unit).

74 Recent cases include *Davis v. Russell*, No. 08–0138, 2011 WL 1770932, at *12 (E.D. Mo. May 10, 2011) ("Petitioner's counsel did not provide ineffective assistance of counsel and the plea court did not violate Petitioner's federal constitutional rights by failing to advise Petitioner that he may be subject to civil commitment ... upon his release from prison...."), *Rigger v. State*, 341 S.W.3d 299, 313 (Tenn. Crim. App. 2010) ("A trial court has no duty to advise a guilty-pleading defendant of a collateral consequence of his plea."), and *Carroll v. Commonwealth*, 701 S.E.2d 414, 420 (Va. 2010) (holding that a plea was not invalid for failure of the court to warn of collateral consequence). See generally Gabriel J. Chin & Richard W. Holmes, *Effective Assistance of Counsel and the Consequences of Guilty Pleas*, 87 CORNELL L. REV. 697, 703–12 (2002) (discussing the general rule that counsel is not required to warn about collateral consequences).
75 130 S. Ct. 1473, 1482 (2010).
76 Margaret Colgate Love, *Collateral Consequences after Padilla v. Kentucky: From Punishment to Regulation*, 31 ST. LOUIS U. PUB. L. REV. 105–11 (2012).
77 217 U.S. 349 (1910).
78 356 U.S. 86 (1958).
79 See *Weems*, 217 U.S. at 364 ("They shall always carry a chain at the ankle, hanging from the wrists; they shall be employed at hard and painful labor, and shall receive no assistance whatsoever from without the institution.").
80 *Id.*
81 See *id.* ("Civil interdiction shall deprive the person punished, as long as he suffers it, of the rights of parental authority, guardianship of person or property, participation in the family council, marital authority, the administration of property, and the right to dispose of his own property by acts inter vivos.").
82 See *id.* at 364–5 ("The penalty of perpetual absolute disqualification is the deprivation of office, even though it be held by popular election, the deprivation of the right to vote or to be elected to public office, the disqualification to acquire honors, etc., and the loss of retirement pay, etc.").
83 See *id.* at 364 (noting that subjection to surveillance required the person punished to lawfully support himself by "some trade, art, industry, or profession," submit to inspection, report his residence to authorities, and obtain permission before moving).
84 *Id.* at 366.
85 See *id.*
86 See *id.* at 377 ("It is cruel in its excess of imprisonment and that which accompanies and follows imprisonment. It is unusual in its character. Its punishments come under the condemnation of the bill of rights, both on account of their degree and kind.").
87 Given this, Justice White, dissenting for himself and Justice Holmes, concluded "that the accessory punishments are the basis of the ruling now made." *Id.* at 412 (White, J., dissenting). White argued that the accessory punishments, even if unconstitutional, were severable. *Id.* The majority's response indicated that White correctly perceived the centrality of the accessory punishment: "It is suggested that the provision for imprisonment in the Philippine Code is separable from the accessory punishment, and that the latter may be declared illegal, leaving the former to have application." *Id.* at 381. Instead of holding that the conditions of imprisonment would themselves have invalidated the sentence, the Court concluded that the accessory punishments were not severable. *Id.* at 381–2.

88 356 U.S. 86, 101–2 (1958) (plurality opinion).
89 *Id.* at 103.
90 See *id.* at 99.
91 *Id.* at 101–2.
92 *Id.* at 102 ("He knows not what discriminations may be established against him, what proscriptions may be directed against him, and when and for what cause his existence in his native land may be terminated.").
93 First, Justice Brennan concluded that because "expatriation is made a consequence of desertion, it must stand together with death and imprisonment – as a form of punishment." *Id.* at 110 (Brennan, J., concurring). In addition, he agreed with the plurality that the uncertainty created by the consequence was central. *Id.* at 110–11; see also *id.* at 110 n.7 ("[T]his very uncertainty of the consequences makes expatriation as punishment severe."). In *Furman v. Georgia*, Justice Brennan indicated his support for the Trop plurality opinion. 408 U.S. 238, 271 & n.13 (1972) (Brennan, J., concurring).
94 See 130 S. Ct. 1473, 1477 (2010).
95 *Id.* at 1486.
96 *Id.* at 1482; see also *id.* at 1481 ("Our law has enmeshed criminal convictions and the penalty of deportation for nearly a century.").
97 See *id.* at 1486.
98 *Ng Fung Ho v. White*, 259 U.S. 276, 284 (1922).
99 Unif. *Collateral Consequences of Conviction Act* § 5 (2009) (http://www.uniformlaws.org/Act.aspx?title=Collateral%20Consequences%20of%20Conviction%20Act) (last visited Apr. 30, 2013). I served as Reporter for this Act.
100 *Parker v. Ellis*, 362 U.S. 574, 593–4 (1960) (Warren, C. J., dissenting), overruled by *Carafas v. LaVallee*, 391 U.S. 234 (1968).
101 As an analogy, no one would claim that each of the individual disadvantages of imprisonment – subjection to classification, prison rules, solitary confinement, mail restrictions, transfer, bad food – is a separate punishment that must be explained at a guilty plea. Yet, imprisonment is punishment.

13

Psychopathy, Criminal Responsibility, Punishment, and the Eighth Amendment

Adam R. Fox and Reid Griffith Fontaine

1. INTRODUCTION

Criminal responsibility is a complex subject, and in a retributive system such as that in the United States, it rests on presuppositions about the cognitive capacities of individuals whom we intend to punish. Under the Eighth Amendment, which prohibits "cruel and unusual punishment," considerations of proportionality limit the extent to which a criminal offender may be punished for a particular crime. In some cases, a defendant's "subrationality" or "cognitive *in*capacities" may serve to mitigate or fully excuse criminal responsibility, but standards tend to be very high when it comes to criminal excuses. The M'Naghten standard for legal insanity, for example, requires that a defendant, at the time of his act, not know the nature and quality of said act or know that it was wrong. In practice, this standard will often only be met by individuals suffering from such a profound mental disturbance (such as a psychotic/thought disorder) that most observers would be compelled to declare the defendant resolutely "insane."

Recently, however, the United States Supreme Court has made a number of rulings aimed at staking out the boundaries of mitigation of responsibility, based upon empirical research on human cognition and psychological development. Defendants who were previously held fully responsible for severe offenses are now held to a reduced standard of responsibility, and certain penalties that were formerly considered acceptable are now prohibited for some classes of criminal offenders. The scope of these rulings has thus far been limited to cases where public sentiment weighed in favor of mitigation, such as in cases of juveniles and individuals with severe mental handicaps. In this chapter, we will explore whether psychopathy, a condition that is considerably less likely to attract public sympathy, may nonetheless be appropriately treated as a mitigating condition given modern research in psychology and neuroscience. We close with a discussion of what this may mean for future developments in Eighth Amendment law.

2. BEHAVIORAL FEATURES OF PSYCHOPATHY

Psychopaths present a number of deficits that appear to contribute to their propensity for chronic, severe antisocial behavior. These include deficits in impulse control, behavioral learning, affect representation and affective response, and understanding of moral norms.

a. Impulse Control

Psychopaths become bored easily and will often act impulsively to create entertainment in the absence of events around them that secure their attention. They may quickly tire of "this week's lover, wife, and type of crime; they move impulsively on to the next, with little appreciation of the meaning of the commitment."[1] Even very young children "learn to postpone pleasure, compromising with restrictions in the environment ... but psychopaths never seem to learn this lesson."[2] The psychopath is "like an infant" in his capacity for self-regulation.[3]

b. Behavioral Learning

Combined with overall impulsivity, psychopaths appear to have substantial impairments in learning to select or alter their behavior appropriately in the face of negative outcomes. First, psychopaths have much greater difficulty than nonpsychopathic subjects in learning to avoid responding to stimuli associated with a negative outcome, a process known as passive avoidance learning.[4] Second, they have greater difficulty learning to alter their behavior in the face of new information or changed circumstances, known as response-reversal and extinction.[5] Third, psychopaths show deficits in aversive conditioning, which involves learning a negative response to a previously neutral stimulus, on the basis of its association with other negative stimuli.[6] This may include learning a negative association with a particular act based on the negative reactions of others or additional negative consequences. Overall, psychopaths appear to be better at learning to act (or not act) to obtain rewards than learning to act (or not act) to avoid punishment, although psychopaths do appear to have some difficulty in learning appropriate responses to appetitive stimuli in some cases.[7]

c. Affect Representation and Affective Response

Psychological evaluation of psychopaths has found that they lack "affect representation," the capacity to perceive and consciously represent the emotions and feelings of others.[8] In addition, psychopaths generally show a reduced affective *response* to the negative affect of others, as compared to nonpsychopaths, and typically find many conditions neutral that others find highly aversive (such as those that tend to provoke fear, shame, or regret).[9]

Robert Hare notes one psychopathic rapist who, in reference to his victims' fear, reported, "I don't really understand it. I've been scared myself, and it wasn't unpleasant."[10] Another psychopath in Hare's research stated that "he did not really understand what others meant by 'fear.'"[11] This individual failed to understand why a bank teller would shake or "become tongue-tied" while he robbed a bank and made "no reference to bodily sensations" when asked to describe how *he* would feel if he were in the teller's place.[12] Hare notes that the psychopathic individual "seemed perplexed" when asked to state how he would feel rather than to describe what he would think or do in the situation.

Overall, it appears that psychopaths' difficulty perceiving and understanding the affect of others, and substantially diminished affective response, may promote their noted lack of empathy and undeveloped (or at least underdeveloped) capacity for aversive conditioning. These are characteristics that would normally inhibit future aggressive behavior toward others.[13]

d. Understanding Norms and Norms Violations

One of the most prominent tools for assessing the capacity for moral reasoning is Eliot Turiel's moral/conventional task, which is designed to test whether an individual is able to differentiate between moral and conventional social-norm violations.[14] Conventional norm violations are considered permissible in the absence of an authority (such as a rule or a governing authority) prohibiting such acts ("authority dependent"), whereas moral norm violations are considered impermissible even in the *absence* of an authority enforcing a prohibition on such acts ("authority independent").[15] Children as young as four years of age are able to draw the appropriate distinction between moral and conventional norms and typically appeal to harm-based justifications for moral norms, and to social-order justifications for conventional norms.[16]

James Blair has found that psychopaths, like normal individuals, report that moral transgressions are more serious than conventional transgressions.[17] However, *unlike* normal individuals, psychopaths appealed almost exclusively to the existence of rules against the violation in the case of *both* moral and conventional rules. Additionally, psychopaths reported that both conventional and moral transgressions would still be wrong even in the absence of a rule prohibiting such acts, and Blair and Cipolotti found that psychopaths overreported the number of conventional transgressions that would be wrong in the absence of a rule.[18]

Blair has theorized that, because participants in these studies were incarcerated, psychopaths may have reported authority independence for both moral and conventional norms in order to give the impression that they had accepted the norms of society in the hope of gaining more favorable treatment, rather than in order to report their beliefs accurately.[19] Nonpsychopathic incarcerated subjects had no less of an apparent desire for more favorable treatment yet made the moral/conventional distinction without difficulty. If psychopaths had an ordinary understanding of norms, or at least a well-developed understanding of *non*psychopaths' views, it seems plausible to expect that psychopathic participants would have been able to emulate nonpsychopaths' responses. In addition, Blair's interpretation appears consistent with Hervey Cleckley and Robert Hare's suggestions that psychopaths do not carry a deep understanding of the significance of moral norms.[20]

In sum, psychopaths appear to have difficulty learning rules and recognizing norms, understanding their justification and significance, understanding their practical application to concrete situations, and regulating their behavior accordingly. Psychopaths also appear to have significant impairments in perceiving the relevant contextual features of a situation that are often critical to detecting that a norm has been violated. Thus, psychopaths do not appear to be just like normal adults, minus the motivation to act appropriately. Rather, psychopaths appear to possess deficits relevant to their capacity for moral *reasoning* in addition to impairments in their ability to follow the norms they may discern.

3. PSYCHOPATHY AND PENAL PROPORTIONALITY

Psychopaths often commit criminal acts in a manner that attracts the most severe forms of punishment, while their deficits fail to qualify as mitigating factors and more commonly *aggravate* the penalties they receive. Psychopaths are more likely to engage in instrumental aggression[21] than ordinary adults (or even nonpsychopathic antisocial adults). This type of aggression is treated as more culpable than reactive aggression, on the basis of the theory that reactive aggression involves a lower degree of cognitive processing and control.[22] Psychopaths also have greater rates of recidivism than ordinary adults, a fact that often leads to increased penalties at sentencing.[23] Finally, psychopaths tend to show a lack of remorse for the crimes they commit and may often fail to acknowledge that wrongdoing has occurred.[24]

The consensus view is that psychopathy does not qualify as a mental illness for the purpose of excusing criminal conduct under the M'Naughten rule.[25] Psychopathy is not recognized in the *Diagnostic and Statistical Manual of Mental Disorders IV Text Revision* of 2000. Instead, it is typically assessed using Robert Hare's Psychopathy Checklist-Revised (PCL-R).[26] While up to 85 percent of incarcerated individuals may meet the clinical criteria for antisocial personality disorder (ASPD; the diagnosis psychopaths typically receive under the *DSM*), less than 15 percent appear to meet the diagnostic criteria for psychopathy.[27] Although psychopathy and ASPD may overlap, they are separate psychological constructs meriting independent analysis under the law.[28]

Psychopaths appear to understand on a basic level that the term "wrong" is associated with punishment or censure, but they appear to lack the ability to understand fully the notion of a moral wrong or *why* a particular act is wrongful. Currently, such deficits do not serve to mitigate criminal responsibility on the part of psychopaths. However, the Supreme Court's view of mitigation on the basis of cognitive deficit is evolving.

The Eighth Amendment prohibits "cruel and unusual punishment," which calls for balancing considerations of penal proportionality with evolving standards regarding acceptable forms of punishment, on the basis that the law "is not fastened to the obsolete but may acquire meaning as public opinion becomes enlightened by humane justice."[29] In the past ten years, the U.S. Supreme Court has ruled on issues regarding the impact of an individual's mental incapacities and behavioral dispositions on penal proportionality through cases such as *Atkins v. Virginia*, *Roper v. Simmons*, and *Graham v. Florida*. *Atkins* provides much of the treatment of impaired agency that is relevant to the case of psychopaths, although *Roper* and *Graham* approach these issues as well. However, each of these cases also contains arguments that suggest that the law will be reluctant to extend mitigation to psychopathy.

In *Atkins v. Virginia*,[30] the Court held that "punishment is 'excessive' ... if it is not graduated and proportioned to the offense," that proportionality review is judged under "prevailing standards of decency," and that "such evolving standards should be informed by objective factors to the maximum possible extent."[31] The Court argued that "because of their disabilities in areas of reasoning, judgment, and control of their impulses ... [mentally retarded persons[32]] do not act with the level of moral culpability that characterizes the most serious adult criminal conduct."[33] While "mentally retarded persons frequently know the difference between wrong and right," their "diminished capacities to understand and process information, to communicate, to abstract from mistakes and learn from experience, to engage in logical reasoning, to control impulses, and to understand the reactions of others" serve to diminish their culpability.[34] Additionally, the Court argued that "the theory of deterrence in capital sentencing is predicated upon the notion that increased severity of the punishment will inhibit criminal actors from carrying out murderous conduct" and that "the cognitive and behavioral impairments" of mentally retarded persons "make it less likely that they can process the information of the possibility of execution as a penalty and, as a result, control their conduct based upon that information."[35]

In *Roper v. Simmons*,[36] the court held that juveniles were "categorically less culpable than the average criminal" and that juveniles show a "lack of maturity and an underdeveloped sense of responsibility" that "often result in impetuous and ill-considered actions and decisions."[37] In *Graham v. Florida*,[38] the Court held that "'the heart of the retribution rationale is that a criminal sentence must be directly related to the personal culpability of the criminal offender.'"[39] The Court argued that "developments in psychology and brain science continue to show fundamental differences between juvenile and adult minds" such that "parts of the brain involved in behavior control continue to mature through late adolescence."[40] Noting that juveniles are less likely to consider the possibility of punishment when deciding how to act, the Court declared that the deterrent function of life imprisonment is not served by subjecting juveniles to such punishment.[41]

Psychopaths' attributes and specific deficits touch upon many of the issues raised in *Atkins*, *Roper*, and *Graham*. As noted extensively in our discussion, psychopaths appear to have a number of processing deficits related to their capacity to learn and *understand* the significance of norms and to perceive relevant facts about their situation to which such norms are relevant. In addition, psychopaths' impairments in aversive conditioning and rule learning suggest that they are much less likely to learn from mistakes or even perceive that a mistake occurred and are unlikely to be moved by considerations of negative consequences. Psychopaths' deficits in affect representation and affective response appear to impair their ability to "understand the reactions of others." Finally psychopaths' impulsivity and need for stimulation resemble those of a juvenile, or worse; Hare, as noted previously, compared their incapacities to those of an infant. However, *Atkins*, *Roper*, and *Graham* contain caveats that may make application to psychopaths difficult – in particular, the emphasis on public consensus in *Atkins* and the characterization of juvenile offenders' antisocial attributes as transient and externally influenced in *Roper* and *Graham*.

In *Atkins*, the Court states that "the large number of States prohibiting the execution of mentally retarded persons" provides strong evidence that prevailing standards have shifted in opposition to their execution.[42] The Court also notes that "there is no evidence that [mentally retarded persons] are more likely to engage in criminal conduct than others, but there is abundant evidence that they often act on impulse rather than pursuant to a premeditated plan, and that in group settings they are followers rather than leaders."[43] In *Roper* the Court held that a juvenile's commission of even a heinous crime is not "evidence of irretrievably depraved character" because the juvenile's personality traits are "more transitory."[44] The Court argued that, since psychiatrists are forbidden to diagnose juvenile patients with ASPD, "a disorder also referred to as psychopathy or sociopathy," states "should refrain from asking jurors to issue a far graver condemnation – that a juvenile offender merits the death penalty."[45] These statements taken together imply that *if* a juvenile offender happened to be diagnosed with ASPD and her character was determined to be *less* "transitory" and instead "characterized by callousness, cynicism, and contempt for the feelings, rights, and suffering of others,"[46] then the Court would be less moved to mitigate punishment. As the Court argues, "It would be misguided to equate the failings of a minor with those of an adult, for a greater possibility exists that a minor's character deficiencies will be reformed."[47]

In sum, the issue of mitigation is complicated. On the one hand, cognitive deficits that inhibit a defendant's capacity for ordinary moral agency,[48] including the capacity for judgment, self-evaluation, and self-control, are suggested as mitigating factors. On the other hand, the Court leans significantly on public consensus, and on factors that are unlikely to apply to psychopaths – notably, the lack of a heightened disposition for violence and the functional capacity for reform and continued moral development. Psychopaths are dangerous and generally intransigent in their disposition for criminal behavior, so courts will likely be wary about endorsing a shift to treating psychopathy as a mitigating factor if these latter considerations are emphasized. Furthermore, the Court's tendency to create categorical rules, in which entire classes of individuals are covered by a particular rule, may poorly accommodate the fact that psychopaths are not uniform in their deficits.

Therefore, treating psychopathy as a mitigating condition to criminal responsibility would depart from the existing focus on a mix of consensus and more popularly accepted forms of cognitive incapacity (e.g., mental retardation) and may require the creation of a categorical rule that is still sensitive to the degree of deficit on the part of the defendant. Future courts would have to take a more nuanced and expansive view of cognitive deficits, such as taking into account the selective executive and affective deficits associated with psychopathy, when determining whether an individual should be treated as an ordinary adult for the purposes of criminal responsibility. Modern research in neuroscience and moral psychology may provide the sort of evidence that would warrant such a change.

4. NEUROSCIENCE, MORAL AGENCY, AND RESPONSIBILITY

Absent strong evidence, people usually favor explaining others' behavior on a model that resembles their own conduct. We generally imagine that those who harm or help us have comparable cognitive capacities and a mental life that would look very much like our own, if only we had the same beliefs, desires, and intentions. However, we can be wrong about the inferences we draw, particularly when explaining the behavior of psychologically unusual individuals. Ordinary ways of explaining behavior, such as by attributing typical or intuitively plausible mental states, may be inappropriate. In the case of psychopaths, behavioral and neuroscientific evidence suggests that psychopaths have an atypical mental life.

Furthermore, in considering whether someone is culpable for his or her behavior, we make distinctions between culpable and nonculpable etiologies of an individual's capacities. To the extent that we believe that mental processes are physical processes of the brain, it will come as no surprise that neuroscience may discover associations between our behavior and physical events in the brain (such as patterns of neuronal activation). The fact that we may populate our account of how someone came to act as she did with reference to facts about her brain does not serve on its own to exculpate her behavior. However, neuroscientific evidence may help us better understand the degree to which an individual's deficits or incapacities are of her own making or are largely unavoidable given inherent characteristics of her neurobiology.

For example, when confronted with behavioral evidence that psychopaths appear to have difficulty learning and understanding moral rules and perceiving or understanding the aversive conditions of others, we may still wonder whether they could *ever* have had such capacities when assessing culpability. In this regard, evidence of neurobiological dysfunction, and of the relationship of such dysfunction with the development of moral agency, may be helpful in providing a complete account of an individual's potential responsibility.

In the next section, we will first consider some relevant evidence on the neurological basis of psychopathy. Then, we will discuss how neurological dysfunction can affect moral reasoning. Finally, we will examine moral agency as a developmental process.

a. Psychopathy and Neuroscience

Psychopaths' lack of empathy, impairments in affect representation and aversive conditioning, and penchant for instrumental aggression have been associated with dysfunction in the limbic areas[49] of the brain, particularly the amygdala.[50] For instance, Rilling and colleagues found that non–clinically diagnosed psychopaths showed reduced amygdala activation during social-economic games.[51] They concluded that this may explain psychopaths' weaker capacity for aversive conditioning, which could account for their lower likelihood of cooperating with a partner after establishing mutual cooperation. While nonpsychopaths appeared to be emotionally biased to cooperate, overcoming this bias only through "effortful cognitive control," psychopaths appeared to be biased toward defection (that again could only be overcome with effort).

While neuroimaging studies indicate that brain dysfunctions bear a strong correlation with psychopathic behavior, psychopathy does not appear to be a simple neurological disorder. Rather, psychopaths are unable to be properly morally socialized because amygdala dysfunction impairs their capacity for aversive conditioning. Thus, psychopaths are able to harm others without feeling a negative emotional response, and this heightens their capacity for instrumental aggression. Dysfunction in other areas such as the ventromedial prefrontal cortex also appears to contribute to the deficits associated with psychopathy.[52]

b. Affect and Moral Judgment

Affective deficits play a broader role in human psychology than simply robbing an individual of the ability to connect with the experiences of others. The ability to perceive and experience the ordinary range of emotions, in ordinary ways, appears to be vital to an individual's capacity for moral judgment.

One popular way of characterizing reason is that it is either opposed to, or separately tracked from, emotion as a source of moral judgment. In fact, emotion is often associated exclusively with *motivation* rather than moral judgment. Consequently, the emotional deficits that psychopaths present could be dismissed as unrelated to potential defects in their capacity for moral reasoning. However, contemporary research in moral psychology suggests otherwise.

People actively judge social norms as they develop into adulthood. These judgments are intimately connected to their emotional response to past outcomes and their expected emotional response to future outcomes.[53] Turiel and Killen argue that "feelings of care for others are necessary for the acquisition of concepts of equality and fairness" and that emotions underlie "patterns of reasoning about rules, authority, generalizability, and common practices."⁵⁴ According to Turiel and Killen, emotions help people evaluate whether actions are right or wrong. Thus, instead of being divisible tracks, emotions are intertwined with reason.⁵⁵

Research in neuroscience appears to vindicate theories that emphasize emotion as integrated in moral cognition. Joshua Greene and Jonathan Haidt have found that emotion features prominently in judgments concerning "personal moral violations," which involve acts likely directly to cause serious harm to a particular person.⁵⁶ Greene and colleagues found that, when a personal moral violation was at issue, increased activity occurs in areas of the brain associated with emotional processing (such as the ventromedial prefrontal cortex [vmPFC] and amygdala), whereas impersonal moral and nonmoral judgments showed little difference in activity. These areas are argued to make up part of an "affective system" that contributes to moral judgments considering such violations.⁵⁷

Colin Klein notes that patients with damage to the vmPFC are "profoundly impaired when it comes to planning and executing actions" and that the medial PFC region appears to manage representation of the value of future actions and that of outcomes.⁵⁸ He argues that increased activation in these areas is not indicative of a noncognitive, emotionally driven form of judgment. Klein places more emphasis on networked interaction between regions of the brain, and thus less emphasis on a modular single-function treatment of many areas. However, psychopaths appear to display abnormal activation in regions associated with moral judgment on either Greene and Haidt's or Klein's interpretation of the neuroimaging data.

Another research track associated with vmPFC dysfunction, and relevant to moral judgment, is Antonio Damasio's somatic markers theory. According to Damasio, "somatic markers" cue attention to negative outcomes by providing an "automated alarm signal which says: Beware of danger ahead if you choose the option which leads to this outcome."⁵⁹ This "alarm" may lead an individual to reject a course of action immediately, protecting her against future harm and narrowing down the options she has to consider.⁶⁰ Damasio is careful to state, however, that "somatic markers do not deliberate for us," appearing to echo Turiel and Killen's view of emotional response.⁶¹ However, somatic markers assist deliberation by "highlighting some options (either dangerous or favorable), and eliminating them rapidly from consideration."⁶²

One way of thinking about what somatic markers do is that they aid in counterfactual reasoning – that is, thinking about how the world *could* be if one were to act in a particular way. As we consider possible actions, we think about the expected outcomes of those actions in order to decide how to act. If we had to think about every option available to us, it would take a considerable amount of time, and we might end up feeling rather ambivalent about our judgments if we had to evaluate every option in thorough detail. Somatic markers help us quickly eliminate actions from consideration, by quickly drawing our attention to features of a hypothetical scenario that we need to know about (e.g., danger). As discussed previously, psychopaths also show vmPFC dysfunction, and Damasio describes psychopathy as "in fact yet another example of a pathological state in which decline in rationality is accompanied by diminution or absence of feeling."[63]

Psychopaths' deficits in moral judgment may arise out of neurological abnormalities. These abnormalities may bias the subsequent development of the core capacities associated with ordinary moral agency. Moral agency involves more than a capacity for moral judgment. Rather, moral agency also requires the capacity to act in accordance with one's moral judgments, to integrate moral reasoning as a fundamental element of one's formation of goals, and to evaluate of the quality of one's actions and one's self-conception. We now look at moral agency in greater detail.

c. Moral Agency

The concept of agency is often difficult to characterize, touching upon notions of rationality, control, introspection, and, in particular, a capacity for counterfactual reasoning. However, agency is an important concept in law and moral responsibility, as we generally think of people as more than passive observers of their environment. Instead, we assume that people actively participate in developing the world around them through intentional action. As such, to be a responsible individual appears to involve not only being a judge, but also an *agent*. There are many models of agency that may be discussed; however, we will focus on one that appears to reflect relatively popular views.

Albert Bandura characterizes human agency as the ability "to influence intentionally one's functioning and life circumstances."[64] An agent forms plans that will govern her actions in order to achieve her goals, anticipates likely outcomes that will help her form her plans, regulates the execution of such plans, and has accurate knowledge of her own abilities, the significance of her goals, and the soundness of her judgments and has the capacity to correct her behavior when necessary. Moral agency under this model involves the adoption of standards of conduct against which people monitor and evaluate their own behavior. Moral agents act in ways that reinforce their sense of self-worth and satisfaction and will refrain from acting in ways that will violate their adopted standards, generally out of aversion toward the self-sanction they will subsequently impose on themselves. Bandura argues that "it is difficult to mistreat humanized people without risking personal distress and self-condemnation."[65] This self-regulation may collapse if an individual inhibits or lacks a capacity for negative self-judgment. In such cases, even an individual with a capacity for moral reasoning and an understanding of moral concepts may become an ineffectual moral agent.

Bandura's description reflects the widely held view that we take ourselves to be consciously active in the formation of our intentions and actions. We believe that we possess the ability to regulate our actions through the accurate representation of the facts of a situation, reasoned inference, and adequate self-evaluation. This picture of the development of moral agency incorporates Blair's finding that deficits in aversive conditioning may contribute to the development of psychopathy. Psychopaths are far less likely to find the suffering of others aversive or develop a conditioned response to such aversive stimuli. Therefore, under this model, psychopaths are less likely to be competent moral agents even in cases where they seem to possess the intellectual capacity to discuss morality on a conceptual level.

Notably, however, this model may not adequately emphasize the role of positive emotions in the regulation of behavior. Turiel and Killen argue that emotions such as "sympathy, empathy, compassion, and affection" are more central to moral development than negative emotions such as "fear, anxiety, guilt, and disgust" because these positive emotions factor critically into individuals' "purposeful, intentional, [and] goal-directed thinking about the world around them," particularly in the case of social relationships.[66] Thus, a complete account of moral development and agency appears to involve the full spectrum of emotional responses. While there is some conflict in the particulars about the role of certain emotional responses, the framework discussed previously does appear instructive about developmental and cognitive features of moral agency. Furthermore, the account provides a model of a normally functioning adult to serve as a comparison class for psychopaths, in order to help situate their deficits in a general account of human behavior and cognition.

d. Mitigation of Criminal Responsibility and Punishment Revisited

Neuroscientific research may help to improve our understanding of psychopaths' deficits and of human agency (including moral cognition) generally, by showing patterns of neural activation associated with various cognitive capacities, to help disambiguate which capacities a particular process (such as moral judgment) appears to rely upon in an individual with ordinary competency. Psychopaths' executive deficits, such as behavioral control and ability to learn or change their behavior appropriately, appear to have an inherited neurological basis. Furthermore, neuroscientific evidence appears to show that psychopaths do not experience the range of emotions associated with the ordinary moral cognition of adults and children.

Behavioral evidence suggests that such conclusions are valid. However, neuroscientific evidence allows us to progress closer to a unified account of an individual's internal phenomenology so that we can distinguish between individuals who may possess the core capacities associated with moral judgment but ignore those judgments and individuals who may often fail to have such judgments to begin with. Psychopaths, because of the very transient nature of their impulses and capacity for follow-through on plans, arguably are considerably more situationally governed than ordinary adults. Furthermore, evidence from neuroscience and moral psychology appears to suggest that psychopaths may not be ordinary or full moral agents and, in severe cases, perhaps not moral agents at all, because of their affective and executive deficits. Given such evidence, future courts will need to reevaluate sentencing practices on the basis of changes in how selective cognitive deficits, such as psychopathy, are conceptualized.

To be clear, psychopaths are not automata who are devoid of any cognizable sense of agency; they are not akin to the legally insane. Thus, partial responsibility is not only defensible, but also the most likely result even from a court sympathetic to the case made previously. Second, psychopathy is not a uniform deficit in which all defendants possess identical incapacities. Courts will likely have to consider a defendant's deficits on a case-by-case basis for purposes of mitigation. However, even if a court does take seriously the case of mitigation,[67] given the danger that a psychopathic defendant may pose to society, courts will likely consider the option of civil commitment.

e. Civil Commitment

Even if psychopathy were to be treated as a mitigating or, in severe cases, an excusing condition in the future, courts may seek to limit a psychopathic defendant's ability to pose a continued threat to the public at large. Recall from earlier discussion that evidence of psychopathy is often used to show propensity for violent recidivism. This concern is unlikely to be overlooked even by courts that are sympathetic to the case for mitigation. So, the question then becomes, can society isolate psychopaths from the general population? Historically, such concerns have been met by the institution of civil commitment, which is often premised upon utilitarian considerations about social welfare. In *Kansas v. Hendricks*, the Supreme Court held that the "constitutionally protected interest in avoiding physical restraint may be overridden even in the civil context."[68] The court relied upon *Jacobsen v. Massachusetts*, which argued that the constitutionally protected interest in liberty is subject to restraint by the state on the basis of "the common good" since, otherwise, "organized society could not exist with safety to its members."[69]

Utilitarian considerations attempt to balance the burdens and benefits of release and detainment and distribute them between the detainee and society at large typically on the basis of general considerations of social welfare. In some cases, however, paternalistic considerations about the detainee's interests may plausibly factor in as well. Kiehl and Hoffman have recently argued that promising treatment options are available for "youth on a putative trajectory to psychopathic personality," which focus "on the slow and methodical rebuilding of the social connections that are absent in psychopaths."[70] Some courts may opt to commit young defendants to such treatment programs, on the basis of paternalistic considerations in addition to concerns of society at large.

While utilitarian concerns feature prominently in the law, some may find them unsatisfying. Civil commitment of an individual imposes constraints on his or her liberty and agency, and utilitarian justifications are often found unpersuasive as they appear to undermine individual rights in favor of the interests of society. One important consideration to bear in mind, however, is that the basis for mitigation (or excuse) made earlier is premised upon psychopaths' possessing a diminished form of agency. As such, their legal rights may differ from those of adults, as is often considered justifiable in the case of children or individuals classified as legally insane. Psychopaths' deficits and incapacities persevere well past the commission of crimes and the conclusion of criminal trials, and a judgment of diminished responsibility does not restore ordinary adult agency to them. Thus, putatively utilitarian considerations involving civil commitment may still respect the rights of psychopathic offenders.

5. CONCLUSION

Psychopathy presents a difficult and complex challenge for the law because concerns about public safety, individual rights, and ambiguities regarding an individual's responsibility will tend to weigh against mitigation for psychopathic defendants. However, psychopaths appear to depart substantially in their capacities, compared to ordinary adults, and their deficits seem to form a diminished type of agency for which full punishment and responsibility may be inappropriate. Recent cases that favor a more nuanced look at defendants' capacities suggest that the Supreme Court may be on an accelerated trajectory in limiting punishment under the Eighth Amendment on the basis of psychological deficit. Courts in the future should consider psychopathy as a mitigating factor rather than as an excusing condition, owing to the fact that psychopaths often do appear to understand that some behaviors are proscribed, even if they are diminished in their capacity to understand the reasons for such prohibitions or control their behavior in accordance with such prohibitions. However, even in cases where criminal responsibility is excused, psychopaths do not possess a right to act without restraint or regulation, and courts should consider civil commitment in order to protect the interests of society and, in some cases, of the defendant.

Notes

1 Kent Kiehl & Morris B. Hoffman, *The Criminal Psychopath: History, Neuroscience, Treatment, and Economics*, 51 JURIMETRICS 355 (2011).
2 ROBERT D. HARE, WITHOUT CONSCIENCE 58 (1993).
3 *Id.*
4 R. J. R. Blair, et al., *Passive avoidance learning in psychopathic individuals: Modulation by reward but not by punishment*, 37 PERSONALITY AND INDIVIDUAL DIFFERENCES 1179 (2004).
5 R. J. R. Blair, *Applying a Cognitive Neuroscience Perspective to the Disorder of Psychopathy*, 17 DEVELOPMENTAL PSYCHOPATHOLOGY 865 (2005).
6 Herta Flor et al., *Aversive Pavlovian Conditioning in Psychopaths: Peripheral and Central Correlates*, 394 PSYCHOPHYSIOLOGY 505 (2002).
7 Blair, supra note 5.
8 *Id*
9 Hare, supra note 2.
10 *Id.* at 44.
11 *Id.* at 53.
12 *Id.* at 54.
13 Blair, supra note 5, at 873.
14 ELLIOT TURIEL, THE DEVELOPMENT OF SOCIAL KNOWLEDGE: MORALITY AND CONVENTION (1983).
15 R. J. R. Blair, *A Cognitive Developmental Approach to Morality: Investigating the Psychopath*, 57 COGNITION 1 (1995).
16 Judith G. Smetana & Judith L. Braeges, *The Development of Toddlers' Moral and Conventional Judgments*, 36 MERRILL-PALMER QUARTERLY 329 (1990).
17 Blair, supra note 5; R. J. R. Blair, et al., *Is the Psychopath Morally Insane?* 19 PERSONALITY AND INDIVIDUAL DIFFERENCES 741 (1995).
18 R. J. R. Blair & Lisa Cipolotti, *Impaired Social Response Reversal: A Case of "Acquired Sociopathy"*, 123 BRAIN 1122 (2000).
19 Blair, supra note 15, at 26.
20 HERVEY CLECKLEY, THE MASK OF SANITY (1941); HARE, supra note 2.
21 Instrumental aggression is associated with calculated efforts toward accomplishing a goal involving personal gain, while reactive aggression is associated with an individual acting in response to a perceived provocation, with the intent of harming the perceived provocateur. Reid Griffith Fontaine, *Disentangling the Psychology*

and Law of Instrumental and Reactive Subtypes of Aggression, 13 PSYCHOLOGY, PUBLIC POLICY, AND LAW 143 (2007).
22 REID GRIFFITH FONTAINE, THE MIND OF THE CRIMINAL: THE ROLE OF DEVELOPMENTAL SOCIAL COGNITION IN CRIMINAL DEFENSE LAW (2012); Stephen Morse, *Diminished Rationality, Diminished Responsibility*, 1 OHIO ST. J. CRIM. L. 289 (2003)
23 David DeMatteo & John F. Edens, *The Role and Relevance of the Psychopathy Checklist – Revised in Court: A Case-law Survey of U.S. Courts (1991–2004)*, 12 PSYCHOLOGY, PUBLIC POLICY, AND LAW 214–41 (2006).
24 Hare, supra note 2.
25 DeMatteo & Edens, supra note 23, at 230.
26 *Id.*
27 Stephen D. Hare & Robert D. Hare (1996), *Psychopathy and Antisocial Personality Disorder*, 9 CURRENT OPINION IN PSYCHIATRY 129 (1996).
28 FONTAINE, supra note 22.
29 *Weems v. United States*, 217 U.S. 349, 378 (1910).
30 563 U.S. 304 (2002).
31 *Id.* at 304.
32 This is the phrase the *Atkins* Court used to describe defendants such as Renard Atkins.
33 *Id.* at 306–7.
34 *Id.* at 318.
35 *Id.* at 320.
36 543 U.S. 551 (2005).
37 *Id.* at 567, 569.
38 130 S. Ct. 2011 (2010).
39 *Id.* at 2028 (quoting *Tison v. Arizona*, 481 U.S. 137, 149 (1987))
40 *Id.* at 2026.
41 *Id.* at 2028–9.
42 *Atkins v. Virginia*, 563 U.S. 304, 315–16 (2002).
43 ID. at 318.
44 *Roper v. Simmons*, 543 U.S. 551, 599 (2005).
45 *Id.* at 573.
46 *Id.*
47 *Id.* at 570.
48 The concept of moral agency will be discussed in greater detail in the next section.
49 The limbic system consists of several regions of the brain associated with functions such as behavioral regulation, motivation, emotional response, and formation of long-term memory (all of which factor into reinforcing behavioral responses in an individual).
50 Blair, supra note 4; Blair, supra note 5. Amygdala dysfunction has also been implicated in increased amounts of instrumental aggression, Blair, supra note 4, while orbitofrontal cortex (OFC) dysfunction in psychopaths has been linked with their penchant for impulsive behavior, Blair, supra note 5. Furthermore, OFC and ventromedial prefrontal cortex (vmPFC) dysfunction has been linked with deficits in response-reversal and extinction. See also R. J. R. Blair, *The Roles of Orbital*

Frontal Cortex in the Modulation of Antisocial Behavior, 55 BRAIN AND COGNITION 198 (2004).
51 James Rilling et al., *Neural Correlates of Social Cooperation and Noncooperation as a Function of Psychopathy*, 61 BIOLOGICAL PSYCHIATRY 1260 (2007).
52 Michael Koenigs, Michael Kruepke & Joseph P. Newman, *Economic Decision-Making in Psychopathy: A Comparison with Ventromedial Prefrontal Lesion Patients*, 48 NEUROPSYCHOLOGIA 2198 (2010).
53 TURIEL, supra note 14, at 220.
54 Elliot Turiel & Melanie Killen, *Taking Emotions Seriously: The Role of Emotions in Moral Development*, in EMOTIONS, AGGRESSION, AND MORALITY IN CHILDREN 40–2 (Frank Arsenio & Elizabeth A. Lemerise, eds., 2010).
55 *Id.* at 37.
56 Joshua Greene & Jonathan Haidt, *How (and Where) Does Moral Judgment Work?* 6 TRENDS IN COGNITIVE SCIENCES 517 (2002); see also Joshua Greene, et al., *An fMRI Investigation of Emotional Engagement in Moral Judgment*, 293 SCIENCE 2105 (2001).
57 Fiery Cushman, Liane Young & Joshua Greene, *Our Multi-System Moral Psychology: Towards a Consensus View*, in THE OXFORD HANDBOOK OF MORAL PSYCHOLOGY (John Doris et al., eds., 2008).
58 Colin Klein, *The Dual Track Theory of Moral Decision-Making: A Critique of the Neuroimaging Evidence*, NEUROETHICS 4: 143–62, at 149 (2011).
59 ANTONIO DAMASIO, DESCARTES' ERROR: EMOTION, REASON, AND THE HUMAN BRAIN 173 (1994).
60 *Id.*
61 *Id.* at 174.
62 *Id.*
63 *Id.* at 178.
64 Albert Bandura, *Toward a Psychology of Human Agency*, 1 PERSPECTIVES ON PSYCHOLOGICAL SCIENCE 164 (2006).
65 Albert Bandura, *Selective Moral Disengagement in the Exercise of Moral Agency*, 31 JOURNAL OF MORAL EDUCATION 101, 109 (2002).
66 Turiel and Killen, supra note 54, 47.
67 For more discussion on the details of mitigation, and our defense of maintaining partial criminal responsibility for psychopaths, see A. R. Fox, T. H. Kvaran & R. G. Fontaine, *Psychopathy and Culpability: How Responsible is the Psychopath for Criminal Wrongdoing*, 37 LAW AND SOCIAL INQUIRY (2012).
68 521 U.S. 346, 356 (1997).
69 197 U.S. 11, 26 (1905).
70 Kiehl and Hoffman, supra note 1.

Part VII

EMERGENCIES AND BORDERS – IMMIGRATION, TERRORISM, NATIONAL SECURITY, AND TRANSNATIONAL CRIME

14

Preemption and Proportionality in State and Local Crimmigration Law

Juliet P. Stumpf

In October 2011, Mercedes-Benz announced a major expansion of its sprawling manufacturing plant in Tuscaloosa County, Alabama, forecasting a $350 million investment and the addition of hundreds of jobs to the forty-eight-hundred-strong workforce. A month later, a Tuscaloosa police officer stopped a rental car without a tag and asked the driver for his license. The driver handed the officer a foreign identity card but no driver's license nor proof of lawful presence in the United States. The officer arrested the noncitizen driver and detained him pursuant to a state immigration law passed just months before. The driver turned out to be Detlev Hager, a German citizen and an executive with Mercedes-Benz.[1]

Hager's arrest galvanized public debate over state laws governing migration across and within their borders. Supporters and critics alike had deemed the Alabama law the harshest state immigration law in the nation. The Beason-Hammon Alabama Taxpayer and Citizen Protection Act gathered in a single piece of legislation the most severe elements of other state laws that had criminalized conduct related to immigration. It expanded police arrest and detention authority, made seeking unauthorized work a crime, criminalized "encouraging" unauthorized immigrants to enter the state, and required parents, under penalty of perjury, to report the citizenship status of their schoolchildren. Relevant to Hager's case, the law provided that a noncitizen lacking federal authorization to be present in the United States committed a crime in Alabama by failing to carry a document evidencing lawful status.[2]

Alabama's response to Hager's failure to carry documentation of his lawful presence in the United States seemed to many to be out of proportion. Hager had lawful immigration status and therefore had not actually violated the Alabama immigration law. Because he did not have proof of lawful status on his person, however, the state's immigration law obligated the officer to treat

Hager as if he had none. According to the chief of police, had Hager been a U.S. citizen, Tuscaloosa practice would have been to issue him a citation for failure to carry his driver's license and let him go. Instead, the state dropped the charges against him only after he produced documentation at a municipal court hearing. It was Hager's noncitizen status that led to his acquaintance with the state's criminal justice system.

Hager's case was newsworthy because it exemplified Alabama's new immigration law functioning as fashioned while missing its target. The arrest and the negative publicity surrounding it seemed to hoist the law on its own petard. Hager's position as an executive of one of Alabama's most important employers and his German national origin placed him well outside the population that Alabama's legislators likely imagined when they passed the immigration law.[3] Public discussion centered on whether the state should single out noncitizens, many of whom were visible ethnic minorities, for harsher treatment and criminal punishment.

Seven months after Hager's arrest, in June 2012, President Obama announced that the federal government would refrain from deporting certain young noncitizen residents who lacked lawful immigration status.[4] The Deferred Action for Childhood Arrivals ("DACA") program formalized the exercise of prosecutorial discretion to indefinitely defer deporting undocumented students, high school graduates, and soldiers without criminal histories, and it granted them temporary work authorization.[5] The premise underlying the President's announcement was that under some circumstances deportation was a disproportionate response to unlawful presence.

The President's DACA initiative and the Alabama immigration law illustrated two divergent approaches to deportation law and policy: one taken by the federal government and the other by a state. The Alabama law was a no-holds-barred effort to rout any and all unauthorized immigrants from the state under threat of criminal punishment. The federal deferred action program, in contrast, sought to distinguish among those unlawfully present, withholding the penalty of deportation for some, depending on their circumstances. The two approaches whetted an ongoing public debate over whether and how much to sanction noncitizens when they have crossed the border unlawfully.

The public debate, in other words, has resonated with themes of equality and proportionality. In the courtroom, in contrast, the issue was framed as a constitutional question of preemption. A year after Hager's arrest, the U.S. Supreme Court in *Arizona v. United States* struck down as preempted parts of a similar state immigration law, leaving other parts at least provisionally intact.[6] The Justices divided sharply over whether federal power over immigration preempted state and local governments from making similar immigration laws, with Justice Scalia reading his strong dissent from the bench.

As Hager's case and the Deferred Action program illustrate, the preemption question is closely linked to the issue of proportionality in crimmigration law – the intersection of immigration and criminal law.[7] If laws like Alabama's immigration statute criminalize migration-related conduct in ways that are inconsistent with federal immigration law or increase the consequences to noncitizens of traditional crimes, issues of proportionality sharpen.

Preemption has become a lightning rod of contention. It has served as the battleground between those who seek to increase state control over immigration enforcement and those who would slow the momentum toward ever-heavier immigration enforcement.[8] In other words, the question whether state immigration laws are disproportionately punitive is also a debate about federalism, about whether federal immigration law bars the states from making and enforcing immigration law.

This chapter examines the tensions inherent in these alternate ways of framing the debate about nonfederal immigration law. Two constitutional threads trace through this contest over state and local control of migration. The first is the Supremacy Clause's proclamation that federal law trumps state law, bolstered by the plenary power doctrine's concern with how immigration policy may impact the nation-state as an entity on the international stage. The second is the constitutional mandate to impose criminal and civil punishment proportionally.[9] Through preemption, the first thread has assumed center stage, while proportionality operates subterraneously as a background norm rather than a doctrinal directive.

The chapter will excavate how state and local crimmigration law has overlain the constitutional issue of preemption upon a submerged norm of proportionality, with potentially tectonic results. The first part of this chapter narrates the postcolonial decline of state and local control of immigration law and the constitutional anointing of exclusive federal immigration power. It describes the recent origin and flourishing of crimmigration law and the problem of proportionality. The second part of the chapter recounts the resurrection of state and local efforts to govern the flow of noncitizens across and within their borders, and the emergence of the preemption issue.

The chapter concludes that the legitimacy of state criminal law as a proportionate response to immigration violations depends on the meaning of unlawful presence. If unlawful presence is usually the result of unlawful border crossing, then determining whether state crimmigration laws disproportionately punish depends on how large or small a transgression unlawful entry is.[10] If, on the other hand, an unlawful border crosser is eligible for lawful immigration status through marriage or other reason, or subject to deferred action, then state criminalization of the unlawful entry appears both oppressive and disproportionate.

1. FEDERAL IMMIGRATION POWER AND THE RISE OF CRIMMIGRATION LAW

While the interest of states in immigration law is long-standing, its intensity and methodology are new. Over and again, states have selected criminal law, the legal tool with which they are deeply familiar, to regulate and often penalize both migrants and the U.S. citizens who associate with them. State criminalization of immigrants is an increasingly prominent facet of crimmigration law.

State crimmigration law has stirred federalism questions about how much the federal government's constitutional dominance in immigration law limits state efforts to criminalize immigration-related conduct. In 2012, the Supreme Court's decision in *Arizona v. United States* shed light on that question but did not fully answer it. The roots of state crimmigration law lie in the peculiar development of federal power over immigration law and the increasingly conflicted significance of unlawful presence.

a. The Establishment of Federal Power over Immigration

The federal government came late into its constitutional power over immigration, but when it did, it engulfed state immigration law. Throughout the nation's first century, states governed the migration of people across borders.[11] Early state and local legislatures sought to prevent the entry of people on the basis of religion, race, ethnicity, and gender, among other reasons.[12] Criminal law was also largely within the bailiwick of the states. At that time, criminal law played only a minor role in immigration enforcement and a much larger role in protecting individuals against expulsion from the country.

Expelling a free white noncitizen after admission to the new nation constituted banishment, a criminal punishment imposed after full criminal process.[13] British loyalists were the early recipients of what was considered an extreme punishment. The criminal justice system was the main channel for decisions about expulsion. As a result, noncitizens were entitled to the sturdier procedural protections of criminal law before the government could remove them from its territory.

Perhaps because of the states' insistence on the power to regulate the movement of free blacks during the era of slavery, there was little federal immigration legislation prior to the Civil War.[14] After the Civil War, the federal government began to regulate immigration actively. Among other laws, Congress passed several statutes meant to prevent the Chinese from settling in the United States. Two men from China, one a resident of California and the other of New York, challenged these laws requiring the exclusion of Chinese laborers from entering and the expulsion of those already in the country. One had left the United States to visit China, only to have Congress pass the exclusion law before he returned. The other was in the United States and sought to prevent his expulsion. They both argued that the Constitution did not bestow on Congress a power to expel people living in the United States.

They both lost. In 1893, the Supreme Court articulated a federal plenary power over immigration law so far-reaching that the Constitution could not cabin it. In that decision, the Court pushed aside state regulation of the entry or expulsion of noncitizens. The power it outlined for Congress, because it was tied so closely to international relations, was exclusively federal, "forbidden to the state governments."[15] The Supreme Court announced that federal power over immigration – over decisions about who may enter and who must leave – were so closely related to foreign policy and the international identity of the nation, so fundamental to its existence, that it preceded the Constitution. The immigration power was not unconstitutional because it was beyond the Constitution's reach.

What flowed from that conclusion was that individual constitutional protections were weaker in immigration law. Beyond the general distinctions drawn between citizen and noncitizen, this weaker constitutional protection resulted from the concern that recognizing noncitizens' claims of rights might undermine foreign affairs and national security efforts. As well, deportation was not a criminal sanction and could be imposed without criminal procedural protections. Instead, less robust due process protections applied.

These early cases framed a new kind of preemption question about whether any room was left for nonfederal governments to regulate migration.[16] As federal immigration legislation proliferated and federal administrative power expanded through the institutions the federal agencies built to process the entry and expulsion of noncitizens, the scope of state and local regulation of migration narrowed.

b. Legislating Unauthorized Migration

The cloudiness of the preemption question became salient when several major policy shifts expanded the population of unlawfully present immigrants.[17] First, in 1965, legislation that ended overtly racial immigration policies also imposed a quota on the number of noncitizens who could lawfully immigrate to the United States from outside the Western Hemisphere. As well, it made the nuclear family the basis for lawful family-based migration.[18] Congress later applied numerical limits on Western Hemisphere immigrants, including those from Mexico.[19] These limitations effectively set a cap on lawful permanent migration that was considerably below the migration flow from Mexico. Lawful immigration from Mexico dropped to 40 percent of its previous level. Noncitizens who had close family ties outside the new law's definition of family or who exceeded the quotas had a choice of sorts: stay where they were or enter the United States unlawfully. Occurring at the end of the Bracero Program, which had established strong ties between agricultural growers and Mexican laborers by creating temporary legal status for Mexican agricultural workers, the constriction of lawful avenues for immigration propagated a rise in unauthorized border crossings.[20]

The second policy change made deportation more prevalent. Legislation passed in 1996 closed many of the avenues for relief from deportation, eliminating most justifications for permitting unlawfully present noncitizens to stay in the United States.[21] Many noncitizens were faced with a choice: leave the United States or live there clandestinely.

Finally, in the 1990s, Congress legislated bars to reentering the United States and increased border enforcement. The bars to reentry, triggered when the noncitizen left the country, prohibited reentering the country for a set term of years and sometimes forever.[22] These two changes made it much harder for unauthorized noncitizens to return lawfully to the United States after leaving.[23]

The combined effect of these legal and policy changes was that some people did not enter the United States and others left for good. Because of the difficulty of returning, however, others stayed who otherwise would have left. By 1990, the population of unauthorized noncitizens had risen to 3.5 million.[24]

Meanwhile, the states explored ways to govern these migration flows. In the 1970s, the efforts of Texas and California to reduce their populations of unlawfully present noncitizens inspired two seminal Supreme Court decisions about how much states could regulate noncitizens. *Plyler v. Doe* severely limited the states' power to exclude noncitizen children from public schools.[25] *DeCanas v. Bica* allowed states some leeway, in the absence of federal legislation, to restrict noncitizens' access to employment.[26] This would be the Supreme Court's last word on preemption in immigration law until the year 2012.

c. The Rise of Crimmigration

Starting in 1986 and accelerating through the following decade, crimmigration law became a defining element of the relationships among the federal and state governments and the noncitizen.[27] It also entered a collision course with the constitutional norm of proportionality.

Federal crimmigration law has evolved in two directions. First, unlawful entry or presence had been a major focus of expulsion from the United States. Deportation law now cants heavily toward criminal grounds that include low-level convictions and misdemeanors. This development has made lawful permanent residents considerably more vulnerable to deportation. In particular, the category of crime that deportation legislation dubbed an "aggravated felony" is now a jumbled list of crimes that trigger deportation. There are few bases for relief from expulsion and almost no lawful pathway to return to the United States after deportation.[28]

Second, violations of immigration law that had been handled in administrative courts are now frequently channeled through the criminal justice system before deportation. Criminal prosecution on top of deportation became more common for unlawful entry as well as for use of false documents to obtain work. New crimes for conduct related to migration expanded the menu for prosecuting noncitizens and those who associated with them. For example, in 1986, when Congress barred employers for the first time from employing noncitizens who lacked government permission to work, the law criminalized employers who repeatedly and knowingly hired undocumented noncitizens.[29]

Deportations increased as Congress provided more funding for immigration enforcement and detention. Immigration agents embraced the full powers of law enforcement, especially the discretion to stop, arrest, and detain noncitizens. Where immigration enforcement and traditional policing crossed paths, formal procedural protections in immigration and criminal law gave way. State and local police stops set the stage for federal immigration authorities to convert the state apprehension into a federal immigration detention, thereby nullifying the right to seek bail under state law.[30] Federal plea agreements closed off access to immigration court to seek relief from deportation.[31] Federal policy makers, responding to state concerns about immigration, announced plans to prioritize criminal aliens for removal.

These developments introduced a significantly harsher edge to immigration law that was exacerbated by two contemporaneous legislative changes. First, the crimmigration laws radically limited judicial review of deportation decisions. The combination of limited judicial intervention and the less forgiving deportation grounds for crimes meant that an arresting officer's decision about what crime to charge could effectively determine whether a noncitizen would be expelled forever from the United States.[32]

Second, in 1996, Congress made deportation retroactive for many crimes.[33] Lawful permanent residents with ancient convictions and long-served sentences suddenly faced deportation as a new consequence of those old convictions. Noncitizens with new reasons for lawful entry such as family ties or jobs found themselves excludable on the basis of crimes punished long ago. Minor crimes began to lead to the deportation of numerous U.S. residents, sometimes well after they had served their sentences, and with little leeway for a court or other official to grant relief from removal. Federal immigration law had become a full-fledged and large-scale deportation power operating well within the border.

Collectively, these developments raised the issue of proportionality. Criminal law, like other areas of law that impose penalties, operates with the norm that minor transgressions are to be matched with minor sanctions, and vice versa. That norm is backed by the Eighth Amendment's prohibition against cruel and unusual punishments and the Fifth and Fourteenth Amendments' guarantees of due process. Federal and state sentencing guidelines illustrate its influence in the intricacies of the formula for calculating a fitting sentence. While there is room for debate about how effectively criminal punishment in the United States succeeds in carrying out proportionate punishment, the proportionality principle serves as a wellspring of argument in criminal law and in challenges to civil punitive damages.

In contrast, the pedigree of proportionality as a source of norms in immigration law is thin. Deportation is the central penalty, available for every transgression of immigration law. As deportation grounds have expanded and complicated criminal process and punishment, the issue of proportionality has advanced to the forefront.

With little flexibility in the legislative framework and limited judicial review, the most flexible tool for the kind of individualized query that proportionality contemplates is the discretion over enforcement decisions that the federal immigration agencies hold. In 2000, in direct response to the 1996 laws limiting relief from deportation, the commissioner of the Immigration and Naturalization Service issued a memo affirming that immigration agents had discretion in enforcing the deportation laws and setting forth a list of factors for immigration agents to consider in individual circumstances.[34] The factors included the existence of a criminal history, the length of time a noncitizen had spent in the United States, the availability of relief from deportation, and the negative effect for future admission to the United States that an enforcement action might create.

In 2011, after repeated stymied attempts at comprehensive immigration reform and a surge in annual deportations to record levels, the immigration agency issued directives similar to the earlier memo to guide the use of federal immigration enforcement resources.[35] This effort to channel prosecutorial discretion similarly emphasized consideration of favorable factors and prioritized crime-based cases for enforcement. These agency directives articulated a theory of prosecutorial discretion as a pathway toward proportionality in immigration law.[36]

2. THE RISE OF STATE AND LOCAL CRIMMIGRATION LAW AND THE SPECTER OF PREEMPTION

a. Crimmigration and the Domestication of Immigration Law

The Alabama immigration law represented the edge of a wave of nonfederal efforts to govern immigration. State and local legislatures began churning out laws and resolutions relating to immigration at a tremendous rate, ratcheting upward from 45 laws passed in twenty-five states in 2005 (when the trend was significant enough to track) to 306 laws passed in forty-two states by December 2011.[37] In April 2010, Arizona passed an omnibus immigration enforcement law overtly meant to drive unlawfully present noncitizens from the state. It included state penalties and enforcement mechanisms for trespassing, failing to carry immigration registration documents, employing undocumented immigrants, harboring and transporting unlawfully present noncitizens, and human smuggling, among other provisions.[38]

The Arizona law generated tremendous national interest and, despite intense civil rights and preemption litigation, inspired several other states to enact copycat laws.[39] The Beason-Hammon Alabama Taxpayer and Citizen Protection Act is a collection of elements from several of these state laws.

Why have we seen this amplification of nonfederal interest in governing immigration? The explanations most commonly offered do not satisfactorily answer this question. Proponents of these laws assert that federal underenforcement of immigration law has forced the states' hands. Unauthorized immigration is out of control and the federal government has failed to control the borders adequately. The impact on the communities receiving the migrant flow is so great that state and local officials should have a role in controlling that flow.

This story is very contested. It is true that estimates of the population size of unauthorized noncitizens in the United States hover around 11 million. On the other hand, federal deportation levels are higher than they have ever been. The Obama administration set a new record early in its first term, deporting almost 400,000 noncitizens, then passed the 400,000 mark for deportations in 2012.

Opponents of state and local regulation of immigration contend that the flood of nonfederal immigration laws stems from illegitimate efforts to use the neutral face of immigration law to control ethnically diverse populations. The demographics of the modern wave of immigration lean heavily toward migrants of color, especially Latinos and Asians. These migrants have settled in areas of the United States that were unaccustomed to heavy migrant flows, such as the Southwest and Midwest. The movement into nontraditional areas, combined with mainstream associations of Latinos and Asians with foreignness, have triggered a public reaction in those areas that manifests as state and local interest in immigration enforcement. This explanation for – and objection to – the intense state and local interest in legislating immigration law arises from a concern that greater power to enforce immigration law would translate to higher levels of discrimination on grounds of bias.

These explanations, however, do not address why nonfederal governments exhibit such an extraordinary level of interest in immigration enforcement at this juncture. State and local governments have sought to control migration since the early years of the United States. Unauthorized migration is not new to the United States. Nor is bias.

The explanation that this chapter offers forefronts the rise of crimmigration law in transforming the nature of federal immigration law. The development of crimmigration law was part of a larger trend toward domesticating immigration law.[40] Crimmigration law expanded the regulation of migration from the border toward the interior of the country. Crimmigration also made the connection between criminal and immigration law more visible to the average citizen and to state and local policy makers. As a result, it constructed the noncitizen as a criminal alien: the undocumented noncitizen because of the spotlight on migration-related criminal offenses and the lawful permanent resident because of the new sanctions for minor crimes and ancient convictions.

Domesticating immigration law paved the way for nonfederal officials to feel competent in setting up shop as immigration regulators. The federal government was now regulating migration in areas that states traditionally regulated, namely, employment, welfare, and especially crime. Immigration enforcement began to resemble the activities that the states engaged in every day, making it easier for state and local governments to reach for the power to regulate immigration. The perception of proximity between immigration law and state and local powers received a boost when Congress established avenues for police to assist with federal immigration enforcement efforts, such as by deputizing police officers as immigration agents.[41] Congress also mandated communication between federal and nonfederal officials when it required the federal immigration agency to respond to state and local agencies' requests for information about an individual's immigration status.[42]

State policy makers reached for a familiar tool – criminal law – to venture into immigration enforcement. New nonfederal laws like those in Arizona and Alabama relied heavily on state criminal law and law enforcement to pursue the state's immigration policies. Preemption moved to the fore as an avenue for curbing the state crimmigration trend. The states defended the legislation against preemption arguments by maintaining that the laws mirrored federal immigration law and merely magnified the level of enforcement.

b. Preemption, Proportionality, and the Courts

A preemption challenge usually connotes a power struggle between the states and the federal legislature. On its face, the constitutional question of preemption is about the breadth of federal supremacy over immigration and the extent to which that federal power limits the states' ability to regulate noncitizens. Once embedded in crimmigration law, however, this pure question of federalism becomes tangled with consequentialist concerns such as equal protection. Nonfederal crimmigration law is usually an effort to discourage unauthorized migrants from settling within state borders. Equal protection concerns arise because the migrants these state laws target are often ethnically different from most of the incumbent population.

Less apparent than equal protection is the connection between preemption and proportionality, particularly the potential for disproportionate sanctions. In general, the U.S. Supreme Court has not looked kindly upon arguments based directly on constitutional proportionality in criminal law;[43] nor has it shown a taste for actively preempting civil state laws using federal immigration law.[44] Moreover, deportation is formally a civil penalty not subject to the Eighth Amendment. If proportionality has any effect, it will be in the nature of a "phantom constitutional norm,"[45] exerting a gravitational pull on the reasoning and outcomes in preemption cases.

The breadth of the Alabama law and its cousin, the Arizona immigration law, usefully illustrates the way in which preemption relates to proportionality. The Alabama law, though more extensive than most state immigration laws, is a prime example of the use of criminal law to regulate both noncitizens and others connected to them. Like the previously passed Arizona law, the Alabama immigration law bore down most heavily on unlawfully present noncitizens. In addition to criminalizing the failure to carry an immigration document, the law created state crimes for passing oneself off as a U.S. citizen when seeking state welfare benefits and for looking for work. It also obligated parents of schoolchildren, under penalty of perjury, to provide to school officials documentation of the citizenship or immigration status of their children. Because perjury is a misdemeanor under Alabama law, this provision criminalized a parent's misrepresentations to school officials about a child's immigration status.[46]

The Alabama law reached beyond unauthorized noncitizens. The new state immigration crimes swept in U.S. citizens and others who have contact with unlawfully present noncitizens. A landlord who rented or attempted to rent property to unlawfully present noncitizens may have committed a felony. Taking a page from Arizona's immigration law, Alabama declared that day laborers and contractors who hired them committed a misdemeanor if the contractor's vehicle impeded traffic during the hire. The measure also made it a state crime for anyone to harbor, transport, or shield from detection an unlawfully present noncitizen or to "encourage" an unauthorized noncitizen to enter the state. It became a misdemeanor for state employees to fail to report if they know or have reason to believe that someone has violated any part of the immigration law.[47]

Alabama relied heavily on the tools of criminal enforcement to implement its goals, empowering police to investigate the immigration status of anyone they stop or arrest if the officer has a "reasonable suspicion" the person is in the United States without authorization. The statute required police who arrest and book a noncitizen to establish the arrestee's immigration status and granted the officer authority to detain the noncitizen for a day for that purpose. The law also required state and local law enforcement to hand over the noncitizen to the federal government upon request.[48]

When states or cities criminalize immigration-related conduct that the federal government has not prohibited, two preemption issues arise. The first is whether nonfederal authorities may use their police powers to govern immigration matters that had previously largely been federal concerns, such as the decision to question or detain a noncitizen and thereby trigger federal immigration law enforcement. The second is whether state and local governments are preempted from implementing new criminal laws, such as prosecution of landlords and school administrators, to enforce federal immigration laws.

The purpose of many of these state laws is to increase federal deportations but also to encourage self-deportation by making life in the state unbearable for unauthorized migrants. Taking those purposes seriously, these nonfederal criminal laws are exacting a penalty on noncitizens for being unlawfully present. They add a criminal sanction to the consequence of deportation (as well as to any federal criminal punishment), which the Supreme Court has acknowledged is closely connected to criminal punishment.[49]

Preemption raises issues of proportionality because allowing one sovereign to sanction noncitizens through crime-based deportation and immigration-related criminal prosecution while the other sanctions through criminal law irretrievably complicates the potential for a proportionate response to immigration violations. Loosening the rein on preemption of state crimmigration law risks losing control over the proportionality of the sanctions that both governments may exact.[50]

In deciding facial challenges to the Arizona and Alabama laws, the courts have had to grapple with these connections between preemption and proportionality. In *Arizona v. United States*, holding that Congress had preempted much of the Arizona immigration law, the theme of proportionality is a steady undercurrent throughout the opinion.[51] The Supreme Court first struck down as field-preempted the state crime of failing to comply with federal alien registration requirements. The Court noted that state criminal punishment would pose a conflict whenever federal officials determined that it was inappropriate to pursue immigration enforcement. Conflict would also arise because the state penalties were harsher than the legislated federal penalties.

Similarly, in holding that Congress had preempted Arizona's criminal penalty scheme for seeking unauthorized employment, the Court compared the federal decision to impose only civil penalties with the state's broader enforcement policy and more severe criminal penalties. Because Congress had decided it would be "inappropriate to impose criminal penalties on aliens who seek or engage in unauthorized employment," state criminal penalties posed an impermissible obstacle to Congress's purposes. Likewise, when invalidating as preempted Alabama's equivalent provision, the Eleventh Circuit contrasted the severity of the state criminal penalties with the noncriminal consequences that federal law imposed for unauthorized employment.[52]

The states' criminal sanctions were preempted because of their severity. The states were foreclosed from altering Congress's "calibrated framework" of sanctions for immigration violations.[53] Because the state laws were more punitive than Congress had in mind, they constituted a disproportionate response to the noncitizens' conduct.

The Supreme Court's *Arizona* opinion continued to connect preemption and proportionality even when addressing the more procedural components of the state law. In striking down the state requirement that Arizona police arrest and detain noncitizens suspected of having committed a removable offense, the opinion played up the comparative severity of the enforcement actions. The majority expressed concern that state enforcement would impose "unnecessary harassment" of noncitizens in the face of federal determinations not to remove them.

In contrast, when upholding the final challenged provision requiring police to perform immigration status checks during stops when the police reasonably suspect the stopped individual is unlawfully present, the majority opinion carefully neutralized the proportionality issue. So long as the requirement of immigration checks did not impose punitive consequences such as prolonged detention or pure immigration stops, the provision was facially lawful. Similarly, the Eleventh Circuit upheld Alabama's analogous provision by conceptualizing it as a mere inquiry between police and noncitizen, and a sharing of information between federal and state officers, not as a consequence triggering proportionality concerns.

The influence of proportionality in these cases is subtextual. It does not flow directly from a constitutional amendment but rather functions as a norm that influences the preemption analysis without overtly governing it. It is a comparative proportionality in which the courts measure the disproportionality of the state law by the difference between the state and federal levels of severity toward noncitizens.

The question of whether federal enforcement preempts state enforcement thus became a question about proportionality. Proportionality, by its nature, assumes that there is a decision maker with control over how much or how little to sanction an individual for unlawful conduct. The states have no control over the reasons for deporting a noncitizen or over whether a federal immigration officer will be available to pursue immigration charges against someone whom state or local police have detained. Deportation grounds are exclusively within Congress's bailiwick. At the same time, the federal government lacks control over whom state and local police will choose to arrest or whom state prosecutors will charge with a crime.

That leaves nobody in charge of figuring out whether the penalty – deportation or criminal punishment or both – is proportionate to the crime, to the immigration-related conduct, or to the circumstances of the individual noncitizen. If both sovereigns are exacting a penalty for the same conduct or status, then there is no one authority regulating how much punishment is exacted. It is this institutional dysfunction that creates disproportionality. At risk in the preemption analysis is the loss of an institutional capacity for a proportionate outcome to interactions between law enforcement and individual noncitizens. Without some level of preemption of state and local power to punish criminally, there is no clear pathway to a proportionate system of deportation.

3. CONCLUSION

Preemption challenges raised in the context of immigration enforcement attract a variety of arguments about sovereignty, international relations, federal-state relations, and equal protection, among others. The arguments that generated the most intense judicial discussion, however, were suffused with the subtextual norm of proportionality stemming from the clash of state crimmigration schemes and federal prosecutorial discretion. The Alabama example shows that state crimmigration approaches are naturally backward-looking, seeking to punish the prior act of border crossing, using criminal law to move noncitizens physically beyond the border and to isolate them from the community, discouraging them from renting homes or attending school. In contrast, the Deferred Action program is forward-looking, stepping away from the notion that unlawful presence is akin to a criminal state of being and looking to the future potential for authorized settlement in the United States.

Measuring proportionality by focusing on the distinctions between the federal and state levels of punitiveness highlights an important aspect of the courts' reasoning in *Arizona* and *Alabama*. When states decide to impose independent punitive consequences for immigration violations, they ignore federal decisions not to enforce the violation or to recognize the kind of potential for a formal or informal status that the deferred action announcement represented. This suggests a deeper distinction between punitive state laws and the potential for federal enforcement discretion.

Whether the state criminal laws are a proportionate response to immigration violations depends on the meaning of unlawful presence.[54] If unlawful presence, like trespassing, can be summed up as entering and remaining where one is forbidden, so that the law's focus is on the unauthorized border crossing, then whether state crimmigration laws disproportionately punish depends on how egregious unlawful entry is. If, on the other hand, an unlawful border crosser is eligible for lawful immigration status through marriage or other reason, or subject to deferred action, then state criminalization of the unlawful entry appears both arbitrary and disproportionate. In other words, if unlawful presence is at least as much about the potential for lawful integration – about redemption – as it is about unlawful entry, then state crimmigration law will always ultimately fall short.

Perhaps what the Constitution requires is a harder look at the preemption question in the immigration context because of that potential for redemption through legalization. Criminalization of immigration law creates more criminalized noncitizens, people who either have been convicted of state immigration crimes or who, as a class, exist in the shadow of the state crimmigration law. When federal immigration law carries the potential for transforming a noncitizen into a resident or a citizen, perhaps preemption in the immigration realm can act as a conduit for concerns about proportionality.

Notes

1 Hager was released after an associate retrieved his driver's license and German passport.
2 ALA. CODE § 31-13-10.
3 See Verna Gates, *Alabama Immigration Crackdown Nabs Mercedes Executive*, REUTERS (Nov. 22, 2011) http://www.reuters.com/article/2011/11/22/us-immigration-a

labama-mercedes-idUSTRE7AL0DT20111122 (last visited Apr. 29, 2013) (referring to Hager's arrest as one of a number of "unintended consequences" of the law); *Illegal Immigration Charges Dropped Against German Mercedes-Benz Executive*, THE WIRE BLOG (Nov. 23, 2011, 12:02 PM) http://blog.al.com/wire/2011/11/illegal_immigration_charges_dr.html (last visited Apr. 29, 2013) (noting that Mercedes-Benz is one of Alabama's largest employers); Dawn Kent, *Mercedes to Build Fifth Model at Alabama Auto Plant*, THE WIRE BLOG (Oct. 20, 2011) http://blog.al.com/business-news/2011/10/mercedes_to_build_fifth_model.html (last visited Apr. 29, 2013) (discussing Mercedes-Benz's plans to expand operations in Tuscaloosa County); Julia Preston, *In Alabama, a Harsh Bill for Residents Here Illegally*, N.Y. TIMES, June 3, 2011, http://www.nytimes.com/2011/06/04/us/04immig.html (last visited Apr. 29, 2013) (quoting a chief sponsor of the bill as stating that the law was "to prevent illegal immigrants from coming to Alabama and to prevent those who are here from putting down roots").

4 Press Release, *The White House, Remarks by the President on Immigration* (June 15, 2012), available at http://www.whitehouse.gov/the-press-office/2012/06/15/remarks-president-immigration (last visited Apr. 29, 2013); see Memorandum from Janet Napolitano, Sec'y of Homeland Sec. to David V. Aguilar, Acting Comm'r, U.S. Customs & Border Prot., Alejandro Mayorkas, Dir., U.S. Citizenship & Immigration Servs., & John Morton, Dir. U.S. Immigration & Customs Enforcement, on Exercising Prosecutorial Discretion with Respect to Individuals Who Came to the United States as Children (June 15, 2012), available at http://www.dhs.gov/xlibrary/assets/s1-exercising-prosecutorial-discretion-individuals-who-came-to-us-as-children.pdf (last visited Apr. 29, 2013).

5 The deferred action program targeted the population that would have benefited from lawful immigration status if Congress had passed the DREAM Act. See Development Relief and Education for Alien Minors Act of 2011, S. 952, 112th Cong. (2011).

6 *Arizona v. United States*, 132 S. Ct. 2492 (2012).

7 Juliet Stumpf, *The Crimmigration Crisis: Immigrants, Crime, and Sovereign Power*, 56 AM. U. L. REV. 367, 376 (2006).

8 See generally Kris W. Kobach, *The Quintessential Force Multiplier: The Inherent Authority of Local Police to Make Immigration Arrests*, 69 ALB. L. REV. 179 (2005) (arguing that state and local law enforcement officers have inherent authority to make civil immigration arrests and sketching counter-arguments).

9 See Juliet Stumpf, *Fitting Punishment*, 66 WASH & LEE L. REV. 1683, 1687 (2009) ("While criminal law is animated by the idea that the punishment must be proportionate to the crime, proportionality is scarce in immigration law."); see also Angela M. Banks, *Proportional Deportation*, 55 WAYNE L. REV. 1651 (2009) (concluding that deportation, as a civil punitive measure, is subject to constitutional limitations requiring proportionality); Michael J. Wishnie, *Proportionality: The Struggle for Balance in U.S. Immigration Policy*, 72 U. PITT. L. REV. 431, 450–65 (2011) (exploring the application of proportionality in immigration law).

10 Hiroshi Motomura, *The Rights of Others: Legal Claims and Immigration outside the Law*, 59 DUKE L.J. 1723, 1780 (2010) (setting out varying views of the meaning of unlawful presence in the United States).

11 GERALD L. NEUMAN, STRANGERS TO THE CONSTITUTION: IMMIGRANTS, BORDERS, AND FUNDAMENTAL LAW 19 (1996).

12 See EMBERSON EDWARD PROPER, COLONIAL IMMIGRATION LAWS: A STUDY OF THE REGULATION OF IMMIGRATION BY THE ENGLISH COLONIES IN AMERICA 17–18, 33, 63 (William S. Hein & Co., 2003) (1900); NEUMAN, supra note 11 at 34–40. See also Kerry Abrams, *The Hidden Dimension of Nineteenth-Century Immigration Law*, 62 VAND. L. REV. 1353, 1395–7 (2009) (describing the historical exclusion of Chinese women in early state and federal immigration law).

13 Peter L. Markowitz, *Straddling the Civil-Criminal Divide: A Bifurcated Approach to Understanding the Nature of Immigration Removal Proceedings*, 43 HARV. C.R-C.L. REV. 289, 325–7 (2008) (discussing early uses of banishment and noting that "[t]he only mechanism to expel persons from the colonies was banishment – a criminal punishment imposed after completion of the criminal process with all the relevant procedures and protections attached thereto.").

14 Gerald L. Neuman, *The Lost Century of American Immigration Law (1776–1875)*, 93 COLUM. L. REV. 1833, 1866 (1993).

15 *Fong Yue Ting v. United States*, 149 U.S. 698, 706 (1893) ("For local interests, the several States of the Union exist; but for international purposes, embracing our relations with foreign nations, we are but one people, one nation, one power.") (quoting *Chae Chan Ping v. United States*, 130 U.S. 581, 606 (1889)).

16 See *Arizona v. United States*, 132 S. Ct. 2492 (2012) (Scalia, J., dissenting) (opining that the states retained a general power to exclude aliens from their territories).

17 See DOUGLAS S. MASSEY ET AL., BEYOND SMOKE AND MIRRORS: MEXICAN IMMIGRATION IN AN ERA OF ECONOMIC INTEGRATION 40–7 (2002).

18 Act of Oct. 3, 1965, Pub. L. No. 89–236, § 3, 79 Stat. 911 (1965) (codified as amended in scattered sections of 8 U.S.C.).

19 *Id.* § 21 (placing a limit of 120,000 immigrant visas applicable to the Western Hemisphere as of 1968); Immigration and Nationality Act Amendments of 1976, Pub. L. No. 94–571, § 7, 90 Stat. 2703, 2706 (1976) (applying the per country limit to Western Hemisphere countries); Act of Oct. 5, 1978, Pub. L. No. 95–412, § 1, 92 Stat. 907, 907 (1978) (combining immigration ceilings for the Eastern and Western Hemispheres).

20 See MASSEY, supra note 17, at 43–5.

21 Illegal Immigration Reform and Immigrant Responsibility Act of 1996 (IIRIRA), Pub. L. No. 104–208, 110 Stat. 3009–546 (1996) (codified as amended in scattered sections of 8 U.S.C., 18 U.S.C.).

22 See 8 U.S.C. § 1182(a)(9)(B)(i)(I) (2006) (applying a three-year bar to reentry to a noncitizen who has accrued more than 180 days but less than one year of unlawful presence and who voluntarily departed prior to the commencement of removal proceedings); 8 U.S.C. § 1182(a)(6)(G) (2006) (applying a five-year bar to reentry to a noncitizen who violates the terms of a student visa); 8 U.S.C. § 1182(a)(9) (2006) (creating bars of between five and twenty years for unlawful presence and reentry after a previous removal or departure under a removal order).

23 MASSEY, supra note 17, at 128–33.

24 JEFFREY S. PASSEL & D'VERA COHN, PEW HISPANIC CENTER, UNAUTHORIZED IMMIGRANT POPULATION: NATIONAL AND STATE TRENDS, 2010, at 23, tbl. A3 (2011), available at http://www.pewhispanic.org/files/reports/133.pdf (last visited Apr. 29, 2013).

25 *Plyler v. Doe*, 457 U.S. 202, 224–6 (1982).

26 *DeCanas v. Bica*, 424 U.S. 351, 365 (1976).
27 See generally Stumpf, supra note 7.
28 See 8 U.S.C. § 1101(a)(43) (2006) (defining "aggravated felony"); Stumpf, supra note 9, at 1723–4.
29 8 U.S.C. § 1324a(f) (2006).
30 See Ingrid V. Eagly, *Prosecuting Immigration*, 104 Nw. U. L. Rev. 1281, 1337 (2010) ("Once inside the formal criminal system, bail hearings are erased, plea bargaining is placed on a fast-track timetable, and adjudication is often funneled into a magistrate court system that lacks the safeguards of Article III and is designed for expediency").
31 See *id.* at 1303–4.
32 See Hiroshi Motomura, *The Discretion That Matters: Federal Immigration Enforcement, State and Local Arrests, and the Civil-Criminal Line*, 58 UCLA L. Rev. 1819, 1858 (2011).
33 8 U.S.C. § 1101(a)(43), (amending INA § 101(a)(43) and applying the "aggravated felony" definition "regardless of whether the conviction was entered before, on, or after the date of enactment").
34 Memorandum from Doris Meissner, Comm'r, Immigration & Naturalization Serv. to Regional Directors, District Directors, Chief Patrol Agents, and Regional and District Counsel, *Exercising Prosecutorial Discretion* (Nov. 17, 2000), available at http://www.scribd.com/doc/22092970/INS-Guidance-Memo-Prosecutorial-Discretion-Doris-Meissner-11-7-00 (last visited Apr. 29, 2013). See also Motomura, supra note 32, at 1829–36 (analyzing discretion in immigration arrest and prosecution decisions).
35 See, e.g., Memorandum from John Morton, Assistant Sec'y, U.S. Immigration & Customs Enforcement to All Field Office Directors, All Special Agents in Charge, and All Chief Counsel, *Exercising Prosecutorial Discretion Consistent with the Civil Immigration Enforcement Priorities of the Agency for the Apprehension, Detention, and Removal of Aliens* (June 17, 2011), available at http://www.ice.gov/doclib/secure-communities/pdf/prosecutorial-discretion-memo.pdf (last visited Apr. 29, 2013)
36 See Shoba Sivaprasad Wadhia, *The Role of Prosecutorial Discretion in Immigration Law*, 9 Conn. Pub. Int. L.J. 243, 292–3 (2010) (exploring whether immigration enforcement operations and practices accord with formal agency policies requiring prosecutorial discretion); Julia Preston, *Deportations Continue Despite U.S. Review of Backlog*, N.Y. Times, June 6, 2012, http://www.nytimes.com/2012/06/07/us/politics/deportations-continue-despite-us-review-of-backlog.html?pagewanted=all (last visited Apr. 29, 2013) (reporting that as of May 29, 2012, fewer than 2% of deportation cases under review for the exercise of prosecutorial discretion had been closed).
37 Compare Brooke Meyer et al., Nat'l Conference of State Legislatures, 2011 Immigration-Related Laws and Resolutions in the States (2011), available at http://www.ncsl.org/issues-research/immig/state-immigration-legislation-report-dec-2011.aspx (last visited Apr. 29, 2013), with Ann Morse, Lindsay Littlefield, and Leya Speasmaker, *A Review of State Immigration Legislation in 2005*, Nat'l Conference of State Legislatures (Jan. 2007), http://www.ncsl.org/issues-research/immig/immigrant-policy-project-state-legislation-117.aspx (last visited Mar. 29, 2013).

38 Support Our Law Enforcement and Safe Neighborhoods Act, S.B. 1070, 49th Leg., 2d Reg. Sess. (Ariz. 2010) (amended by H.R. 2162, 49th Leg., 2d Reg. Sess. (Ariz. 2010)).
39 See MEYER, supra note 37.
40 See Juliet P. Stumpf, *States of Confusion: The Rise of State and Local Power over Immigration*, 86 N.C. L. REV. 1557, 1581–2 (2008) (describing the domestication of federal immigration law).
41 See 8 U.S.C. § 1357(g) (2006) (often referred to as the "287(g) program").
42 8 U.S.C. § 1373(c) (2006).
43 See, e.g., EWING V. CALIFORNIA, 538 U.S. 11, 25 (2003) (upholding California's three strikes law against a challenge that it constituted cruel and unusual punishment in violation of the Eighth Amendment).
44 *Chamber of Commerce v. Whiting*, 131 S.Ct. 1968 (2011) (upholding an Arizona law suspending or revoking the licenses of businesses that knowingly hired undocumented workers and rejecting arguments that license loss was a "death penalty" for employers).
45 See Hiroshi Motomura, *Immigration Law after a Century of Plenary Power: Phantom Constitutional Norms and Statutory Interpretation*, 100 YALE L. J. 545 (1990).
46 ALA. CODE §§ 13A-10-101–13A-10-103 (West 2012) (defining three degrees of perjury); H.B. 56 § 27, ALA. CODE § 31-13-27 (West 2012).
47 H.B. 56 § 6 (stating that any employee of the State "or a political subdivision thereof" will be guilty of "obstructing governmental operations" if the employee fails to report violations of the Act when there is reasonable cause to believe that a violation has occurred); ID. § 11 (prohibiting unlawfully-present noncitizens from applying for work in Alabama and making it unlawful for "an occupant of a motor vehicle that is stopped ... to attempt to hire or hire and pick up passengers for work at a different location" if the vehicle blocks traffic); *Id.* § 13 (establishing that it is a crime to conceal or shield an unlawfully-present noncitizen, to "[e]ncourage or induce" the noncitizen to come to or live in Alabama, or to "[h]arbor an alien ... by entering into a rental agreement ... to provide accommodations").
48 *Id.* § 12.
49 See *Padilla v. Kentucky*, 130 S. Ct. 1473, 1480 (2010).
50 See Wishnie, supra note 9.
51 *Arizona v. United States*, 132 S. Ct. 2492 (2012).
52 *United States v. Alabama*, 691 F.3d 1269, 1282–83 (11th Cir. 2012) cert. denied, 2013 WL 210698 (U.S. April 29, 2013) (No. 12–884).
53 *Id.* at 1286.
54 See Motomura, supra note 10.

15

Embattled Paradigms

The "War on Terror" and the Criminal Justice System

Susan N. Herman

1. INTRODUCTION

The post-9/11 "War on Terror" has profoundly challenged American criminal law in two very different ways. First, directing some suspected terrorists to a regime of military detention and military tribunal prosecutions for war crimes circumvents the criminal justice system altogether, making it easy to create a watered-down version of justice. But absorbing terrorism prosecutions of Guantánamo detainees and other suspected terrorists in the civilian courts also provokes the dilution of our accustomed criminal law and procedure guarantees for a group of defendants regarded as exceptional. And once accepted as legitimate, these exceptions and watered-down rights are positioned to become the new normal for all criminal defendants. While I believe that suspected terrorists should be treated as criminals rather than as soldiers in a metaphorical "war," the widespread assumption that terrorism prosecutions are categorically unique has led us to a true Hobson's choice: isolating prosecutions of foreign terrorism suspects to avoid compromising the civilian justice system or affording these suspects full due process in civilian courts with the understanding that the meaning of full due process is then likely to be altered.

a. Circumventing Criminal Justice

Beginning in the fall of 2001, President George W. Bush[1] and later Congress[2] proclaimed authority for the president to treat suspected terrorists as prisoners of war or war criminals rather than charging them with crimes in the civilian courts. Adoption of this "war" paradigm was based on the assumption that terrorism presents an inherently different challenge from crime.[3] This paradigm shift resulted in the establishment of a law-free zone in Guantánamo, where suspects might be detained indefinitely without charges and might also be charged with war crimes before military tribunals that, from the outset, were designed not to follow the usual constitutional criminal trial norms.[4] Indeed, the idea that a custom-designed model of what counts as due process might facilitate convictions was one of the chief attractions of the military venue.

The fundamental question of whether this exceptional treatment is justified – whether we are at "war" with terror in anything other than a metaphorical sense – has dominated political and legal debate about our responses to terrorism.[5] I will not rehearse those arguments here. Notably, the Bush administration did not simply opt for the war model. Instead, it attempted to straddle two very different paradigms. In a traditional war, pitting nation against nation, the Geneva Conventions would prohibit criminal prosecution of soldiers for doing their lawful job of killing their nation's enemies but would allow detention of those enemy soldiers for the duration of the hostilities to prevent them from continuing to kill.[6] But because terrorists like members of al-Qaeda do not represent a nation, the Bush administration also declared those designated as enemy combatants to be "unlawful" enemy combatants and thus not even entitled to the detention hearings the Geneva Conventions would have required.[7] The Supreme Court, of course, in a historic series of cases, insisted that the treatment of terrorists be moved somewhat closer to the criminal justice paradigm, insisting that detained Americans were entitled to some form of due process,[8] that detainees in Guantánamo were entitled to some form of habeas corpus review of their detention,[9] and that military commission trials for war crimes must meet certain minimal due process standards.[10] Yet twelve years after 9/11, the question of what should count as adequate due process in military commission proceedings is still not fully resolved, as that system has not yielded convictions tested on appeal.[11]

In the second decade after 9/11, the question of where to hold trials of suspected foreign terrorists remains controversial. President Bush asserted authority to make ad hoc decisions to channel suspected terrorists either to the indefinite detention/military commission model (as long as the suspects were not American citizens)[12] or to prosecution in the civilian criminal justice system.[13] This choice was considered possible because these enemy combatants were deemed "unlawful" combatants, who therefore were not to enjoy the immunity from criminal prosecution the Geneva Conventions afford prisoners of war – although they could still be held indefinitely for the duration of the War on Terror.

In the fall of 2011, Congress enacted a National Defense Authorization Act authorizing indefinite detention of suspected terrorists.[14] President Obama, expressing "serious reservations" about the indefinite detention power, initially threatened to veto the bill but reversed his position and instead issued a signing statement promising not to use that authority during his time in office.[15] This position was part of a compromise in which Congress dropped proposed provisions that would have required President Obama to try *all* foreign national or all al-Qaeda–related terrorism suspects in military commissions.[16] Thus terrorism prosecutions, for now, can still be brought either in civilian court or in military tribunals, although the statute favors military commissions.

b. Retrofitting Criminal Law

In this chapter, I will discuss the consequences of trying terrorism suspects in civilian court rather than in an isolated military justice system, offering three examples of how the criminal law has been or may yet be retrofitted to accommodate the fight against terrorism. First, substantive criminal laws have been expanded to serve preventive rather than purely punitive goals, particularly in post-9/11 laws criminalizing "material support" of terrorism. Material support laws have been fashioned into dragnets, increasing the potential to catch innocent people in addition to actual supporters of terrorism, and increasing the likelihood that this preventive model will seep throughout the criminal law. Second, constitutional criminal procedure guarantees, including Sixth Amendment, Fourth Amendment, and *Miranda* rights, have been subjected to pressure. Various Sixth Amendment guarantees, starting before 9/11, have been reconfigured to accommodate terrorism prosecutions. Since 9/11, exceptions to other rights have been proposed, as with *Miranda* warnings, or adopted, as with the "sneak and peek" authority (dispensing with notice of certain government searches and seizures), which entered the law as part of the USA PATRIOT Act. Although adopted in the fall of 2001 with the primary motivation of easing terrorism investigations, the "sneak and peek" authority is a good example of "mission creep," having been used overwhelmingly in criminal cases having nothing to do with terrorism. Third, investigative techniques that were condemned pre-9/11, including forms of racial profiling and infiltration of political and religious meetings, have been resurrected and deemed permissible in terrorism investigations. And once these exceptions and techniques are regarded as acceptable in the context of terrorism investigations, how long will it be before this permissive attitude allows them to migrate to enforcement of other criminal laws?

2. THE PREVENTION PARADIGM AND THE CRIMINAL LAW

The material support laws[17] are a prime example of how the criminal law can be repurposed to prevent rather than just punish. Terrorists and would-be terrorists may, of course, be prosecuted for traditional crimes like murder, attempted murder, conspiracy to commit murder, assault, or arson. Current material support laws provide a potential additional charge against someone who has caused one of these forms of harm, as well as allowing leeway to prosecute those who have not actually caused or even intended any act of violence.

The material support law first added to the United States Code in 1994[18] made it a crime to provide terrorists with material support (such as weapons or cash), allowing law enforcement to intervene at an earlier point even if agents and prosecutors did not have sufficient evidence to prove a conspiracy or attempt. This original material support law tried to accommodate First Amendment freedoms. It provided, first, that no one could be prosecuted for supplying humanitarian assistance (such as medical care) to a terrorist or sympathizer "not directly involved" in such violations, and second, that investigations could not be initiated on the basis of "activities protected by the First Amendment, including expressions of support or the provision of financial support for the nonviolent political, religious, philosophical, or ideological goals of any person or group."[19] And this law required prosecutors to prove that the accused intended to support a suspected group's terrorist activities and not, for example, a nursery school run by a suspect organization.[20]

The Oklahoma City bombing led to the first expansion of this law, in the Antiterrorism and Effective Death Penalty Act of 1996 [AEDPA].[21] The 1996 revised material support statute embraced the theory that money is fungible,[22] and thus a person with no intent of supporting terrorism could nevertheless be prosecuted for donating money to a terrorist-run nursery school because that donation would free up other money for terrorists to use in committing acts of violence.[23] The provision affording protection to First Amendment activities was eliminated.[24] AEDPA also drastically narrowed the exception for humanitarian relief, declaring instead that only provision of medicine (not medical services) or religious books would be exempt.[25] Five years later, the USA PATRIOT Act expanded the range of actions that would count as material support to include the provision of "expert advice or assistance"[26] to those deemed terrorists. This vague term covers some acts that should indeed be crimes (and would be even without this statute), such as giving terrorists guns or money to buy guns, but it also expands the potential for the statute to be used to punish many other kinds of conduct, including well-intentioned humanitarian aid.

What difference do these changes make? By narrowing what the prosecution has to prove and simultaneously narrowing the range of available defenses, the material support statutes give prosecutors a broader dragnet capable of catching a lot more than terrorists who otherwise might have slipped away. In my recent book, *Taking Liberties: The War on Terror and the Erosion of American Democracy* (Oxford University Press 2011), I tell the stories of three cases that show the alarming consequences of allowing humanly fallible investigators and prosecutors to wield this broad a dragnet.

Sami al-Hussayen. A material support statute was used to prosecute University of Idaho graduate student Sami al-Hussayen for providing "expert advice or assistance" to terrorists by posting links on an Islamic organization's Web site. The wide variety of material posted, intended to offer a fair depiction of the entire range of Islamic thought, included anti-American writings and even the point of view of jihadists.[27] It seems evident that agents became suspicious of al-Hussayen because, as a Muslim, he made charitable donations to Islamic charities, something they found out by reviewing his bank records (as post-9/11 law allowed them to do even without any basis for suspicion).[28] But as the jury at his trial later concluded, there was no evidence that al-Hussayen supported terrorism in any way. In fact, he had led a candlelight vigil on the Idaho campus after 9/11 to denounce the terrorist actions of that day.[29] There was so little evidence of any connection between al-Hussayen and any form of terrorism that the theory of the prosecution about what terrorists he was supporting bounced from al-Qaeda to Hamas to Chechen rebels.[30] And this prosecution, brought under the vague and expansive material support law, was fundamentally inconsistent with our First Amendment freedoms of speech, association, and religion.[31] As al-Hussayen's lawyer pointed out at trial, if this man could be convicted for providing "expert advice or assistance" to terrorists by posting links to controversial speech on a Web site, then CNN would be equally guilty for airing a speech by a member of al-Qaeda explaining that organization's point of view.[32] An Idaho jury, after a crash course in the First Amendment, acquitted al-Hussayen on all terrorism charges.[33]

The loosening of the criminal law itself was what enabled this ill-conceived prosecution, threatened First Amendment values, and invited a form of religious profiling. Even one publicized prosecution like this can chill the First Amendment rights of others, frightening people from engaging in speech or discussion of controversial ideas.[34] Another Webmaster might be deterred from posting links to a discussion of jihad; library patrons might decide not to check out a biography of Osama bin Laden, for fear the government might investigate or prosecute them for getting too close to terrorist ideas. Despite the acquittal in this case, others might well be deterred in their speech, association, or religious contributions by the fact that al-Hussayen was prosecuted at all and that he spent seventeen months in solitary confinement awaiting trial – most of it alone, because his family was deported.[35] And future defendants in a similar prosecution might well confront a jury less inclined to honor First Amendment principles and more willing to convict an Arab Muslim man just in case he actually was a terrorist after all.

"*Roya Rahmani*." Another material support prosecution shows the ease with which critical questions in material support cases can be withheld from juries, again enabling this kind of law to act as a sweeping dragnet.

"Roya Rahmani" is the pseudonym of an Iranian woman who was jailed by her government for supporting a prodemocracy group, the People's Mujahedin Organization of Iran (PMOI, sometimes also known as the MEK). After three and a half years of suffering horrific conditions in an Iranian prison, she was released and left the country.[36] Still quite reasonably fearing reprisals from the Iranian government, she decided to immigrate to the United States. She applied for and was granted political asylum.[37] After living in the United States for twenty months, however, she found herself arrested and prosecuted for providing material support to that same prodemocracy group – because she had been working with a group aiding Iranian refugees that had ties to the PMOI.[38] The PMOI had been designated as a terrorist group by the State Department, which meant that Rahmani could be prosecuted under another material support law, allowing conviction for supporting any group designated as a terrorist organization.[39] This designation occurred in 1997, evidently at the demand of the Iranian government, which made branding its political opponent as a terrorist group a condition of any U.S.-Iran rapprochement.[40]

Under this material support law, Rahmani and her codefendants, some of whom were American citizens, could not defend themselves on the ground that they had no intention of supporting terrorism because the law made their intent irrelevant.[41] Money is fungible. So they decided instead to explain to the jury why they believed the government's designation of the PMOI was erroneous.[42] In their view, supported by a number of experts in the United States and by official decisions in other countries, the PMOI was not a terrorist group but a prodemocracy group.[43] But the United States Court of Appeals for the Ninth Circuit ruled that Rahmani and her colleagues were not allowed to raise this defense either.[44] The secretary of state's designation of the group as a terrorist organization is conclusive for purposes of a criminal prosecution.[45]

Humanitarian Law Project. As Roya Rahmani's story shows, the "War on Terror" is not only a war on al-Qaeda. Most of the changes in law developed in response to 9/11 apply to many groups designated as terrorist entities in a highly politicized, clandestine process.[46] Other designees have included Hamas and the African National Congress,[47] but never the IRA.[48]

Also in 1997, the secretary of state designated as a foreign terrorist organization a Kurdish group known as the Kurdistan Workers Party (PKK),[49] whose supporters complained of systematic repression of the Kurds by the Turkish government.

The Humanitarian Law Project (HLP) was established to promote peace and humanitarianism. Its members tried to persuade national forces to respect the human rights of subject populations and worked to persuade insurgent groups to use peaceful dispute resolution methods rather than violence to achieve their goals.[50] The members of the HLP became increasingly alarmed as the language of the material support law broadened from AEDPA through the Patriot Act.[51] The increasingly expansive language of the successive statutes – prohibiting provision of "services" or "personnel" or "training" to any group and then, under the Patriot Act, prohibiting provision of "expert advice or assistance" – might on its face be thought to include their efforts to persuade terrorists to stop being terrorists, illogical though that might seem.

So HLP engaged in what turned into more than a decade of litigation in the California federal courts to try to clarify whether its members were vulnerable to prosecution and whether the law was unconstitutional.[52] Their litigation culminated in a Supreme Court decision, *Holder v. Humanitarian Law Project*,[53] which declared that their activities were indeed covered by the language prohibiting "expert advice or assistance."[54] Dissenting Justice Sonia Sotomayor asked wryly at oral argument whether under the government's theory someone could be prosecuted for teaching a terrorist to play the harmonica.[55] The Court also rejected HLP's argument that being prohibited from talking to terrorists violates the First Amendment.[56]

The material support laws aim to prevent terrorist acts and terrorist conspiracies by cutting off the flow of any form of support to anyone believed to be a terrorist. They seek to serve this goal by lowering the law's bar in a number of different ways, as shown by the sample cases just discussed. First, the statute criminalizing material support for a terrorist organization makes it relatively easy for a prosecutor to gain a conviction. It does not by its elements require proof of intent to support terrorism or proof of actual support of terrorist acts or conspiracies.[57] Second, the form that "support" may take within the meaning of the statute – provision of "expert advice or assistance" – is sweeping and vague, permitting prosecutors to target even those who are trying to talk terrorists out of being terrorists.[58] Third, where material support of terrorism is premised on an individual's connection with a designated group, there is no opportunity for the accused to show that the designation is incorrect, again lightening the prosecutor's burden and minimizing the defenses available to the accused.[59] The list of designated terrorist groups includes not only al-Qaeda, which has directly threatened the United States of America, but organizations that are designated for complex foreign policy reasons, allowing prosecutions of people who become political pawns.[60]

The assumption that reshaping the criminal law in these ways is necessary to neutralize terrorists encourages courts to disregard serious First Amendment and due process challenges to these laws or to particular prosecutions, even though the utility of these laws is far from having been established. The Supreme Court in the *Humanitarian Law Project* case swept the First Amendment out of the way;[61] the trial judge in the prosecution of Sami al-Hussayen for posting links on a Web site denied a defense motion to dismiss the prosecution on First Amendment grounds, saying that an opinion would follow. No opinion followed. It would indeed have been hard to defend the constitutionality of a prosecution that twelve average Idaho residents understood to be an affront to the First Amendment.

Once these procrustean uses of the criminal law are accepted as valid on the assumption that they are necessary to meet the challenge of terrorism, it becomes far more likely that similar expansions will eventually be viewed as acceptable in nonterrorism prosecutions as well. As Justice Robert Jackson said in his now-celebrated dissent in *Korematsu v. United States*, once an exception to principle is made, "The principle then lies about like a loaded weapon ready for the hand of any authority that can bring forward a plausible claim of an urgent need."[62]

There have already been signs of such mission creep in the substantive criminal law. When a Patriot Act–enhanced money laundering statute was used to investigate the activities of the owner of a Las Vegas strip club who was suspected of bribery, Senator Harry Reid remarked, "The law was intended for activities related to terrorism and not to naked women."[63] The impetus for revising the money laundering law was to keep money away from terrorists.[64] But, like some other Patriot Act innovations, the measure was worded broadly enough to allow the newly defined crime to be used for money laundering having no relation to terrorism.

One author coined the evocative term "mission amnesia" to describe how post-9/11 measures initially adopted in an attempt to prevent violent acts of terrorism have become less connected with that objective and ultimately become ends in themselves.[65] As one DOJ employee put it, "I think any reasonable person would agree that we have an obligation to do everything we can to protect the lives and liberties of Americans under attack, whether it's from terrorists or garden-variety criminals."[66]

By 2021, to what extent will the new normal for antiterrorism prosecutions have become the new normal for our criminal law generally?

3. MISSION AMNESIA AND CRIMINAL PROCEDURE

Diverting prosecutions of suspected terrorists to military tribunals offered an opportunity to redefine what would count as a fair trial in this context. In civilian courts, criminal defendants enjoy a series of rights set out in the Sixth Amendment, including the right to jury trial, right to counsel, right to a speedy and public trial, and right to confront the witnesses against them. But the Sixth Amendment, by its terms, only applies to "criminal prosecutions."[67] Debates about what should count as due process in military tribunal proceedings not specifically covered by the Sixth Amendment have centered, again, on the notion that there is something unique about terrorism prosecutions: the defendants are more dangerous; the evidence against them is more likely to be classified; the need for conviction is more urgent. William Blackstone famously remarked that our system is willing to let ten guilty people go free to avoid convicting one innocent.[68] Michael Chertoff, as head of the Department of Homeland Security, asserted that with respect to terrorists, that ratio should be radically readjusted. Criminal procedure could be reconfigured in military commissions to allow detention and conviction of those who might be innocent, in the name of national security.

When trials of suspected terrorists do take place in civilian courts, similar challenges to traditional procedures arise. Will the Sixth Amendment apply in the same manner to suspected terrorists as to other defendants? The law already provides accommodations to preserve national security interests during criminal proceedings. The Classified Information Procedures Act (CIPA), for example, enacted before 9/11, provides special procedures under which certain defendants may be prevented from viewing certain classified information, an exception to the defendant's right of confrontation.[69] Special administrative measures (SAMs) have been adopted to control interactions between civilian court terrorism defendants and their attorneys, a gloss on the right to counsel.[70] When the government finally decided to bring a criminal prosecution against Ahmed K. Ghailani after holding him as an enemy combatant in secret detention sites and at Guantánamo Bay for five years, the defense argued that Ghailani was being denied his Sixth Amendment right to a speedy trial. The court disagreed, finding that this trial was speedy enough under the circumstances.[71] Once the speedy trial bar – in addition to the confidential relationship with counsel, a defendant's right to confront the witnesses against him, and the right to be present at trial – are lowered in civilian court terrorism prosecutions, how long will it be before any or all of those bars are lowered for other reasons deemed important?

The Fourth Amendment can be perceived as an impediment to antiterrorism investigations, as it generally requires individualized suspicion and some form of court order or warrant before government agents can search or seize.[72] But many provisions of the Patriot Act and subsequent laws have lowered the statutory bar (sometimes significantly higher than the current Supreme Court's interpretations of Fourth Amendment protections) on the government's ability to eavesdrop, to obtain private records from a third party, and conduct other forms of surveillance. Some of these provisions apply only in terrorism investigations; others are more general.[73] And almost all of these provisions have proved impervious to constitutional challenge.[74]

One example of a Patriot Act surveillance authority not restricted by its terms to terrorism investigations is the deferred notification of search provision, usually referred to as the "sneak and peek" provision.[75] This provision allows the government to seek a court's permission to defer notifying the target of a search warrant that a search (or perhaps even a seizure) has taken place. The court may grant this permission on finding, among other factors, that immediate notification might have "an adverse result."[76] Although there had been some judicial decisions allowing a form of delayed notification,[77] it was not until the fall of 2001, during the panicky days following 9/11, that Congress decided to codify this permission in a manner that encourages more frequent exceptions to the norm of notice.[78]

As it turns out, the sneak and peek provision has overwhelmingly been used in investigations having no relation to terrorism. In fiscal year 2008, for example, law enforcement agencies used delayed notification warrants 763 times, but only 3 times in terrorism investigations.[79] And, as critics had predicted, use of this authority escalated rapidly. In fiscal year 2010, the Administrative Office reported 2,395 sneak and peek requests. In that year, federal magistrate and district judges granted 2,327 of the applications made outright, granted an additional 48 of those requests after some modification, and rejected only 20.[80] More than three-quarters of these deferred notification requests were made in drug investigations; the second highest categories were extortion/racketeering and fraud.[81] Fewer than 1 percent of the requests made were in terrorism investigations.[82] Sen. Russell Feingold (D-Wis.), the only senator to vote against the Patriot Act,[83] fought unsuccessfully to limit the scope of the sneak and peek provision in 2001. In 2009, he tried again, grilling a testifying assistant attorney general about mission creep and insisting that the Patriot Act's broad powers were not intended to be used in the very different "war" on drugs.[84]

The application in terrorism prosecutions of the ruling in *Miranda v. Arizona*,[85] created to implement the Fifth Amendment's privilege against self-incrimination, has also sparked calls for new exceptions to established law.[86] Believers in the war model argue that it would be ludicrous to give *Miranda* warnings to an enemy soldier taken into custody on the battlefield, and therefore it must also be ludicrous to *Mirandize* terrorism suspects. But the war metaphor is misleading here. Because the law of war generally prohibits the criminal prosecution of soldiers (unless they have committed war crimes), when enemy soldiers are questioned, it is only for intelligence and not with potential prosecution in mind. But when suspected terrorists are interrogated beyond a battlefield and prosecuted in civilian court, *Miranda* becomes relevant. In a prosecution of defendants charged with involvement in the 1993 World Trade Center bombing, Judge Leonard Sand correctly concluded that *Miranda* would bar use of a criminal defendant's statement as evidence against him in a civilian court if he had not received *Miranda* warnings.[87]

This decision, and the *Miranda* warnings themselves, have been widely misunderstood. *Miranda* focuses not on the moment of apprehension of a suspect, but on the introduction of evidence at trial. The Fifth Amendment privilege against self-incrimination does not prohibit interrogation of suspects without warnings, but only the use of unwarned statements at trial.[88] Therefore, those who apprehend suspected terrorists need not provide warnings if they are only seeking intelligence. But, because the Fifth Amendment prohibits courts from compelling a witness at a criminal trial to provide evidence against him- or herself, evidence obtained from the defendant before the trial also cannot be used against him or her if that evidence is deemed to have been compelled – and *Miranda* establishes a conclusive presumption that a suspect's statement is not tolerably freely given if the suspect was not advised, as he would have been advised at trial, of the right to remain silent.[89]

On the premise that the terrorism context is unique, critics have proposed various exceptions to the *Miranda* rules to allow "unwarned" evidence to be admitted at terrorism trials. Proposals have included creation of a legislative terrorism exception,[90] or, more broadly a "foreign interrogation" exception,[91] which obviously would then apply to all prosecutions involving testimony obtained abroad. The Holder Department of Justice originally took the position that there is no need to create a new exception to *Miranda* because interrogation of suspected terrorists falls within the already existing "public safety" exception the Supreme Court created in *New York v. Quarles*.[92] This limited exception allowed police to defer giving warnings when they were asking a suspect about the whereabouts of a gun that might pose an immediate danger to the public, rather than seeking evidence.

Following this reasoning, in December of 2009 and February of 2010, Attorney General Holder maintained that the public safety exception was flexible enough to allow the interrogation of Umar Farouk Abdulmutallab, the "Christmas Day bomber," for an hour, and of Faisal Shahzad, the Times Square bombing suspect, for three hours before proffering *Miranda* warnings.[93] But then in October 2010, a Department of Justice memorandum interpreted *Quarles* as providing authority for agents to continue un-Mirandized interrogation in "exceptional cases" when continued interrogation was deemed necessary to collect valuable and timely intelligence, even if that intelligence is "not related to any immediate threat."[94] This position would substantially expand the exception defined in *Quarles*, which only applied to immediate threats to public safety. And this administratively declared extension of *Quarles* would also apply to non-terrorism-related interrogations.[95]

The debates over the scope of *Miranda* also highlight another feature typical of the antiterrorism context: the idea that both Congress and the executive branch have a more important policy-making role to play in this context than they do in formulating non-terrorism-related criminal procedure. When Congress tried to overrule *Miranda* legislatively in the Omnibus Crime Control and Safe Streets Act of 1968,[96] an indignant Supreme Court in *Dickerson v. United States*[97] found the attempt unconstitutional, announcing that *Miranda* was a constitutionally based rule and therefore was not subject to dilution by Congress. If Congress or the Department of Justice were to expand the public safety exception, would the Supreme Court be as unyielding as it was in *Dickerson*, or would the Court accede? Might this depend on whether the constitutional question first arises in the context of a terrorism-related prosecution?

Justice Hugo Black once noted, in the context of a discussion of the Constitution's double jeopardy guarantee, that after the Supreme Court had found reprosecution by a second sovereign permissible, people had apparently "become more accustomed to double trials, once deemed so shocking, just as they might, in time, adjust themselves to all other violations of the Bill of Rights should they be sanctioned by this Court."[98] The idea that the guarantees of the Fourth, Fifth, and Sixth Amendments can be outweighed by the desire to convict terrorists could, similarly, lead to devaluation of any of these rights, and spread to criminal prosecutions generally.

4. RACIAL PROFILING REDUX

By 1999, sardonic references to the "offense" of "Driving while Black" had gone viral. Americans were finally coming to terms with the fact that racial profiling – mostly of African-American men – was rampant in law enforcement. The ACLU published a special report in 1999 called *Driving while Black: Racial Profiling on Our Nation's Highways*.[99] Law review and news articles documented and deplored racial profiling;[100] class action lawsuits challenging reliance on race as a factor in traffic stops were filed in Oklahoma, New Jersey, Maryland, Illinois, Florida, Pennsylvania, and Colorado.[101] A Gallup poll in December of 1999 showed that 59 percent of Americans believed that there was widespread racial profiling by police, and 81 percent said that they disapproved of this practice.[102] Because of the galvanization of public opinion, by 1999 fifteen legislatures had introduced bills outlawing racial profiling or requiring the collection of traffic stop data to expose racially biased patterns and practices.[103] It seemed that awareness of and opposition to law enforcement based on stereotyping and biases, conscious or unconscious, would continue to grow, and that we were becoming committed as a society to insisting that law enforcement judge people only by their conduct rather than by the color of their skin.

Since 9/11, however, many Americans seem to have forgotten what they had learned about the wisdom, fairness, and efficacy of racial profiling. Post-9/11 public opinion polls have shown that 60–70 percent of those polled explicitly favor profiling Arabs and Muslims, at the airport and elsewhere.[104] Although many officials, including President George W. Bush, urged the nation not to generalize about or condemn Arabs and Muslims as presumptively terrorists,[105] other official statements have endorsed ethnic or religious profiling as a legitimate antiterrorism tactic. In the words of one member of the 9/11 Commission, "If there is an Arab, a young Arab male or female, and a little old lady from Pasadena, you pick the Arab to pull aside."[106]

Arguments have raged in this context too about whether terrorism is exceptional – different enough from ordinary law enforcement that we should accept racial profiling as necessary to our safety, and perhaps even as fair enough.[107] And these arguments flare up periodically as we continue to learn about governmental activity targeting Muslims – like the FBI's mapping of Muslim communities, including "mosque counting"[108] – or FBI training materials portraying Muslims as having a "proclivity for terrorism."[109]

Acceptance of religious and ethnic profiling in this context also seems to have triggered mission amnesia. Once we are willing to ignore the unfairness of treating people as presumptively guilty because of their race, religion, or ethnicity in one context, it may be unrealistic to expect that we will remain indignant about the same phenomenon in other contexts. Since 9/11, a number of states have repealed or are in the process of repealing their traffic data reporting efforts. Wisconsin, for example, recently ended its data collection[110] and Illinois failed to appoint members to a panel required by law to review its reporting results.¹¹¹ Googling "Driving while Black" or similar content today yields few articles written on this subject post 9/11. A good deal of our resolve on this issue seems to have crumbled in the face of a widespread desire to make exceptions for terror investigations.

In what may be an additional ripple effect of the public tolerance of racial profiling as part of the "War on Terror," antiimmigrant sentiments seem to undergird a wide variety of post-9/11 federal and state laws and policies. In the fall of 2001, many Arab and Muslim men were swept from the streets and placed in harsh custody, deported, and targeted for questioning in connection with immigration violations, even though there was little or no actual basis for suspecting these men of any connection with terrorism.¹¹² In November 2001, a special waiting period for men applying for visas was imposed – but only for men from a list of specified countries, almost all of which were Arab and/or Muslim.¹¹³ The NSEERS program required registration by more than ninety-three thousand men and boys from Muslim-majority countries who were seeking entry to or already within the United States on temporary visas. This particular program was finally suspended indefinitely in 2011 when it was found, not surprisingly, to be ineffective as an antiterrorism measure.¹¹⁴ But not all measures singling out Arab and Muslim men for special treatment have been disavowed.

Domestic intelligence gathering and federal-local cooperative law enforcement efforts originally designed as antiterrorism measures have increasingly been employed in "Secure Communities" immigration programs and in the war on drugs, under the rubric of unified "homeland security."¹¹⁵ States including Alabama and Arizona have adapted the "war on terror" paradigm to regional "wars" on illegal immigration. Profiling techniques deployed against perceived undocumented workers¹¹⁶ and arrestees¹¹⁷ inevitably sweep lawful permanent residents and even United States citizens into their dragnets.¹¹⁸ While it is probably impossible to pinpoint the extent to which 9/11 has triggered these developments, the resemblance of the patterns is indisputable.

5. CONCLUSION

What will the criminal law look like ten years from now?

That depends on several factors. Depending on which party controls the White House and Congress, we could see changes in our antiterrorism strategies. Barack Obama continued Bush-era policies in most of the areas I have discussed. He did, however, abandon the term "enemy combatants," and expressed reluctance to detain indefinitely suspects who have not had a fair hearing. It seems unlikely that a Democratic president would voluntarily change course, either in the direction of increasing the military role or in the direction of increasing due process protections. Terrorism prosecutions would be likely to continue to take place in criminal courts as well as, perhaps, in military tribunals; prosecutorial and investigative dragnets would continue to lurk; the present level of surveillance would likely continue; limited exceptions to our criminal procedure regime would probably continue to be proposed.

Under a Republican president, with or without a Republican-dominated Congress, we would not be likely to see any of the Obama-approved policies rolled back in the interests of due process. A Republican Congress might well continue to push the idea of treating terrorists as a military rather than criminal problem. But utilizing a military tribunal regime more frequently does not mean that the criminal justice system would remain pure. There will always be prosecutions of alleged terrorists in the civilian courts too – like the domestic material support prosecutions of al-Hussayen and Rahmani – and so there would continue to be opportunities for the president or Congress to press for additional exceptions to criminal procedure guarantees, to generate even broader surveillance authority, and perhaps to tolerate investigative techniques that a Democratic administration likely would regard as unacceptable racial profiling.

The other unpredictable variable in forecasting the future of our criminal justice ideals is whether or not any additional terrorist incidents occur, increasing our level of fear and further decreasing our level of resolve to maintain our principles. As Harold Hongju Koh, now legal adviser to the State Department and a Yale Law School faculty member at the time, put it in 2002:

> In the days since [September 11], I have been struck by how many Americans – and how many lawyers – seem to have concluded that, somehow, the destruction of four planes and three buildings has taken us back to a state of nature in which there are no laws or rules. In fact, over the years, we have developed an elaborate system of domestic and international laws, institutions, regimes, and decision-making procedures precisely so that they will be consulted and obeyed, not ignored, at a time like this.[119]

Will we adhere to those laws and procedures or, particularly if another terrorist incident occurs, will we continue the pattern of trying to buy safety by carving out exceptions to our principles – even when there is no real evidence that these exceptions will make us any safer? And in 2021, will the war on crime look more like the war on terror, or vice versa? My crystal ball reveals several possible paths ahead, but no reliable basis for identifying which is most likely to prevail.

Notes

1. Military Order of November 13, 2001, *Detention, Treatment, and Trial of Certain Non-Citizens in the War against Terrorism*, 66 FED. REG. 57,833 (Nov. 16, 2001) (denying Article III court review for persons detained as terrorism suspects).
2. Detainee Treatment Act of 2005, 42 U.S.C. §§ 2000dd–dd-1 (2006) (revoking judicial jurisdiction over habeas claims of persons detained as "enemy combatants"); Military Commissions Act of 2006, Pub. L. No. 109–366, 120 Stat. 2600 (codified as amended by Pub. L. No. 111–84, 10 U.S.C. ch. 47a (2006)) (authorizing military commissions and suspending habeas corpus); National Defense Authorization Act for Fiscal Year 2012, P.L. 112–81, 125 Stat. 1298 (2011) (expanding military detention power over U.S. citizens and non-citizens).
3. See, e.g., George W. Bush, President, Address to the Nation on the Terrorist Attacks (Sept. 11, 2001) (transcript available at http://www.presidency.ucsb.edu/ws/index.php?pid=58057) (last visited May 8, 2013); George W. Bush, President, Address to a Joint Session of the Congress on the United States Response to the Terrorist Attacks of September 11 (Sept. 20, 2001) (available at http://www.presidency.ucsb.edu/ws/?pid=64731)(last visited May 8, 2013) (first declaring an undefined "war on terror").
4. Robert Chesney & Jack Goldsmith, *Terrorism and the Convergence of Criminal and Military Detention Models*, 60 STAN. L. REV. 1079, 1084–92, 1122 (2008). For critical views of the results, see DAVID COLE & JULES LOBEL, LESS SAFE, LESS FREE 51–3 (2007); Gregory S. McNeal, *Beyond Guantanamo: Obstacles and Options*, 103 NW. U. L. REV. COLLOQUY 29 (2008) (identifying structural flaws in the current military commission system including undue political influence, unsupervised delegation, and absence of meaningful oversight); Stephen I. Vladeck, *On Jurisdictional Elephants and Kangaroo Courts*, 103 NW. U. L. REV. COLLOQUY 172 (2008) (critiquing personal jurisdiction deficiencies in military commissions); Kent Roach & Gary Trotter, *Miscarriages of Justice in the War Against Terror*, 109 PENN. ST. L. REV. 967 (2005) (discussing likelihood of wrongful seizure of innocent people); Michael Ratner, *Moving Away from the Rule of Law: Military Tribunals, Executive Detentions and the Rule of Law*, 24 CARDOZO L. REV. 1513 (2003) (arguing military commissions lack proper processes to establish jurisdiction over detainees); Jenny S. Martinez, *Process and Substance in the "War on Terror,"* 108 COLUM. L. REV. 1013 (2008) (recounting how judicial review of Guantanamo detentions fails to protect detainees' substantive rights).
5. See BRUCE ACKERMAN, BEFORE THE NEXT ATTACK: PRESERVING CIVIL LIBERTIES IN THE AGE OF TERRORISM 13–14 (2006) (arguing that describing counterterror measures as "war" is inaccurate and dangerous because it distorts nature of threat and legitimizes inappropriate responses); William H. Taft IV, *War Not Crime*, in THE TORTURE DEBATE IN AMERICA 223, 225 (Karen J. Greenberg, ed., 2006); Chesney & Goldsmith, supra note 4; Frances M. Kamm, *Terrorism and Several Moral Distinctions*, 12 LEGAL THEORY 19 (2006); Tom Gerety, *The War Difference: Law and Morality in Counter-Terrorism*, 74 U. CIN. L. REV. 147 (2005); Paul Hoffman, *Human Rights and Terrorism*, 26 HUM. RTS. Q. 932 (2004); Mary Ellen O'Connell, *The Legal Case against the Global War on Terror*, 36 CASE W. RES. J. INT'L L. 349, 350 (2004) ("The claim of global war is a radical departure from mainstream legal

analysis."); Dana Priest, *Bush's 'War' on Terror Comes to a Sudden End*, WASH. POST, Jan. 23, 2009, at A1; Susan Sontag, Comment, *Real Battles and Empty Metaphors*, N.Y. TIMES, Sept. 10, 2002, at A25. See also Susan N. Herman, Comment, *Five Years Later: Law and the Fog of 9/11*, JURIST, Sept. 11, 2006, available at http://jurist. law.pitt.edu/for-umy/200–6/09/five-years-later-law-and-fog-of-911.php (last visited May 8, 2013) (discussing implications of paradigm uncertainty).

6 Geneva Convention Relative to the Treatment of Prisoners of War, art. 118, Aug. 12, 1949, 6 U.S.T. 3316, 75 U.N.T.S. 135 ("Prisoners of war shall be released and repatriated without delay after the cessation of active hostilities.").

7 *Id.* at art. 5 ("Should any doubt arise as to whether persons, having committed a belligerent act and having fallen into the hands of the enemy, belong to any of the categories enumerated in Article 4 [defining prisoners of war], such persons shall enjoy the protection of the present Convention until such time as their status has been determined by a competent tribunal.").

8 *Hamdi v. Rumsfeld*, 542 U.S. 507, 519–20, 533–35 (2004) (requiring judicial review of the grounds of a U.S. citizen's military detention and limiting detention powers to the duration of "the relevant conflict").

9 *Rasul v. Bush*, 542 U.S. 466, 480–85 (2004) (finding Guantanamo military base within federal court jurisdiction under the habeas corpus statute, 28 U.S.C. § 2241); *Boumediene v. Bush*, 553 U.S. 723, 787–92 (2008) (holding the Military Commissions Act's judicial review limitations an unconstitutional suspension of habeas corpus).

10 *Hamdan v. Rumsfeld*, 548 U.S. 557, 623–26, 633–35 (2006) (holding some of the rules specified for Hamdan's military commission trial "illegal" under the Uniform Code of Military Justice and the Geneva Convention).

11 Salim Hamdan, the Guantanamo detainee who successfully challenged the constitutionality of the Bush military commissions system in 2006, brought the first appeal over a tribunal conviction to an American civilian court. *Bin Laden Ex-Driver's Appeal Heard in US Court*, N.Y. DAILY NEWS, May 4, 2012, http://india.nydailynews.com/newsarticle/4fa3e478b7445cf462000000/bin-laden-ex-driver-s-appeal-heard-in-us-court (last visited May 8, 2013). See Chisun Lee, *Gitmo Challenges Could Endanger Half of Convictions*, PROPUBLICA (July 23, 2010), http://www.propublica.org/article/gitmo-challenges-could-endanger-hal f-of-convictions, for a summary of pending appeals (last visited May 8, 2013).

12 Military Order of November 13, 2001, 66 FED. REG. 57, 833–4.

13 For a discussion of the Bush-era trial outcomes of each executive decision, see Scott Shane, *Terrorism Fight Creates Battle over Prosecution*, N.Y. TIMES, Feb. 11, 2010, http://www.nytimes.com/2010/02/12/us/12detain.html (last visited May 8, 2013).

14 See National Defense Authorization Act for Fiscal Year 2012, Pub. L. No. 112–81, §§ 1021–25, 1028, 1029, 125 Stat. 1298 (2011) (codified in scattered sections of 10 U.S.C. 167, 949).

15 Presidential Statement on Signing the National Defense Authorization Act for Fiscal Year 2012 (Dec. 31, 2011), available at http://www.gpo.gov/fdsys/pkg/ DCPD-201100978/html/DCPD-201100978.html (last visited May 8, 2013).

16 Section 1027 of the 2012 National Defense Authorization Act makes it more difficult to transfer or release cleared detainees, thwarting the President's order to close Guantanamo in 2009. Section 1029 requires the Attorney General to consult

with the Director of National Intelligence and the Defense Department before deciding to prosecute an individual in civilian court. See *id.*

17 Providing Material Support to Terrorists, 18 U.S.C. § 2339A (2006); Providing Material Support or Resources to Designated Foreign Terrorist Organizations, 18 U.S.C. § 2339B (2006); Designation of Foreign Terrorist Organizations, 8 U.S.C. § 1189(a) (2006). Material support for terrorism is also covered by Money Laundering Control Act, 18 U.S.C. §1956(a)(2)(A) (2006) (criminalized transmission of funds "with the intent to promote the carrying on of specified unlawful activity," including related to terrorism); USA PATRIOT Act, Pub. L. No. 107–56, §§ 301–376, 115 Stat 272 (2001) (augmenting investigation and prevention of money laundering related to terrorism); Racketeering Influenced and Corrupt Organizations Act, 18 U.S.C. § 1961(1) (2006) (defining fundraising for terrorist activity as criminal racketeering).

18 Violent Crime Control and Law Enforcement Act of 1994, Pub. L. No. 103–322, § 120005(a), 108 Stat. 1796, 2022 (1994).

19 *Id.* at § 120005(c)(2).

20 *Id.* at § 120005(c)(1). For a comparison of the pre- and post-9/11 applications of the material support statutes, see Robert M. Chesney, *The Sleeper Scenario: Terrorism-Support Laws and The Demands of Prevention*, 42 HARV. J. ON LEGIS. 1, 18–22 (2005).

21 Antiterrorism and Effective Death Penalty Act of 1996 (AEDPA), Pub. L. No. 104–132, §§ 303, 323, 110 Stat. 1214, 1215 (1996).

22 See H.R. REP. NO. 104–383, at 81 (1995).

23 For a dissenting view on this philosophy, see, e.g., *id.* at 176 n.3.

24 See AEDPA § 323.

25 USA PATRIOT Act § 805(2)(B).

26 *Id.* at § 805.

27 SUSAN N. HERMAN, TAKING LIBERTIES: THE WAR ON TERROR AND THE EROSION OF AMERICAN DEMOCRACY 23–38 (2011) [hereinafter HERMAN, TAKING LIBERTIES].

28 Superseding Indictment at 3–4 *United States v. al-Hussayen*, No. CR 03–048 (D. Idaho Jan. 9 2004), available at http://www.investigativeproject.org/documents/case_docs/179.pdf (last visited May 8, 2013).

29 Richard Schmitt, *Saudi Cleared of Charges He Spread Terror Online*, BALT. SUN, June 11, 2004, http://articles.baltimoresun.com/2004-06-11/news/0406110425_1_terror-usa-patriot-patriot-act (last visited May 8, 2013).

30 Bill Morlin, *Access to Lab Part of UI Terrorism Case*, SPOKESMAN-REVIEW, Dec. 7, 2003, http://www.spokesmanreview.com/news-story.asp?date=120703&ID=s1452096 (Al-Qaeda theory); Second Superseding Indictment at ¶ 16, *United States v. al-Hussayen*, No. CR 03–048 (D. Idaho Mar. 4, 2004), available at news.findlaw.com/hdocs/docs/terrorism/usalhussyn304sind2.pdf (last visited May 8, 2013).

31 HERMAN, TAKING LIBERTIES, supra note 27, at 27–8.

32 Besty Z. Russell, *Free Speech or Terrorism? Eye on Boise Blog*, (May 4, 2004 8:29 AM), http://www.spokesman.com/blogs/boise/2004/may/04/free-speech-or-terrorism (last visited May 8, 2013).

33 HERMAN, TAKING LIBERTIES, supra note 27, at 29–30.

34 See *id.* at 61–5, 127, for discussion of the chilling of American Muslims' First Amendment activities because of increased scrutiny by law enforcement and intelligence agencies.

35 David Nevin, Esq., Keynote Address at the Nat'l Ass'n for Civil Oversight of Law Enforcement Annual Conference: The Rule of Law in a Time of Terror (Oct. 14, 2006).
36 HERMAN, TAKING LIBERTIES, supra note 27, at 39–40.
37 *Id.* at 40.
38 *Id.*
39 8 U.S.C. § 1189(a)(4)(B).
40 See Shahin Gobadi, Letter to the Editor, *Taking Iranian Opposition Group off U.S. Terror List*, N.Y. TIMES, Oct. 11, 2011, http://www.nytimes.com/2011/10/11/opinion/taking-iranian-opposition-group-off-us-terrorist-list.html (last visited May 8, 2013).
41 Section 2339B provides that a person has the requisite intent to support a designated organization as long as she has "knowledge that the organization is a designated terrorist organization [defined in subsection (g)(6)], [or] that the organization has engaged or engages in terrorist activity [defined in 8 U.S.C.S. § 1182(a)(3)(B)] ...." 18 U.S.C. § 2339B(A)(1). Proof that Roya Rahmani intended to support terrorism apparently would not have been possible, given her transcribed statements to an undercover informant that she was not interested in supporting armed struggle but only in providing humanitarian aid to refugees. HERMAN, TAKING LIBERTIES at 40.
42 *United States v. Afshari*, 426 F.3d 1150 (9th Cir. 2005), *reh. & reh. en banc denied*, 446 F.3d 915 (9th Cir. 2006), *cert. denied sub nom. Rahmani v. United States*, 549 U.S. 1110 (2007).
43 See Scott Shane, *Across Party Lines, Lobbying for Iranian Exiles on Terrorist List*, N.Y. TIMES, Nov. 26, 2011, at A1 (describing movement seeking State Department review of PMOI's status). The PMOI's designation as a terrorist group was subsequently removed in September 2012, see Scott Shane, *Iranian Dissidents Convince U.S. to Drop Terror Label*, N.Y. TIMES, Sept. 21, 2012; http://www.nytimes.com/2012/09/22/world/middleeast/iranian-opposition-group-mek-wins-removal-from-us-terrorist-list.html?pagewanted=all (last visited May 8, 2013).
44 426 F.3d 1150 at 1155–6 ("Under § 2339B, if defendants provide material support for an organization that has been designated a terrorist organization under § 1189, they commit the crime, and it does not matter whether the designation is correct or not.").
45 The court was unwilling to question the Designation of Foreign Terrorist Organizations statute, which specifically provides that "a defendant in a [§ 2339B] criminal action or an alien in a removal proceeding shall not be permitted to raise any question concerning the validity of the issuance of such designation or redesignation as a defense or an objection at any trial or hearing." 8 U.S.C. § 1189(a)(8).
46 Besides additions to the Foreign Terrorist Organization list, travellers are grounded and unable to fly into the country if they are on "No-Fly" and "Automatic Selectee" lists, while private sector financial institutions have been enlisted to police the blacklist against "Specially Designated Nationals" and to create their own blocked "No-Buy" lists from among their clients. See HERMAN, TAKING LIBERTIES, supra note 27, at 66–98. Section 1189(a)(2) prescribes the process of FTO designation. The Secretary must notify select members of Congress by classified communication of her findings establishing that the organization engages in terrorism and poses a threat to U.S. security interests. The FTO designation goes into effect seven days

later, without statutory process for congressional advice or assent; Congress may only prevent a designation through bicameral legislation. 8 U.S.C. § 1189(a)(2)(A) & (B). The designated organization must wait at least two years before seeking administrative revocation of the designation. 8 U.S.C. § 1189(a)(4)(B)(ii). The petitioning organization must show changed circumstances; no process is provided for wrongful designations and the petitioner may not challenge classified information used against it. 8 U.S.C. § 1189(a)(4)(B)(iii). Only the designated organization may petition for revocation or challenge the designation in court, and review must be based "solely on the administrative record," including ex parte and in camera review of classified materials. 8 U.S.C. § 1189(c).

47 Office of the Coordinator for Counterterrorism, U.S. State Dep't, *Current List of Designated Foreign Terrorist Organizations* (Sept. 15, 2011), http://www.state.gov/j/ct/rls/other/des/123085.htm (last visited May 8, 2013) *Mandela Taken off US Terror List*, BBC NEWS (July 1, 2008), http://news.bbc.co.uk/2/hi/7484517.stm (last visited May 8, 2013)(quoting Secretary of State Condoleezza Rice calling the long-standing restrictions on former South African President and anti-apartheid activist Nelson Mandela "rather embarrassing").

48 Kathryn Gregory, *Provisional Irish Republican Army (IRA)*, COUNCIL ON FOREIGN RELATIONS (Mar. 16, 2010), http://www.cfr.org/terrorist-organizations/provisional-irish-republican-army-ira-aka-pira-provos-glaigh-na-hireann-uk-separatists/p9240 (last visited May 8, 2013) (explaining that the IRA has never been designated as an FTO). Two Irish Republican Army splinter groups, Real and Continuity IRA, were listed as terrorist organizations in 2001 and 2004, respectively. Marc Lacey, *State Department Adds the Real I.R.A. to List of Terror Groups*, N.Y. TIMES, May 17, 2001, http://www.nytimes.com/2001/05/-17/world/state-department-adds-the-real-ira-to-list-of-terror-groups.html (last visited May 8,2013) *CIRA Added to US Terror List*, BBC NEWS (July 13, 2004), http://news.bbc.co.uk/2/hi/uk_news/northern_ireland-/3891791.stm (last visited May 8, 2013).

49 Office of the Coordinator for Counterterrorism, U.S. State Dep't, *Country Reports on Terrorism 2008* (Apr. 30, 2009), http://www.state.gov/g/ct/rls/crt/2008/122449.htm.

50 HERMAN, TAKING LIBERTIES, supra note 27, at 44.

51 *Id.* at 44–5.

52 The odyssey began with *Humanitarian Law Project v. Reno*, 9 F. Supp. 2d 1176 (C.D. Cal. 1998).

53 *Holder v. Humanitarian Law Project*, 130 S. Ct. 2705 (2010).

54 *Id.* at 2790.

55 Nina Totenberg, *Supreme Court Examines Limits of Material Support*, NPR, (Feb. 23, 2010), http://www.npr.org/templates/story/story.php?storyId=124012925 (last visited May 8, 2013).

56 130 S. Ct. at 2729–31.

57 18 U.S.C. § 2339A(a) requires knowledge that support provided will or is intended to be used to commit a narrow list of enumerated crimes of violence; 18 U.S.C. § 2339B(a)(1) was designed to close this "loophole" by requiring only knowledge that the organization was designated a terrorist organization, or that the organization has engaged or engages in terrorist activity. The absence of any requirement of specific intent or purpose to support terrorist activities has been upheld in numerous

decisions. Jason Binimow, *Validity, Construction, and Application of 18 U.S.C.A. § 2339B*, 184 A.L.R. Fed. 545 (2011) (citing *United States v. Assi*, 414 F. Supp. 2d 707 (E.D. Mich. 2006) (holding due process was not violated by knowledge standard since the statute did not prohibit mere association with an FTO, and could not be used against unwitting donors); *United States v. Warsame*, 537 F. Supp. 2d 1005 (D. Minn. 2008) (§ 2339B prohibited the conduct of providing material support to a designated FTO but not mere membership in the FTO or espousal of its views); *United States v. Assi*, 414 F. Supp. 2d 707, 717 (E.D. Mich. 2006) ("[E]ven assuming that statute might in a rare case criminalize protected First Amendment activity, such fact would not justify its wholesale invalidation.").

58 *Humanitarian Law Project*, 130 S. Ct. at 2790.
59 Affected parties, such as defendants and immigrants charged with supporting designated organizations, may not seek judicial review of the designation. See discussion supra at note 46.
60 See supra text accompanying note 45–6 for discussion of the designation process.
61 See HERMAN, TAKING LIBERTIES, supra note 27, at 45–8.
62 323 U.S. 214, 246 (1944) (Jackson, J., dissenting).
63 HERMAN, TAKING LIBERTIES, SUPRA note 27, at 11 (citing J. M. Kalil & Steve Tetreault, *PATRIOT Act: Law's Use Causing Concerns*, LAS VEGAS REV. J., Nov. 5, 2003).
64 Chesney, SUPRA note 20, at 13–17.
65 Kent Roach, *Preventing What? Post 9/11 Mission Amnesia and Mission Creep*, in THE LONG DECADE: HOW 9/11 HAS CHANGED THE LAW (David Jenkins et al. eds., 2012) (defining "mission amnesia" as measures specifically taken in an attempt to prevent acts of violent terrorism that become less connected to that objective and ultimately ends in themselves, and "mission creep" as interventions taken for other objectives but presented as counter-terrorism measures).
66 Eric Lichtblau, *U.S. Uses Terror Law to Pursue Crimes from Drugs to Swindling*, N.Y. TIMES, Sept. 28, 2003, at A1; see also Eric Lichtblau, *Justice Dept. Defends Patriot Act Before Senate Hearings*, N.Y. TIMES, Apr. 5, 2005, http://www.nytimes.com/2005/04/05/politics/05patriot.html?scp=11&sq=%-22sneak%20and%20peek%22&st=cse (last visited May 8, 2013).
67 U.S. CONST. amend. VI ("In all criminal prosecutions, the accused shall enjoy the right to a speedy and public trial, by an impartial jury …").
68 William Blackstone, 4 COMMENTARIES ON THE LAWS OF ENGLAND 27, 358 (Univ. of Chicago Press 1979) (1765), available at http://lonang.com/exlibris/blackstone/bla-427.htm (last visited May 8, 2013).
69 18 U.S.C. appx. §§ 1–19 (2006).
70 Prevention of Acts of Violence and Terrorism, 28 C.F.R. § 501.3(a) (2012) (allowing the Attorney General to impose restrictions on attorney-defendant communications in the interest of national security).
71 *United States v. Ghailani*, 751 F. Supp. 2d 515, 518 (S.D.N.Y. 2010).
72 See Susan N. Herman, *The USA Patriot Act and the Submajoritarian Fourth Amendment*, 41 HARV. C.R.-C.L. L. REV. 67, 74 (2006) [hereinafter Herman, *The USA Patriot Act*].
73 *Id.* at 73–105.
74 *Id.* For example, Section 505 of the USA PATRIOT Act allows the federal government to use national security letters (NSLs) to demand customer information,

without a warrant, from Internet and telephone service providers and libraries providing public Internet access. USA PATRIOT Act of 2001, Pub. L. No. 107–56, § 505, 115 Stat. 272, 365 (codified at 18 U.S.C. § 2709(b) (2006)). The government only needs to certify that information relevant to a terrorism investigation might be obtained. *Id*. The ACLU's John Doe litigation, on behalf of an Internet service provider from whom client information had been demanded, succeeded in striking down the gag order imposed on NSL recipients (which seemed even to bar recipients from seeking legal advice), but the court affirmed that the targets of the NSL subpoenas have only "a limited Fourth Amendment interest in records which they voluntarily convey to a third party" and no Fourth Amendment right to prohibit further disclosure of information they communicate to their Internet service providers. *Doe v. Ashcroft*, 317 F. Supp. 2d 488, 494 n.118 & 508 n.171. (S.D.N.Y. 2004); see also *Muslim Community Ass'n of Ann Arbor v. Ashcroft*, 459 F. Supp. 2d 592 (E.D. Mich. 2006).

75 Pub. L. No. 107–56, § 213, 115 Stat. 272 (2001) (codified at 18 U.S.C. § 3103a(b) (2006)). See HERMAN, TAKING LIBERTIES, supra note 27, at 113–14; Herman, *The USA Patriot Act*, supra note 72, at 99–102.

76 18 U.S.C. § 3103a(b)(1). The term "adverse result" is defined in 18 U.S.C. § 2705(a) (2) (2000) and includes physical or other harms to a person, or damage to a prosecution. See Herman, *The USA Patriot Act*, supra note 72, at 99.

77 Kevin Corr, *Sneaky but Lawful: The Use of Sneak and Peek Search Warrants*, 43 U. KAN. L. REV. 1103, 1103 (1995); John Kent Walker, Jr., Note, *Covert Searches*, 39 STAN. L. REV. 545 (1987). Before the Patriot Act passed, some federal circuit courts were crafting standards for deferred notification. The Ninth Circuit required notification within seven days of the search. *United States v. Freitas*, 800 F.2d 1451, 1456 (9th Cir. 1986). The Second Circuit required a showing of necessity, an inventory of seized property, and a flexible but limited notification delay. *United States v. Villegas*, 899 F.2d 1324 (2d Cir. 1990). The courts' authority to actually approve the deferred notification warrants was unsettled. See, e.g., *United States v. Pangburn*, 983 F.2d 449, 453–5 (2d Cir. 1993).

78 President Bush advocated for broad sneak and peek authority to seize tangible evidence with greater delays of notice to enable extensive investigations of terror cells. Some congressmen expressed reservations but felt on balance that more expansive authority was needed in an age of terrorism and advanced information technology. Wayne Washington, *House Passes Bill Targeting Terrorism*, BOSTON GLOBE, Oct. 25, 2001, at A1. At the time, Rep. Robert C. Scott (D-Va.) warned that "[t]his bill is general search warrants and wiretap law. It is not just limited to terrorism." Reassured by the provision's sunset clause and reporting requirements, Democratic leaders did not heed prescient concerns of mission creep. Jack Torry, *War on Terrorism; Bill Adds To Police Powers*, COLUMBUS DISPATCH, Oct. 25, 2001, at 1A.

79 See DIR. OF THE ADMIN. OFFICE OF THE UNITED STATES COURTS, REPORT ON APPLICATIONS FOR DELAYED-NOTICE SEARCH WARRANTS AND EXTENSIONS (2009), available at http://big.assets.huffingtonpost.com/SneakAndPeakReport.pdf) (last visited May 8, 2013).

80 DIR. OF THE ADMIN. OFFICE OF THE UNITED STATES COURTS, REPORT ON APPLICATIONS FOR DELAYED-NOTICE SEARCH WARRANTS AND EXTENSIONS 2 (2011) (reporting applications received between Oct. 1, 2009, and Sept. 30, 2010), available at http://www.aclu.org/blog/national-security/tool-governments-war-privacy-absolutely-its-war-terror-not-so-much (last visited May 8, 2013).

81 *Id.* at 2 & 6 Table 2. See also Robyn Greene, *A Tool in the Government's War on Privacy? Absolutely. But in Its War on Terror? Not So Much ...*, ACLU BLOG OF RIGHTS, Oct. 28, 2011, http://www.aclu.org/blog/national-security/tool-governments-war-privacy-absolutely-its-war-terror-not-so-much (last visited May 8, 2013). One sneak and peek warrant appears to have been used to help shut down a cockfighting ring in Cocke County, Tennessee. Affidavit, Thomas E. Farrow, FBI Special Agent, signed by Dennis H. Inman, U.S. Magistrate Judge (May 10, 2004) 3 & 33, available at http://web.knoxnews.com/pdf/delriosearchwarrant.pdf (last visited May 8, 2013) & http://web.knoxnews.com/pdf/delriosearch2.pdf (last visited May 8, 2013). The Federal Bureau of Investigations was permitted to delay notification to the owner of the Del Rio Cockfighting Pit for three months. J.J. Stambaugh, *Sneak-and-Peek Warrants Debated; Patriot Act Used to Search for Evidence in Cockfighting Case*, KNOXVILLE NEWS SENTINEL, Aug. 13, 2007, http://www.knoxnews.com/news/2007/aug/13/sneak-and-peak-warrants-debated/ (last visited May 8, 2013).

82 See Robert M. Duncan Jr., Note, *Surreptitious Search Warrants and the USA Patriot Act: "Thinking Outside the Box but Within the Constitution," or a Violation of Fourth Amendment Protections?* 7 N.Y. CITY L. REV. 1 (2004).

83 HERMAN, TAKING LIBERTIES, supra note 27, at 6 & 219 n.3 (citing 147 CONG. REC. S10990–02, S11020 (daily ed. Oct. 25, 2001) (statement by Sen. Feingold) ("Of course, there is no doubt that if we lived in a police state, it would be easier to catch terrorists ... [but] that would not be America").

84 Ryan Grim, *DOJ Official Blows Cover off PATRIOT Act*, HUFF. POST (Nov. 23, 2009), http://www.huffingtonpost.com/2009/09/23/watch-doj-official-blows_n_296209.html (last visited May 8, 2013) (quoting Sen. Feingold stating: "That's not how this was sold to the American people. It was sold – as stated on DOJ's website in 2005 – as being necessary (quote) 'to conduct investigations without tipping off terrorists.'")

85 396 U.S. 868 (1969).

86 Peter Baker, *Obama Challenges Terrorism Critics*, N.Y. TIMES, Feb. 8, 2011, at A12; Paul Kane, Shailagh Murray & Matt DeLong, *Times Square Bombing Arrest Allows GOP to Revive 'Miranda' Debate*, WASH. POST, May 4, 2010, http://voices.washingtonpost.com/44/2010/05/gop-seizes-on-times-square-arr.html (last visited May 8, 2013).

87 *United States v. Bin Laden*, 132 F. Supp. 2d 168, 188 (2001), *aff'd sub nom* In re Terrorist Bombings of U.S. Embassies in East Africa, 552 F.3d 177 (2d Cir. 2008) (suppressing confession by defendant interrogated in Kenya for 1998 bombings of the American embassies in East Africa because he was not informed of *Miranda* rights; admitting Mirandized confessions of three defendants interrogated in South Africa).

88 *Miranda v. Arizona*, 384 U.S. 436, 429 (1966) ("[W]e deal with the admissibility of statements obtained from an individual who is subjected to custodial police interrogation and the necessity for procedures which assure that the individual is accorded his privilege under the Fifth Amendment to the Constitution not to be compelled to incriminate himself.").

89 *Id.* at 504.

90 Charlie Savage, *Holder Backing Law to Restrict Miranda Rights*, N.Y. TIMES, May 9, 2010, at A1; Charlie Savage, *Obama Said to Be Open to New Miranda Look*,

N.Y. Times, May 10, 2010, at A11 (reporting President Obama's support for a new exception to the *Miranda* rule). The administration did not ask Congress for a legislative expansion of the *Miranda* exception, citing pushback from congressional Democrats and libertarian Republicans. Evan Perez, *Rights Are Curtailed for Terror Suspects*, Wall St. J., Mar. 24, 2011, http://online.wsj.com/article/SB100014-24052748704050204576218970652119898.html (last visited May 8, 2013).

91 Mark A. Godsey, *Miranda's Final Frontier – the International Arena: A Critical Analysis of United States v. Bin Laden, and a Proposal for a New Miranda Exception Abroad*, 51 Duke L.J. 1703 (2002).

92 467 U.S. 649, 655–8 (1984) (creating public safety exception for any statement responsive to question reasonably perceived to be relevant to immediate need to protect the public).

93 Warren Richey, *Holder Letter: Why We Read Christmas Day Bomber His Rights*, Christian Sci. Monitor, Feb. 3, 2010, http://www.csmonitor.com/USA/Justice/2010/0203/Holder-letter-why-we-read-Christmas-Day-bomber-his-rights (last visited May 8, 2013); Perez, supra note 88.

94 Fed. Bureau of Investigations, *Internal Memorandum on Custodial Interrogation for Public Safety and Intelligence-Gathering Purposes of Operational Terrorists Inside the United States* (Oct. 21, 2010), available at http://www.nytimes.com/2011/03/25/us/25miranda-text.html?_r=0 (last visited May 8, 2013); Savage, *Holder Backing Law to Restrict Miranda Rights*, supra note 90; Perez, supra note 90.

95 See Amos N. Guiora, *Relearning Lessons of History: Miranda and Counterterrorism*, 71 La. L. Rev. 1147, 1164–8, 1170 (2011).

96 Pub. L. 90–351, 82 Stat. 197 (codified at 42 U.S.C. § 3711 et seq. (2006)).

97 *Dickerson v. United States*, 530 U.S. 428, 415 (2000) ("Congress may not legislatively supersede our decisions interpreting and applying the Constitution.").

98 *Bartkus v. Illinois*, 359 U.S. 121, 162–3 (1959) (Black, J., dissenting).

99 David A. Harris, American Civil Liberties Union Special Report (1999), available at http://www.aclu.org/racial-justice/driving-while-black-racial-profiling-our-nations-highways (last visited May 8, 2013).

100 David A. Harris, *"Driving While Black" and All Other Traffic Offenses: The Supreme Court and Pretextual Traffic Stops*, 87 J. Crim. L. & Criminology, 544 (1997); Lisa Helem, *Bills Would Ban Racial Profiling; Mayor of Detroit Testifies About His Firsthand Experience*, Atlanta Journal-Constitution, Aug. 2, 2001, at 6A; Jane Prendergast, *Officers' Hearts Hold Racial Profiling Solution, Chief Says*, Cincinnati Enquirer, March 6, 2001, at 1A; Charles Levendosky, Comment, *Racial Profiling Is a Hate Crime*, St. Paul Pioneer Press, Oct. 11, 2000, at 19A; Leland Ware, Comment, *Racial Profiling Cannot Be Tolerated*, St. Louis Post-Dispatch, Oct. 7, 1999, at B7; Editorial, Zero in on Racial Profiling, Hartford Courant, May 5, 1999, at A16.

101 Harris, supra note 100, at 582.

102 Frank Newport, *Racial Profiling Is Seen as Widespread, Particularly among Young Black Men*, Gallup News Services (Dec. 9, 1999), http://www.gallup.com/poll/3421/racial-profiling-seen-widespread-particularly-among-young-black-men.aspx (last visited May 8, 2013).

103 U.S. General Accounting Office, Racial Profiling: Limited Data Available on Motorist Stops 15 tbl. 1 (2000), available at http://www.gao.gov/new.items/gg00041.pdf (last visited May 8, 2013).

104 Sam Howe, *A Nation Challenged: Civil Liberties; Americans Give in to Race Profiling*, N.Y. TIMES, Sept. 23, 2001, at A1 (post-9/11 polls revealed 60% polled were in favor of profiling of Arabs and Muslims); *Terrorism in the United States*, GALLUP (Jan. 8, 2010), http://www.gallup.com/poll/4909/Terrorism-United-States.aspx (last visited May 8, 2013) (71% of Americans polled felt those who "fit the profile" of suspected terrorists should be subjected to more intensive security checks before being permitted to board airplanes); ACLU, SANCTIONED BIAS: RACIAL PROFILING SINCE 9/11 4–5 (2004), available at http://www.aclu.org/FilesPDFs/racial%20profiling%20report.pdf (last visited May 8, 2013) ("This report details how the trauma of 9/11 has made general anti-immigrant sentiment acceptable in the guise of law enforcement and how national security initiatives incorporate discrimination into their application."); see generally HERMAN, TAKING LIBERTIES, supra note 27, at 197.

105 President Bush, Address to Joint Session of Congress (Feb. 27, 2001), available at http://www.justice.gov/opa/pr/2003/June/racial_profiling_fact_sheet.pdf (last visited May 8, 2013) (stating that racial profiling is "wrong and we will end it in America."). The USA PATRIOT Act itself included a "sense of Congress resolution" condemning discrimination against Muslims. USA Patriot Act § 102. Attorney General John Ashcroft condemned racial profiling as "wrong and unconstitutional no matter what the content" during his confirmation hearings. *Confirmation Hearing on the Nomination of John Ashcroft to Be Attorney General of the United States: Hearing Before the S. Comm. on the Judiciary*, 107th Cong. 492 (2001). Following his confirmation, Attorney General Ashcroft issued new guidelines in 2003 purporting to ban racial profiling in the Federal law enforcement agencies. U.S. Dep't of Justice, Guidance Regarding the Use of Race by Law Enforcement Agencies (2003), available at http://www.justice.gov/crt/about/spl/documents/guidance_on_race.pdf (last visited May 8, 2013).

106 *Hearing on Reforming Civil Aviation Security: Next Steps – Before the Nat'l Comm'n on Terrorist Attacks Upon the United States*, 108th Cong. (2003) 115 (comments of John F. Lehman, 9/11 Commissioner), available at http://govinfo.library.unt.edu/911/archive/hearing2/9-11Commission_Hearing_2003-05-23.htm (last visited May 8, 2013).

107 See, e.g., Bernard Harcourt, *Muslim Profiles Post-9/11: Is Racial Profiling an Effective Counterterrorist Measure and Does It Violate the Right to Be Free from Discrimination?* in SECURITY & HUMAN RIGHTS (Benjamin J. Goold & Liora Lazarus, eds., 2007); Paul Sperry, *When the Profile Fits the Crime*, N.Y. TIMES, July 28, 2005, http://www.nytimes.com/2005/07/28/opinion/28sperry.html (last visited May 8, 2013)); Sharon Davies, *Profiling Terror*, 1 OHIO ST. J. CRIM. L. 45, 76–81 (2003); Christopher Edley, Jr., *The New American Dilemma: Racial Profiling Post-9/11*, in THE WAR ON OUR FREEDOMS 180–6 (Richard C. Leone & Greg Anrig, Jr. eds., 2003); W. Kip Viscusi & Richard J. Zeckhauser, *Sacrificing Civil Liberties to Reduce Terrorism Risks*, 26 J. RISK & UNCERTAINTY 99 (2003); Samuel R. Gross & Debra Livingston, *Racial Profiling under Attack*, 102 COLUM. L. REV. 1413, 1437 (2002); William J. Stuntz, *Local Policing after the Terror*, 111 YALE L.J. 2137, 2161, 2179 (2002).

108 See Eric Lichtblau, *F.B.I. Tells Offices to Count Local Muslims and Mosques*, N.Y. TIMES, Jan. 28, 2003, http://www.nytimes.com/2003/01/28/politics/28MOSQ.html; Charlie Savage, *F.B.I. Scrutinized for Amassing Data on Ethnic and*

Religious Groups, N.Y. TIMES, Oct. 21, 2011, at A20; ACLU, MAPPING THE FBI: EXPANDED FBI AUTHORITY (Oct. 19, 2011), http://www.aclu.org/national-security/expanded-fbi-authority (last visited May 8, 2013).

109 Savage, supra note 108 (citing ACLU, EYE ON THE FBI (Dec. 1, 2011), available at http://www.aclu.org/files/assets/aclu_eye_on_the_fbi_engaged_in_unconstitutional_racial_profiling_and_racial_mapping.pdf (last visited May 8, 2013).

110 Ben Poston, *City's Disparities Are Greater Than Other Large Metro Police Departments, Milwaukee*, JOURNAL SENTINEL, Dec. 3, 2011, available at http://www.jsonline.com/watchdog/watchdogreports/racial-gap-found-in-traffic-stopd-in-milwaukee-ke1hsip-134977408.html (last visited May 8, 2013).

111 Daniel C. Vock, *Racial Profiling Data Often Unstudied*, WASH. POST, Aug. 9, 2011, at A13. No data for traffic stops in Maryland were collected in 2010 because the reporting law had expired, but the law was subsequently reauthorized for 2012. *Cardin Reviving Legislation to End Racial Profiling*, ANNAPOLIS CAPITAL, Sept. 15, 2011, at A5.

112 See Neil Lewis, *Detentions After Attacks Pass 1,000 U.S. Says*, N.Y. TIMES, Oct. 30, 2001, at B1 (quoting Justice Department official reporting 1,017 arrests); Amy Goldstein, *A Deliberate Strategy of Disruption: Massive, Secret Detention Effort Aimed Mainly at Preventing More Terror*, WASH. POST, Nov. 4, 2001, at A01 (reporting an "official tally" of 1,147 detainees). Minor immigration violations were considered potentially connected with terrorist activity, and used as a proxy for detention purposes.

113 Raymond Bonner, *New Policy Delays Visas for Specified Muslim Men*, N.Y. TIMES, Sept. 10, 2002, at A12 (adding "[t]he visa applicants are primarily university students, many of whom had gone home for the summer vacation and are now unable to resume their studies, and business executives with American companies....").

114 Chris Rickerd, *Homeland Security Suspends Ineffective, Discriminatory Immigration Program*, ACLU BLOG OF RIGHTS (May 6, 2011, 11:23 AM), http://www.aclu.org/blog/immigrants-rights-racial-justice/homeland-security-suspends-ineffective-discriminatory-immigrat (last visited May 8, 2013).

115 GOV'T ACCOUNTABILITY OFFICE, INFORMATION SHARING: FEDERAL AGENCIES ARE HELPING FUSION CENTERS BUILD AND SUSTAIN CAPABILITIES AND PROTECT PRIVACY, BUT COULD BETTER MEASURE RESULTS 8–9 (2010), available at http://www.gao.gov/assets/320/310268.pdf (last visited May 8, 2013) (reporting that while all "fusion centers" combining federal-state or federal-local law enforcement agencies were "generally created ... to prevent terrorism or other threats," their missions "vary based on the environment in which the center operates"; adding, for example, that Customs and Border Protection and Drug Enforcement Administration agents are often placed in fusion centers to support a comprehensive "all-hazards" approach rather than only addressing terrorism). See also *Homeland Security and Intelligence: Next Steps in Evolving the Mission: Hearing before the H, Permanent Select Comm. on Intelligence*, 112th Cong. (2012) (statement of Philip Mudd, Member, Aspen Homeland Security Group), available at http://intelligence.house.gov/sites/intelligence.house.gov/files/documents/MuddSFR01182012.pdf (last visited Jun. 27, 2013) ("[T]he DHS intelligence mission should be threat

agnostic. Though the impetus for creating this new agency, in the wake of the 9/11 attacks, was clearly terrorism-based, the kinds of tools now deployed, from border security to cyber protection, are equally critical in fights against emerging adversaries.").

116 Letter from Thomas E. Perez, Assistant Att'y Gen. Civil Rights Div., U.S. Dep't of Justice, to Bill Montgomery, Esq., Maricopa Cty. Att'y, Re: United States' Investigation of the Maricopa County Sheriff's Office (Dec. 15, 2011), available at http://s3.documentcloud.org/documents/274910/justice-department-findings-in-its-investigation.pdf (last visited May 8, 2013).

117 AARTI KOHLI, PETER L. MARKOWITZ & LISA CHAVEZ, SECURE COMMUNITIES BY THE NUMBERS: AN ANALYSIS OF DEMOGRAPHICS AND DUE PROCESS (2011), available at http://www.law.berkeley.edu/files/Secure_Communities_by_the_Numbers.pdf (last visited May 8, 2013).

118 The Warren Institute reported that 1.6% of individuals who were arrested and reported to federal immigration agents under the Secure Communities program have been U.S. citizens. *Id.* at 4–5. Several U.S. citizens have been detained or even deported in the past few years. See, e.g., *American Teen Mistakenly Deported to Colombia Returns to Texas*, CNN (Jan. 6, 2012), http://www.cnn.com/2012/01/06/us/texas-colombia-teen (last visited May 8, 2013).

119 Harold Hongju Koh, *The Spirit of the Laws*, 43 HARV. INT'L L.J. 23, 23 (2002).

16

The Civilianization of Military Jurisdiction

Stephen I. Vladeck

Most discussions of current and future issues in American criminal law and procedure tend to ignore completely the role of the military in shaping that body of jurisprudence. Perhaps this lacuna reflects widespread – if tacit – acceptance of the maxim that "military law is to law as military music is to music."[1] Or it may represent generations of lawyers inculcated with Justice Black's oft-quoted characterization of the U.S. court-martial system as a "rough form of justice."[2] Regardless, the assumption appears to be that there is little for true criminal law scholars to learn from judicial proceedings presided over by jurists – and juries – in uniform. As a particularly notorious case in point, when the Supreme Court in 2008 held that the Eighth Amendment forbids imposition of the death penalty for child rape (at least where the offense neither resulted nor intended to result in the death of the victim),[3] its survey of the apparently vanishing number of U.S. jurisdictions authorizing such a punishment notoriously overlooked federal military law – which *did* so provide.[4]

The Court's unfortunate oversight in *Kennedy v. Louisiana* obfuscates the well-documented harmonization of U.S. military law with the procedural and substantive constitutional protections enjoyed by defendants in civilian criminal trials over the past three decades.[5] Although the procedures deployed by courts-martial still differ in substantial ways from those one would find in a federal (or state) civilian court,[6] U.S. military tribunals have, perhaps surprisingly, been active participants – if not trailblazers – in the articulation of constitutionally grounded principles of both criminal law and procedure.

This phenomenon, which some have described as the "civilianization" of military law,[7] may well have been precipitated by Congress's progressive investiture of *civilian* appellate courts – including the Court of Appeals for the Armed Forces (CAAF) and the U.S. Supreme Court – with direct appellate jurisdiction over, and thus better control of, military trial courts.[8] It may also have been aided by the Supreme Court's gradual relaxing of the scope of *collateral* review of military convictions in the civilian courts,[9] which until the 1950s only encompassed claims that the military courts lacked jurisdiction.[10] But regardless of what caused this development,[11] it is now difficult to disagree with a sentiment expressed by CAAF Judge Margaret Ryan in 2009: "Whatever its beginnings, far from being 'a rough form of justice,' the military justice system today, including this Court, generally provides 'substantial procedural protections and provision for appellate review by independent civilian judges [to] vindicate servicemen's constitutional rights.'"[12]

At the same time as the substance of military criminal law has been subject to such "civilianization," however, the past quarter-century has also witnessed subtle but decisive expansions in the scope of military jurisdiction – allowing far more criminal prosecutions to be brought in military courts than was previously the case. In *Solorio v. United States*, for example, the Supreme Court held that courts-martial could constitutionally try servicemembers for *any* offense, including those with no relation whatsoever to their military service.[13] In the process, the Court overruled a 1969 decision that had conditioned the assertion of military jurisdiction on a connection between the underlying offense and the defendant's military service,[14] and thereby opened the door to military trials of servicemembers for entirely ordinary civilian crimes that just happened to be committed by men and women formally (if not actually) in uniform.[15]

More recently, in 2006, Congress quietly expanded the scope of military jurisdiction over civilians, as well. Whereas the Uniform Code of Military Justice (UCMJ) had previously authorized the trial of "persons serving with or accompanying an armed force in the field" only during a "time of war,"[16] Congress amended that proviso additionally to authorize such trials during "a contingency operation" – a statutory term that encompasses virtually all overseas (and some domestic) deployments of U.S. troops.[17] And in a controversial decision in July 2012, CAAF unanimously upheld this expansion against constitutional challenge – at least in cases in which the defendant is a noncitizen tried outside the territorial United States for offenses committed overseas.[18]

A similar theme can be found in the more visible use of military commissions by the U.S. government at Guantánamo over the past decade to try noncitizens alleged to have committed war crimes as part of the war on terrorism.[19] Although the government initially defended these commissions as merely exercising the jurisdiction that the Supreme Court endorsed in the Nazi saboteur case during World War II,[20] that line of reasoning was repudiated by the Court in its 2006 decision in *Hamdan v. Rumsfeld*.[21] Congress responded by placing the commissions on a different jurisdictional footing,[22] but as a result, the current defense of the commissions' legality (in *Hamdan II* and *United States v. al-Bahlul*) rests on a more subtle – but necessarily broader – understanding of the power of such military courts, one that would allow the military trial of at least some defendants and/or offenses that are not subject to military jurisdiction under international law.[23] As with the expansion of court-martial jurisdiction, this expansion is also currently under attack, but thus far, the government's newfound theory has been only partially repudiated.[24] In short, as Parts 1 and 2 of this chapter will detail, both courts-martial and military commissions have witnessed another kind of "civilianization" in recent years: the "civilianization" of their jurisdiction – to encompass offenses previously triable only in civilian courts and/or classes of defendants who were not previously subject to military jurisdiction. And although the courts may yet have the last word on the issues raised in *Ali* and *al-Bahlul*, Part 2 concludes by suggesting that, rather than being *at* a critical juncture in the civilianization of military jurisdiction, we have in fact already passed the turning point, for better or worse.

In Part 3, I turn to whether this development *is* for better or for worse. Inasmuch as the civilianization of *substantive* military law has been seen largely as a positive development by courts and commentators, I do not think we can so quickly say the same thing about the civilianization of military jurisdiction. Although it might appear at first blush that the civilianization of substantive military law reduces the risks that might otherwise have followed from unduly expansive military jurisdiction, Part 3 concludes by offering a structural defense of a principle first expressed by Justice Johnson almost two hundred years ago – that, where military jurisdiction is concerned, Congress should be confined to "the least possible power adequate to the end proposed."[25] Whether or not the civilianization of substantive military law has been a positive development, my thesis is that, in the long term, the civilianization of military jurisdiction would be to the detriment of American constitutional law in general, and the constitutional rights of criminal defendants, in particular.

1. THE CIVILIANIZATION OF COURT-MARTIAL JURISDICTION

The debate over the proper scope of U.S. military jurisdiction has its historical foundations in the seventeenth-century struggle between Parliament and the Crown over control of the English military, and a series of Mutiny Acts that gradually expanded the ability of the military to try soldiers for "peacetime" (and, in some cases, "nonmilitary") offenses.[26] For jurisprudential purposes, however, the richness of this history only began to matter in the 1950s, when various factors led to a dramatic expansion in the statutory scope of court-martial jurisdiction with respect to both offenses and offenders – and a series of Supreme Court decisions interposing incremental but increasingly significant limits on Congress's power over military jurisdiction.[27]

Thus, although the Court in *Madsen v. Kinsella* upheld the use of military courts in occupied Germany to try U.S. citizen dependents of American servicemembers,[28] Justice Burton's reasoning turned largely on the unique nature of occupation courts as supplanting, rather than supplementing, ordinary civilian jurisdiction.[29] When the Court returned to the power of military courts over civilians in 1957, a majority in *Reid v. Covert* rejected such authority in capital cases during peacetime,[30] with Justice Black's four-justice plurality opinion appearing to reject *any* military jurisdiction over civilians.[31] Three years later, the Court handed down a trilogy of decisions that extended *Covert* to encompass (1) capital offenses by civilian contractors,[32] (2) noncapital offenses by civilian dependents,[33] and (3) noncapital offenses by civilian contractors.[34] After the 1960 trilogy, it therefore appeared that military jurisdiction over civilians would be categorically unconstitutional during "peacetime." In light of those holdings, the Court of Military Appeals (CAAF's predecessor) even held in 1970 that the statutory authorization to try civilian employees of the military "in time of war" would raise serious constitutional questions unless that phrase were interpreted to require a formal declaration of war – thereby rejecting the assertion of such jurisdiction during the hostilities in Vietnam (and in any other episode since the end of World War II).[35]

And even with regard to servicemembers, the Court during the same period also rejected their amenability to military jurisdiction for offenses committed while in the service if they had been honorably discharged in the interim.[36]

Although these decisions involved military jurisdiction over individuals no longer (or never) part of the military, they left untouched the military's power over active-duty servicemembers – which was largely thought to be a matter left to the discretion of the political branches.[37] That changed in 1969, however, when a 6–3 majority in *O'Callahan v. Parker* articulated a "service connection" test – a constitutionally grounded requirement that a servicemember's offense be in some way related to, or at least affecting, his military service in order to be properly subject to military jurisdiction.[38] As Justice Douglas explained for the Court,

> We have concluded that the crime to be under military jurisdiction must be service connected, lest "cases arising in the land or naval forces, or in the Militia, when in actual service in time of War or public danger," as used in the Fifth Amendment, be expanded to deprive every member of the armed services of the benefits on an indictment by a grand jury and a trial by a jury of his peers. The power of Congress to make "Rules for the Government and

Regulation of the land and naval Forces," need not be sparingly read in order to preserve those two important constitutional guarantees. For it is assumed that an express grant of general power to Congress is to be exercised in harmony with express guarantees of the Bill of Rights.[39]

As Justice Harlan predicted in his dissent in *O'Callahan*,[40] the "service-connection" test proved somewhat difficult to administer over time, at least at the margins.[41] But at least into the 1980s, it provided an important – if not always easily discernible – constraint on the power of military courts to try nonmilitary offenses, even when committed by active-duty servicemembers. When servicemembers committed wholly civilian offenses with no connection whatsoever to their service, *O'Callahan* mandated that they be tried – if at all – in civilian courts.

As noted previously, the Supreme Court abandoned the "service connection" test in 1987, holding in *Solorio v. United States* that the Constitution allows Congress to subject active-duty servicemembers to military jurisdiction for *any* offense committed while in the service.[42] According to Chief Justice Rehnquist, *O'Callahan* had misread English history and otherwise misunderstood American precedents.[43] Instead, "In an unbroken line of decisions from 1866 to 1960, this Court interpreted the Constitution as conditioning the proper exercise of court-martial jurisdiction over an offense on one factor: the military status of the accused."[44] For the majority, this understanding followed from the "plain text" of the make rules clause of Article I,[45] which did not appear to brook any distinction based upon whether or not the rule was directed toward service-connected conduct.[46]

To be sure, such analysis arguably neglects the additional work done by the Fifth Amendment's grand jury indictment clause, which only exempts cases "*arising in* the land or naval forces,"[47] and not just cases in which the defendants are *members* of the land and naval forces. Thus, as Justice Marshall pointed out for the dissenters in *Solorio*, whether Congress could make the underlying conduct a criminal offense in general and whether it could subject the same to military jurisdiction in particular were, in fact, two *different* questions – and the "unbroken line of decisions" on which the majority relied were therefore inapposite.[48]

But regardless of which side had the better of the constitutional argument in *Solorio*, or whether the majority's logic applies to *all* offenses, including capital charges,[49] there is an important upshot to Chief Justice Rehnquist's analysis:

> the logic of *Solorio*, pursuant to which U.S. servicemembers may be tried for virtually any offense, cuts very much against congressional power to subject individuals outside the scope of the Make Rules Clause to military

jurisdiction, unless another source of such legislative authority can be identified. And even then, the constitutional rights to grand jury indictment and trial by petit jury may nevertheless furnish their own constraint.[50]

Thanks to *Averette* and the Supreme Court's earlier decisions concerning military jurisdiction over civilians, that issue did not return to the forefront until 2006. Then, spurred by Senator Lindsey Graham, Congress quietly expanded the scope of the UCMJ to authorize trial by court-martial of civilians "serving with or accompanying an armed force in the field" during a "time of declared war *or* a contingency operation."[51] Given that "contingency operation" could include *any* "operation in which members of the armed forces are or may become involved in military actions, operations, or hostilities against an enemy of the United States or against an opposing military force,"[52] it would only be a matter of time before the Graham Amendment squarely presented the constitutional question that the Supreme Court ducked in the 1950s and the 1960 trilogy, and that the Court of Military Appeals sidestepped in *Averette*.

After a false start,[53] that question arose in the case of Alaa Mohammad Ali, a dual Canadian-Iraqi citizen who was hired by L3 Communications/Titan Corporation as part of its contract to provide interpreters for the U.S. military in Iraq. Ali, who was issued military equipment and provided pre-deployment training at Fort Benning, Georgia, was subsequently arrested for his role in a violent altercation with another translator in Iraq.[54] Because of his Iraqi citizenship, Ali could not be prosecuted in civilian court under the Military Extraterritorial Jurisdiction Act (MEJA),[55] which only applies to crimes committed by military contractors who, inter alia, are "not a national of or ordinarily resident in the host nation."[56] Instead, the military chose to pursue court-martial proceedings, charging Ali both for his role in the assault and for false statements he made in conjunction with the government's investigation thereof. Eventually, and in exchange for the government's dropping of the assault charge, Ali agreed to plead guilty to the false statement charges – preserving his right to contest military jurisdiction on appeal.[57]

On appeal, the Army Court of Criminal Appeals upheld the Graham Amendment, concluding that, in contrast to the Supreme Court cases from the 1950s, "the appellant in this case committed all of his offenses and was court-martialed (1) during a time of actual hostilities and (2) in a location where actual hostilities were taking place."[58] Moreover, the court explained, "there is no such danger of the broad application of the UCMJ to civilians because Congress has chosen to specifically limit the exercise of military jurisdiction over civilians by requiring either a formal declaration of war by

Congress or the existence of a 'contingency operation,' as that term is narrowly defined by statute."[59]

Exactly one year later, CAAF unanimously affirmed – albeit with fairly sharp internal disagreements as to the reasoning.[60] Writing for the CAAF majority, Judge Erdmann chose not to follow the Army CCA's reasoning (or the arguments offered by the government or its *amici* before CAAF). Instead, his opinion rested on the (thoroughly debatable) conclusion that, as a noncitizen tried outside the territorial United States, Ali was not protected by either the Fifth or Sixth Amendments.[61] As such, there was no constitutional provision that Ali's trial by court-martial would offend.[62]

Leaving aside both the factual and analytical shortcomings of Judge Erdmann's opinion,[63] it is also methodologically incomplete. For even if the Fifth and Sixth Amendments do not *bar* courts-martial of noncitizen civilian contractors for offenses committed outside the territorial United States, there is still the question of whether Congress has the affirmative power to subject such offenses to military jurisdiction – the question *Solorio* left unanswered for non-servicemembers. Thus, although the majority's reasoning therefore rested on exceedingly narrow grounds – authorizing military jurisdiction over civilians only in cases in which the defendants are not protected by the Fifth or Sixth Amendment – it left unclear the critical question as to the scope of Congress's power to act in the first place.

After criticizing the majority's failure carefully to consider that issue, Chief Judge Baker's opinion concurring in the result grappled with it in detail, concluding that "a functional approach should be taken when determining the narrow and extraordinary limits of court-martial jurisdiction over civilians."[64] To that end, Chief Judge Baker's opinion focused on the fact that Ali was in a zone of active combat operations at the time of his offense and that it would not be "feasible or practicable to suspend military operations to pursue the transfer of [military contractors in the field with U.S. forces] back to the United States for trial" whenever they commit criminal offenses – especially relatively minor offenses – overseas.[65]

Put another way, although the majority rested on its view of the categorical inapplicability of the Fifth and Sixth Amendments to noncitizens overseas, Chief Judge Baker rested instead on a more functional inquiry that has more to do with the nature and location of the offense than with the citizenship of the offender.[66] And as for the slippery slope that would potentially allow such logic to justify military trials for civilians even within the United States, Chief Judge Baker concluded, "While jurisdiction could, in theory, be exercised under Article 2(a)(10) … in the context of domestic security operations within the continental United States, we do not face that situation here."[67]

And yet, although Chief Judge Baker's analysis focused on the fact that Ali was accompanying U.S. armed forces overseas during "combat operations," it is not immediately clear what that term will mean – or, as such, where he would draw the constitutional line – going forward, since jurisdiction under Article 2(a)(10) turns on the contractor's involvement in a "contingency operation," and not the existence of hostilities.

A second critique of Chief Judge Baker's functional approach can be found in Judge Effron's separate opinion concurring in the result.[68] In contrast to Chief Judge Baker, Judge Effron argued that one should approach the constitutional question as turning upon the existence *vel non* of an Article III forum.[69] To that end, because of the government's demonstrated ability to use MEJA to prosecute contractors (whether citizens or not) in civilian court even for offenses committed in foreign combat zones,[70] the availability and utility of civilian courts in the typical case militate against military jurisdiction – and would also thereby undercut Chief Judge Baker's functional case for military jurisdiction in such cases.[71] Thus, for Judge Effron, because MEJA has a textual exception for nationals of the "host" country, Ali's is one of the few cases in which an Article III forum would be unavailable – and military jurisdiction therefore permissible.[72]

As with Chief Judge Baker's opinion, there is a superficial attractiveness to Judge Effron's approach. At the same time, it is difficult to square Judge Effron's approach with decisions like *McElroy v. United States ex rel. Guagliardo*, which rejected the constitutionality of military jurisdiction over civilian contractors (during peacetime) even though no alternative forum was available.[73] More fundamentally, Judge Effron's approach would give Congress control over the answer to the constitutional question because it would mean that the Constitution authorizes military jurisdiction *whenever* Congress has failed to provide a civilian forum – and so Congress could expand the permissible constitutional scope of military jurisdiction – and contract the scope of the jury-trial guarantees – merely by contracting the statutory scope of civilian jurisdiction.[74]

As should ideally be clear, these three competing approaches are largely irreconcilable. And yet each of them presupposes an expansion of military jurisdiction over civilians – whether to noncitizens overseas (under the majority's approach), to anyone who cannot be tried in a civilian court (under Judge Effron's reasoning), or under a functional analysis balancing the practical difficulty of civilian trials with the rights of the defendant (per Chief Judge Baker's concurrence). Whichever of these three rationales ultimately prevails,[75] the critical point for present purposes is that they each would result in greater military jurisdiction over civilian offenders than that which was available prior to the Graham Amendment's enactment. Indeed, even if Article 2(a)(10) is eventually invalidated, the fact remains that the military justice system has far more power to hear cases arising out of civilian life today than it did thirty years ago – and that, as such, it should be far more relevant to students and scholars of civilian criminal law and procedure.

2. THE CIVILIANIZATION OF MILITARY COMMISSION JURISDICTION

Whereas court-martial jurisdiction over civilians and nonmilitary offenses has produced the substantial body of case law summarized in the preceding pages, the same cannot be said for the constitutional scope of the jurisdiction of military *commissions*. Instead, the relevant constitutional rules can largely be divined from two Supreme Court decisions: *Ex parte Milligan*[76] and *Ex parte Quirin*.[77]

In *Milligan*, the Court unanimously struck down military commissions unilaterally created by President Lincoln during the Civil War.[78] And yet, the Court's unanimity as to the result belied a fundamental division as to the reasoning. Although Justice Davis famously declared that "martial rule can never exist where the courts are open, and in the proper and unobstructed exercise of their jurisdiction,"[79] Chief Justice Chase, writing for himself and three of his colleagues, was not convinced that *Congress* could not authorize military commissions in appropriate circumstances, even where there *was* functioning civil authority.[80] Thus, although *Milligan* appeared to articulate a categorical "open court" rule based upon the jury-trial protections of Article III and the Fifth and Sixth Amendments, there was at least some prospect that the Court might adopt a narrower accommodation in a case in which Congress had authorized the tribunals at issue.[81]

So it was that, in 1942, the Court unanimously *upheld* military tribunals utilized by President Roosevelt to try eight Nazi saboteurs who had surreptitiously entered the United States with plans to commit industrial sabotage.[82] To reach that result, the Court first relied on a less-than-obvious interpretation of the Articles of War as providing the congressional authorization that had been lacking in *Milligan*.[83] As Chief Justice Stone explained for the Court,

> By the Articles of War, and especially Article 15, Congress has explicitly provided, *so far as it may constitutionally do so*, that military tribunals shall have jurisdiction to try offenders or offenses against the law of war in appropriate cases. Congress, in addition to making rules for the government of our Armed Forces, *has thus exercised its authority to define and punish offenses against the law of nations* by sanctioning, within constitutional limitations, the jurisdiction of military commissions to try persons for offenses which, according to the rules and precepts of the law of nations, and more particularly the law of war, are cognizable by such tribunals.[84]

In other words, the source of Congress's power to subject enemy belligerents to trial by military commission differed from the source of its authority vis-à-vis courts-martial, deriving from the define and punish clause rather than the make rules clause (or a more amorphous conception of the "war powers").[85] And just as the define and punish clause empowered Congress to prescribe offenses against the law of nations, so too it confined Congress's power to those offenses *recognized* as such.[86] As for the jury-trial protections that had been central to the repudiation of military jurisdiction in *Milligan*, the Court identified a new atextual exception thereto:

> An express exception from Article III, § 2, and from the Fifth and Sixth Amendments, of trials of petty offenses and of criminal contempts has not been found necessary in order to preserve the traditional practice of trying those offenses without a jury. It is no more so in order to continue the practice of trying, before military tribunals without a jury, *offenses committed by enemy belligerents against the law of war.*[87]

Thus, separate from the controversial *substance* of the *Quirin* Court's analysis, its methodology appears to echo that which the Supreme Court has also used in the court-martial cases: military jurisdiction is only permissible for a specific class of offenses, and only when there is a specific exception to the jury-trial protections of Article III and the Fifth and Sixth Amendments. Moreover, and critically for contemporary purposes, the *Quirin* Court tied both Congress's power and the jury-trial exception to the law of war – a body of international law the substance of which is not entirely controlled by the United States.[88]

These understandings proved crucial when the Court next revisited the permissible scope of military commission jurisdiction in *Hamdan v. Rumsfeld*, a challenge to military tribunals unilaterally established by President Bush after September 11.[89] Writing for a 5–3 majority, Justice Stevens noted that "the *Quirin* Court recognized that Congress had simply preserved what power, under the Constitution and the common law of war, the President had had before 1916 to convene military commissions – with the express condition that the President and those under his command comply with the law of war."[90] Because, in the Court's view, the commissions created by President Bush did *not* comply with the law of war, they therefore *exceeded* the statutory authorization that Congress had provided.

Tellingly, part of Justice Stevens's reasoning for why the commissions were inconsistent with the laws of war was that the offense with which Hamdan was charged – conspiracy – was not recognized as a war crime under international law. Although he wrote only for a four-justice plurality on this point, Justice Stevens explained that

Congress, through Article 21 of the UCMJ, has "incorporated by reference" the common law of war, which may render triable by military commission certain offenses not defined by statute. When, however, neither the elements of the offense nor the range of permissible punishments is defined by statute or treaty, the precedent must be plain and unambiguous. To demand any less would be to risk concentrating in military hands a degree of adjudicative and punitive power in excess of that contemplated either by statute or by the Constitution.[91]

But the precedents supporting conspiracy as a war crime were not unambiguous – except perhaps in the other direction. Thus, Justice Stevens concluded that Congress had not thereby authorized military jurisdiction over such an offense: "Because the charge does not support the commission's jurisdiction, the commission lacks authority to try Hamdan."[92]

Congress responded in the Military Commissions Act of 2006 by specifically identifying who could be tried by military commissions, and for which offenses.[93] With regard to the former, the 2006 MCA provided that commissions could try any offense prescribed by the statute committed by a noncitizen "who has engaged in hostilities or who has purposefully and materially supported hostilities against the United States or its co-belligerents who is not a lawful enemy combatant (including a person who is part of the Taliban, al Qaeda, or associated forces)."[94]

With regard to substantive offenses, the MCA set forth as its "purpose" to "codify offenses that have traditionally been triable by military commissions. This chapter does not establish new crimes that did not exist before its enactment, but rather codifies those crimes for trial by military commission."[95] This language was particularly telling, given that, in addition to traditional war crimes, the 2006 MCA included as substantive offenses the crimes of "terrorism,"[96] "providing material support for terrorism,"[97] and, notwithstanding *Hamdan*, "conspiracy."[98] In the Military Commissions Act of 2009, Congress made a series of significant changes to the 2006 statutory language.[99] But it nevertheless reenacted as stand-alone offenses the same three crimes (along with twenty-six others).[100]

Thus, the MCA raises two constitutional questions with which the Supreme Court has never grappled: may Congress subject to trial by military commission (1) individuals who are not recognized as belligerents under international law and (2) offenses not recognized as war crimes under international law?

The latter question (albeit not the former) has been at the heart of several prosecutions brought under the MCA, including *United States* v. *Hamdan* (*Hamdan II*), in which the government charged the defendant with conspiracy and "providing material support to terrorism."[101] The commission ultimately acquitted Hamdan on the conspiracy charge but convicted on the charge of material support, largely on the basis of the trial judge's conclusion that material support *was* recognized as a war crime under international law.[102] A different defendant – Ali Hamza Ahmad Suliman *al Bahlul* – was also convicted of conspiracy. On appeal, the Court of Military Commission Review affirmed both convictions.[103] But when Hamdan and al-Bahlul appealed *those* decisions to the D.C. Circuit, the government shifted the focus of its position from the view that material support is an *international* war crime to the distinct argument that, even if it is not, it is nevertheless triable by a military commission because it is a violation of the "U.S. common law of war."[104]

Thus, whereas *Quirin* had held that the Constitution's jury-trial protections do not encompass "offenses committed by enemy belligerents against the law of war," and that Congress could subject such offenses to military jurisdiction so long as they were recognized as such under international law, the government's position in *Hamdan II* and *al-Bahlul* goes an important step past *Quirin*: on the government's view, the jury-trial protections similarly do not extend to offenses against the "U.S. common law of war," and Congress may subject such offenses to military jurisdiction whether or not they are recognized as war crimes under international law.

In reversing Hamdan's conviction, the D.C. Circuit rejected this argument on narrow grounds, holding that individuals could not be tried for *pre*-MCA conduct unless that conduct was recognized as a violation of the international laws of war – given the ex post facto issues that would otherwise arise.[105] As Judge Kavanaugh explained for a unanimous panel, "imposing liability on the basis of a violation of 'international law' or the 'law of nations' or the 'law of war' generally must be based on norms firmly grounded in international law."[106] Because "material support to terrorism" was not such a crime, the D.C. Circuit reversed Hamdan's conviction.[107] Three months later, a different panel reversed *al-Bahlul's* conspiracy conviction, holding, at the government's suggestion, that the result was compelled by *Hamdan II*.[108] As this chapter went to press, the D.C. Circuit granted rehearing en banc in *al-Bahlul*, ostensibly to revisit the panel's analysis of the 2006 MCA in *Hamdan II*.[109]

At the same time, Judge Kavanaugh, writing only for himself on this point in *Hamdan II*, was more receptive to the government's power to try non-law-of-war (or "U.S. common law of war") offenses in military commissions for conduct that *post*-dates the MCA.[110] To be sure, Judge Kavanaugh nowhere considered the Article III issues that such a result would precipitate. But if his view were followed, it would effectuate a subtle – but decisive – expansion in military commission jurisdiction over offenses not previously triable by such courts.

Moreover, notwithstanding the D.C. Circuit's decisions in *Hamdan II* or *al-Bahlul*, there are a number of additional cases coming down the pipeline that might implicate additional questions about the relationship between the MCA and the laws of war, including the question whether an individual can be tried for conduct that predated the September 11 attacks (at which point there was arguably no "armed conflict"),[111] whether the bombing of a French tanker could be a violation of the laws of war if there was no "armed conflict" between France and al-Qaeda,[112] and others. Unless the ultimate bottom line is a categorical rejection of Congress's power to invest military commissions with *prospective* jurisdiction beyond that contemplated by the international laws of war, then the reality will be the same regardless of the holding in *Hamdan II* or the outcome of the pending en banc proceedings in al-Bahlul– military jurisdiction will have been expanded to cover offenses (and potentially offenders) previously subject to the exclusive jurisdiction of civilian criminal courts.

3. CRITIQUING THE CIVILIANIZATION OF MILITARY JURISDICTION

As the preceding analysis suggests, there have been a series of important expansions in the scope of military jurisdiction over the past quarter-century, including several critical developments in the past few years. At the same time, these expansions have occurred alongside dramatic and well-documented improvements in the substantive and procedural protections afforded to defendants in military courts, at least as compared to what was previously true. To be sure, differences still abound. But whereas the Supreme Court in prior generations invoked the "rough form of justice" dispensed by military courts as one of the principal justifications for narrowly construing the constitutional scope of their jurisdiction, the civilianization of military law might well be invoked as a basis for worrying far less about the civilianization of military jurisdiction today.[113]

Before jumping to that conclusion, however, a few points bear consideration: *First*, even if one assumes relative procedural parity (which is hardly a given),[114] the justifications for a distinct system of military justice have historically focused on the unique nature of military *service*. As Justice Jackson explained in 1953, "The military constitutes a specialized community governed by a separate discipline from that of the civilian. Orderly government requires that the judiciary be as scrupulous not to interfere with legitimate Army matters as the Army must be scrupulous not to intervene in judicial matters."[115] That is to say, "The need for special regulations in relation to military discipline, and the consequent need and justification for a special and exclusive system of military justice, is too obvious to require extensive discussion; no military organization can function without strict discipline and regulation that would be unacceptable in a civilian setting."[116]

But to the extent that the principal analytical justifications for a separate and distinct system of military justice center on the need to preserve such "good order and discipline" within the military, and thereby to avoid undue judicial interference in the military chain of command, the force of those arguments wanes (1) the more that the military justice system grows to resemble its civilian counterpart, as has resulted from the civilianization of military law; and (2) in contexts in which those concerns are implicated to a lesser extent, as in cases in which military jurisdiction is directed toward nonmilitary offenses or offenders. After all, the "strict discipline and regulation that would be unacceptable in a civilian setting" would presumably also be unacceptable as applied *to* civilians, perhaps even when those civilians are performing comparable functions to active-duty servicemembers. Thus, even if one is willing to accept the need for military jurisdiction over nonmilitary offenses by servicemembers, as in *Solorio*,[117] the same simply cannot be said for military jurisdiction over *any* offense by non-servicemembers, especially given the extent to which MEJA provides far greater civilian criminal jurisdiction than that which existed when the Supreme Court decided *Covert* and its progeny.

In the military commission context, an alternative justification was offered by the Court in *Quirin*, namely, that it would be anomalous to provide enemy belligerents during wartime with greater procedural and substantive protections at trial than those enjoyed by our own servicemembers.[118] Even assuming *arguendo* that such a result *would* be anomalous, *Quirin* itself emphasized that the relevant exception to civilian trials is therefore circumscribed by the laws of war – the same laws that would presumably govern war crimes trials of U.S. servicemembers by foreign sovereigns. As a result, extending the jurisdiction of military commissions beyond that recognized by international law also cuts against *this* underlying justification.

Related to this tension is the movement away from expansive conceptions of military jurisdiction in other jurisdictions, as documented by Peter Rowe in *The Impact of Human Rights Law on Armed Forces*[119] and as manifested in the "Draft Principles Governing the Administration of Justice through Military Tribunals" promulgated by the UN Commission on Human Rights in 2006.[120] To be sure, there is far more to say about these comparative developments than space permits. For present purposes, however, it should suffice to note that, in these foreign and international contexts as well, concerns have continued to be voiced about the fairness and independence of separate military justice systems for nonmilitary offenses or offenders even as these other military justice systems have undertaken or otherwise undergone much of the same "civilianization" as the U.S. military courts. No amount of procedural or substantive harmonization appears to have redressed the concern that "military courts can be seen as being both unjustifiably favourable and unfavourable to the defendant" in relation to civilian courts, depending on the circumstances.[121] Put differently, the point is not that military courts are more likely to judge a defendant *harshly*; the point is that the outcome is likely to *differ* from that of the civilian courts, one way or the other, in a large enough class of cases to justify circumscribing the size of that class on the basis of the underlying justification for the exception.[122]

Finally, as the preceding discussions should suggest, there is an intrinsic value to drawing bright constitutional lines in this context – clarity that is necessarily obfuscated by the civilianization of military jurisdiction. Thus, even if the expansion of court-martial jurisdiction over civilians is limited under the Graham Amendment to a small class of cases (depending on which of the CAAF opinions ultimately prevails), it may be difficult fully to appreciate the significance of such minimal incursions into the judicial power of Article III courts seriatim. Indeed, it is a common refrain of the Supreme Court's jurisprudence with regard to the constitutional limits on non–Article III courts in general that "a statute may no more lawfully chip away at the authority of the Judicial Branch than it may eliminate it entirely."[123] To similar effect, the minuscule expansion of military commission jurisdiction endorsed by Judge Kavanaugh in *Hamdan II* would also cross a critical constitutional line observed by the Supreme Court for more than seventy years, giving far greater power to Congress to expand the scope of military jurisdiction based entirely on *its* understanding of what the laws of war proscribe.[124]

All of these considerations help to explain the principle first given voice by Justice Johnson that Congress should be confined in defining military jurisdiction to "the least possible power adequate to the end proposed."[125] Chief Justice Rehnquist tried to dismiss this observation in *Solorio* by suggesting that it only applied to the case in which it was articulated (which he wrongly identified as the Court's 1955 decision in *Toth*).[126] In fact, however, there is a subtle depth to Justice Johnson's insight – that Congress and the courts cross a dangerous line whenever they begin to countenance military jurisdiction wholly untethered to the principles justifying the departure from civilian authority in the first place.[127] The civilianization of military law may to some degree mitigate the effects of such line crossing in individual cases, but it cannot eliminate them altogether, nor remedy the systemic concerns that greater military jurisdiction over nonmilitary offenders and offenses necessarily raise.

4. CONCLUSION

If one is inclined to agree that the civilianization of military jurisdiction is a troubling development, or even a relevant one in understanding the relationship between civilian and military criminal justice in the United States, then the next few years may prove crucial in setting the stage for that which follows. To be sure, the fact that *al-Bahlul* is still pending introduces at least an element of uncertainty into the analysis of the preceding pages. Indeed, if the federal courts eventually use these cases to *reassert* constitutional limits on military jurisdiction, then the expansion of military jurisdiction documented previously will effectively reduce to the Court's abolition of the "service connection" test in *Solorio* – an important development, to be sure, but also one that is more than a quarter-century old. To be frank, I very much doubt that the Supreme Court will so hold in either of the contexts discussed herein. But if they do, this chapter will, at bottom, help to explain why such decisions are so significant. To similar effect, this chapter will also illuminate the significance of these cases if the existing rationales are left intact.

But the purpose of this chapter has not simply been to explain why the *Ali* and *al-Bahlul* cases place the courts at a critical crossroads in policing the lines between civilian and military jurisdiction. Instead, my goal has been to explain why students and scholars of American criminal law and procedure in the twenty-first century should care deeply about how the courts resolve these issues – and, more generally, how they police the lines between civilian and military jurisdiction – one way or the other.

Notes

1 This quip is often attributed to Georges Clemenceau, although it is unclear if he ever actually said it. See L. H. LaRue, *What Is the Text in Constitutional Law: Does It Include Thoreau?* 20 GA. L. REV. 1137, 1142 n.2 (1986).
2 *Reid v. Covert*, 354 U.S. 1, 35 (1957) (plurality opinion).
3 See *Kennedy v. Louisiana*, 554 U.S. 407 (2008).
4 See *Kennedy v. Louisiana*, 129 S. Ct. 1, 1–3 (2008) (statement of Kennedy, J., respecting the denial of rehearing); see also *Kennedy*, 554 U.S. at 426 n.*; ID. at 459 n.6 (Alito, J., dissenting).
5 See, e.g., *United States v. Marcum*, 60 M.J. 198, 205 (C.A.A.F. 2004) ("[T]his Court has consistently applied the Bill of Rights to members of the Armed Forces, except in cases where the express terms of the Constitution make such application inapposite.").
6 See, e.g., Jennifer K. Elsea, Cong. Res. Serv., Comparison Of Rights In Military Commission Trials And Trials In Federal Criminal Court 13–27 tbl. 2 (2012), http://www.fas.org/sgp/crs/natsec/R40932.pdf (last visited May 22, 2013); R. Chuck Mason,

Cong. Res. Serv., Military Justice: Courts-Martial, an Overview 9–15 tbl.1 (2012), http://www.fas.org/sgp/crs/natsec/R41739.pdf (last visited May 22, 2013).

7   See, e.g., Edward F. Sherman, *The Civilianization of Military Law*, 22 ME. L. REV. 3 (1970); Karen A. Ruzic, Note, *Military Justice and the Supreme Court's Outdated Standard of Deference*: Weiss v. United States, 70 CHI.-KENT L. REV. 265, 273 & n.78 (1994).

8   See, e.g., Military Justice Act of 1983, § 10(a)(1), 97 Stat. 1393, 1405 (codified at 28 U.S.C. § 1259)). See generally Stephen I. Vladeck, *Exceptional Courts and the Structure of American Military Justice*, in GUANTÁNAMO AND BEYOND: EXCEPTIONAL COURTS AND MILITARY COMMISSIONS IN COMPARATIVE AND POLICY PERSPECTIVE (Fionnuala D. Ní Aoláin & Oren Gross, eds., Cambridge Univ. Press, forthcoming).

9   See, e.g., *Burns v. Wilson*, 346 U.S. 137 (1953) (plurality opinion).

10 See, e.g., *Hiatt v. Brown*, 339 U.S. 103, 110–11 (1950) (citing IN RE GRIMLEY, 137 U.S. 147 [1890]).

11 What has been described within the United States as the "civilianization" of military justice has been characterized more generally as the effect of modern international human rights law on military justice across the world. See, e.g., PETER ROWE, THE IMPACT OF HUMAN RIGHTS LAW ON ARMED FORCES (2006).

12 *Loving v. United States*, 68 M.J. 1, 28 n.11 (C.A.A.F. 2009) (Ryan, J., dissenting) (alteration in original; citations omitted), cert. denied, 131 S. Ct. 67 (2010).

13 483 U.S. 435 (1987).

14 See *O'Callahan v. Parker*, 395 U.S. 258 (1969).

15 At least four Justices have suggested that, notwithstanding *Solorio*, the Constitution might still require a "service connection" in capital cases. See *Loving v. United States*, 517 U.S. 748, 774 (1996) (Stevens, J., concurring in the judgment); see also *United States v. Gray*, 51 M.J. 1, 11 (C.A.A.F. 1999). Since *Solorio*, however, this question has not been squarely presented.

16 See 10 U.S.C. § 802(a)(10) (2006); see also *United States v. Averette*, 41 C.M.R. (19 U.S.C.M.A.) 363 (1970) (interpreting the phrase "time of war" in Article 2's predecessor to require a formal declaration of war in order to avoid constitutional questions).

17 See John Warner National Defense Authorization Act for Fiscal Year 2007, Pub. L. No. 109–364, § 552, 120 Stat. 2083, 2217 (codified at 10 U.S.C. § 802(a)(10)). For the definition of "contingency operation," see 10 U.S.C. § 101(a)(13).

18 See *United States v. Ali*, 71 M.J. 256 (C.A.A.F. 2012), cert. denied , No. 12–505, 2013 WL 1942430 (U.S. May 13, 2013).

19 See Military Order – Detention, Treatment, and Trial of Certain Non-Citizens in the War against Terrorism (Nov. 13, 2001), 66 FED. REG. 57,833 (Nov. 16, 2001).

20 See *Ex parte Quirin*, 317 U.S. 1 (1942); see also *In re Yamashita*, 327 U.S. 1 (1946).

21 548 U.S. 557 (2006).

22 See Military Commissions Act of 2009, Pub. L. No. 111–84, tit. XVIII, 123 Stat. 2190, 2574–614 (codified in scattered sections of 10 U.S.C.); Military Commissions Act of 2006, Pub. L. No. 109–366, 120 Stat. 2600 (codified as amended in scattered sections of 10, 18, and 28 U.S.C.).

23 See Stephen I. Vladeck, *The Laws of War as a Constitutional Limit on Military Jurisdiction*, 4 J. NAT'L SEC. L. & POL'Y 295 (2010).

24 See *United States v. Al-Bahlul*, 820 F. Supp. 2d 1141 (Ct. Mil. Comm'n Rev. 2011) (en banc), rev'd, No. 11–1324, 2013 WL 297726 (D.C. Cir. Jan. 25, 2013) (per curiam); *United States v. Hamdan* (HAMDAN II), 801 F. Supp. 2d 1247 (Ct. Mil. Comm'n Rev. 2011) (en banc), rev'd, 696 F.3d 1238 (D.C. Cir. 2012).In *Hamdan II*, the D.C. Circuit held that an individual could not be subjected to trial by military commission for conduct that predates the Military Commissions Act of 2006 if that conduct was not recognized as a violation of the laws of war at the time of the offense. Whatever the merits of that holding, it leaves intact the possibility that individuals *could* be subjected to such trials if their conduct postdated the MCA – a possibility explicitly endorsed by Judge Kavanaugh. See 696 F.3d at 1246 n.6; see also infra text accompanying notes 105–110.
25 *Anderson v. Dunn*, 19 U.S. (6 Wheat.) 204, 231 (1821).
26 See generally FREDERICK BERNAYS WIENER, CIVILIANS UNDER MILITARY JUSTICE (1967) (providing a comprehensive historical overview of the exercise of military jurisdiction over civilians leading up – and during – the American Revolution).
27 This is not to suggest that there were no cases prior to the 1950s raising the amenability of civilians to military jurisdiction – quite the contrary. But the Supreme Court did not begin to take up the question until this time period, which is why my focus begins here. For a concise summary of pre-1950 examples, see Brittany Warren, *The Case of the Murdering Wives: Reid v. Covert and the Complicated Question of Civilians and Courts-Martial*, 212 MIL. L. REV. 133, 137–41 (2012). See also *Ex parte Henderson*, 11 F. Cas. 1067 (C.C.D. Ky. 1878) (No. 6349) (striking down a Civil War-era Act of Congress that subjected military contractors to court-martial jurisdiction for fraud related to their governmental contracts.).
28 343 U.S. 341 (1952).
29 See, e.g., *id.* at 345–9 & n.7.
30 Initially, the Court actually came out the other way, upholding such jurisdiction 6–3 in *Kinsella v. Krueger*, 351 U.S. 470 (1956). But after a virtually unprecedented grant of rehearing (itself by a 5–3 vote), see *Kinsella v. Krueger*, 352 U.S. 901 (1956) (mem.), Justices Harlan and Frankfurter changed their votes, providing the KRUEGER dissenters (joined by Justice Brennan, who joined the Court in the interim) with a majority – at least as to the result. See *Reid v. Covert*, 354 U.S. 1 (1957). For the fascinating – and complex – story behind the litigation in *Reid* and *Krueger*, see Warren, supra note 27.
31 See *Reid*, 354 U.S. at 38–40 (plurality opinion).
32 See *Grisham v. Hagan*, 361 U.S. 278 (1960).
33 See *Kinsella v. United States ex rel. Singleton*, 361 U.S. 234 (1960).
34 See *McElroy v. United States ex rel. Guagliardo*, 361 U.S. 281 (1960).
35 See *United States v. Averette*, 41 C.M.R. (19 U.S.C.M.A.) 363 (1970).
36 See *United States ex rel. Toth v. Quarles*, 350 U.S. 11 (1955). The practical significance of *Toth* has arguably been diluted by subsequent decisions allowing the military to recall reservists to active duty for the sole purpose of trying them for offenses committed while on active duty. See *Willenbring v. Neurater*, 48 M.J. 152 (C.A.A.F. 1998); see also *Willenbring v. United States*, 559 F.3d 225 (4th Cir. 2009). Nevertheless, it seems clear in hindsight that the decision in *Toth* helped to precipitate the subsequent litigation over civilian dependents and employees. See Warren, supra note 27, at 160 (noting that the habeas petition in *Covert* was filed just 10 days after the decision in *Toth*).

37 See, e.g., *Hiatt v. Brown*, 339 U.S. 103, 111 (1950) ("The correction of any errors [the court-martial] may have committed is for the military authorities which are alone authorized to review its decision."); see also *Burns v. Wilson*, 346 U.S. 137, 146–7 (1953) (Minton, J., concurring in the judgment).
38 See 395 U.S. 258 (1969).
39 *Id.* at 272–73 (footnote and citations omitted).
40 See *id.* at 281–4 (Harlan, J., dissenting).
41 See, e.g., *Relford v. Commandant*, U.S. DISCIPLINARY BARRACKS, 401 U.S. 355 (1971); see also *Solorio v. United States*, 483 U.S. 435, 449–50 & nn. 14–17 (1987).
42 483 U.S. 435.
43 See *id.* at 442–50.
44 *Id.* at 439.
45 See U.S. CONST. art. I, § 8, cl. 14 (empowering Congress "[t]o make Rules for the Government and Regulation of the land and naval Forces").
46 See *Solorio*, 483 U.S. at 439–41.
47 U.S. CONST. amend. V (emphasis added).
48 See *Solorio*, 483 U.S. at 454–5 (Marshall, J., dissenting).
49 See supra note 15.
50 Vladeck, supra note 23, at 311–12.
51 See John Warner National Defense Authorization Act for Fiscal Year 2007, Pub. L. No. 109–364, § 552, 120 Stat. 2083, 2217 (codified at 10 U.S.C. § 802(a)(10)). Careful readers will note that, in addition to adding the "contingency operation" language, the amendment otherwise codifies the holding of *Averette* by adding the word "declared" to the statutory text.
52 10 U.S.C. § 101(a)(13)(A).
53 See Vladeck, supra note 23, at 308 n.76 (describing litigation in *Price v. Gates*).
54 For the background, see *United States v. Ali*, 70 M.J. 514, 515–17 (C.A.A.F. 2011), aff'd on other grounds, 71 M.J. 256 (C.A.A.F. 2012), cert. denied, No. 12-805, 2013 WL 1942430 (U.S. May 13, 2013).
55 18 U.S.C. §§ 3261–67.
56 See *id.* §§ 3267(1)(C), 3267(2)(C).
57 See *Ali*, 70 M.J. at 517.
58 *Id.* at 519.
59 *Id.* at 520.
60 See *United States v. Ali*, 71 M.J. 256 (C.A.A.F. 2012), cert. denied, No. 12-805, 2013 WL 1942430 (U.S. May 13, 2013).
61 See *id.* at 266–9.
62 See *id.*
63 In particular, the majority refused to consider whether the Supreme Court's decision in *Boumediene v. Bush*, 553 U.S. 723 (2008), might alter the calculus with regard to the extraterritorial Fifth and Sixth Amendment rights of a non-citizen such as Ali. See, e.g., *Ali*, 71 M.J. at 269 n.25. And even if the result would have been the same, the majority also refused to take seriously Ali's substantial, voluntary connections to the United States – to wit, his training at Fort Benning and his employment by a U.S. military contractor. For more on these points, see Steve Vladeck, *Analysis of U.S. v. Ali: A Flawed Majority, Conflicting Concurrences, and the Future of Military Jurisdiction*, LAWFARE, July 19, 2012, http://www.lawfareblog.com/2012/07/analysis-of-caaf-decision-in-ali/ (last visited May 22, 2013).

64 See Ali, 71 M.J. at 275 (Baker, C. J., concurring in part and in the result).
65 Id. at 274.
66 See id. at 275–9.
67 Id. at 276.
68 See id. at 279–82 (Effron, J., concurring in part and in the result).
69 See id. at 280.
70 In support of this point, Judge Effron invoked *United States v. Brehm*, No. 1:11-cr-11, 2011 WL 1226088 (E.D. Va. Mar. 30, 2011), in which the district court upheld the constitutionality of MEJA as applied to prosecution of non-citizen contractor for offense committed against another non-citizen on a NATO airbase in Afghanistan. Not long after *Ali* was decided, the Fourth Circuit affirmed Brehm's conviction, holding that Brehm's contacts with the United States *were* sufficient to justify the United States' assertion of criminal jurisdiction over him. See *United States v. Brehm*, 691 F.3d 547 (4th Cir.), cert. denied, 133. S. Ct. 808 (2012).
71 See *Ali*, 71 M.J. at 279–81 (Effron, J., concurring in part and in the result).
72 See id. at 282.
73 See 361 U.S. 281 (1960).
74 For example, if Congress were to amend MEJA to exclude categorically offenses committed in certain countries (e.g., Afghanistan), it would presumably follow from Judge Effron's concurrence that military jurisdiction would be more appropriate.
75 The Supreme Court may yet have the last word. In *Ali*, however, the Justices denied certiorari on May 13, 2013. See *United States v. Ali*, No. 12-805, 2013 WL 1942430 (U.S. May 13, 2013) (mem.).
76 71 U.S. (4 Wall.) 2 (1866).
77 317 U.S. 1 (1942).
78 See 71 U.S. (4 Wall.) at 118–27.
79 Id. at 127.
80 See id. at 136–42 (Chase, C. J.).
81 See, e.g., Trial of Spies by Military Tribunals, 31 OP. ATT'Y GEN. 356 (1918).
82 *Quirin*'s background has been often recounted – and is highly relevant to understanding critiques of the Court's decision. For representative accounts, see LOUIS FISHER, NAZI SABOTEURS ON TRIAL: A MILITARY TRIBUNAL AND AMERICAN LAW (2d ed., 2005); Michael R. Belknap, *The Supreme Court Goes to War: The Meaning and Implications of the Nazi Saboteur Case*, 89 MIL. L. REV. 59 (1980); David Danelski, *The Saboteurs' Case*, 1996 J. S. CT. HIST. 61; Carlos M. Vázquez, "Not a Happy Precedent": The Story of Ex parte Quirin, in FEDERAL COURTS STORIES 219 (Judith Resnik & Vicki C. Jackson, eds., 2009); and G. Edward White, *Felix Frankfurter's "Soliloquy" in Ex parte Quirin: Nazi Sabotage's Constitutional Conundrums*, 5 GREEN BAG 2d 423 (2002).
83 Article 15 of the Articles of War merely provided that "the provisions of these articles conferring jurisdiction upon courts-martial shall not be construed as depriving military commissions ... of concurrent jurisdiction in respect of offenders or offenses that by statute or by the law of war may be triable by such military commissions." See *Quirin*, 317 U.S. at 27. Given that the text appears as more of a reservation of authority than an explicit grant thereof, Justice Stevens would later describe *Quirin*'s characterization of Article 15 as "controversial." See *Hamdan v. Rumsfeld*, 548 U.S. 557, 593 (2006).
84 *Quirin*, 317 U.S. at 28 (emphases added).

85 See U.S. CONST. art. I, § 8, cl. 10 (empowering Congress "[t]o define and punish ... Offences against the Law of Nations").
86 See generally Vladeck, supra note 23.
87 *Quirin*, 317 U.S. at 41 (emphasis added).
88 To that end, the Court's one other World War II-era foray into the law governing military commissions – its 1946 decision in *In re Yamashita*, 327 U.S. 1 (1946) – accepted and applied *Quirin's* framing of the jurisdictional considerations without any reconsideration.
89 548 U.S. 557 (2006). For the order establishing the tribunals, see *Military Order–Detention, Treatment, and Trial of Certain Non–Citizens in the War against Terrorism* (Nov. 13, 2001), 66 FED. REG. 57,833 (Nov. 16, 2001).
90 *Hamdan*, 548 U.S. at 593 (citation omitted).
91 *Id.* at 602 (plurality opinion) (citations omitted).
92 *Id.* at 611–12.
93 See Military Commissions Act of 2006, Pub. L. No. 109–366, 120 Stat. 2600 (codified as amended in scattered sections of 10, 18, and 28 U.S.C.).
94 See 10 U.S.C. § 948a(1) (2006). For the relevant provision as amended by the 2009 MCA, see *id.* § 948a(7)(C) (2012).
95 *Id.* § 950p(a) (2006); see also *id.* § 950p(b) ("[T]he provisions of this subchapter ... are declarative of existing law," and so "do not preclude trial for crimes that occurred before the date of the enactment of this chapter.").
96 See *id.* § 950v(b)(24).
97 See *id.* § 950v(b)(25).
98 See *id.* § 950v(b)(28).
99 See Military Commissions Act of 2009, Pub. L. No. 111–84, tit. XVIII, 123 Stat. 2190, 2574–614 (codified in scattered sections of 10 U.S.C.); see also Vladeck, supra note 8 (discussing key changes between the 2006 and 2009 MCAs).
100 See 10 U.S.C. § 950t (2012).
101 See *United States v. Hamdan*, 2 M.C. 1 (Mil. Comm'n July 14, 2008).
102 See *id.*
103 See *United States v. Hamdan*, 801 F. Supp. 2d 1247 (Ct. Mil. Comm'n Rev. 2011) (en banc) (per curiam).
104 See Brief for the United States, *United States v. Hamdan*, 696 F.3d 1238 (D.C. Cir. 2012) (No. 11–1257), available at http://www.lawfareblog.com/wp-content/uploads/2012/01/Hamdan-Brief-for-US-As-Filed.pdf (last visited May 22, 2013). For more discussion of the change in position – and its implications – see Steve Vladeck, *Government Brief in Hamdan: The Looming Article III Problem*, Lawfare, Jan. 17, 2012, http://www.lawfareblog.com/2012/01/government-brief-in-hamdan-the-looming-article-iii-problem/ (last visited May 22, 2013).
105 See HAMDAN, 696 F.3d at 1252 ("[T]he statutory constraint here imposed by 10 U.S.C. § 821 is the INTERNATIONAL law of war." (emphasis added)).
106 *Id.* at 1250 n.10.
107 *Id.* at 1248–53.
108 See *al-Bahlul v. United States*, No. 11–1324, 2013 WL 297726 (D.C. Cir. Jan. 25, 2013) (per curiam).
109 See Steve Vladeck, *DOJ Seeks Rehearing En Banc in Bahlul to Overturn Hamdan II*, LAWFARE, Mar. 5, 2013, http://www.lawfareblog.com/2013/03/doj-seeks-rehearing-en-banc-in-bahlul-seeks-to-overturn-hamdan-ii/. On April 23, 2013, the D.C.

Circuit granted the government's petition. See *Al-Bahlul v. United States*, No. 11-1324 (D.C. Cir. Apr. 23, 2013) (en banc) (mem.).

110 See *Hamdan II*, 696 F.3d. at 1246 n.6 ("Although material support for terrorism is not yet an international-law war crime, Congress's war powers under Article I are not defined or constrained by international law. The Declare War Clause and the other Article I war powers clauses do not refer to international law, unlike the Define and Punish Clause.").

111 See, e.g., *Al-Nashiri v. McDonald*, No. 11-5907, 2012 WL 1642306 (W.D. Wash. May 10, 2012), appeal docketed, No. 12-35475 (9th Cir. argued June 3, 2013).

112 See, e.g., U.S. Dep't of Def., News Release, *DOD Announces Charges Sworn against Al-Darbi*, Aug. 29, 2012, http://www.defense.gov/releases/release.aspx?releaseid=15544 (last visited May 22, 2013).

113 For example, in *United States v. Denedo*, 556 U.S. 904 (2009), the Court held that military courts had the power to issue post-conviction writs of error coram nobis in at least some circumstances, even though individuals in such cases might also have access to the Article III courts. As Justice Kennedy wrote for the majority, "[t]he military justice system relies upon courts that must take all appropriate means, consistent with their statutory jurisdiction, to ensure the neutrality and integrity of their judgments." *Id.* at 917.

114 See, e.g., MASON, supra note 6.

115 *Orloff v. Willoughby*, 345 U.S. 83, 94 (1953).

116 *Chappell v. Wallace*, 462 U.S. 296, 300 (1983).

117 *Solorio v. United States*, 483 U.S. 435 (1987).

118 See *Ex parte Quirin*, 317 U.S. 1, 44 (1942).

119 ROWE, supra note 11.

120 United Nations Economic and Social Council, Commission on Human Rights, 62nd Sess., Civil and Political Rights, Including the Question of Independence of the Judiciary, Administration of Justice, Impunity: Issue of the Administration of Justice through Military Tribunals, UN Doc. E/CN.4.2006/58 (Jan. 13, 2006).

121 Rain Liivoja, Book Review, 7 HUM. RTS. L. REV. 813, 815 (2007) (reviewing ROWE, supra note 11).

122 See generally Vladeck, supra note 8.

123 *Stern v. Marshall*, 131 S. Ct. 2594, 2620 (2011). Tellingly, the very next sentence of Chief Justice Roberts's opinion in *Stern* quoted Justice Black's plurality opinion in *Covert*: "Slight encroachments create new boundaries from which legions of power can seek new territory to capture." *Id.* (quoting *Reid v. Covert*, 354 U.S. 1, 39 (1957) (plurality opinion)); see also *Commodity Futures Trading Comm'n v. Schor*, 478 U.S. 833, 861 (1986) (Brennan, J., dissenting) ("These important functions of Article III are too central to our constitutional scheme to risk their incremental erosion.").

124 See, e.g., *Hamdan v. United States*, 696 F.3d 1238, 1246 n.6 (D.C. Cir. 2012); see also Michael Stokes Paulsen, *The Constitutional Power To Interpret International Law*, 118 YALE L.J. 1774, 1820 (2009) ("Congress must define the 'Offences'; the regime of international law may not dictate to Congress what those offenses may or must be."); *id.* at 1821 ("It is worth pausing for a moment to absorb just how sweeping this legislative power may be. Congress may define what it understands to be a violation of 'the Law of Nations' and use this judgment as the basis for legislative enactments.").

125 *Anderson v. Dunn*, 19 U.S. (6 Wheat.) 204, 231 (1821).
126 See *Solorio v. United States*, 483 U.S. 435, 440 n.3 (1987) (quoting *United States ex rel. Toth v. Quarles*, 350 U.S. 11, 23 (1955)). *Toth* itself quoted *Anderson v. Dunn*. See *Toth*, 350 U.S. at 23 & n.23.
127 Cf. *Ex parte Milligan*, 71 U.S. (4 Wall.) 2, 127 (1866) ("As necessity creates the rule, so it limits its duration ....").

17

Crime across Borders

Globalization, Executive Power, and the Transformation of Criminal Justice

John T. Parry

In recent years, criminal activity and criminal enforcement efforts have become increasingly transnational and international. This chapter considers these developments alongside the rise of what I call the "national security sovereign" in the United States. I use the term "national security sovereign" to refer, not to a unitary sovereign with power over all aspects of political life, but rather to a federal executive branch with enormous power and discretion over the movements, well-being, and lives of people around the world. This power is so extensive and so independent that it transcends ordinary ideas of executive power in a democratic regime of divided sovereignty and deserves to be treated as a distinct manifestation of sovereignty in a Schmittian sense.[1] The national security sovereign justifies its power through the necessity of managing events – sometimes denominated "crises" – that impact anything that can be classified as a national security concern, as well as, more generally, the ever-present need to advance national security interests. I argue that the rise of the national security sovereign will present growing challenges to criminal justice and criminal practice in the years ahead, particularly but not exclusively at the federal level.

Many aspects of the national security sovereign are reasonable, and some may even be desirable. Nonetheless, the national security sovereign puts pressure on traditional separation of powers and rule of law values. While it is true that these values have never matched up completely with actual practices, they have overlapped enough that it has made sense to use them as normative standards or analytical tools. As the national security sovereign grows, however, the widening gap between these values and actual practice threatens to make such comparisons meaningless.[2] Nor is this threat confined to the international or foreign relations aspects of criminal law. This chapter, accordingly, argues that judges, legislators, and commentators must make a self-conscious doctrinal and political effort to restrain the national security sovereign in the field of criminal law, and elsewhere.

The first section of this chapter addresses the internationalization of crime and law enforcement and highlights the possibilities that this internationalization creates for expanding executive power. The second section describes the rise and authority of the national security sovereign. The third section explores the interactions between the national security sovereign and criminal justice. The last section concludes by briefly speculating about the future of the national security sovereign.

1. INTERNATIONAL AND TRANSNATIONAL CRIME
AND LAW ENFORCEMENT

Criminal conduct does not have to take place within political borders. Yet borders have long been important to crime. People suspected of committing crimes sometimes become fugitives, and their flight from law enforcement typically involves the effort to get across a border, in the belief that they will be safer from prosecution in the territory of a different sovereign. Indeed, certain criminal conduct, such as the variety of crimes associated with the term "smuggling," exists precisely because of borders. Or, to take a very different example, pirates operate outside borders altogether and take advantage of the vulnerability of their victims – a vulnerability that itself derives from the borderless nature of the high seas.[3] The fact that piracy does not take place within (or even across) political borders is one of the important reasons why it became the first international crime and the first example of universal jurisdiction.

Another significant moment in the history of international criminal law was the effort to stifle the slave trade and, ultimately, slavery itself. Like piracy, the slave trade often included conduct on the high seas. More recently, the targets of international criminal law enforcement have expanded to include such matters as human trafficking, drug trafficking, arms dealing, trade in endangered species or products derived from them, money laundering, cybercrime, organized crime (which encompasses many of the specific crimes in this list), and, of course, terrorism.[4] Most of this conduct is criminalized by individual states, and it would be criminal even if it took place entirely within the borders of an individual state. At a formal level, therefore, this crime is "international" simply by virtue of the fact that it has crossed borders (with no requirement that it take place outside any border at all). Commentators thus frequently label such crimes "transnational," to distinguish them from "international criminal law in the strict sense."[5]

"International criminal law in the strict sense" involves the prosecution of war crimes and similar forms of state violence. The 1949 Geneva Conventions, for example, require signatory countries to criminalize "grave breaches" of their provisions, which include "willful killing, torture or inhuman treatment [and] willfully causing great suffering or serious injury to body or health."[6] Enforcement, in other words, is to take place in national courts.

The precedent of the Nuremburg trials, however, has inspired more recent efforts to pursue grave breaches and related crimes outside national courts, in international tribunals such as the International Criminal Tribunal for the Former Yugoslavia and the International Criminal Court (ICC). The ICC has jurisdiction over acts that fall within the general categories of genocide, crimes against humanity, war crimes, and the "crime of aggression."[7] Although state action is not an element of every crime within the ICC's jurisdiction, the focus continues to be on conduct associated with armed conflict and large-scale violence.

International and transnational crimes have received more scrutiny from law enforcement and other government officials in recent decades. To some extent, this increased attention results from a rise in criminal activity. After all, transnational crimes such as money laundering have benefited from globalization and the growing speed of transportation and communications networks. Moreover, as criminal conduct across borders proliferates, so too do international and transnational law enforcement efforts: "as crime problems become more global, ... so do the responses to these problems."[8] But although the frequency explanation is important, it is insufficient on its own to explain the increased scrutiny that this conduct has received.

War crimes, for example, have long been proscribed, and they have never been rare. But the willingness to treat them seriously has been sporadic. Much of the conduct that is the focus of transnational criminal law has not always been regarded as criminal domestically, let alone as an object of international concern. Or, as Peter Andreas and Ethan Nadelmann have claimed, "there is nothing natural, permanent, or inevitable about what states choose to criminalize or decriminalize."[9] International and transnational law enforcement do not simply respond to an objective phenomenon known as international or transnational crime. Instead, they reflect decisions about what should be criminal, and what kinds of responses are appropriate to the conduct classified as criminal.

Andreas and Nadelmann suggest a three-part narrative to explain the expansion of international criminalization:

> A liberal story emphasizing the growth of international police cooperation propelled by mutual interests between increasingly interdependent states in a context of more intensive and expansive transnational interactions; ... a realist story stressing the enduring importance of power, conflict, and the priorities and influences of dominant states in shaping the agenda, reach,

and intensity of international crime control; and ... a constructivist story highlighting how and why certain cross-border activities once considered "normal" are redefined and condemned as "deviant" – often through the proselytizing activities of transnational moral entrepreneurs – and become the subject of prohibition norms possessed of powerful symbolic appeal regardless of their effectiveness.[10]

At the risk of oversimplifying, this passage urges attention not just to rational interests and international cooperation, but also to political and military power, advocacy, and the importance of change and contingency. Perhaps more important, Andreas and Nadelmann's analysis makes clear that the rise of enforcement networks is not simply responsive to crime but also plays a role in the creation of crime.

For a variety of reasons, then, the categories of international and transnational crime have grown at the same time that international law enforcement has expanded. Federal criminal law demonstrates this expansion by regulating and frequently criminalizing a variety of overseas conduct (1) engaged in by U.S. nationals, (2) affecting U.S. nationals wherever they may be, or (3) having effects in the United States. The topics covered by these statutes include antitrust, securities law, trade regulation, bribery, drugs and other forms of contraband, money laundering, fraud, human trafficking and sexual activity with minors, as well as torture, war crimes, and, of course, terrorism. Immigration law likely provides the largest percentage of transnational crime prosecuted in the United States, as well as a significant percentage of all U.S. prosecutions, through its criminalization of illegal entry into the country (the crime of crossing the border).[11]

International conventions have likewise established numerous crimes and have called upon signatory countries to enact new criminal laws or revise old ones to address problems of transnational scope.[12] Alongside these new or revised crimes one typically finds a treaty-based obligation to extradite fugitives or prosecute them domestically. Bilateral extradition treaties also create a web of obligations to arrest and return fugitives, and many of the limitations that these treaties traditionally contained – such as a limited list of eligible crimes and relatively robust political offense exceptions – are giving way to a more categorical approach.[13] Most of these agreements contemplate prosecution in domestic courts, but, as noted previously, the establishment of a permanent International Criminal Court creates an additional forum for certain international crimes.

In addition, countries have entered into formal mutual assistance treaties or less formal assistance agreements. These treaties and agreements help investigators and prosecutors exchange information, gather evidence that will be admissible in court, freeze assets, and otherwise smooth the transnational investigation of criminal activity. Officials often also engage in informal cooperation on a case-by-case basis with their colleagues in other countries.[14]

These developments produce real benefits. While there may be nothing natural about what states choose to criminalize, the topics covered by transnational and international criminal law include conduct that causes meaningful harm and that does so across borders. Certainly, some topics could be excluded, others could be included, and one can always question the allocation of enforcement resources among crimes. Even more, as Andreas and Nadelmann point out, transnational and international crime control efforts often reflect domestic politics and power imbalances among countries. But none of these points fatally undermines the conclusion that policy makers in good faith could decide that these crime control efforts are a reasonable response to conduct that causes transnational and international harm.

Yet even if one assumes that the growth and increasing institutionalization of international and transnational crime control generate benefits, important questions remain. To some extent, these questions mirror the significant but also familiar human and constitutional rights issues that always accompany the investigation and prosecution of crime (such as those discussed in many of the other chapters in this volume). But the cross-border aspects of crime control efforts add a new dimension to the issues raised by domestic law enforcement practices. Saskia Sassen's work on globalization helps provide an analytical framework for these issues. Sassen contends that the economic aspects of globalization have important consequences for the distribution of power within countries. Specifically, she argues that increasing internationalization leads to a concentration of power in the executive officials who have primary responsibility for foreign relations. These gains come at the expense primarily of the legislature, while the judiciary's relative position is less clear (although it certainly has not gained power).[15] In other words, whether or not globalization weakens national sovereignty, it enhances executive power. Further, as Sassen observes, the existence of "a national security emergency" such as the war on terror will resonate with and accelerate the already existing trend toward greater executive power.[16]

2. THE NATIONAL SECURITY SOVEREIGN

This section considers the national security sovereign in the United States. I begin by briefly outlining some of the factors in the growth of federal executive power during the past eighty or so years. Next, I describe the failure of courts to prevent this increase in power. Finally, I sketch the scope and power of the contemporary national security sovereign.

a. The Growth of Executive Power

In the United States, the executive branch has primary authority for foreign relations. Although there is ample reason to debate the extent to which the Constitution actually vests the executive branch and/or the president with this power,[17] as a practical matter the executive branch has enormous authority. First, the president easily becomes a focal point for national authority vis-à-vis other countries, in part because the executive branch often can act quickly, and in part because it is easier for other countries to deal with one person, or with people who are beholden to only one person, than it is to deal with a legislative body. Second, presidents and other executive branch officials have persistently sought to increase their ability to make policy, often at the expense of Congress. Third, Congress has frequently collaborated in those efforts and in particular has vested the president with significant discretionary authority. Some of this authority consists of everyday regulatory authority to craft regulations that control the implementation of statutes and that can be changed by successive administrations without congressional control. Other grants of authority focus on empowering the president to act in a crisis. By the 1970s, for example, more than four hundred pieces of legislation provided the executive branch with emergency power in particular sets of circumstances, often dealing with international issues.[18]

As Sassen points out, the expansion of executive authority occurs most easily during national security crises – and war is perhaps the ultimate "crisis." The United States has been at war, or engaged militarily in some way, for most of the last seventy-five years, beginning with World War II, followed by the cold war that lasted until 1989 and included numerous subwars and proxy wars in Asia, Africa, the Middle East, and Central America. After the cold war ended, the United States fought the Gulf War in 1991. The wars in Afghanistan and Iraq followed a decade later, with the conflict in Afghanistan continuing as this book goes to press. Throughout this period, the United States has also been the dominant economic and military power in the world. As one would expect, it has sought to use that power to advance its national interests. Along the way, these interests have been increasingly redefined as national security interests – to the extent that one now frequently encounters the argument that economic policy *is* national security policy.[19]

b. Judicial Deference to Executive Foreign Relations Authority

Although foreign relations and national security issues often reach the federal courts, the Supreme Court usually defers to executive action in these areas.[20] This deference extends beyond policy judgments. It includes, for example, questions about the legal meaning of treaties. The Supreme Court has held that "the Executive Branch's interpretation of a treaty 'is entitled to great weight.'"[21] Courts sometimes also defer to executive branch determinations of factual issues in national security cases.[22]

The reasons for this deference are in part pragmatic. The federal courts lack the tools to second-guess policy decisions that may turn on confidential communications. Even when the issue appears to be one of law, judges are reluctant to intrude or create clear rules when Congress has not done so in an area that they likely see as requiring discretionary evaluation of factors such as possible "diplomatic consequences."[23]

These pragmatic attitudes find theoretical and doctrinal reinforcement in the case law. In *United States v. Curtiss-Wright Export Corporation*, the Supreme Court declared that the foreign relations power is different from other types of federal power. "The investment of the federal government with the powers of external sovereignty did not depend upon the affirmative grants of the Constitution." Instead, the various aspects of the foreign relations power are "vested in the federal government as necessary concomitants of nationality." The Court also addressed the division of authority over this nontextual power: "participation in the exercise of the [foreign relations] power is significantly limited. In this vast external realm, ... the President alone has the power to speak or listen as a representative of the nation." The Court stressed "the very delicate, plenary and exclusive power of the President as the sole organ of the federal government in the field of international relations – a power which does not require as a basis for its exercise an act of Congress."[24]

In *Youngstown Sheet & Tube v. Sawyer*, the Court rejected the Truman administration's claim that the various grants of executive power allowed it to take over private steel mills during the Korean War.[25] But *Youngstown* is most famous for Justice Jackson's concurring opinion, which suggested three categories for the exercise of presidential power: (1) the president acts pursuant to congressional authority; (2) the president acts in the absence of any grant or denial of authority from Congress; and (3) the president acts against the will of Congress, such that he must rely on a claim of authority that Congress cannot reach. Justice Jackson also suggested a sliding scale of deference by the courts, with great deference paid to actions in the first category, little deference to those in the third category, and a case-by-case approach to those in the second category.[26]

In *Dames & Moore v. Regan*, the Court adopted but also modified Jackson's analysis, stating, "it is doubtless the case that executive action in any particular instance falls, not neatly in one of three pigeonholes, but rather at some point along a spectrum running from explicit congressional authorization to explicit congressional prohibition. This is particularly true as respects cases ... involving responses to international crises the nature of which Congress can hardly have been expected to anticipate in any detail."[27] By framing the inquiry in this way, *Dames & Moore* encourages judicial deference to executive power unless Congress has explicitly and legitimately exercised its authority to constrain the president.[28]

Even the set of cases that appears to reject deference – the detention cases involving people imprisoned at Guantánamo Bay Naval Base[29] – ultimately rejects only the more extreme claims of executive power made by the George W. Bush administration. The cases boil down to the propositions that the president does not have an inherent power to detain people indefinitely or to create ad hoc military commissions to try them, and that persons detained by the executive branch presumptively have a constitutional right of access to the courts to test the legality of their detentions. In the wake of these cases, the administration created an administrative review process that provided little in the way of concrete remedies; Congress passed the Military Commissions Act, which created a statutory structure within which the executive branch could exercise its discretion about whether and how to try suspected terrorists; lower courts frequently invoked deference principles and ruled in favor of the government in individual cases; and the Supreme Court receded into silence.[30]

The federal judiciary, in brief, is reluctant to interfere in issues that have foreign relations or national security overtones unless the president is acting in fairly clear violation of the Constitution or a federal statute.[31] Even when it addresses these issues, it is reluctant to create clear and constraining boundaries for the exercise of executive power. As a result, Congress and the president are usually left to resolve these issues on their own. The conventional wisdom is that in such cases, the president "almost always wins."[32]

c. *The Scope and Power of the National Security Sovereign*

Speaking broadly, the result of executive efforts to gain power, legislative delegations of authority, judicial accommodation, an expanding definition of national security interests, and the near-constant projection of military power overseas is an enormous amount of authority within the executive branch to make policy across a wide range of topics. Congress certainly plays an important role, but it does not set, or even in most cases control, the agenda. The courts check but do not seriously impede executive authority.

What does this expanded executive power allow? In addition to a fairly free hand with diplomacy and other forms of international engagement, the national security sovereign must manage the various crises and events that arise regularly in international affairs. The ultimate goal is to advance the interests of the United States – which usually means advancing the goals of the administration in power (although on many issues there is rough consistency across administrations). Among the tools available to the president are nearly unregulated power to deploy military forces, seize or kill people anywhere in the world – and in the era of drone warfare, this is not a hyperbolic statement – or disrupt national governments and economies in ways that cause serious hardship for the residents of those countries.[33] The executive's power over national security and its enormous influence over what counts as a national security issue also give it enormous influence over the agendas and outcomes of national domestic politics.

Whether or not it is appropriate to speak of a national security sovereign (rather than of, say, an imperial presidency) in the late twentieth century, the term certainly became apt after September 11, 2001. Rahm Emmanuel, President Obama's first chief of staff, famously declared that "you never want a serious crisis to go to waste,"[34] and the George W. Bush administration wasted little time in asserting executive authority that went beyond previous responses to terrorism. Among other things, the Bush administration claimed extensive and unilateral power to engage in surveillance, use military force, detain people without a hearing, conduct coercive interrogations, convene military commissions to conduct criminal trials, and move people from one country to another without process and for the purpose of coercive interrogation (the process known as "extraordinary rendition").[35] Initially, Congress went along with this assertion of executive power. It passed an Authorization to Use Military Force that allowed the executive branch to militarize the response to the 9/11 attacks. Soon after, it passed the USA PATRIOT Act, which expanded the powers of law enforcement officials to investigate criminal activity, whether or not that activity could be defined as "terrorist," and cleared the way for greater sharing of information between law enforcement and military officials. Subsequent legislation confirmed that counterterrorism and national security concerns had expanded and enveloped other areas of government activity, with the consequence that more executive power and discretion and new organizational structures (such as the Homeland Security Department) were necessary.[36] Although the Obama administration has stepped back from the more extreme claims of the Bush administration, it has not rejected very much of the broad authority that it inherited.[37]

Having suggested the relentless expansion of executive power, I also want to avoid exaggerating that power or its cohesiveness. The president wields enormous authority, but that does not mean he gets whatever he wants. Most foreign relations decisions and initiatives are implemented through the federal bureaucracy, which allows turf fighting and impedes White House efforts to oversee and control the details of that implementation. Initiatives and exercises of power often fail to accomplish all of their goals, or they have unintended consequences – as with the war in Afghanistan or the furor over coercive interrogation. Congress and the federal courts can limit executive initiatives – as with the Supreme Court's refusal to sanction some of the Bush administration's practices at Guantánamo and some of the provisions that Congress inserted into the Detainee Treatment Act to restrain coercive interrogation[38] (as well as, more generally, through such factors as Congress's appropriations and advise and consent powers and its ability to hold hearings and conduct investigations). Media scrutiny and the efforts of public interest and advocacy organizations can also hinder or deflect executive efforts.[39]

None of these counterforces currently operates to *prevent* the continued overall expansion of executive power. Indeed, I would argue that congressional second-guessing and judicial intervention have done more to ratify and stabilize the national security sovereign than to undermine it. The rise and expansion of the national security sovereign, therefore, are real and ongoing. And, as the next section suggests, the power of the national security sovereign may be particularly strong in matters related to criminal law. But it is also important to recognize, first, that the expansion of the national security sovereign proceeds in fits and starts and, second, that tools exist for limiting and perhaps even controlling it.

3. THE NATIONAL SECURITY SOVEREIGN AND CRIMINAL LAW

Terrorism is a focal point for the intersection of criminal law with national security law and policy. But the national security sovereign's involvement with criminal law, particularly transnational crime and crime control, is much broader. From a formal perspective, the existence of national borders and the resulting need to interact with the governments of other countries mean that the executive branch must be involved in some way. But the scope of executive involvement in transnational criminal issues owes at least as much to the fact that those issues increasingly are defined as national security issues.

a. Criminal Law as a National Security Issue

Historically, the military has sometimes been involved in transnational and international criminal law enforcement.[40] Also, in 1800, the controversy over the extradition of Jonathan Robbins to Britain required executive and legislative officials to navigate the overlap of criminal justice, foreign relations, and executive powers issues. During the intense debate about Robbins in the House of Representatives, John Marshall famously described the president as "the sole organ of the nation in its external relations."[41] Even today, some federal judges assert that international extradition – which involves the forcible transfer of a person across a national border, after a hearing of some kind, for the purpose of facing criminal charges in the receiving country – is within the president's "plenary authority."[42] And federal courts repeatedly reject individual rights claims in extradition cases on the ground that they must defer to the executive branch in this area.[43] The border, after all, is the place where government power and legal rights shift from one sovereign authority to another. Where criminal law touches a border, the extradition cases suggest, executive power may be more important than due process.

Still, the intersection between national security and criminal law did not emerge as a persistent and central aspect of governance in the United States until after World War II. As the world's dominant economic and military power, the United States played a leading role in pushing for international criminal enforcement in various areas, including drugs and terrorism.[44] Well before 9/11, political figures in the United States spoke of the "war on drugs" as a national security issue.[45] President Clinton referred to "international criminals" as "our enemies,"[46] and Deputy Attorney General Jamie Gorelick declared that "'both conceptually and on the ground' there has been 'a real shift in the paradigm of national security'" to include transnational crime issues.[47] Military and intelligence operations began to include law enforcement functions.[48] And as the United States internationalized these issues, other countries felt increasing amounts of pressure to go along.[49]

After surveying these developments, two commentators advanced the following conclusions in the fall of 2001:

> With security policy focusing increasingly on policing, the traditional distinctions between external and internal security – so central to the old security paradigm – begin to break down. As they break down, the distinction between law enforcement and military missions breaks down, too: military tasks become increasingly domesticated and civilianized, and policing tasks become increasingly internationalized and militarized. In short, there is a growing fusion between the world of military affairs and the world of

police affairs, not to mention the world of security scholars and the world of criminologists.[50]

These empirically based conclusions dovetail with more theoretical assessments. Wars traditionally have been bounded in terms of duration and objectives. Policing, by contrast, is an ongoing effort, part of the modern state's efforts to maintain social order. When the functions of policing are defined in terms of war, the idea of war itself transforms, for "[a] war to create and maintain social order can have no end. It must involve the continuous, uninterrupted exercise of power and violence."[51] As war becomes "virtually indistinguishable from police activity," "international relations and domestic politics become increasingly similar and intermingled," and "there is ever less distance between inside and outside the nation state: low-intensity warfare meets high-intensity policing."[52]

The overlaps between national security and criminal justice, and between the activities of war and policing, affect and potentially transform both fields. And this potential became starkly clear after 9/11, when antiterror efforts became an increasing focus of U.S. military strategy as well as a more central part of traditional federal law enforcement.[53] But the recent antiterror campaigns are not a break with the past. Instead, they accelerate and intensify an already existing trend toward greater executive branch involvement with overseas and transnational crime control efforts and toward defining these efforts in national security terms.

b. Power and Discretion

No federal statute spells out the specific powers of federal law enforcement officials. Their authority derives from ideas about the nature of executive authority, common law, and constitutional restrictions on particular investigative techniques. Thus, unless the Constitution prohibits a particular practice, law enforcement officials have broad discretion to investigate crimes. Nor do specific constitutional rights always provide a clear limit on investigative authority. Constitutional criminal procedure doctrine tends to rely on reasonableness tests, which often means "an assessment of what accommodation between governmental need and individual freedom is reasonable."[54]

When the federal government engages in law enforcement efforts overseas, its powers are even greater, because the constraints on its authority become more amorphous as a matter of domestic law, particularly when the target of federal power is not a U.S. citizen. There is no agreement on the extent to which the Constitution controls the actions of the federal government outside its borders. Some argue that it can never act without constitutional authority; some argue that it has inherent authority as a sovereign nation to act; and others attempt to stake out intermediate positions. No recent Supreme Court majority has clearly adopted one of these positions.[55]

The courts impose few if any restrictions on the manner in which foreign nationals residing overseas end up in the United States to face criminal proceedings. In response to a defendant's claim that he had been kidnapped by U.S. agents, the Supreme Court held that it "need not inquire as to how respondent came before it."[56] A federal circuit court once suggested that it could dismiss an indictment based on outrageous government conduct, but no court has ever done so and most circuits have found ways to distance themselves from the earlier case.[57] Recent administrations have responded by using "rendition," which is simply the effort to obtain criminal suspects without having to address the limits of extradition treaties and delays in the legal systems of other countries. These renditions usually have taken place with the cooperation of officials in the other country, but U.S. officials have also resorted to kidnapping. The Bush administration famously expanded this effort to include transferring people to counties that would interrogate and torture them (or that would allow the CIA to do so). The Obama administration ended this program of "extraordinary rendition," but it did not reject rendition itself.[58]

With respect to other rights claims, the Supreme Court has held that the Fourth Amendment does not apply (or rarely applies) to overseas law enforcement activity.[59] Lower courts have held that the self-incrimination clause does apply, because it is a trial right, but that the *Miranda* doctrine applies in a relaxed way.[60] Noncitizens held by U.S. officials at Guantánamo Bay Naval Base have the right to seek habeas corpus relief in federal court, but it is not clear whether this right extends to people held in locations over which the United States does not have de facto sovereignty.[61] Military officials have made it difficult for lawyers to gain adequate access to their clients at Guantánamo – a group that includes people who are eligible for criminal prosecution.[62]

When enforcement of criminal law is entwined with military operations, constitutional constraints become even more relaxed. For example, when President Obama authorized the killing of Anwar al-Awlaki, who was associated with al-Qaeda and involved in terrorist activities, but who was also an American citizen and was not participating in hostilities in Afghanistan, "the Justice Department's Office of Legal Counsel prepared a lengthy memo … asserting that while the Fifth Amendment's guarantee of due process applied, it could be satisfied by internal deliberations in the executive branch."[63] Was al-Awlaki a potential criminal defendant, or was he an enemy combatant whom the president was able to target pursuant to Congress's Authorization to Use Military Force? He was both, and regardless of his citizenship, the executive branch had discretion to choose the category that best accorded with its policies and priorities.[64] The same basic dynamic plays out for many of the people the United States has captured during the war on terror. They could be classified as criminal defendants and brought to trial before a federal court, or they could be prosecuted before military commissions for violations of the laws of war – and federal courts have little or no say about the choice of forum.[65]

In addition to the flexibility of constitutional constraints, the executive branch has significant authority in criminal law because of the prosecutorial power. "No government official in America has as much unreviewable power and discretion as the prosecutor."[66]

> Beyond the decision of whether or not to prosecute, a federal prosecutor also has discretion in deciding how to prosecute. The Prosecutor chooses which crime to charge.... The prosecutor chooses when to grant immunity, accept a plea bargain, and dismiss charges. Once those choices are made, "no court has any jurisdiction to inquire into or review" a prosecutor's decision to treat differently "[t]wo persons [who] may have committed what is precisely the same legal offense.[67]

Importantly, one of the primary justifications for prosecutorial discretion is that it reflects separation of powers values, yet although "in theory the separation of powers should check prosecutors, in practice it does not."[68] Still, prosecutors do face constraints in ordinary cases. But, the joining of prosecutorial discretion and transnational criminal enforcement further magnifies the power of the national security sovereign, including the power to decide what laws, and what exceptions to those laws, apply in particular situations.[69]

c. Risks

The intersection of executive power over transnational criminal law enforcement and the national security sovereign creates a series of risks, three of which I will highlight here. First, to the extent that law enforcement activities produce criminal cases, the defendants in those cases will raise the same kinds of rights claims that defendants raise in domestic cases. Because of the pressures of national security, courts likely will try to avoid these claims by, for example, finding that the rights have no extraterritorial force. But courts sometimes will have to reach the merits, and the same national security pressures will probably produce rulings in favor of the government – similar to the way in which the war on drugs put pressure on constitutional criminal procedure doctrine.[70] Importantly – and again as with the war on drugs – the holdings in these cases will generalize; the changes in doctrine that they create will apply to all criminal cases, in state and federal court.[71]

Second, the pressures of criminal cases that have national security overtones could also lead to changes in the definitions of crimes. To some extent, this has already started to happen with conspiracy law.[72] Perhaps, too, the emphasis on investigation and prosecution of terrorism will lead to more prosecutions of domestic defendants as "domestic terrorists" under federal law, where before such people would have been tried in state courts or under federal statutes that do not target terrorism.[73] Relatedly, national security concerns can lead Congress to define new crimes or to expand existing ones to cover a wide variety of conduct. The crime of material support to terrorism, created in 1994 and modified several times since then, is an important example.[74] These new or expanded crimes may impact behavior that not only was law-abiding before the new statutes but also does not pose significant risks of harm.[75]

Third, to the extent that transnational criminal law becomes a tool of foreign policy and diplomacy, criminal justice will increasingly become a creature of policy rather than of law. Criminal justice has never been entirely separate from politics, but those politics typically have been domestic in focus. As criminal enforcement efforts become increasingly entwined with national security, and as the distinction between foreign and domestic affairs becomes increasingly blurred, the politics of criminal justice will increasingly overlap with the politics of foreign relations and national security. Decisions about investigation, arrest or detention, and prosecution increasingly will be the province of an executive discretion that is not confined by the legal and institutional constraints that restrain traditional prosecutions. Importantly, moreover, federal officials have little incentive to pay much attention to the rights claims of foreign defendants and others caught up in law enforcement activity. Particularly when criminal investigations merge with national security and military objectives, so that actual prosecution may take a back seat to other goals, such as obtaining information, courts may never have the chance to assess the conduct of executive officials.[76]

At present, these paragraphs describe risks, not reality, except in extradition cases. But to the extent the risk increases, traditional rule of law values will erode.

4. CONCLUSION: CONTROLLING THE NATIONAL SECURITY SOVEREIGN

I have raised the prospect of an increasingly powerful national security sovereign that will fundamentally upset separation of powers and alter the rule of law. I have also tried to make clear that although this prospect does not match current reality, it could be an important part of criminal law's future.

Against that prospect, a variety of tools are available for limiting the power of the national security sovereign. First, Congress should increase its oversight of national security issues, and it should resist efforts to obfuscate or classify information about executive activity. Congress should also become more aggressive with respect to its enumerated powers to make appropriations and regulate the military.

Litigants must continue to press courts to hear cases that challenge executive excess. Familiar separation of powers and individual rights claims could still gain traction. In addition, international law provides significant support for rule of law-based challenges, either on its own or in conjunction with domestic law claims. International human rights law has expanded at the same time that international criminal enforcement efforts have increased, and litigants should press the claim that this is not a coincidence and that it makes sense for the former to limit the latter. Even though U.S. courts are sometimes dismissive of international law claims, newer generations of lawyers and judges are increasingly comfortable with international human rights law and the demands it makes on government officials.

At the very least, policy makers, journalists, and other analysts and commentators should ask hard questions about the national security sovereign. How much do we want to restrict it? What are the potential risks and benefits of stepping back from the present, nearly unbounded, conception of foreign affairs and national security power vested in the executive branch? How should the United States respond to international and transnational crime? How much do national or constitutional rights depend on the executive's discretionary power over borders and the people moving across them? How far do constitutional rights and constitutional limitations extend – are they only for some people in some places, or do they limit the government wherever, however, and against whomever it acts?

At the end of the day, the most likely results are that executive power will continue to expand in the next decades and that this expansion will have increasing consequences for criminal justice and domestic activities more generally. If this prediction of continued expansion is accurate, then self-restraint on the part of the national security sovereign becomes a necessary, albeit limited, goal. The Obama administration has presented itself as a kind of "enlightened" national security sovereign, but it would be naïve to expect much from this kind of self-imposed constraint. James Madison argued that, for separation of powers to work, "ambition must be made to counteract ambition." The failure to counteract executive ambition has allowed a "gradual concentration" of power that, in turn, has produced the national security sovereign.[77] The rule of law that results from these developments is itself a work in progress.

Notes

1. E.g., CARL SCHMITT, POLITICAL THEOLOGY: FOUR CHAPTERS ON THE CONCEPT OF SOVEREIGNTY 1 (George Schwab trans., University of Chicago Press, 2006) (1922) ("Sovereign is he who decides on the exception.").
2. Cf. MARK TUSHNET, EMERGENCIES AND THE IDEA OF CONSTITUTIONALISM, IN THE CONSTITUTION IN WARTIME: BEYOND ALARMISM AND COMPLACENCY 45 (2005) ("The already long duration of the 'war on terrorism' suggests that we ought not to think of it as a war in the sense that the Second World War was a war. It is, perhaps, more like a condition than a war – more like the war on cancer, the war on poverty, or, most pertinently, the war on crime. Suspending legality during a time-limited war is one thing. Suspending it during more or less permanent condition is quite another. The latter is the end of the rule of law itself.").
3. Pirates themselves are not necessarily stateless, and they eventually must come to port somewhere. Often, they have dropped anchor in the harbors of sympathetic or weak governments. "Prior to the seventeenth century,... piracy was widely sanctioned in much of the world [as a] source of wealth and political power." PETER ANDREAS & ETHAN NADELMANN, POLICING THE GLOBE: CRIMINALISATION AND CRIME CONTROL IN INTERNATIONAL RELATIONS 22 (2006).
4. See *id*. at ch. 1; ROBERT MANDEL, DARK LOGIC: INTERNATIONAL CRIMINAL TACTICS AND GLOBAL SECURITY (2011). "Terrorism" is a notoriously difficult word to define, or at least to define in a consistent fashion and with a broad consensus, and I will not venture a definition here. For brief discussion of this point and a survey of U.S. definitions of terrorism, see DAVID LUBAN, JULIE R. O'SULLIVAN & DAVID P. STEWART, INTERNATIONAL AND TRANSNATIONAL CRIMINAL LAW 669–77 (2010). For some of the issues relating to the European effort to define terrorism, see Matthias J. Borgers, *Framework Decision on Combatting Terrorism: Two Questions on the Definition of Terrorist Offences*, 3 NEW EUR. J. CRIM. L. 68 (2012).
5. Luban, et al., supra note 4, at 4. For a helpful discussion of the differences among transnational crimes, international crimes, and treaty-based domestic crimes, see *id*. at 3–5.
6. Convention (No. III) Relative to the Protection of Prisoners of War, arts. 129, 130 (1949), 75 U.N.T.S. 135.
7. Rome Statute of the International Criminal Court, arts. 5, 9, 25 (1998); Official Journal of the International Criminal Court: Elements of Crimes (2002). The ICC's ability to implement its jurisdiction presents a set of issues that are well beyond the scope of this chapter.
8. Andreas & Nadelmann, supra note 3, at 7.
9. *Id*. at 13. See also Eugene Kontorovich, *The Piracy Analogy: Modern Universal Jurisdiction's Hollow Foundation*, 45 HARV. INT'L L.J. 183, 188–94 (2004) (making the point that piracy and slavery have not always been subject to universal condemnation and that efforts to restrict them have sometimes conflicted with the practices of states).
10. Andreas & Nadelmann, supra note 3, at 7.

11 See 8 U.S.C. §§ 1325, 1326. Juliet Stumpf's chapter in this collection provides a helpful overview of the rise of what she has termed "crimmigration" law.
12 E.g., Convention against Torture and Other Cruel, Inhuman or Degrading Treatment or Punishment, art. 4, Dec. 10, 1984, 1465 U.N.T.S. 85 ("1. Each State Party shall ensure that all acts of torture [as defined by the Convention] are offences under its criminal law. The same shall apply to an attempt to commit torture and to an act by any person which constitutes complicity or participation in torture. 2. Each State Party shall make these offences punishable by appropriate penalties which take into account their grave nature.").
13 For a useful overview of extradition, see M. CHERIF BASSIOUNI, INTERNATIONAL EXTRADITION: U.S. LAW AND PRACTICE (5th ed., 2007).
14 For useful overviews of formal and informal mutual assistance, see Andreas & Nadelmann, supra note 3, at 141–9, and Luban, et al., supra note 4, at 374–87.
15 SASKIA SASSEN, TERRITORY, AUTHORITY, RIGHTS: FROM MEDIEVAL TO GLOBAL ASSEMBLAGES 168–84 (2006).
16 *Id.* at 176–7.
17 My reference to "the executive branch and/or the President" is simply an effort to sidestep the textual and originalist aspects of the unitary executive debate.
18 See Jules Lobel, *Emergency Power and the Decline of Liberalism*, 98 YALE L.J. 1385, 1408 (1989). Congress does not always go in one direction, of course. The War Powers Resolution of 1973, 50 U.S.C. §§ 1541–1548, is an effort to control the President's ability to use military force overseas, but few commentators believe that it has significant constraining force. Perhaps the most significant piece of relevant legislation is the National Security Act of 1947, which centralized executive authority over and propelled the growth of the national security bureaucracy. See DOUGLAS T. STUART, CREATING THE NATIONAL SECURITY STATE: A HISTORY OF THE LAW THAT TRANSFORMED AMERICA (2008).
19 E.g., Sydney J. Freedberg Jr., *Biggest Security Threat: Economic Crisis*, NAT'L SEC. EXPERTS BLOG (Mar. 2, 2009, 7:34 AM) http://security.nationaljournal.com/2009/03/biggest-security-threat-econom.php (last visited May 1, 2013); Walter Pincus, *Keys to National Security Start with the Economy, Group Says*, WASHINGTON POST, Apr. 30, 2010, http://www.washingtonpost.com/wp-dyn/content/article/2010/04/12/AR2010041203959.html (last visited May 1, 2013).
20 E.g., *Jama v. Immigration & Customs Enforcement*, 543 U.S. 335, 348 (2005) (refusing to interpret a statute in a way that "would run counter to our customary policy of deference to the President on matters of foreign affairs").
21 *Abbott v. Abbott*, 130 S. Ct. 1983, 1993 (2010).
22 See Robert M. Chesney, *National Security Fact Deference*, 95 VA. L. REV. 1361 (2009).
23 *Abbott*, 130 S. Ct. at 1993.
24 *United States v. Curtiss-Wright Exp. Corp.*, 299 U.S. 304, 315–20 (1936).
25 *Youngstown Sheet & Tube Co. v. Sawyer*, 343 U.S. 579 (1952).
26 *Id.* at 635–8 (Jackson, J., concurring).
27 *Dames & Moore v. Regan*, 453 U.S. 654, 669 (1981).
28 For criticism of *Dames & Moore* for "champion[ing] unguided executive activism and congressional acquiescence in foreign affairs over the constitutional principle of balanced institutional participation," see HAROLD HONGJU KOH, THE NATIONAL

SECURITY CONSTITUTION: SHARING POWER AFTER THE IRAN-CONTRA AFFAIR 140 (1990). Koh later asserted that pre-2001 national security policy rested on the premise of "an energetic executive, to be sure, but one checked by an energetic Congress and overseen by a searching judicial branch." Harold Hongju Koh, *America and the World, 2020*, in THE CONSTITUTION IN 2020, at 316 (Jack M. Balkin & Reva B. Siegel, eds., 2009). Both statements exaggerate, but the earlier one is closer to the mark.

29 See *Rasul v. Bush*, 542 U.S. 466 (2004); *Hamdi v. Rumsfeld*, 542 U.S. 507 (2004); *Hamdam v. Rumsfeld*, 548 U.S. 557 (2006); *Boumediene v. Bush*, 553 U.S. 723 (2008).

30 For the administrative review process, see Mark Denbeaux et al., *No-Hearing Hearings: An Analysis of the Proceedings of the Combatant Status Review Tribunals at Guantanamo*, 41 SETON HALL L. REV. 1231 (2011). For the Military Commissions Act and its aftermath, see JOHN T. PARRY, UNDERSTANDING TORTURE: LAW, VIOLENCE, AND POLITICAL IDENTITY 200–1 (2010). For discussion of lower court cases in the D.C. Circuit, see Stephen I. Vladeck, *The D.C. Circuit after Boumediene*, 41 SETON HALL L. REV. 1451 (2011).

31 The political question doctrine provides a concrete example. Although the doctrine has relatively little traction in domestic law disputes, it is more robust in the foreign relations area as a way for courts to avoid litigation of foreign policy disputes. For a useful and succinct overview of political question doctrine and foreign relations, see CURTIS A. BRADLEY & JACK L. GOLDSMITH, FOREIGN RELATIONS LAW 58–62 (4th ed., 2011). Another example is the rule of non-inquiry in international extradition. Courts refuse to inquire into the treatment that a person might receive in the country that is seeking the extradition, and a chief reason is deference to executive foreign relations authority. See John T. Parry, *International Extradition, the Rule of Non-Inquiry, and the Problem of Sovereignty*, 90 B.U. L. REV. 1973, 1994–5 (2010).

32 See Harold Hongju Koh, *Why the President (Almost) Always Wins in Foreign Affairs: Lessons of the Iran-Contra Affair*, 97 YALE L.J. 1255 (1988).

33 By "nearly unregulated power," I mean to highlight the fairly limited role of judicial and congressional oversight. The executive branch has internal processes that guide the exercise of power, but I would not call those processes "regulation" in a separation of powers sense.

34 Gerald F. Seib, *In Crisis, Opportunity for Obama*, WALL ST. J., Nov. 21, 2008, http://online.wsj.com/article/SB122721278056345271.html (last visited May 1, 2013).

35 Many of these assertions appear in memoranda prepared by the Justice Department's Office of Legal Counsel. For a brief discussion, see Parry, *Understanding Torture*, supra note 30, at 168–77.

36 See John T. Parry, *Terrorism and the New Criminal Process*, 15 WM. & MARY BILL RTS. J. 765, 779–82 (2007).

37 For the claim of important differences between the George W. Bush and Obama administrations on these issues, see David Cole, *Obama and Terror: The Hovering Question*, N.Y. REV. OF BOOKS (July 12, 2012), http://www.nybooks.com/articles/archives/2012/jul/12/obama-and-terror-hovering-questions/ (last visited May 1, 2013). For the argument that the similarities are more important than the differences, see JACK GOLDSMITH, POWER AND CONSTRAINT: THE ACCOUNTABLE PRESIDENCY AFTER 9/11 (2012); see also Tung Yin, *"Anything But Bush?": The*

Obama Administration and Guantanamo Bay, 34 HARV. J. L. & PUB. POL'Y 453 (2010).

38 For general discussion, see Parry, *Terrorism and the New Criminal Process*, supra note 36, at 780–2.
39 For the claim that these factors played an important role during the George W. Bush administration, see Goldsmith, *Power and Constraint*, supra note 37. See also *Binding the Executive (by Law or Politics)*, 79 U. CHI. L. REV. 777, 781 (2012) (arguing that "even in the heart of crisis, and even on matters where executive competence is supposedly at an acme, legislators employ formal institutional powers not only to delay executive initiatives but also affirmatively to end presidential policies.").
40 For example, the British and U.S. Navies attacked pirates and their bases. See Andreas & Nadelmann, supra note 3, at 23–4. The British Navy and, to a much lesser extent, the U.S. Navy, also helped suppress the slave trade. See *id.* at 27, 110. The Mexican Revolution in the early twentieth century also led to military involvement in border control issues. See *id.* at 119–20.
41 Quoted in John T. Parry, *The Lost History of International Extradition Litigation*, 43 VA. J. INT'L L. 93, 112 (2002). See also Ruth Wedgwood, *The Revolutionary Martyrdom of Jonathan Robbins*, 100 YALE L.J. 229 (1990); Michael Van Alstine, *Taking Care of John Marshall's Political Ghost*, 53 ST. LOUIS U. L. J. 93 (2008).
42 *LoDuca v. United States*, 93 F.3d 1100, 1103 n.2 (2nd Cir. 1996). For extensive discussion of executive power and international extradition, see Parry, *International Extradition*, supra note 41.
43 E.g., *Trinidad y Garcia v. Thomas*, 683 F.3d 952, 961 (9th Cir. 2012); see also Parry, *International Extradition*, supra note 41.
44 See Andreas & Nadelmann, supra, at 37–58, 97, 106–7, 171–4.
45 E.g., Victoria Churchville, *Dole: Use Military in Drug War; Candidate Links Issue to National Security*, WASHINGTON POST, Mar. 4, 1988, at A14.
46 Quoted in Andreas & Nadelmann, supra note 3, at 158.
47 Quoted in *id.* and in Peter Andreas & Richard Price, *From War Fighting to Crime Fighting: Transforming the American National Security State*, 3 INT'L STUD. REV. 31, 37 (2001).
48 Andreas & Price, supra note 47, at 40–51. The Posse Comitatus Act prohibits the use of the military "as a posse comitatus or otherwise to execute the laws," 18 U.S.C. § 1385, but Congress has enacted numerous exceptions to the statute. For an overview, see NORMAN ABRAMS, ANTI-TERRORISM AND CRIMINAL ENFORCEMENT 745–69 (4th ed., 2012).
49 Andreas & Nadelmann, supra note 3, at 107.
50 Andreas & Price, supra note 47, at 52. Mandel, supra note 4, is an example of the scholarly aspect of this phenomenon; he calls for an international effort against organized crime that would, among other things, combine police and military action.
51 MICHAEL HARDT & ANTONIO NEGRI, MULTITUDE: WAR AND DEMOCRACY IN THE AGE OF EMPIRE 14 (2004).
52 *Id.* at 341.
53 See Parry, *Understanding Torture*, supra note 30, at 166–70.

54 *Anderson v. Creighton*, 483 U.S. 635, 644 (1987). For elaboration of these points, see Parry, *Terrorism and the New Criminal Process*, supra note 36, at 799–807.
55 For extraterritoriality in general, see Kal Raustiala, Does the Constitution Follow the Flag: The Evolution of Territoriality in American Law (2009). For extraterritoriality and constitutional rights, see Luban, et al., supra note 4, at 297–357.
56 *United States v. Alvarez-Machain*, 504 U.S. 655, 662 (1992).
57 See *United States v. Toscanino*, 500 F.2d 267 (2d Cir. 1974); Arthur D. Hellman, *By Precedent Unbound: The Nature and Extent of Unresolved Intercircuit Conflicts*, 56 U. Pitt. L. Rev. 693, 786 & n.358 (1995) (citing *Toscanino* as an example of a decision "repeatedly distinguished, even in the circuit of origin").
58 For rendition, see Ethan A. Nadelmann, *The Evolution of United States Involvement in the International Rendition of Fugitive Criminals*, 25 N.Y.U. J. Int'l L & Pol. 813 (1993). For extraordinary rendition, see Margaret L. Satterthwaite, *Rendered Meaningless: Extraordinary Rendition and the Rule of Law*, 75 Geo. Wash. L. Rev. 1333 (2007). For the Obama administration, see Jo Becker & Scott Shane, *Secret 'Kill List' Proves a test of Obama's Principles and Will*, N.Y.Times, May 29, 2012, http://www.nytimes.com/2012/05/29/world/obamas-leadership-in-war-on-al-qaeda.html?pagewanted=all (last visited May 1, 2013); Scott Horton, *Target of Obama-Era Rendition Alleges Torture*, Huffington Post (Sept. 11, 2009, last updated May 25, 2011), http://www.huffingtonpost.com/2009/08/11/target-of-obama-era-rendi_n_256499.html (last visited May 1, 2013).
59 *United States v. Verdugo-Urquidez*, 494 U.S. 259 (1990).
60 E.g., *In re Terrorist Bombings*, 552 F.3d 177 (2d Cir. 2008).
61 Compare *Boumediene*, supra note 29 (habeas rights for persons at Guantánamo), with *Al Maqaleh v. Gates*, 605 F.3d 84 (D.C. Cir. 2010) (habeas rights do not always extend to people held at U.S. military bases, particularly those in a theater of war).
62 E.g., Lyle Denniston, *Details of New Limits on Detainees' Lawyers*, Scotusblog (Aug. 7, 2012, 2:31 PM), http://www.scotusblog.com/2012/08/details-of-new-limits-on-detainees-lawyers/ (last visited May 1, 2013). As this book goes to press, a federal district court has blocked this specific set of limitations, but access to and free communication with the detainees has been and remains a challenge for their attorneys.
63 Becker & Shane, supra note 58.
64 For brief discussion of the constitutionality of drone strikes against non-citizens outside the United States, see John T. Parry, *Responses to the Ten Questions*, 36 Wm. Mitchell L. Rev. 5141, 5145–50 (2010) (concluding the Constitution does not impose meaningful constraints).
65 Steve Vladeck's chapter in this volume elaborates on these issues.
66 Stephanos Bibas, *Prosecutorial Regulation verses Prosecutorial Accountability*, 157 U. Pa. L. Rev. 959, 960 (2009).
67 Rebecca Krauss, *The Theory of Prosecutorial Discretion in Federal Law: Origins and Developments*, 6 Seton Hall Circuit Rev. 1, 6 (2009) (citations omitted). For general discussion of prosecutorial power, see Brian Forst, *Prosecution*, in Crime and Public Policy 437–66 (James Q. Wilson & Joan Petersilia, eds., 2011).
68 Bibas, supra note 66, at 961; see also Krauss, supra note 67, at 11–12.

69 See Schmitt supra note 1. Note that Congress has restricted the President's prosecutorial authority in cases involving people at Guantánamo by making it very difficult to try them in domestic Article III courts.
70 One can already see this happening with the *Miranda* doctrine. Although it applies in transnational cases, it does not carry the same force. See *In re Terrorist Bombings*, supra note 60.
71 See William J. Stuntz, *Local Policing after the Terror*, 111 YALE L.J. 2137, 2140 (2002).
72 See Robert M. Chesney, *Beyond Conspiracy: Anticipatory Prosecution and the Challenge of Unaffiliated Terrorism*, 80 S. CAL. L. REV. 425 (2007). Susan Herman's chapter in this volume elaborates on the pressures that anti-terror activities have put on substantive criminal law and constitutional criminal procedure.
73 For the federal distinction between international and domestic terrorism, see 18 U.S.C. § 2331(1) & (5).
74 18 U.S.C. § 2339B.
75 See *Holder v. Humanitarian Law Project*, 130 S. Ct. 2705 (2010) (rejecting vagueness and First Amendment challenges to 18 U.S.C. § 2339B).
76 Civil suits raising abuse allegations against Bush administration officials have largely failed on various procedural grounds.
77 THE FEDERALIST NO. 51 (James Madison).

Index

Abdulmutallab, Umar Farouk, 271
admissibility of confessions, 187
adverse selection, 89
agora, 33
al-Awlaki, Anwar, 322
al-Hussayen, Sami, 264
Ali, Alaa Mohammad, 292
American Law Institute (ALI), 34, 36
American Revolution, 27, 28, 33, 34
anatomists, 30
Andreas, Peter, 312, 313, 314
Antiterrorism and Effective Death Penalty Act of 1996, 263
Arizona v. United States, 242, 244, 253
arrest, 94, 103, 104, 105
arrest efficiency, 59, 71
assumption of risk doctrine, 155, 158, 160
Atkins v. Virginia, 226
attorneys
    competent, 17
Authorization to Use Military Force, 318, 323
autonomy, 33, 37, 38, 96

Bachmann, Talis, 113
Baker, Chief Judge James E., 293
Bandura, Albert, 232
Beason-Hammon Alabama Taxpayer and Citizen Protection Act, 241, 249
Beaumont, Joseph, 122
Beccaria, 28
Bill for Proportioning Crimes and Punishments (1777–79), 29
Bill of Rights, 30
Black, Justice Hugo, 154, 271, 287, 290
Blackstone, 30
Blackstone, William, 268
Blair, James, 224
Bracero Program, 246
Brennan, Justice William, 171
broken windows theory, 49

Burdine, Calvin, 16
Burger, Chief Justice Warren, 155
Burton, Justice Harold, 290
bus sweeps, 96, 102

Camera surveillance, 161
Canada, 27, 38, 39
caseloads
    reasonable, 20
Chertoff, Michael, 268
Civil Commitment, 234
Civil War, 27
Civil War amendments, 33
Classified Information Procedures Act, 268
Cleckley, Hervey, 225
coercion, 174, 181
Coercion error, 173
coercive interrogation, 173
Coke, 29, 30
collateral consequences, 6, 205, 206, 207, 208, 214
colonies, 28
Colorado v. Connelly, 184
compliance, 94, 96, 106
compulsion, 95, 96, 97, 100
Connecticut Department of Public Safety v. Doe, 143
consent, 93, 94, 95, 96, 97, 98, 99, 100, 101, 102, 103, 104, 105
consent searches, 4
conspiracy, 296, 297, 324
contamination, 179, 181
contamination error, 174, 183
cooperation, 93, 96, 97, 106
Court of Appeals for the Armed Forces, 287, 293
Court of Military Appeals, 290, 292
courts-martial, 8, 287
criminal responsibility, 222, 233

crimmigration, 7, 241, 244, 246, 249, 250, 254, 255
critical analysis, 28, 39
cruel and unusual punishment, 212, 214, 222, 226, 248
custodial interrogation, 189, 192

Damasio, Antonio, 231
Dames & Moore v. Regan, 317
debiasing, 71
debtors, 32
DeCanas v. Bica, 246
Declaration of Independence, 29
Define and Punish Clause, 296
deportation, 206, 245, 246, 247, 248, 252
Deskovic, Jeffrey, 169
Detainee Treatment Act, 319
deterrence, 138
Diagnostic and Statistical Manual of Mental Disorders IV, 226
Dickerson v. United States, 197, 271
Dickinson, Emily, 122
dignity, 98, 105
Discipline and Punish, 31
discretion, 93, 99
DNA testing, 14
Douglas, Justice William O., 290
Dow Chemical v. EPA, 157
Draft Principles Governing the Administration of Justice Through Military Tribunals, 300
Drayton, 97, 98, 101, See also *United States v. Drayton*
DSM, 35
ducking, 30
Due Process, 175, 177, 184, 187, 206

EEG, 110, 111, 120, 122, 123
effective assistance of counsel, 21
Effron, Judge Andrew, 294
Eighth Amendment, 7, 31, 35, 212, 222, 226, 248, 251, 287
emergency power, 315
English Bill of Rights of 1689, 31
Enlightenment, 27, 28
Equal Protection Clause, 209
Erdmann, Judge Charles, 293
Ex parte Milligan, 295
Ex parte Quirin, 295, 300
ex post facto, 298
exclusionary rule, 4, 46, 47, 50, 52, 79, 80, 81, 82, 83, 84, 85, 86, 87, 88, 89, 90, 91
execute, 17
executed, 16
exonerated, 14
extradition, 313, 320, 322, 324
extraterritoriality, 323

false confessions, ix, 5, 171, 173, 174, 175, 176, 177, 178, 181, 182, 183, 184, 189
familia, 28, 33
Farahany, Nita, 123
Federal criminal law, 313
Feige, David, 49, 50
Fifth Amendment, 88, 91, 94, 95, 100, 101, 109, 110, 113, 114, 115, 116, 117, 118, 121, 124, 175, 187, 189, 192, 270, 291
First Amendment, 36, 37, 263, 264
Fisher, James T., 15, 22
fMRI, 112, 113, 120, 122
foreign relations, 310, 316, 319, 324
forum, 33
Foucault, 31
Founding Fathers, 28, 31
Founding Generation, 29, 31
Fourteenth Amendment, 175, 184, 187
Fourth Amendment, v, vi, x, 4, 5, 40, 45, 46, 47, 48, 50, 52, 53, 56, 57, 58, 59, 63, 66, 68, 74, 76, 79, 81, 85, 88, 89, 90, 92, 93, 94, 95, 98, 99, 100, 101, 104, 105, 107, 109, 110, 113, 117, 118, 119, 120, 121, 122, 123, 124, 125, 126, 127, 130, 131, 133, 152, 153, 154, 155, 156, 157, 158, 159, 160, 161, 162, 163, 165, 166, 262, 269, 280, 281, 282, 322
Friedman, Barry, 198
fundamental fairness, 175
funding for lawyers
 adequate, 17, 22
 insufficient, 17
Furman v. Georgia, 35

Garrett, Brandon, 174
Gay, Kenneth Earl, 21
general public use doctrine, 155, 156
Geneva Conventions, 261, 311
Germany, 27, 38, 39
Ghailani, Ahmed K., 268
gibbet, 30
good government, 28, 35
governance, 28, 29
Graham, Lindsey, 292
Graham v. Florida, 227
Greene, Joshua, 231
Guantánamo. See Guantánamo Bay Naval Base
Guantánamo Bay Naval Base, 268, 288, 317, 322
guilt principle, 39

Hager, Detlev, 241
Haidt, Jonathan, 231
Hamdan v. Rumsfeld, 288, 296
hanging, 30

Hare, Robert, 224, 225, 226, 227
Harlan, Justice John Marshall, 154, 291
harm principle, 38
Henry Hart, 36
Herbert Wechsler, 34
heteronomy, 33
Hines v. Davidowitz, 146
hit rates, 68
hit-rate data, 68, 71
Hoffman, Morris, 235
Holder v. Humanitarian Law Project, 266, 267
household, 28, 31, 33, 34
Howes v. Fields, 100
human trafficking, 311, 313
Humanitarian Law Project, 266

ignorantia legis non excusat, 34
immigration, 7, 244, 313
Implicit Association Test (IAT), 71
implicit bias, 60, 62, 66, 67, 68, 69, 70, 71, 72, 73, 74, *See also* unconscious bias
implicit racial biases. *See* unconscious racial bias
implicit social cognition, 59, 60, 72, 74
implicit stereotypes, 70, 73,
  See also unconscious stereotypes
In re Grand Jury Proceedings (T.S.), 125
incentives, 79, 89, 90
indigent defense, 18
insanity, 222
International Criminal Court, 312, 313
international criminal law, 311, 314
International Criminal Tribunal for the Former Yugoslavia, 312
International human rights, 325
international law, 296, 298, 300, 325
interrogation, 94, 95, 100, 101

J.D.B. v. North Carolina, 198
Jacob Wetterling Act, 138
Jacobsen v. Massachusetts, 235
Jefferson, Thomas, 29, 30, 31
Johnson, Carl, 16
Johnson, Justice Thomas, 289, 301
Jones v. United States, 155
juries, 81
juror resistance, 80, 81, 83, 85, 87

Kamisar, Yale, 197
Kansas v. Hendricks, 234
Kant, 28
Karton, Inga, 113
Kassin, Saul M., 83
Katz v. United States, 121, 154, 163
Kavanaugh, Judge Brett, 298, 301
Kennedy, Justice Anthony, 193
Kennedy, Randall, 51

Kennedy v. Louisiana, 287
Kennedy v. Mendoza-Martinez, 209
Kiehl, Kent, 235
Killen, Melanie, 230, 233
king, 28, 29
Klein, Colin, 231
Koh, Harold Hongju, 274
Korematsu v. United States, 267
Kurdistan Workers Party, 266
Kyllo v. United States, 121, 157

Lambert v. California, 210
larceny, 30
law and economics, 141
law of war, 296, 298, 300
Lawrence v. Texas, 3, 37
lawyer
  contract, 20, 21
lawyers
  incompetent, 17
legal process, 34, 35, 36
legal representation, 14, 18
  competent, 16, 21, 22
  deficient, 16
  effective, 20
  good, 17
  inadequate, 21
  ineffective, 21
  perfunctory, 17
  poor, 17
  quality, 18
legality, 33
legitimacy, 27, 29, 33, 36, 37, 39
Leo, Richard, 189
lie detection, 111, 112
Lightfoot Lee, Thomas, 30

macro household, 29, *See also* macro householder
macro householder, 28, , *See also* macro household 28
Madison, James, 325
Madsen v. Kinsella, 290
maiming, 30
Make Rules Clause, 296
Malone, Dumas, 30
Marshall, John, 320
Marshall, Justice Thurgood, 291
Mason, 30, *See also* Mason, George
Mason, George, 30
Mass Conviction, 207
material support to terrorism, 262, 263, 266, 297, 324
McElroy v. United States ex rel. Guagliardo, 294
McFarland, George, 16
Megan's Law, 139

Methodist, 32
micro household, 28
micro householder, 28
military commission, 7
military commissions, 8, 261, 262, 288, 295
Military Commissions Act, 317
Military Commissions Act of 2006, 297
Military Commissions Act of 2009, 297
military courts, 8
Military Extraterritorial Jurisdiction Act, 292, 294, 300
military jurisdiction, 288, 289, 294, 300, 301
military justice, 8
military tribunals. *See also* military commissions, 260
Miller v. United States, 158
Miranda v. Arizona, 2, 175, 176, 177, 187, 189, 194, 197, 262, 270, 322
Miranda warnings, 96, 100, 175, 177, 187, 189, 190, 191, 192, 193, 196, 262, 270, 271
misclassification error, 172, 181, 182
Missouri v. Seibert, 6, 10, 177, 186, 187, 188, 190, 193, 197, 199, 200, 201
mitigation, 226, 228, 233
Model Penal and Correctional Code, 35
Model Penal Code, 34, 35, 36
money laundering, 311, 313
moral agency, 229, 232
moral judgment, 230, 232
Moreno, Joelle Anne, 199
Morissette v. United States, 37
motorists, 96, 102, 103
MRI, 110, 111, 117
Murder by, 30
  dueling, 30
mutual assistance treaties, 313

Nadelmann, Ethan, 312, 313, 314
National Defense Authorization Act, 261
national security, 8, 310, 316, 318, 319, 320, 321, 323, 324
national security sovereign, 310, 314, 317, 318, 319, 323, 324, 325
neuroimaging, 110
neuroscience, 5, 110, 111, 230
neurotechnology, 4
New York v. Quarles, 270
non facit reum nisi mens sit rea, 34
nuisance, 29

O'Callahan v. Parker, 290
Ofshe, Richard, 178, 179
oikonomikos, 28
oikos, 28, 33
order, 39
outrageous government conduct, 322
overcriminalization, 48

Padilla v. Kentucky, 206, 211, 213
pat-downs, 53
paterfamilias, 28
patriarchal, 28, 33
peace, 29, 34
peace, order, and good government, 28
peace, welfare, and government, 28
Pendleton, Edmund, 30
penmanship, 30
Pennsylvania v. Muniz, 115, 116
People's Mujahedin Organization of Iran, 265
petit treason, 30, 31
Philadelphia Society for Alleviating the Miseries of Public Prisons, 32
pillory, 30
pirates, 311
plea bargains, 205, 214
Plyler v. Doe, 246
police, 28, 34
police misconduct, 79
police power, 28, 29, 33
police practices, 93, 94, 96, 101, 103, 106
police science, 28
police-citizen interactions, 95
post-admission narrative, 179
pragmatic implicature, 99
preemption, 241, 242, 243, 245, 250, 251, 252, 253, 254, 255
pretext, 103, 104
pretext searches, 48, 52, 53
pretextual searches, 53
prison law, 33
prison reform, 32
privacy, 59
private law, 29
probable cause, 63, 67
proportionality, 222, 225, 241, 242, 243, 246, 248, 251, 252, 253, 254, 255
proportionality principle, 161
prosecutorial discretion, 323
providing material support for terrorism, 297
psychological coercion, 173, 182
psychological costs, 102
psychologically coercive, 173
psychopathy, 7, 223, 225
public defender offices, 18, 19
Public Defender Service in Washington, D.C., 22
public harm, 29
public peace, 29
public safety exception, 196

quality of life policing, 48

racial bias
  unconscious, 65

Index

racial profiling, 60, 70, 106, 272, 273
Rahmani, Roya, 265
rational basis review, 209
reasonable suspicion, 63, 64, 66, 67, 68, 69, 93, 99, 102, 103, 105
Rechtsgut principle, 38, 39
registration and community notification, 137, 144, 146
registration and community notification laws, 5
Rehnquist, Chief Justice William, 197, 291, 301
Reid, Harry, 267
Reid v. Covert, 290
Reliability, 178
rendition, 322
right to counsel, 20, 21
"right to remain silent", 187
Rilling, James, 230
Robbins, Jonathan, 320
Roper v. Simmons, 227
Rosen, Jeffery, 142
Rowe, Peter, 300
Rubenfeld, Jed, 106
rule of law principle, 39
Ryan, Judge Margaret, 288

Sand, Judge Leonard, 270
Sassen, Saskia, 314, 315
Scalia, Justice Antonin, 97, 243
Schmerber v. California, 115, 119, 123
Schuldprinzip, 39
search and seizure, 90, 113, 115, 119, 123, 124, 125
searches, 93, 94, 98, 99, 100, 101, 102, 104, 105, 106
Secure Communities, 273
security, 103, 105, 106
seized, 97, *See also* seizure
seizure, 95, 101, *See also* seized
self-government, 27, 29, 31, 32, 37
self-incrimination, 113, 114, 187, 189, 192, 270
sex offenders, 138, 143
Shahzad, Faisal, 271
shooter bias, 72
Simon, Jonathan, 140
Sixth Amendment, 20, 175, 176, 214, 262, 268
slave of the state, 33
slave trade, 311
Smith v. Doe, 143
Smith v. Maryland, 158
sneak and peek, 269
social control, 137, 138, 139, 146, 147
Solorio v. United States, 288, 291, 301
Solove, Daniel, 141
Sommers, Samuel R., 83
Sotomayor, Justice Sonia, 160, 198, 266

Souter, Justice David, 177
sovereignty, 28, 310, 314
Special Administrative Measures, 268
Special Needs Doctrine, 160
special needs searches, 52
speedy trial, right to a, 268
stereotype
 unconscious, 64
stereotypes, 60, *See* cultural, unconscious
 unconscious, 60, 65
stop and frisk, 3, 45, 50, 51, 52, 53, 63, 64, 67, 68, 73, 104, 105
stops and frisks, 4, 59
Supremacy Clause, 243
surveillance, 156

Tappan, Paul W., 209
taxation without representation, 31
terrorism, 297, 311, 313, 319, 324
Terrorism Information Awareness, 159
Terry, 64, 65, 68, 73, 105, *See also Terry v. Ohio*
Terry stops, 50, 68
Terry v. Ohio, 3, 45, 46, 47, 48, 52, 53, 62, 63, 105, 161, 162, *See also Terry*
Thirteenth Amendment, 33
Tomkovicz, James J., 193
Total Information Awareness, 159
totality of the circumstances, 175
trade in endangered species, 311
traffic regulations, 103
traffic stops, 104
Treason Act 1351, 31
Trop v. Dulles, 206, 213
Turiel, Elliot, 224, 230, 233

U.N. Commission on Human Rights, 300
unconscious bias, 59, *See also* implicit bias
Uniform Code of Military Justice, 288, 292
Uniform Collateral Consequences of Conviction Act, 214
Unitarian, 32
United States ex rel. Toth v. Quarles, 301
United States v. Curtiss-Wright Export Corporation, 316
United States v. Drayton, 97, *See* Drayton
United States v. Hamdan, 297
United States v. Knotts, 155
United States v. Nicolosi, 124
unlawful entry, 247, 255
USA Patriot Act, 262, 263, 267, 269, 318
Uviller, Richard, 95

Virtual searches, 163
voluntariness, 177, 184, 187, 189, 192
voluntary, 98
voluntary action, 95

voluntary waiver, 95, 100
voluntary confession, 175

waiver, 94, 95, 100
Walnut Street Jail, 32
Walsh, John, 140
war crime, 296
war crimes, 312, 313
war on crime, 1, 2
war on drugs, 320, 324
War on Terror, 2, 7, 260, 261, 273
Warren, Chief Justice Earl, 215
Warren Court, 1, 36, 46, 47
Weems v. United States, 206, 212
Weisselberg, Charles D., 193

whipping, 30
Whitman, James, 141
Whren v. United States, 53
Willingham, Todd, 14, 15
Willis, Ernest Ray, 14, 15
Winbrone, Jacqueline, 16
Winston v. Lee, 119
witchcraft, 30
wrongful convictions, ix, 6, 19, 171, 172, 178, 181
Wythe, George, 30

Youngstown Sheet & Tube v. Sawyer, 316

Zimmerman, Diane, 141